MACCABEE

David C. Carson

Outskirts Press, Inc.
Denver, Colorado

This is a work of fiction. The events and characters described here are imaginary and are not intended to refer to specific places or living persons. The opinions expressed in this manuscript are solely the opinions of the author and do not represent the opinions or thoughts of the publisher.

Maccabee
All Rights Reserved
Copyright © 2007 David C. Carson

This book may not be reproduced, transmitted, or stored in whole or in part by any means, including graphic, electronic, or mechanical without the express written consent of the publisher except in the case of brief quotations embodied in critical articles and reviews.

Outskirts Press
http://www.outskirtspress.com

ISBN-10: 1-4327-0165-7
ISBN-13: 978-1-4327-0165-9

Outskirts Press and the "OP" logo are trademarks belonging to Outskirts Press, Inc.

Printed in the United States of America

To all who worship the God of Abraham, Isaac, and Jacob in spirit and in truth.

Preface

The story told in these pages comes down to us through the writings of the ancient Jewish historian Flavius Josephus and the anonymous authors of the apocryphal works *1* and *2 Maccabees*. Though the history is recorded in the space of only a few pages, it has been my effort to put a human face to the figures of whom so little is actually known.

While making every effort to remain true to the ancient records in the inclusion of key people, the cultural and political environment, and the primary events of this volatile period of Jewish history, some secondary characters and events have been added for the flow of the story. The reader is encouraged to consult the "Author's Historical Notes" found at the end of the book for clarification on what parts of the story are recorded history and where I have used license in the telling of the story. A glossary has also been included in order to help with unfamiliar terminology.

David C. Carson
October 26, 2006

Prologue

332 BCE

The brisk morning air did nothing to pacify the young king as he stepped from his tent. He spit on the ground as a cobra spits venom. The siege had not yet begun, nevertheless the anger from which he drew his strength had reached its peak. Who was this gnat Jaddua to resist him, to refuse his will? He was Alexander. No one had been able to stand up to him. Even Darius, the Persian everyone from the Great Sea to the rising sun called the King of Kings, had fled from him at Issus. Alexander already had Darius's wife and children in his possession, spoils of battle. Before it was over, he would have his throne as well. But before he could meet Darius again, he would have to deal with troublesome mites like the one he would confront this day. Today, he would reduce Jerusalem to dust, and Jaddua, its high priest, would be but a memory.

Jaddua had been given the opportunity to side with Alexander. During the seven-month siege of Tyre, a city that seemingly would never fall, Alexander had called upon Jerusalem to send auxiliaries and provisions for his army. The high priest had sent messengers back saying he had made an oath to Darius and could offer no support so long as Darius remained in the land of the living. Alexander recalled his dark musings upon receiving the word from the messengers: *Darius has more time left in that land than do you, my dear high priest.*

Alexander's attendants read his demeanor as he strode toward his horse. No one dared speak. They loved and admired their king and usually spoke freely in his presence. However, they knew when it was best to maintain silence. They had all heard about what had transpired between Alexander and the priest of Jerusalem, and they knew this had been a festering sore to him for months. Besides this, they could see their king rubbing his shoulder, reminding him that an enemy's sword had made its mark during the siege of Gaza weeks earlier. Alexander was not invincible. This in itself soured his spirits. Those attending the king knew it would be best to simply stand quiet this day and only speak when spoken to.

Parmenio, the man second only to Alexander, arrived on a snorting steed as the tent flaps fell behind Alexander. Parmenio dismounted and took the reins from the young attendant caring for Alexander's horse. Only Parmenio would freely address the king on a day like this. There were other generals – most notably Antigonas, Seleucus, and Ptolemy – but it was Parmenio who was Alexander's right hand, having served under Alexander's father, Philip, and who wielded the power of half of Alexander's army. Parmenio passed the reins to the young king as the attendant backed out of ear shot, knowing anything that would be said between these two powerful men was not meant for him.

Alexander took the reins from Parmenio and swung himself onto the back of the horse that itself had become a legend. The black stallion named Bucephalus was rumored to have been tamed by Alexander when no else could. According to the stories, none of Philip's men had been able to break the horse. A then 10-year-old Alexander had approached and said he could break it. The men had laughed at the child, but Alexander had looked directly at the horse, speaking softly and reassuringly. The horse had appeared to come to attention as a soldier before his commander and walked to Alexander and stood before him. The boy had then mounted the horse and claimed it as his own, and seemingly the horse had claimed the boy also. Those watching had exclaimed that it must be a sign from the gods.

"Everything is ready, Sire," Parmenio said, mounting his own steed. "The men are rather excited. They know how you feel about this one."

Alexander answered with a caustic sneer. "Probably the Chaldeans and Phoenicians most of all, if my thoughts are correct."

"I would say you are correct, Sire," Parmenio agreed, recognizing that though he saw Alexander's cause as noble, he certainly did not see such nobility in all who served under him. The Chaldeans and Phoenicians, as mercenaries in every war, fell in this latter category. They would as quickly fight for the enemy if they believed there was profit in it.

The mercenaries were known for their thirst for blood. The Greeks, mainly Macedonians, fought more out of pride in the spread of the Greek empire and its king. The mercenaries, however, just wanted blood and plunder. They had no particular desire to see the world Hellenized, but they did have a yearning to satisfy their worst lusts. They knew from the rumors that had spread, that Alexander would not deny them anything they wanted from this city. By the end of this siege, they anticipated that there would be scarce a Jewish woman who had not been raped and scarce a Jewish man left alive. There had already been talk of what means would be used to torture Jaddua the high priest to death. There was always delight in seeing those who had held power brought as low as possible before they begged for death. The imagination was the only limitation to what cruelties would be employed before this was over.

Alexander and Parmenio galloped their horses to the front of the lines. The walls of Jerusalem rose in the near distance, their visibility somewhat obscured by the glare of the sun cresting the horizon behind the city. Alexander sat astride his mount considering the siege towers behind him that would be pushed by shielded men to the city walls during the next few hours. This city should be easier to take than Gaza. It had been reported to him that at one time Jerusalem had been a formidable fortress, withstanding long sieges by powerful kings. However, Jerusalem had finally fallen to the Babylonian king Nebuchadnezzar. Jerusalem's seemingly impenetrable walls had been destroyed and the people had been led away as slaves. Many years later the descendents of those slaves had been permitted by the Persian king to return and rebuild their city. That had been almost a hundred years before this morning in which Alexander sat astride his horse visualizing the events of the next few hours. Jerusalem was nothing like it had been during the times of its kings. What a fool, this man Jaddua, not even a king, to refuse him. The world would be better without such fools. Jerusalem would certainly not offer him any protection. Even the indomitable Tyre had eventually fallen before Alexander. Who would think they could hide behind the walls of Jerusalem?

"What do you know about these people, Parmenio?" Alexander asked, as if trying to understand what made people act so foolishly.

"Who, Sire? The Jews?" Parmenio said the word "Jews" as if he were speaking of something for which one would not care to even ask.

"Yes. What do you know about the Jews?" Alexander mockingly repeated "Jews" in the same tone as had Parmenio.

"Well, Sire. They are a strange people to say the least, from what I've heard."

"Strange? You and I have seen a lot of strange things together, Parmenio. I almost don't know what the word means anymore."

"Well, the Jews don't sound like anyone we have ever come across. They have some very unusual practices. For one thing, they mutilate their children shortly after birth, only the boys, I think."

"How so? What do they do?"

"They cut their genitals. It's something they have done for generations."

Alexander cringed upon his saddle as Parmenio continued.

"And another thing, they will only eat certain foods. They

say for them to eat pork is like cursing their god."

"You said 'their god,'" Alexander queried. "Do they only have *one*?"

"Yes, Sire, and they put great stock in him."

"They will need more than one god to help them before this day is over. It would seem prudent for them to find some more."

"That is one thing they will most surely *not* do, if what people have told me is true. Their god seems to be a jealous god. From what I've heard, they say that the Babylonians conquered them almost 200 years ago because they offended their god by worshipping other gods. Had they stayed with just the one, their god would have protected them. These Jews today say it was their ancestors' fault that they were conquered because they worshipped other gods."

"One god." Alexander could not seem to make any sense of what he was hearing. "These are a strange people indeed. It's almost a shame to destroy them. The world needs some variety so the philosophers can have more to think upon."

"But, Sire," continued Parmenio, "in the end, they are of little significance. There are empires, the Egyptians, the Persians, and probably others that we do not even know about. But these people are few. They are just an insignificant drop among the peoples of the world. They do not even have a king of their own, just this high priest who has defied *my* king. The world will not miss them."

At the mention of the high priest Alexander's face hardened. After a moment's hesitation, Alexander seemed to take on new energy. "You are right, my friend. If someone who is less than a fly is allowed to defy me, others will do the same. We will put an end to this fly today. Begin advancing the towers."

Parmenio gave the order to a nearby commander who passed the order down the line. Muscular men took up long poles that were joined to four tall, partially enclosed towers. Ten or twelve men held each pole, pushing the towers on their massive wooden wheels as other men pulled on ropes from the front. Each tower was more than the height of twenty men. When the towers grew close to the city, the men in front would leave their ropes for they would be without protection. Infantry soldiers and archers, who were already arrayed behind the towers, would fill the towers for the final push to the city wall. The archers would return the hail of arrows that would be coming from the battlements on the wall of the enemy city until the wall was attained. Then the soldiers, with sword and shield, would come in an endless stream across the wall.

The units of *phalangites* remained in the rear holding their long spears in vertical fashion. The *phalanx* made famous by Alexander in field battle was of little use in the siege of a city. Likewise, the cavalry, while ready for battle, remained in the flank upon restless horses. What was going to happen in the next few hours was for men who were fast upon their feet and whose swords could disembowel an enemy before its flash was seen.

The wood on the towers creaked amidst the grunts of those pushing and pulling. The whole army moved in slow motion behind them. Alexander and Parmenio along with two cavalry commanders trotted their horses about a furlong ahead of the towers where they would have a better view of the city and at the same time watch the slow progress of the siege towers. All but Alexander turned their horses to face their own troops. They sat silently upon their mounts while the towers, like clumsy wooden giants, covered another half furlong of distance in their direction.

Parmenio, who was beside Alexander but facing the opposite direction, suddenly felt a strong hand grip his arm. He turned and looked at Alexander, who was holding tightly to his arm. All the color seemed to have drained from the king's face.

"Sire, are you ill?" Parmenio blurted.

Alexander tightened his grip. The hand digging into Parmenio's arm was speaking where words failed to come forth. Parmenio followed Alexander's gaze toward the city. Peering into the glare of the sun, he suddenly realized there were people coming from the city. In fact, there appeared to be an army of people pouring out of the city gates.

"By the gods, they are attacking *us*," cried out Parmenio. "I can't believe it." He quickly spoke to the two commanders, first to one then to the other. "Call the archers forward. Tell them to array immediately in front of the towers. You, order the phalanxes into formation and tell the cavalry to stand ready."

The commanders dug their heels into their steeds when Alexander suddenly shouted, "No! Stay those orders!"

"Sire?" Parmenio was utterly confused. Never before had the king countermanded one of his orders. He could make no sense of it.

"Look," said Alexander, motioning with his head in the direction of the city. "They are not coming to do battle."

Parmenio looked again at the multitude approaching from the city. They were all dressed in white, all except for one. In the midst of all the white, there was one man who was robed in purple and scarlet. Upon this man's head there appeared to be an unusual headdress. The people moved along in procession, not seeming to be armed in any way. "Only the gods know what is happening here!" Parmenio exclaimed.

Suddenly, Alexander looked at him and said simply but firmly, "Do nothing." Before Parmenio could respond, Alexander made his horse bolt toward the procession coming towards them.

Parmenio sat dumbfounded. His king was riding alone into the midst of the enemy yet had given orders to do nothing. Besides this, he had countermanded his own orders to prepare for battle. The two commanders, having stopped at Alexander's countermand, were now looking to Parmenio for direction. Parmenio just shook his head, quietly muttering, "I don't know, I don't know." He had never been in a situation like this before. Finally he said to one of the men. "Stop the advance of the towers."

The commander to whom he had spoken made the short jaunt across the field and gave the order. The creaking of the towers ceased and the men who had been pushing and pulling came and stood in front of the towers looking toward the city.

With his army behind him, Parmenio watched as Alexander came close to the crowd in white. Alexander stopped his horse and dismounted, approaching the figure in purple and scarlet on foot. Parmenio and his subordinate commander beside him hardly breathed as they watched what was unfolding in front of them. Alexander appeared to stand for several minutes some distance from the figure in purple as if discussing something. Then, as the crowd now stood still, Alexander approached the man and bowed down before him, touching his face to the ground.

"He's gone mad," Parmenio said under his breath. The commander beside him heard him but sat still upon his horse, feeling the same as his general but not daring to voice it.

Alexander then stood up and the crowd in white appeared to envelope him. Parmenio grew tense and came to the verge of breaking Alexander's orders. He was about to order his commander to call up the cavalry when suddenly the crowd began to melt away. The procession slowly returned to the city.

Alexander mounted Bucephalus and trotted back toward his army. Parmenio ordered the commander to remain in place while he rode to meet the king. Both Alexander and Parmenio pulled up their horses as they came together. Parmenio was unable to speak. He did not know what question to ask first. Confusion was written all over his face.

Alexander was in exuberant spirits. He was certainly not the same man that had walked out of his tent a short while before.

Parmenio finally stammered out, "Sire, who was that man . . . why did you bow . . . what is happening here . . . the gods." Then Parmenio lapsed into silence with a huge sigh, still staring inquiringly at the king.

Alexander responded simply, "That man was Jaddua, the high priest."

"But you bowed down to him."

"No, I didn't. I bowed down to his god. Upon the miter that sits upon the priest's head is a gold plate with the name of their god."

"The name of their god? What *is* his name?"

"I don't know. The priest would not say the name. For some reason they don't like to say his name, but it was written there in their language."

Parmenio was beside himself. "Sire, you don't even know the name of this god and yet you bowed down to him. Your whole army saw you, the great Alexander, bow down to this unknown god of an insignificant people. What are we to think?"

Alexander paused for a moment. Sitting erect upon his mount, he looked toward his army and then back at the crowd clothed in white as they steadily retreated into the city.

"Parmenio, you have been with me from the beginning. You served my father. Do you recall when I was agonizing over whether or not to cross over the sea and seek the dominion of Asia?"

"I remember too well, Sire. We were in Dios, still in Macedonia. You were not easy to live with during those days, but then one morning you walked out of your tent and gave the orders to prepare to cross over. No one has been able to stand up to you since. Everything and everyone has fallen before you. You made the right decision, though I am not sure how you came to make it."

"That is just it, Parmenio. On the night before I ordered the army into Asia, I had a dream. Do you believe in dreams, Parmenio?"

"Dreams?" replied Parmenio. "That's when the gods play in our minds."

"This was not play that night, Parmenio. That night, I saw what we have seen today. I saw Jaddua in that dream. I did not know who he was, but I saw him, dressed in that very robe he was wearing today, and that miter upon his head, the miter with the name of his god. In my dream, he told me to pass over the sea, and that he would conduct my army and would give me dominion over the Persians."

"That who would conduct your army? Jaddua?" retorted Parmenio.

"No, the god of Jaddua. The jealous god you were telling me about, the god who will allow for no other gods. In these years since we left Macedonia, this dream has always been with me, and I have known that one day I would see this in the light. Today I have. This is the god who will give me the world. We will honor this god. I believe that by honoring this god, I will conquer Darius, and will destroy the power of the Persians, and will succeed according to everything that is in my mind. But it is not just what I think. This day, Jaddua has told me that one of their prophets, someone called Daniel, predicted that a Greek would destroy the empire of the Persians."

"So what will you do with Jerusalem? What will you do with the Jews?"

"Tomorrow I will go into the city and worship their god. I will give them what they need to prosper. I will give them freedom to follow their laws and their religion. I do not know about some of the strange things these people do, but I do not want their god to be strange to me. We will not try to change these people as we do others. The rest of the world needs what Greece has brought to the world, but these people will be left alone. We need these people, and we need their god."

Alexander's thoughts were strange to Parmenio. He would probably never understand how the mind of his king worked, but he was glad that this day, at least, there would be no bloodshed. Now if he could just explain it to the Chaldeans and the Phoenicians.

Chapter 1

Kislev 167 BCE

The blood drained from Mattathias's face as his mind surrendered to the vision of the Syrian officer standing in the doorway of the synagogue. Somehow he had known this day would come, but he had hoped to rest with his fathers before it actually arrived.

"Are you the one called Mattathias?" shouted the Syrian rudely.

Every eye in the synagogue was looking at the Gentile who had dared interrupt the Sabbath reading of Torah. The Syrian glanced around the room of about thirty men. Their ages ranged from young men who would soon have their bar mitzvah to old men close to the age of Mattathias. Every face looking back dripped with disdain. The Syrian was by his very appearance an abomination in their place of worship. The flimsy short skirt he wore, typical of the Greek upper class, boasted of his disregard for any standard of decency. The danger of a man like this was not the shortness of his clothing, however, but the lack of his conscience.

"Are you Mattathias?" the Syrian shouted again.

Mattathias lifted his head from the scroll he had been reading and called out strongly and proudly, "I am Mattathias ben John ben Simon ben Hasmoneus, priest of the order of

Joarib. What do you want here?"

The Syrian paused for a moment, debating whether or not to make some snide remark about Mattathias's giving his ancestry for three generations rather than simply answering the question. These Jews and their genealogies. It was as if they thought their bloodline made them better than everyone else. If a nobody begets a nobody, he is still a nobody. They were a conquered people.

"I am Apelles," he said, "officer of your illustrious king Antiochus IV."

Mattathias thought, "He is not *my* king," but he held his tongue.

Apelles, lost in his own self-importance, waited as if expecting some sort of eloquent greeting or an invitation into the synagogue. When no invitation was forthcoming, he walked brazenly to the front where Mattathias stood behind the lectern with the open scroll. Murmurs arose in the group. One young man was on the verge of jumping up to bar his path, but a hand reached out and grabbed him. The same hand then pointed out the door. Through the doorway could be seen a detachment of what appeared to be more than forty soldiers, all armed with spears, swords, and shields.

Stationing himself directly in front of Mattathias, Apelles said, "Mattathias, I have come to you because I understand you to be the chief elder of this town, but what I have to say is for everyone."

Turning to the group of men who sat on stone benches, he held out a rolled up parchment. Without unrolling the parchment but holding it up in his right hand he announced, "I have here an edict from the king. By his orders, all practice of the religion of the Jews will cease. We have gods enough. We do not need your god. Besides, you are a conquered people, so your god is obviously too weak to be worth your time."

Apelles paused. As his eyes surveyed the reddening faces, one corner of his mouth turned up in a sinister grin. He took on the posture of a military officer reprimanding his troops.

"You have an opportunity to comply with the king's

desires. If you refuse, there will be consequences. Understand me clearly, from this day forward there will be no more Sabbath observances. There will be no more reading of your holy books. In fact, what books you have must be destroyed. You will cease your insane rules about what you will eat and what you will not eat. You will no longer practice this barbaric rite of circumcision on your children. Whoever does so will do so at the cost of his own life. Finally, you will offer sacrifice to Zeus, the chief god of our nation and of our king, who is himself a god.

"I will return in one month. Your books are to be destroyed, and you are to be prepared to offer your sacrifice. As I have said, you have the opportunity to comply. I advise that you do so. Your high priest in Jerusalem has agreed to these matters, and I suggest you do the same."

With those words Apelles turned to Mattathias. "Will you comply?"

Mattathias's face was like flint. He spoke not a word but stared at the Syrian through unblinking eyes. The room was silent, more like a grave than a place of worship. After what seemed like several minutes without a word from either man, Apelles turned again to the group.

"I will be back. Do not disappoint me," he said. Then without turning his head to either side, he walked out.

Everyone in the synagogue remained silent and still. Outside could be heard the clatter of shields being raised to shoulder level for marching. As the sound of many footsteps was heard receding in cadence, a young man in his late teens ran to the door and peered out. There he saw the soldiers divided into two groups, twenty soldiers in front and twenty soldiers behind a litter borne by a dozen slaves. Upon the litter rode the pompous Apelles. Before the day was over he would carry his bitter message to yet another town.

After a long while, the young man said simply, "They're gone."

Mattathias broke his silence. "Come sit down, Jonathan. We must continue with the reading."

As soon as the silence was broken, a voice as hot as a blacksmith's forge pierced the air. "Father, why didn't you answer him? Why didn't you tell that Syrian bastard that we will die before we agree to the things he said?"

Mattathias looked sharply in the direction of the voice. "Judas," he rebuked, "remember where you are. And remember what day this is."

Judas lowered his eyes to avoid his father's piercing glare. It mattered not what insult they may have endured, the Sabbath remained the Sabbath and would not be profaned.

With every eye turned upon him, Mattathias, looking older than his already advanced years, said quietly, "When the sun has set this Sabbath day, there will be a meeting at the home of Mattathias ben John ben Simon ben Hasmoneus. All who love Israel are asked to come."

The old man lowered his eyes once again to the scroll open before him. He tried to focus on the words, but they were a blur. He blinked back the tears that marred his vision. Even if he could see the words, at the moment, his mind could make no sense of them, for his thoughts were racing through the years that had led to this day.

Mattathias had just wanted to live out his days quietly honoring God and teaching Torah to the young men who would follow in his footsteps. That was why, upon retiring from his priestly duties in the temple, he had moved his family from Jerusalem to Modin, a Levite town a full day's journey from Jerusalem. Though every Jew's heart was in some way tied to Jerusalem, the things Mattathias had seen there had made him want never to return. If he could only retire to his corner of the world and live out his days in peace. Jerusalem, whose name meant peace, held no peace, not for those who wanted to honor the God of Abraham.

Ever since Alexander the Macedonian, Jerusalem along with all the land thought of as Israel had been a vassal to warring kings. But they had respected her enough to not try to change her. Even when the Ptolemies of Egypt had held power over Jerusalem, they had sought nothing more than the usual tributes. Now, however, things had changed, and would change even more.

The Syrian king Antiochus, the one they called Epiphanes – the illustrious one – had come on the scene brandishing great ambition. He called himself the King of Kings and was determined to control the lives of his subjects down to the smallest detail. Antiochus was against anyone who was not like himself. Unlike Alexander, Antiochus would not defer to anyone being different. The Jews were perhaps more different than anyone else. For that reason, he hated them. They would be *Hellenized* or they would be destroyed.

Antiochus had marched his army of Macedonian cutthroats, those ruthless mercenaries, into Jerusalem and plundered the temple. Mattathias could still hear the screams of the people as cohorts of soldiers had moved through the streets slaughtering even women and children as a show of force. Antiochus had taken what he wanted and left, leaving a contingent of his army in charge to eventually reshape the city and its people.

Mattathias raised his eyes momentarily and looked out the open door of the synagogue. He saw the top of the Syrian officer's litter just as it went out of sight over a rise on the edge of town. The officer had mentioned the complicity of their own high priest. "Menelaus," whispered Mattathias contemptuously as the tears dried from his eyes to be replaced by a silent rage that boiled in his stomach. Menelaus had bargained with Antiochus for the high priesthood and had sold the heart and soul of Israel by surrendering to Antiochus's plans of *Hellenization*. Little by little, he began to turn the people from the Law of God to the idolatrous culture of Greece. The foundations of Israel were crumbling. Mattathias had wept openly before his family over what was happening, but he was only one man. What could he do? So he had left Jerusalem, retiring to the small town of Modin to live out his days.

Mattathias lowered his eyes to the scroll again and stared at the text he had been reading before the arrival of the Syrian. After a few moments, he started unrolling the scroll until he arrived at the text he was searching. In a renewed voice, he began to read. "These are the statutes and the ordinances, which ye shall observe to do in the land which the Lord, the God of thy fathers, hath given thee to possess, all the days that ye live upon the earth. Ye shall surely destroy all the places, wherein the nations that ye are to dispossess served their gods . . ."

Chapter 2

Mattathias quietly watched his daughter-in-law kindle a fire in the small stone oven in the corner of the room. All the while pulling his cloak more tightly around him to keep out the frigid Kislev night air, he said, "Don't make the fire too big, Leah. There will likely soon be more heat in this room than we want."

Leah turned her dark eyes toward him and nodded. "Yes, Father." She knew the heat he was referring to had nothing to do with the fire and lamps she was lighting at the pronouncement that Sabbath was ended. Nevertheless, she was glad for the warmth the fire brought to her hands as she fueled it with small sticks. This house always strictly observed Moses' command: "Ye shall kindle no fire throughout your habitations upon the Sabbath day." But now Sabbath was over, and the fires were relit.

Continuing to observe Leah going about her activities, Mattathias retreated into his thoughts. How thankful he was for Leah. Since his own dear Hannah had died two years earlier, Leah had carried a heavy load, being the only woman to cook and care for six men. Yet never a complaint crossed her lips.

Leah was the wife of Mattathias's oldest son, John. Mattathias had done well in arranging the marriage between John and Leah. Though they had only met each other twice before their wedding day, they had grown to love each other deeply. Mattathias, along with John and Leah, was anxious to see children begin arriving as part of this union. But now, thought Mattathias, it's probably just as well. A dark cloud loomed on the horizon, a cloud filled with blood. These were not good days to have the care of children.

Mattathias had four other sons. Simon, the second son, was the thinker. From boyhood he had always wanted to understand why things were the way they were. For him, just knowing what Torah said was not enough. He wanted to know why it said what it did. Simon's quest for reason carried over into how he related to others, for he was always trying to assert his reasoning upon them. Even as a child, when a disagreement would arise with his brothers or with other children, Simon would try to reason with them and persuade them of his side rather than become embroiled in a fight.

Judas, the third son, was a different story. Mattathias could not count the times Judas had come home with his face bloodied and his clothes torn because of scuffles resulting from childhood disagreements. The only word to adequately describe Judas was passion. Judas could be like a wild stallion one day and like a mother grieving over a lost son the next. Whatever seized Judas's heart consumed him. He was a lover and a fighter, one extreme or the other. There was no middle ground with Judas. Whereas Simon was the diplomat, Judas was the warrior who would win without compromise. Judas was also the leader. His passionate disposition inspired others to follow where simple reason would not.

Two of his followers were his younger brothers, Eleazar and Jonathan. Eleazar and Jonathan worshipped the ground Judas walked on. If Judas got in a fight, both of them were immediately involved in the same fight. If Judas was zealous about something, their own zeal melded itself with his. Though now growing out of the emotional years of youth, their regard for their brother had changed little.

The dim light of the small fire and three oil lamps was chasing the darkness away as Mattathias came away from the corners of his mind. John came in from caring for the animals.

"Father, some of the men are starting to arrive."

"Very well," said Mattathias with a sigh. "Tell them to come in. Go get Simon and Judas. And tell Eleazar and Jonathan to go find a dark spot some distance from the house and keep watch for anyone that looks suspicious. We can't be too careful."

John nodded and left, leaving the door hanging open. As soon as he had gone, men began appearing out of the darkness into the lighted doorway. The first through the door was Eliud. A smile crossed Mattathias's lips at the sight of an old friend being the first to arrive. Behind him came Azariah, another friend. One by one the men came through the door and gathered around the walls of the small room. Those of greatest years were given places on the three simple benches that had been pulled away from the table behind which Mattathias sat. Soon the room was crowded, and indeed, the air began to warm just from the heat of the bodies, though Mattathias had meant a different kind of heat in his words to Leah earlier, the heat of temper and passion.

John returned with Simon and Judas. John and Simon found a bare spot on the floor and seated themselves, but Judas remained standing just beside the doorway, leaving the door partially open to allow ventilation. No one spoke. All eyes were on Mattathias.

Mattathias surveyed the group with his eyes before beginning. "Thank you for coming tonight. All of you were at the synagogue today. You all know . . ."

Just at that moment a piercing voice cut through the air. "I guess I'm not surprised that you would start without me."

Every head turned to the door that had been pushed open wide. The rotund owner of the voice was Matthan. All breathing momentarily stopped as Mattathias and Matthan's eyes met. Judas turned as if to bar the way, but Mattathias simply said, "Judas."

Judas's eyes met his father's. With an almost imperceptible shake of his head, Mattthias indicated to Judas that he was to let Matthan enter. Judas stepped back. Matthan insolently combed Judas with his eyes and stepped into the room, followed by his son, Akim. For a long moment Matthan stood in the middle of the room looking at the already filled benches. Surely no one expected him to stand or sit on the floor. Finally, seeing that no one would give way, he walked to the nearest wall. The men along the wall parted and made a place for him and his son, squeezing against one another but leaving a gap on either side of Matthan and Akim so as not to touch them. Matthan's visage reflected the insult back upon everyone in the room.

Matthan was the wealthiest man in Modin. He was also the only Sadducee in Modin. The two often seemed to go together. The Sadducees, while more and more common in Jerusalem and other larger towns and cities, were still a rarity in places like Modin. The Sadducees did not believe that God controlled their destiny. They believed that everything that happened was by their own doing. And even that only lasted for the present time, for they did not believe in such a thing as eternal reward or retribution. The soul died with the body, and that was the end of a man. Therefore, since whatever good or evil there was would be experienced in this life only, what truly mattered was the present pursuit of comfort and the avoidance of pain and unpleasantness. Many wondered how the Sadducees could call themselves Jews. Nevertheless, they laid claim to the name by continuing to observe the basic laws of Torah, though they ignored the writings of the prophets. They had found various ways to use the religious system for their own profits and insisted that they were part of it.

Matthan and Mattathias had come to sharp words more than once. Matthan had held considerable influence in Modin until Mattathias had come. But Mattathias had not only returned to the town of his birth as the elder of one of the most important families to have its roots in Modin, Mattathias and his sons had built the synagogue that was now the hub of communication in Modin. As such, the center of power had shifted from the marketplace to the synagogue. What was more, because of Mattathias's teaching in the synagogue, the people were becoming more educated in the meaning of the Torah and were finding themselves more and more in sharp disagreement with the things Matthan had been telling them for so many years.

The momentary interruption having passed, Mattathias began again. "You all know what occurred today and what we have been asked to do."

Mattathias looked around the room to see if there were any questioning looks. Seeing none, he continued. "You also know that we cannot do what has been required of us. This is the law of God. When we broke it before, the nation was led into captivity by the Babylonians. If we break it now, we will certainly . . ."

"Just a moment, Mattathias." As expected, it was Matthan who had broken in. Holding out a fleshy hand that had seen no work for quite some time, Matthan said, "Surely you are going farther than what any of us can really know. To be sure, our nation has had its enemies, and those enemies have at times held power over us, but it was because they were more powerful than we, not because we had offended God. If God wanted to punish us, he could have done it himself, like with Sodom and Gomorrah."

"I am just stating what the prophets have written," said Mattathias indignantly. Grunts of agreement were heard around the room.

"The prophets?" Matthan riposted. "They were just stating their point of view. That's how they saw things back then. We live in a different day. We know better now. That's why there hasn't been a so-called prophet for over two hundred years. Besides, when it was all over, we came back. It will be that way again. If we will just get along with this newest power, we will save ourselves a lot of grief."

"Get along with it?" It was Judas who had everyone's attention now. "You don't get along with a snake! You kill it!"

Everyone was suddenly shocked to silence, feeling the import of what Judas had said. This was not just rhetorical language. This was a proposal.

"Do you know what you are saying?" Even in the dim light, it could be seen that Matthan was going red from the neck up. "You could bring war on the whole nation. Haven't we seen enough of that? Besides, when Alexander the Macedonian came a hundred years ago, our people didn't fight him. They embraced him, and he let them live in peace. If we would just make some concessions to these people, we can all profit from it."

"From what I understand, Alexander didn't ask them to break the law," Simon commented timidly from his place on the floor.

"The law." Matthan held out both hands condescendingly, palms up as if presenting an offering. "It's all a matter of interpretation, isn't it? We just need to have open minds."

Mattathias had remained silent as the interchange played itself out. He was about to speak when Eliud, seated on a bench situated diagonally from him, said in a steady voice, "Mattathias, I agree with you that we cannot do what has been asked of us. However, I do want to know that we are not alone. Here in our little town, it's easy to just see ourselves and forget that we are part of a nation, and it is the nation that must take a stand, not just a few insignificant people in a little place called Modin. We need to know what our leaders in Jerusalem are saying. How are they responding to this threat? After all, the most important place in all of Israel is the temple, and the temple is the heart of Jerusalem. What is happening there?"

Mattathias appreciated Eliud's thoughts, but as he turned his own thoughts to Jerusalem, his memories could only shout the name Menelaus. If Menelaus was all they had as a leader, then all was already lost. Menelaus would give the nation away for a drachma. However, Eliud was right, they should not act in isolation. They needed the support of others, and since all Israel revolved around Jerusalem, they needed to know how the people there were responding to this newest threat. There was one man Mattathias knew he could trust in Jerusalem, another Levite, Hananiah. Hananiah would see things rightly and would give good counsel.

Before Mattathias could speak, Matthan had taken the floor again. His disposition had suddenly become more affable. "Of course, Eliud is right. We must not act alone. Now as you can well imagine, I have many contacts in Jerusalem. I know people of influence there. I do business with them all the time. Let me offer my services. I understand that this can't wait, so I am willing to go to Jerusalem tomorrow. I will speak with . . ."

A low murmur had already begun to circle the room as Matthan was speaking, but it was Judas who cut Matthan short. "Nobody here wants you to represent us *or* report to us. We don't trust you, Matthan. I know I don't. I know you would only represent your own selfish interests."

Matthan was crimson with rage. "You dare speak to me that way, you young . . ." Further words failed Matthan as he could think of nothing adequate to express the insult he wanted to rain upon Judas.

Akim came to his father's defense by jumping into the fray. Taking a step toward Judas and shaking his finger at him he said "You Hasmoneans think you are the only people anybody should listen to, all because you have this great genealogy that you are so proud of. Sure, we hear it every time you say you're something ben something ben something ben Hasmoneus. Nobody else does that. We don't always need to be telling who some ancestor a hundred years ago was to make us somebody. We can do that on our own. My father has done more on his own than anybody here. He has accumulated more wealth than any ten men together here tonight."

"And sold his soul to do it!" retorted Judas.

Akim lunged at Judas but was caught on both sides as men jumped out in front of him. Judas stepped forward to meet his challenge.

"Judas!" Mattathias shouted, "Step back!"

Judas stepped back, but the fire in his eyes did not cool. Matthan put his hand on Akim's shoulder from behind. Akim backed away to the wall and stood beside his father, a morose expression remaining on his face. The air had grown thick and all anybody wanted was to go outside and breathe freely in the cool night.

With a firm but subdued voice, Mattathias again took control. "We will accomplish nothing by fighting among ourselves." Maintaining his calm demeanor but aiming a piercing gaze at Akim, he said, "I am sorry that our occasional reference to our ancestry offends you. But if we forget from whence we came, we will have no point of reference for where we are to go. Every time Israel has abandoned her roots, it has been at great cost."

Akim looked away from Mattathias's glare to his father beside him. Matthan, feeling his son's inquiring look, did not turn his head but muttered under his breath, "Don't say any more. You can't talk to these people."

There was a long silence in the room. Most of the men stood looking down at their feet, but some glanced about to see who would speak next.

"I think Mattathias should go to Jerusalem." It was Azariah who had broken the silence.

A buzz of agreement came from various parts of the room. Eliud voiced his accord. "Mattathias knows Jerusalem better than anyone here. Not only that, he served in the temple for many years. He will know who to talk to."

All eyes were upon Mattathias. Mattathias looked down as he weighed his thoughts. As his mind neared resolution, he raised his eyes. "I have already been thinking of an old friend, someone I know I can trust to tell me the truth. He is Hananiah ben Zechariah. If it is your desire, I will leave for Jerusalem on the morrow."

There were nods and whispers of approval around the room, but eventually every eye came to rest on Matthan. Everyone knew he would not agree. Coming to the sudden realization that everyone was looking at him, Matthan said curtly, "This is madness. I think we all know what this will lead to. What is the point? Come, Akim. We should not have come here tonight."

Matthan took as long strides as his portly body would allow him, stomping across the room and out the door, which Judas swung open wide for him. Akim followed but stopped at the door just long enough to exchange a caustic glare with Judas.

With Matthan and Akim gone, Mattathias spoke again. "When you go home tonight, pray for me that I will see and hear what God wants me to know. And pray for Israel."

Eliud spoke up, "You will not go alone, will you? These are dangerous times."

"No, my friend," assured Mattathias with a half smile. "I will go with some of the protection God has provided for me in my old age. I will take Simon and Judas with me."

In that moment, Judas's countenance changed. Every ireful thought of his encounter with Akim was suddenly chased away. The prophet had spoken of receiving beauty for ashes. That was how he felt at this moment. Tonight it had been Akim, the ashes. But because of this encounter tonight in Modin, before the sun set tomorrow in Jerusalem, it would be the beauty. Rebekah!

Chapter 3

Reclining against the large cushion at the end of his couch, Antiochus IV picked at the delicacies before him as a shapely young female slave poured wine into his goblet. Antiochus looked up into the young woman's face, but the slave consciously kept her eyes averted so as not to meet those of the king. She knew that if Antiochus desired something more than wine, she would be required to give it, or else she would die.

"Which would you prefer as a gift, my friends," Antiochus said to those at the table with him, "a shipload of this exquisite wine?" The king gestured toward his filling goblet. "Or would you prefer this?" Antiochus reached out and took the edge of the slave girl's filmy clothing, pulling it tight against her body so as to display her shape. The girl stoically stood in place, not daring to appear in any way resistant. Antiochus's two guests understood the question to be all in jest and answered by impish grins and shrugs.

To the right of Antiochus at the end of the thick marble table was Lysias, Antiochus's highest minister, supreme governor from the borders of Egypt to the river Euphrates. Lysias knew Antiochus better than anyone. He knew that even though Antiochus called himself Epiphanes and the King of Kings, and insisted on being revered as a god, he was as dependent as anyone else on money and men and good strategies on the battlefield. Lysias sipped sparingly on his wine, knowing it was never wise to have one's senses dulled in the presence of Antiochus. Not even high officials were exempt from the wrath of this king for a word hastily spoken.

At the other end of the table from Lysias sat Apollonius. Apollonius, as military governor of Judea, was responsible not only to Antiochus the king, but answered to Lysias as well. Apollonius had come from Samaria, the seat of his own authority, to report on conditions in Judea. Unlike Lysias, Apollonius had been drinking freely of the wine and had become very talkative. This was exactly according to Antiochus's design. Antiochus had no friends and cared for none. All he wanted was servants, people he could control, and he would control them one way or the other, be it by intimidation or by ruse.

"So then, my dear Apollonius," said Antiochus as the slave girl returned to the recesses of the room, her job momentarily completed, "have you succeeded in bringing Judea into the fold?" As was his habit, the king had suddenly changed the subject, turning a genial conversation into a serious discussion. This was one of his many ways of always maintaining control, not allowing anyone to anticipate him.

"More than you know, Sire," replied Apollonius confidently, hardly realizing a new subject had been broached.

"I certainly hope so." Antiochus quickly conveyed ill-humor. Lysias had grown accustomed to the king's sudden changes of mood, but to Apollonius it was unsettling. "You have been emptying the royal coffers in the process."

Apollonius was suddenly on the defensive, forcing himself out of his wine-induced glibness. "I assure you, Sire, that it has been money well spent. It is accomplishing what we have intended."

"Explain." The king settled a piercing gaze on Apollonius.

"Well, Sire, there is nothing that turns the hearts of men better than the promise of a more desirable life. And as the hearts of men turn, so turns the heart of the nation. The young people, the future of the nation, are attracted more and more by everything Greek. The new gymnasium is the most popular place in Jerusalem for the young men, so much so that these Jewish lads are having surgery to reverse their circumcisions so they will look Greek. It would seem to me that is quite a cost in order to become like us, and they are doing it of their own accord. So I would say that our tactics appear to be working."

Antiochus feigned a shudder. "I'm not even going to ask how one reverses a circumcision, but do go on."

Apollonius continued. "Not only is this younger generation turning, but the wealthier class is seeing the advantage of the new ways. They understand that this is where the money is. And of course, Menelaus the high priest has been a great asset, though a few talents have naturally changed hands in the process. As from the beginning, he is a man easily bought."

Antiochus nodded knowingly at the mention of Menelaus. "Just make sure our enriching of Menelaus does not become a habit. He should be giving to us, not us giving to him."

From the beginning, Antiochus had played a game of give and take with Menelaus. All that was needed in order to gain the cooperation of Menelaus was to find a way to give him more wealth and an appearance of power. That was easily done with the simple matter of tax farming. Menelaus had bribed Antiochus in order to receive the high priesthood, and in turn had received the power to collect taxes for Antiochus, of which he naturally retained a substantial amount for himself.

"I assure you, Sire," Apollonius defended, "that it's only a temporary way of gaining further support from Menelaus. Once we have what we want, Menelaus will be the one doing the giving once again. This is part of the process, a process that is working."

Antiochus grimaced. He did not like the idea of being entangled in a process. Processes were slow. Processes took lifetimes. Hellenization had been in process since Alexander. Alexander had forced thousands of his soldiers to marry Persian women in order to raise a generation of Greek children all over Asia. Seleucus, the successor of Alexander, and the three Antiochuses that followed him had all established Greek colonies over all their territories. Tremendous progress had been made. The world had become more and more Greek. Antiochus IV, however, had no intention of waiting for a process. He was not an idealist who surrendered to some heavenly impression. His only ideal was himself. The world that would exist by his permission had to accord itself with *him*, and he, though ruling from Syria and known as a Syrian, was Greek. The world must be Hellenized, not because the ideal world was Greek, but because Antiochus was Greek.

Antiochus voiced his impatience. "That is all well and good, but are things moving quickly enough? We do not have a whole generation to see Judea become part of the civilized world."

Not missing the intended rebuke, a smile nevertheless grew across Apollonius's face. "Sire, I anticipated that of which you speak months ago. Everything up to this point has been a softening process." There was that word again, thought Antiochus, though he did not interrupt as Apollonuis continued. "We have been dividing the forces, so to speak. The Jews can no longer be said to be of a common mind. As such, their resolve about their way of life is much less than it was formerly. What is getting ready to take place will have a far different result than it would have had we moved sooner.

"Now, as per your directives a year ago, the people are being informed of the changes that will come about, in essence, the abolishment of their religion. During the past month, starting at Jerusalem, every town down to the smallest village has been informed of this decree. Within one month, the decree will be enforced all over Judea. This enforcement will start as early as this week.

"The great inauguration of all this is only two days away. During the past month, the Jewish temple has been altered so as to no longer be Jewish, but rather to be Greek. Quarters have been prepared for the prostitutes just as in every other temple throughout the Greek world. The day after tomorrow, sacrifice will be made in the temple in Jerusalem to the great Zeus.

From that point on, there will be no more separate religion for the Jews. They will become as one of us."

Lysias had been quietly fingering the edge of his goblet until this moment. "You speak with great optimism, my friend, but I wonder if all is as well as you believe. I wonder if you have gotten a true picture of what the Jews are like from your palace in Samaria. Do you not expect resistance to this sacrifice that is about to take place?"

Apollonius's composure was clearly shaken. He did not like having his judgment questioned in front of the king. Anger rose within him even as he forced himself to remember that Lysias, too, was his superior. A slight tremble found its way into his voice. "I assure you that I have good men that serve me well. Our king well knows one of them, Apelles, whose heart fully belongs to the king."

Antiochus nodded agreeably at the name of Apelles. Apollonius found some degree of comfort at the king's gesture as he continued. "It does not matter that I am in Samaria, since just as you my dear Lysias, I cannot be in all places in Judea at the same time. We all depend upon those who serve us, and I am confident that I have well chosen those upon whom I depend to both inform me and to enforce on my behalf.

"There *will* be some resistance. I have no doubt of this. In fact, I have planned on it. The commander of the Syrian garrison occupying Jerusalem has actually gained information concerning who our enemies are. We expect to use the sacrifice day after tomorrow to deal them a fatal blow."

"And how is that?" the king interrupted.

"Sire, according to our information, our biggest problem is a group that are called in their language the *Hasidim*."

"The Hasidim?" said the king. "What does that mean? Who are they?"

"The best translation I can get," continued Apollonius, "has something to do with being pious. They are fanatics about holding on to their religion in its purest form. They are dead set against even the slightest modification even if it means it would be more appealing to more people."

"So how will the coming sacrifice bring this fatal blow?" Antiochus inquired.

"Well, Sire, we have allowed news about the sacrifice to be disseminated among the people. The Hasidim are sure to be there in protest. We will have a small contingent of soldiers present as they would expect but nothing that would induce enough fear so as to keep them away. We want them to have a false sense of security. As you know, the Acra, the citadel in which our garrison is barracked, overlooks the temple. Not only can all temple activity be seen from there, but from the citadel our forces can quickly block all access to or from the temple area. The entire garrison will be standing ready inside the citadel gates.

"If the Hasidim or anyone else is there protesting what is happening, then at just the right moment, when the temple courts are at their fullest and the protesters are at their loudest, our soldiers will come out in force, trapping the entire crowd in the temple area. Then in phalanx formation, they will proceed to systematically kill everyone right up to the walls of the temple. The message will be heard throughout Judea. The days of everything Jewish will be over. We will be purified of these purists. Then those who have wanted to take on the new ways but have been hindered from doing so by this crowd of troublemakers will come to our side and Judea will be truly ours."

Antiochus was pleased with the plan. At the other end of the table, Lysias also nodded approval. He understood the language of force.

"Do you believe the resistance is limited to these Hasidim?" Lysias again entered the conversation.

"There are others, but they are few." Apollonius was feeling more confident now. "There will be some in the rural areas, in the towns and villages. Some of these we will search out and destroy, that is the primary task of Apelles. Others will simply be brought to their senses when they see what happens to those who refuse to cooperate. It will be impossible to survive under the old system. Life can be good under the new system, but it will most certainly be miserable under the old.

Many in Jerusalem have already seen this, especially, as I have said, among the young and the wealthy. It will not be long before the rest of the country sees this as well."

Antiochus rose from his couch. "I like your spirit, my dear Apollonius. I trust you will send steady communication of how things go. As for me, I must direct much of my attention toward matters with Rome, who continues to be a thorn in my side, as well as with the cities of Persia, who are slow to pay their taxes. I leave this affair concerning Judea with you and Lysias. Manage it well, and you will be richly rewarded." The king paused for a moment and then said again in very deliberate fashion, "Manage it well."

Antiochus's last three words held an unmistakable warning. Apollonius caught their meaning.

He and Lysias rose as the king turned to leave the room. They both bowed their heads slightly in obeisance as the king walked away toward his chambers. As Antiochus came to the edge of the large columned room, he stopped and turned momentarily. Looking across the room at the young slave girl, showing no expression of desire, only of expected obedience, he made a shallow motion with his right hand for her to follow. Dropping her eyes to the floor, the young woman timidly crossed the room and followed the king out. Tonight her body would not be her own.

Walking around the table to where Apollonius stood, Lysias spoke to his subordinate in a subdued voice. "You certainly have won over the heart of the king. I hope you have not misjudged, for your sake. The king is convinced, as am I, that if he can consolidate his power by Hellenizing Judea, then he will be vindicated against Rome, who stopped his advance against Egypt. If you succeed in doing this, you will have both the shipload of fine wine *and* the woman. If you fail ..." Lysias left a pregnant pause in his sentence before continuing. "... well, you had best fall on your own sword. You have the king's heart today. Let's just hope that when this is all over he will not have *your* heart on public display. Manage it well."

Lysias turned and walked away. Apollonius blanched at the echo of Antiochus's words. It mattered not whether one was a general or a peasant. There was no safe place on earth. Power never creates security, it only changes the source of danger.

Chapter 4

Mattathias and his two sons were well on their way by the time the sun crested the eastern ridge the next morning. Though the distance from Modin to Jerusalem was no more than a half day's brisk walk for a healthy man in ideal circumstances, the steady increase in altitude along less than ideal terrain made the journey longer. Besides this, there were towns along the way that could not be passed by without greetings being given to kinsmen. All said, it would be dusk before they would reach Jerusalem.

This was the Way of Beth-horon, famous from ancient times. Bordered on both sides by rough low-lying mountains, this was the primary passage from the coastal plain to the central highlands, wherein was situated Jerusalem. Over a thousand years earlier, the Canaanites had fled down this way before Joshua's army. Almost two centuries later, the first king of Israel, Saul, had pursued the Philistines here, littering the ground with their corpses. The Way of Beth-horon had not always been witness to victories for Israel, however. Over the centuries at various times, enemies from Egypt, Assyria, and Babylon had gained the upper hand by seizing control of this passage. The Way of Beth-horon was of such importance that the kings of Israel had built two fortified cities along its way, designating them simply as Lower Beth-horon and Upper Beth-horon.

As Mattathias squinted into the rising sun, he pondered the history of this strategic piece of land. When Israel had been faithful to God, she had pursued her enemies along its ground, but when her faithfulness had declined, this same ground had provided access to her enemies. Who would have control of this valley in the days to come?

A few feet ahead, Judas stopped and leaned against an outcropping of rock. He held a skin of water up to his lips and took a couple of short sips while his father and brother caught up to him. Unlike his father, Judas had not been thinking about land or history. His mind was filled with visions of Rebekah. Unlike with John and Leah, Judas and Rebekah had known each other since childhood. Before the move to Modin when Judas had been in his early teens, they had been the closest of friends. Since their fathers had developed a closeness, agreeing on practically everything from religion to politics, they had spent many hours in each other's homes as children.

Judas recalled vividly the day many years earlier when what had begun in jest had turned into a serious agreement between Mattathias and Rebekah's father, Hananiah. Only nine or ten years old at the time, Judas and Rebekah had been climbing a tree in the small garden area behind Hananiah's house as Mattathias visited with Hananiah. The two men had been walking along in the garden discussing some matter of the Levitical code when Hananiah had looked into the tree.

"Rebekah," he had called. "That doesn't look to be the place for a daughter of Israel. That looks rather to be the place for a monkey."

Mattathias, peering into the branches as if to discover something, had joined in. "I think I see more than one monkey up there. Why there are two monkeys!"

"Two? Why yes, I believe you are right," Hananiah had continued the jest.

Then Mattathias had turned the conversation in a way that had made Judas's heart warm with delight. "Hananiah, my friend, do you believe in the purity of the race?"

"Yes, you know I do," had been the reply.

"Then I believe that should also be the case between young monkeys. I think these two belong together, don't you?" Mattathias, in a uniquely unorthodox way, had proposed the future marriage of Judas and Rebekah.

"I think it would be wrong to consider anything but that." Hananiah had accepted the proposal, and then the two Levites had continued their discussion of their religion's codes as they strolled away.

The two children had remained hanging to tree limbs staring at each other. As if simultaneously directed to do so, their eyes had gradually grown wide and their lips had broadened to a smile. From that moment on, they knew they belonged to each other.

Every time Judas had seen Rebekah over the years, she had grown more beautiful. Next year, she would become his wife. The only thing holding the wedding back was that Simon would be married first. Simon's future wife, Mahlah, lived in Mizpah with her family. Simon did not express his feelings for her as Judas had for Rebekah so many times, but this was Simon's way. Much of what Simon felt remained in the privacy of his own thoughts. Mizpah was not far off the Way of Beth-horon. Mattathias had suggested that they stop there on the way back to Modin. Judas hoped that discussion would be made of a wedding so that his own could proceed.

Mattathias took the skin of water from Judas's hands, breaking his reverie. As Mattathias drank from the skin, Simon came up behind him. Looking through the morning haze at Lower Beth-horon in the distance, Simon inquired, "Will we be stopping in the city?"

Mattathias lowered the skin and passed it to Simon. "Yes, I want to stop in at the synagogue and see what I can learn. Whatever happens in these coming days, it involves all of Israel."

Judas received the water skin back from Simon and hung it over his shoulder. He then took the lead again. Lower Beth-horon was no longer the fortified city it had once been. Though some reconstruction had taken place, partial breaches made during past sieges remained in the walls. The city would be dependent upon the forces within it rather than its walls in order to mount a defense, if it ever came to that.

As they neared the city, Judas suddenly leapt off the rocky road to the shadows of a fig tree. Motioning quickly to the others, he said in a loud whisper, "Come here! Get out of sight!" Mattathias and Simon were quickly at his side. Soldiers were coming from the city. In their midst was a litter borne by slaves, upon which sat a government official.

Judas squinted to see better. "It's that Syrian that was in Modin yesterday. There's nothing between Modin and here. This must be where they spent the night."

Mattathias nodded. "You are probably right. We had better wait here until they are gone. If they were to see us, it would only raise questions, questions that we don't need anyone asking just yet."

The three men squatted under the tree until the detachment of soldiers and the one they were protecting were out of sight. They then rose and entered the city. The streets were quiet, as if it were the Sabbath. There were no sounds of children out playing. Mattathias and his sons wound around the streets until they arrived a block away from the synagogue. When they turned the corner the sound of angry voices reached their ears.

A minute later, they saw the source of the uproar from the doorway of the synagogue. There seemed to be two sides in contention, one side much larger than the other. It was difficult to discern what was being said since so many were trying to speak at one time.

Mattathias stepped into the room holding up both hands. Those nearest the door turned his way, not sure who had entered, thinking possibly the Syrian had returned. Immediately they recognized him to be a Levite from the material in the thin sash around his waist. Those toward the front of the room partially quieted themselves as they realized something was happening at the entrance. From the front of the room, an elderly man peered through the crowd and exclaimed, "Mattathias! Mattathias ben Hasmoneous!" He skipped all the intervening generations and went right to the name everyone knew. There was instant silence.

The elderly man who had spoken made his way through the crowd and embraced Mattathias. "Mattathias ben Hasmoneous! What a day for you to arrive in our presence! It must be the hand of God."

Mattathias clutched arms with the old man, "Abiezer ben Judah, I see this is not a day of peace. I think I already know, but you tell me, what has happened here?"

Several men tried to speak at once but Mattathias held up his hands again to quiet them. "Just let my dear friend here speak."

Abiezer began. "Yesterday, toward the end of the Sabbath, a Syrian officer came to our city. He had soldiers with him. He told us that from now on it would be unlawful to practice the religion of the Jews. We would be required to adopt the ways of the Syrians and the Greeks. Some of our people argued with him, but most said nothing. We were simply hoping that he would have his say and leave us. But then he required several of our families to board his soldiers and himself during the night. It was bad enough having these uncircumcised Gentiles under our roofs, but this morning we learned that during the night two of our women, our daughters, have been raped."

Mattathias gasped and then let out a long sigh. Judas ground his teeth in silent rage while Simon quietly surveyed the room.

Abiezer continued. "This morning the word about what had happened during the night moved quickly through the city and our men came out ready to challenge the Syrians. We would have fought with them, but as you know, it is illegal for us to have weapons. All we have is cooking utensils and farm tools. The soldiers drew their swords and we knew we would all die if we tried to fight them. Besides that, this Apelles, this animal, has insisted that what happened was our own fault, that this should be a lesson to us for the future."

Weariness etched itself deeper in every line of Abiezer's face as he finished relating the events. Mattathias muttered under his breath, "May hell consume him."

Someone in the back of the room called out, "It wouldn't have happened if no one had argued with him. They would have just gone on their way. We brought it on ourselves."

Another voice burned through the air, "Did Jesimiel bring it on himself to see his daughter defiled by these dogs? Or Shimon, his daughter?"

The room was suddenly a barrage of shouts again. No sense could be made of what anyone was saying. Mattathias held up his hands, but this time his gestures went unheeded.

All that had been said had reignited the passions Judas had felt the day before. Spying a bare spot on a bench, Judas leapt upon it, placing himself above everyone else. Looking up and seeing a body that looked more like a warrior than a farmer, everyone was momentarily silenced. Judas seized the moment to make his voice heard.

"My brothers, God has never intended that we live this way. A thousand years ago God gave this land to us to live in it in freedom. If we compromise with dogs like Apelles it will be worse than death. It is better to die than to give in to them."

A voice interrupted from the crowd, "And you will cause the death of the rest of us. Some of us aren't all that ready to die."

Judas couldn't see who had spoken but responded hotly, "Cowards never are!"

A cacophony of mumbles began growing across the room when Mattathias put up his hands. "Brothers! Men of Israel! Let me tell you why I am here today." The commotion died and Mattathias continued. "This same Apelles visited our small town of Modin yesterday. He brought the same message to us, though we did not suffer the things you did during the night. Today, I and two of my sons are on the way to Jerusalem to see what can be done. Just as my son who has spoken just now, I am more than willing to die for the purity of our nation, a purity that will only come when we are free of men such as this Syrian. However, I know if only a few resist those who enslave us, our efforts will not only be futile, but will bring even more suffering upon our nation. Therefore, I ask you to pray for us as we seek to understand what course of action to take."

The same voice that had spoken before, the voice that Judas had accused of cowardice, was heard again. "Who are you that you should be deciding a course of action?"

Judas angrily looked into the crowd from his vantage point, trying to discern the owner of the voice. Abiezer answered the voice in a firm tone, "This is Mattathias ben Hasmoneus, a priest of the order of Joarib. He is a man to be respected."

Mattathias held up his hands before another commotion could begin. "I am nobody. But the God of Abraham, Isaac, and Jacob can take a boy from the sheepfold and make him a king of Israel."

"So you want us to believe you are the next David?" the voice said insolently.

Mattathias had held his calm demeanor up to this point. Now the sparring with the unknown figure had caused a fire to rise within him. "There was only one David, but unless we have the faith of David, we will not endure. You can live by faith or fear. You choose. We are the people of Moses who stood up to Pharaoh, Joshua who brought down great cities, Gideon who defeated the Midianites with only three hundred men, David – a boy who killed Goliath, Daniel who saw the mouths of lions closed, and the three Hebrews who withstood the fires of Babylon. That's the people we are. If you are going to run from that, then don't call yourself a Jew. Being circumcised on the eighth day of your life when you don't have any choice doesn't make a Jew. Being a Jew is a state of mind, a condition of the heart, it's our life. Either live the life, or leave."

Turning and walking out the door, Mattathias called back, "Come my sons, some of these aren't worth saving. We're fighting for those who are." Silence reigned in the synagogue as Mattathias and his sons walked up the dusty street.

Upon leaving the city gates, they continued toward Jerusalem. When they arrived at Upper Beth-horon, they continued without stopping, believing Apelles to be in the city spreading his deadly news.

They were hungry by the time they reached the gates of Jerusalem. They had planned to find the source of their midday meal in Upper Beth-horon, but those plans had changed and nothing else had offered itself along the way. They knew the rumbles in their stomachs would be quickly silenced at the home of Hananiah ben Zechariah.

The shadows were growing long across the city as they wound their way through its streets. In another hour, torches would be all that would light the streets and alleyways. It was with relief that they spied the door of Hananiah's house at the end of a narrow lane. Coming to the door, it was Judas who knocked. His heart turned over at just the anticipation that it might be Rebekah who would open the door.

After what seemed like several minutes, longer than it normally took someone to arrive at a door, a weak voice came from the other side. It wasn't the voice of Rebekah. "Who is it?"

The voice was weak, but Mattathias recognized it and responded. "It's an old friend from Modin."

The door opened just a crack at first and then swung open wide. The smiles suddenly vanished from the faces of the three travelers. Something was very wrong.

Chapter 5

The gaunt figure standing before them hardly seemed alive. His thin shoulders appeared scarcely able to hold up the woolen tunic he wore. A thin hoary beard barely covered his caved in cheeks. Peering back at them through eyes mounted in dark hollows, a glimmer of life appeared as a faint smile crept across his thin lips.

"Mattathias, is that really you?"

The appearance of his old friend had caught Mattathias off guard. It took him a moment to recapture his thoughts. "Yes, my dear friend, it is I. I have come this day with my two sons to seek your assistance. Could you provide us a place for the night?"

New life seemed to flow into Hananiah's body. "Oh, yes. Welcome. Welcome to our home. It is also your home. Welcome, my brothers." The profusion of welcomes went on for some time as Hananiah ushered them into the house. He called out with new energy, "Miriam! Rebekah! Come quickly! We have guests!"

Hananiah's wife, Miriam, peered from the doorway of the neighboring room to see who was there. Despite the smile, her countenance also revealed yet unspoken troubles. She looked at the travelers and called back into the dimly lit room, "Bring a basin and water, Rebekah. We have travelers to tend to."

Miriam then entered the front room, welcoming them and

taking their light travel bundles from them before returning to the other room. Hananiah motioned for the men to be seated on a low bench that backed up to the side of the room. He pulled a small three-legged stool from the corner and sat facing them.

At that moment, Rebekah appeared in the doorway holding a basin, a towel draped over her shoulder. She almost dropped the basin when she realized who their guests were. Judas's heart momentarily stopped as he looked into her big dark eyes that were focused solely on him. His memories had fallen short of the warm beauty of her presence. Her simple white woolen tunic hung over a body that made his heart burn with desire. However, it was the finely sculptured face that took his eyes captive. The black hair draped across her shoulders perfectly framed every fine feature. One could easily become lost in the eyes that were as pools of ink, but it was the full lips that called to Judas to be kissed.

Hananiah rolled his tired eyes toward Rebekah then toward Judas and back. Giving a knowing look at Mattathias, who had a gentle smirk on his face, he said, "Rebekah, my daughter, those feet will not wash themselves."

Rebekah, suddenly coming to her senses, stepped into the room. "Sorry, Father. I was just coming. I didn't want to spill the water."

"If you do," Hananiah laughed weakly, "spill it on their feet." Mattathias and Simon laughed along with him. Judas just sighed, an involuntary expression of his own deep longing.

Rebekah knelt down in front of Mattathias and helped him settle his feet into the basin of water. As in most Jewish homes, the travelers had left their sandals by the door. Using a small cloth, Rebekah washed away the dust of the road before drying Mattathias's feet with a towel. Next, she proceeded to Simon and did the same. Mattathias had begun speaking with Hananiah concerning the reason for their visit, but she was hardly hearing what was said, for next she came to Judas.

The world stopped for Judas as he felt the touch of Rebekah's hands, even though they were only touching his dusty feet. Each rub of the cleaning cloth was a caress.

Rebekah did not look at Judas's feet the whole time she was washing them as she had with the others. They were lost in each other's eyes.

While Rebekah was lingering over Judas's feet, Miriam came into the room and stood before each man with another basin of water with which each washed his hands in typical Jewish fashion. As soon as this was done, she left and came back with a skin of wine and poured it into simple clay cups, handing one to each of the four men before leaving the room again. The travelers all commented on how good the wine was after the day's journey. A few moments later, Miriam returned with round, flat loaves of bread along with bowls of figs and dates, placing them on a cloth that she spread over the straw mat that covered the floor. Miriam and Rebekah seated themselves on the mat opposite the men. Seeing that the food was ready, simple though it may have been, Hananiah stopped the conversation and lowered his eyes, holding his hands palms up before him as he repeated the prayer of thanks heard for generations: "Blessed are Thou, Jehovah our God, King of the world, who causes to come forth bread from the earth, Amen." Everyone repeated a low "Amen" as they lifted their eyes.

Miriam began encouraging everyone to eat. Judas and Simon slid from the bench and reclined on the mat in front of the food. Mattathias and Hananiah remained on their seats but reached across to receive fruit and bread as it was handed to them. For a few moments, the atmosphere became jovial as they enjoyed the food and wine. Before long, though, Mattathias returned to the reason for their coming.

After a period of listening to Mattathias recite the events of the past couple of days, Hananiah said to his daughter, "Rebekah, it's growing rather dark. Can you see to the lamps?"

As Rebekah stood up to go, Judas rose with her, saying, "I'll go help her."

"Those lamps are heavy at that," said Hananiah. Despite his frail appearance, Hananiah had not lost his sense of humor.

Rebekah took two small clay lamps from shelves on the wall and went into the other room, followed by Judas. She walked directly to a wooden chest in the corner of the room. Turning and handing the lamps to Judas, lingering for a look in his eyes despite the dimness of the room, she did not say a word but turned and bent down, extracting a narrow clay jar of oil from the chest. When she straightened up and turned back toward Judas, she suddenly felt strong arms reach around her as Judas pulled her to himself. Looking down, she saw that Judas had quickly set the lamps on the floor while she was finding the oil.

Feeling herself encumbered by the pitcher in her hands, she said, "Wait!" Judas appeared puzzled at first, but seeing her hold up the pitcher, understood. He released her partially so she could set down the pitcher. Then, not only did his arms reach around her body, her arms reached around his neck as they fully embraced. They lingered over the kiss, feeling the warmth flow between their touching bodies. After a long moment, Judas pulled back his head, keeping Rebekah pressed tightly against him, and smiled. "That was better than the wine."

"Shhh!" Rebekah retorted as she looked toward the room where the others sat. "They'll hear us."

They both listened for sounds from the doorway. All was momentarily quiet until they heard Hananiah's feeble yet mirthful voice. "It really is getting dark in here."

Rebekah pushed away from Judas, rolling her eyes laughingly at him as she bent down to the lamps and jar of oil. "I'll just be a minute, Father." A moment later, they heard Mattathias continue with his monologue. Rebekah began filling a lamp as Judas crouched in front of her. Not looking away from her work, she said to Judas in a low voice, "I'm so glad you are here. You have no idea how I've longed to see you. But not just that, I'm glad for Father's sake."

Judas took on a more serious tone, speaking almost in a whisper. "He doesn't look well. Has he been ill?"

"Ill in his spirit," replied Rebekah, "and that's made him ill in his body. You know what Solomon's proverb says: 'A merry heart is a good medicine; but a broken spirit drieth the bones."

"What has happened?" asked Judas, as Rebekah filled the second lamp.

"I suppose it is what is happening everywhere, the Syrian occupation, the unrest among our own people. He takes it all upon himself." Then after a moment's hesitation, she added, "But most of all, it's Shimri."

Judas immediately thought of Rebekah's brother and wondered where he was. "Is something wrong with Shimri?"

"According to Father, everything is wrong with Shimri. Shimri has joined the Sadducees, and it has broken Father's heart. I don't know much of such things, but I see what it has done to Father, and to Mother as well. Shimri still lives here, but it's as though he is not a part of the family any more. He and Father disagree on everything, and Father has taken it so hard that he hardly even eats any more. He is just wasting away from grief as if his son had died."

"I didn't know," was all Judas could say as Rebekah handed him the lamps and turned to put the oil away. She then crossed to the far corner of the room and lit a straw from the glowing coals in the small stone oven. Judas held out the lamps as she touched the flame to each of them.

Rebekah threw the straw into the coals and stood for a moment just looking at Judas. "It's so good to have you here. Maybe your father can help mine. But more than anything, it's just good to see you, to be with you." Then, after a long pause, she said in a whisper, "Next year."

Judas took her meaning, and repeated, "Next year." Their hearts burned within them as they thought of the day only a few months away on which they would finally be free to fully express their love for one another. For just a moment, they were in another time at another place as their minds caught a glimpse of that day. How long they had dreamed of it. Their reverie was suddenly awakened by the strength of Mattathias's voice exclaiming something about the Syrians. Rebekah took the lamps from Judas and led the way back to where the others were involved in deep conversation.

No one looked up as Judas and Rebekah returned to the

front room. A moroseness that the light from the lamps refused to dispel had taken over the mood of the room.

Mattathias looked Hananiah in the eyes. "I have come specifically to you, my old friend, because I knew you would know what is happening here in Jerusalem, and that you could perhaps give us some guidance."

Hananiah sat very still for a moment, and then a single tear rolled down his sunken cheek as he lowered his head. "I know what's happening, all right. But as to what to do, if I knew what to do I would already have done it. All of what you have spoken is not just destroying our country, it has taken my very son. Our son has been stolen from us."

At this, Hananiah broke down and wept openly. Miriam rose and came beside Hananiah and put her arms around him as tears rolled down her own face. Mattathias, not understanding what was meant by Hananiah's words was momentarily at a loss for what to say.

Judas looked at Mattathias and quietly commented, "Shimri has become a Sadducee."

"Oh," said Mattathias somberly. "I see."

Hananiah spoke again through his tears. "He has not just become a Sadducee. For all purposes, he has become Greek. He has abandoned our ways. I saw it happening in other families, but I never thought it would happen here, in my own home. All over Jerusalem, our Jewish boys who we named after our fathers are becoming Greeks."

Mattathias sat for a long moment then ventured to ask, "Where does Shimri live now?"

"He lives here, or at least he sleeps here," came the reply.

"But how could he?" said Mattathias hesitantly. Mattathias had to work to temper an instinctive hardness that overcame him. "Surely if he renounces his heritage, he is dead to us all. Why have you not put him out?"

Hananiah and Miriam clung to one another. "I couldn't, Mattathias," Hananiah said through his tears. "I couldn't. He is our only son. We do not have four other sons as do you. We love him too dearly."

Tears ran down Rebekah's face as she witnessed the grief of her parents. She had heard them weep over Shimri many times in recent months. Judas leaned against a wall, looking down at his feet. Simon, seated on the floor, put his head against his knees. No one said anything for several minutes.

When the moment of grief seemed to have passed, Miriam stood up from where she had been crouched beside her husband. "Let me pour us some more wine." Everyone seemed to be in agreement and held out empty cups. When each cup was filled, they sat quietly drinking. Only Simon spoke, making a brief comment that it was indeed good wine.

The silence was suddenly broken as the door opened. Shimri took a step into the room and stopped, surprised to see that they had guests. No one spoke for a long moment. Mattathias and his sons looked at Shimri incredulously. Had they not known his parentage, they would have thought a Greek was standing in the doorway. The young man before them stood with an air of pride. His coiffed hair and clean shaven face immediately set him apart from the other men in the room. His short tunic was very similar to the one they had seen worn by the hated Apelles the day before. Shimri was well built, his clothing easily allowing one to see his muscular arms and legs. Though strong, he was smooth, not as those who gain their strength from heavy labor.

Judas remembered Shimri as a child. Shimri was two years older than he and Rebekah. Shimri had always reflected an air of superiority, rarely willing to take part in their activities, considering them beneath him. Judas recalled the many times that Shimri had spoken of how he would not be like his father when he grew up, that he would become wealthy and be looked up to. Even in those early years, he had been a source of grief for Hananiah, who had named his son after two Levites, one who had been a gatekeeper in David's sanctuary, and another who had helped renovate the temple under King Hezekiah. His was a name any Levite would be proud of, but Shimri was not content with being a Levite.

Miriam rose and ushered Shimri into the room. Hananiah

spoke dispassionately. "Come in, Son. We have guests."

Miriam found another cup and filled it with wine for Shimri while he surveyed their guests in the dim light of the oil lamps. Shimri knew their guests well, though it had been some time since he had seen them. There was an awkward silence. Shimri sipped his wine and then reclined on the straw mat in front of the bowls of fruit that remained there. Glancing around the room at the three visitors, Shimri broke the silence.

"Have you come all the way from Modin today? How are things in the country?" Shimri said, arrogantly insinuating the inferiority of rural life to life in the city.

Mattathias spoke after a moment's hesitation. "You must forgive us, Shimri. We were a bit startled at your appearance when you arrived in the doorway. You no longer look like a son of Israel."

The young man glanced back and forth between his father and Mattathias. Hananiah hung his head, unable to look either at his son or at his old friend.

After an awkward pause, Shimri burst out, "Oh, but I am. I *am* a son of Israel, but this is the *new* Israel. This is the future. Either we embrace the future, or we die with the past."

"And what is the future?" Mattathias asked suspiciously.

"If we embrace the new thinking, the future is wealth. Privilege. It's no longer having to be slaves to these archaic ways that have held us down for so long."

"What do you mean, 'held us down?'" Mattathias challenged.

"Well just look around you. Here I am sitting on the floor drinking from a clay cup. Why, in some of my friends' homes I lie on a couch at a marble table, drinking from a silver goblet. They have learned how to be a part of this world, not separated from it. The new world is a better world, a richer world. It's also a world that admires the strong rather than the weak, the way it ought to be. Just come to the gymnasium tomorrow. You will see." Shimri looked at Judas with this comment about the gymnasium. It was clear for anyone to see that Judas was physically a very powerful man. Shimri's assumption was that

Judas would admire others of strength.

Mattathias paused and then turned to Hananiah. "What about this gymnasium, Hananiah? Is this new? I haven't heard speak of it before."

Hananiah did not look up. He only muttered, "I *can't* speak of it."

Mattathias formed his plans out loud. "Perhaps we *should* see this gymnasium." Shimri looked pleased, but Hananiah raised his eyes in a look of distress as Mattathias continued. "I must learn everything I can of what is happening here and what the leaders of our people are thinking. One thing I *must* do tomorrow is go to the temple. Will you go with me Hananiah?"

A sudden look of fear and uncertainty crossed Shimri's face and he blurted out, "Uh ...," stopping himself before he said more.

Hananiah looked at his son. "What is it Shimri? Is something the matter?"

Shimri hesitated. He could be in trouble if he said too much and it was traced back to him. He was suddenly caught between two worlds, his family or the world he so wanted to be a part of. Stumbling across the words, he said, "It . . . might . . . not be a good day to go to the temple."

"Why?" said Mattathias. "What is going to happen at the temple tomorrow?"

Still groping for the words to circumvent the truth, Shimri stammered, "Probably . . . nothing. It's just that I heard a rumor that there may be trouble there tomorrow."

"Trouble? What kind of trouble?" Mattathias continued to pry.

"I've just heard that the high priest is going to be offering a sacrifice that certain ones might object to, especially the Hasidim. But then, the Hasidim cause trouble wherever they are."

That last statement spelled out clearly for Mattathias where Shimri's loyalties lay. The Hasidim may be extremists in some things, but it was far better to be an extremist in pursuit of the truth than to be a Sadducee and abandon truth altogether.

Mattathias made a mental note of Shimri's warning, but it made his plans all the more imperative. One thing he *must* do tomorrow was to visit the temple.

Later that evening, thin straw mattresses were taken from where they leaned against the wall during the day. As it was the custom to always to be prepared for guests, there were enough mattresses for everyone, though the members of the family were less comfortable than usual. When they were alone as a family they would stack the extra mattress so as to have the thickness of more than one. However, tonight, the floor was a bit harder, though no one bemoaned the discomfort.

Hananiah slept with his wife and daughter in the back room. The three guests along with Shimri lay on their mattresses in the front room. Mattathias and Simon fell asleep quickly, tired from the day's journey. Shimri, too, was soon in a deep sleep, as could be told from his long steady breathing. Judas, however, was wide awake. His mind was alive with the picture of the woman lying in the next room. Not since they were children had he slept in the same house as Rebekah, and that only one time, on the night before they moved to Modin. Now, only a few feet away, lay the woman he loved.

In the next room, listening to the breathing of her parents, Rebekah lay staring at the ceiling. An agreeable nervousness stirred her blood and chased sleep from her eyes. Just on the other side of the wall on a straw mattress lay Judas ben Mattathias. Soon there would be no wall between them. They belonged to each other.

Chapter 6

When everyone arose the next morning, Shimri was already gone. He would willingly argue with his father, but one against four was not the odds he favored. Besides this, they might ask him further about what he knew of the coming day's events at the temple. He hoped his warning was enough.

Few words were exchanged as Mattathias and his two sons shared barley cakes that they dipped in honey with Hananiah, Miriam, and Rebekah. Hananiah did not seem to want to talk, perhaps embarrassed by what he perceived Mattathias's opinion of him to be due to his position concerning Shimri. He had thought much about it during the night, awakening periodically and reliving the previous evening's conversation. Judas and Rebekah just watched each other with playful eyes as they ate, hardly aware that anyone else was in the room.

Mattathias broke the silence. "Hananiah, do you feel able to go with us today? I want to see this gymnasium that Shimri spoke of. It seemed an important part of the life of Jerusalem in his opinion. I really want to see it. Perhaps you could direct us there. I would like your input along the way."

Hananiah was pleased that Mattathias still valued his opinion, but mention of the gymnasium caused a knot to form in his stomach. He wrestled within himself. He knew what Mattathias would see, things that he was unable to speak of himself. "I'm not strong, you know. I could tell you how to get there, since you already know the city."

"That would be all right, my friend, if you do not feel able," said Mattathias.

Rather than feeling relieved, Hananiah immediately felt overcome by defeat. He had not stood up to his son, and now he was choosing the coward's way out when his friend beseeched his help. After a long pause, he suddenly raised his eyes and said with certainty, "No. I will go with you. I will show you the way."

"Are you sure you are able?"

"Yes, I'm sure. There are things you must see. Things I have tried to shut out. I cannot speak of them, but you will see them, and you will understand." Hananiah felt a new boldness, even though the weight upon his heart refused to lift.

"Very well. I'm thankful to have a friend like you on whom I can depend."

Hananiah was pleased by the words but still felt a heaviness. If only God could depend on him, he thought. What he was allowing in his own home had beckoned the judgment that had come upon previous generations.

"I also want to go to the temple," Mattathias added.

Hananiah simply nodded, resigning himself to whatever the day held.

A few minutes later the four men walked away from the simple dwelling. Judas looked back at Rebekah's smiling face in the doorway. The glow of the morning sun upon her face gave her an angelic appearance. He secretly hoped they would not be gone long.

Hananiah's short, feeble steps slowed the progress of the small group. There was ample time to absorb the flavor of the streets of Jerusalem as they proceeded. Though the morning air was brisk, it was not overly so. As they wound their way through the narrow streets, they recognized changes. The change was not so much in the streets or the buildings as it was in subtle differences in the people. Many living in Jerusalem probably did not even notice the change, but for someone who had not lived there for some time, the change was obvious. People dressed differently. Most conspicuous was the shorter tunics some of the men now wore. These same men almost always had shaven faces and closely coiffed hair. To the tuned ear, sounds were different. Aramaic was still the prevalent language, but it was polluted with a mixture of Greek words. Some, those who appeared more Greek even though they were Jews, had abandoned Aramaic altogether and proudly spoke only Greek. Even the smells were different. As they passed some of the wealthier homes, aromas came from cooking pots that were quite foreign to the olfactory senses of any of the men, all except for Hananiah, that is. He did not want to make mention of the meats that were producing the odors drifting through the air. Jerusalem was no longer the city of the Jews. Other influences were gradually taking over.

It was midmorning when their trek across the city brought them to an open space in which stood an immense elaborate structure. This structure was obviously of a different world from most of the dwellings, large and small, along the streets that had brought them there. The building must have been as tall as any in Jerusalem. A portico completely surrounded the edifice, making one mindful of the temples the Greeks erected to their many gods. The Corinthian columns which supported the portico reached two-thirds the height of the building. Just inside the portico was a wide entrance, bordered by two columns several times larger than those on the outside.

After pausing to visually take in the huge structure, Mattathias proceeded to enter. Judas and Simon followed, looking up to survey the elaborate carvings that became visible once they entered under the portico. Most of the stone carvings were of nude men engaged in feats of strength. Mattathias observed the carvings without turning his head, only rolling his eyes up toward them as he maintained an austere look on his face. Hananiah did not look up, but lowered his eyes to the ground as he followed closely behind Mattathias.

Entering the gymnasium, they saw that to either side of the entrance were sizeable open rooms. The room on the right was some sort of lecture hall. Several young men in casual Greek attire sat on risers as an older man stood before them, appearing to give instruction. Mattathias stopped to listen, as did the others behind him. The discussion – for it seemed to be more discussion than lecture, though everyone appeared to be of the same opinion – was extolling the virtues of Greek culture. After a moment, Mattathias realized that some, including the instructor, were looking their way with disdainful expressions. Mattathias moved his small group away from the entrance of the lecture hall.

On the other side of the entrance was a large vestibule onto which several smaller rooms opened. From what could be seen through the entrances to those rooms, they appeared to be dressing rooms and baths.

Mattathias continued to lead the group forward into the building until the entranceway opened into an immense room that was open to the sky. As he approached the opening to the room, he could see that above the ground level was a mezzanine from which some sat observing the activities on the floor below.

Mattathias's attention was quickly drawn from the architecture of the building, however, when he stepped into the room and looked about. Throughout the huge room, a space large enough to race horses, nude men were engaged in various forms of sports and exercises. Some of the men wore broad-brimmed felt hats. Other than that, they were completely nude.

Mattathias and his two sons stood momentarily dazed, their mouths hanging open. Hananiah refused to look up. They all jumped out of the way as a naked young man ran past them on a track that ran the circumference of the room. It took them some minutes to convince themselves that what they were seeing was not an illusion. To their right, several young men were taking turns throwing a discus. To their left, a pair was wrestling, their well-oiled bodies shining in the sunlight that filtered into the room from the open ceiling. From time to time, a shout of encouragement would come from the mezzanine to one of the athletes.

The suspension of their thoughts due to the astonishment at what they were witnessing was suddenly broken by a voice from behind. "You *did* come." It was Shimri.

Everyone turned to see Shimri standing there wearing nothing but a long white linen towel around his waist. His body was shiny with oil. Shimri was in good spirits.

Mattathias, barely able to speak from consternation, stammered out his words. "Shimri, what is this place? Everyone is naked?"

Shimri laughed. "What did you expect? This is a *gymnasium*. You surely know enough Greek to know that gymnasium comes from the word *gymnos*, which means "naked." We exercise naked. The Jews need to learn from this." Shimri took on a condescending tone. "The body is nothing to be ashamed of. God gave us our bodies. It's because of the old archaic ideas that we fear showing ourselves to each other. A well developed body is a thing of beauty."

No one knew quite how to respond. Simon, looking out at the young men throwing the discus asked, "Why do they wear those hats?"

Shimri hesitated. "The felt hats." He answered slowly and reluctantly, knowing his response would only cause more questions. "The hats represent Hermes."

"Hermes?" burst in Mattathias. "The Greek god Hermes?"

"It's all just a symbol," Shimri defended. "Hermes is the messenger god. He represents swiftness. And much more than that, Hermes is about commerce and invention. This is what we are learning from Greek culture, not their gods, but what they stand for. Good things, things that make life better, richer, stronger." Shimri held up a muscular arm and tightened his fist to emphasize his last word.

Mattathias was about to respond with a sharp rebuke when he was interrupted by a shout from a young man standing close by who had a linen towel similar to that of Shimri's, only his towel was draped over one shoulder. "Antigonus, are you coming?"

Shimri was suddenly flushed in the face. The young man

called again. "Antigonus, come on."

"Who is Antigonus?" said Mattathias. "This young man seems to be talking to you."

Shimri, still red in the face, looked toward his father then back at Mattathias. "That's what they call me here." Then he turned and walked away with the young man to the middle of the room where a pair had just finished wrestling.

"Hananiah," said Mattathias, "did you know about this?"

"I didn't know about the name," the old man replied, appearing weaker than ever before.

"But, did you ..." Mattathias stopped and waited. Shimri had just removed his towel and was facing the young man who called him earlier. They faced off and suddenly locked arms with each other, twisting one another in various contorted positions.

Mattathias suddenly gasped. He leaned in as if to see better. Backing and turning to Hananiah, with wide incredulous eyes he exclaimed, "Hananiah, did you not circumcise your son on the eighth day of his life?"

Judas and Simon squinted their eyes to see what their father was seeing. Hananiah was about to answer when Mattathias continued. "You did! I know you did! I was there."

Hananiah looked up with mournful eyes.

Mattathias was still unable to believe what he saw. "Then how is it I'm seeing what I'm seeing?"

Hananiah backed toward the wall and collapsed on a marble bench. "I knew of it, but had not seen it until today."

"But, how?" said Mattathias.

"I don't know how they do it, but there is an operation to remove the marks of circumcision. Sometime last year, Shimri didn't come home for several days. He said he was on a trip carrying on some business, but a friend told me that he had heard that Shimri had this operation."

"But why would he do such a thing?"

Hananiah broke down and wept. "He doesn't want to look like a Jew."

"Why? So he can run naked with a bunch of Greeks?" A

fire was rising in Mattathias. "That's all I see in here. Nothing but Greeks. How could this happen?"

Hananiah put a weak hand on Mattathias's arm. "Don't be fooled by what you see, Mattathias. Most of these young men are Jewish. I know some of them. I know their parents." Then he added, "So do you."

No more words would come to Mattathias's lips for the moment. He looked around the room examining every face, trying to determine whether he was seeing Jew or Greek. Finally he sighed sorrowfully, "May God forgive us. He gave us circumcision as a sign of His covenant with us. Are our sons saying they no longer want His covenant?"

Hananiah continued to sob. A group of young men walked by, headed toward the baths. One was heard to say arrogantly, "Get the old man out of here. This is a place for the strong. If he wants to cry, let him go somewhere else."

Judas overheard the remark and was about to go after the one who had said it. Mattathias put out his hand to stop him. "Not now. There will come a day to fight, but not now, not here." Then he motioned toward the way they had come in. "Let's leave this place."

Mattathias helped Hananiah to his feet and began to lead him out, Simon on Hananiah's other side. Their progress being slow, Judas lingered in the gymnasium, looking at the wrestling match going on in the middle of the room. In a sudden surge of strength, Shimri threw his opponent. Standing straight up, flexing his shining muscles, obviously proud of his appearance, he looked toward Judas and called out. "Judas, you should come try this. You can be much more than you are."

Judas stood for a moment longer, then turned and walked away. He could hear Shimri's snort of laughter behind him, a laughter joined by others. He wondered, would he one day have to fight Rebekah's brother, a fight that would be much more than a nude wrestling match.

Chapter 7

Outside the gymnasium the four men stopped and looked at one another. Mattathias spoke, though to no one in particular.

"Moses warned us not to become like the nations that surround us. The prophets warned us that if we became *like* them, in the end we would be defeated *by* them. It has always been that way, from the times of the judges to Israel's fall to Babylon. Why can't our people see? Why can't they understand? God called us apart to be a separate people, *his* people. But when we reject his ways we reject him, and he no longer protects us. God help us. This is just like the times of the judges. The people did what was right in their own eyes, and it always led to Israel's defeat. Oh God, give us a Gideon."

Mattathias's pensive comments had been spoken mournfully, but the mention of Gideon aroused a passion in Judas. He recalled the many times as a child when his father would tell him of the celebrated figure in their history, one of the judges before Israel ever had a king, who had begun by destroying the idols in his own town and had gone on to lead the nation to victory over their occupiers against overwhelming odds. The mention of this hero of their people gave birth to a thought that took up permanent residence in Judas's heart. Israel needed a hero.

With no further comments, the men stood looking around

them. Young men, and some not so young, passed by going in and out of the gymnasium. Most wore Greek fashion and looked askance at the four men standing just outside the entrance whose striped woolen cloaks with tasseled corners marked their Jewish loyalties. After a long silence, Simon ventured, "Are we going to the temple?"

Pulled away from his thoughts, Mattathias said, "Yes. At least *there* maybe we will find someone who still knows what it means to be a son of Israel."

As the men proceeded slowly toward the temple mount, the others allowing for Hananiah's lagging pace, they occasionally got a glimpse of the top of the temple through gaps between the buildings. The temple was the highest point in Jerusalem and could be seen from any approach. This was the temple built by Zerubbabel over 250 years earlier upon the return of Israel from captivity in Babylon. It was said that this temple did not have the magnificence of the first temple, the one constructed by Solomon. Nevertheless, Zerubbabel's temple had taken over 20 years to complete and was looked upon with pride and reverence by all who held to the traditions of their ancestors. The temple was the heart of Israel.

Arriving on the western side of the temple mount, the side on which lay the major part of the city, the men looked toward the southern end of the mount. There loomed the Acra, the citadel housing the Syrian garrison. From the towers of the Acra one would be able to see all activity that went on in the temple courts. The sacrilege of Gentile eyes being able to constantly observe the intimate workings of Israel's worship served in no small measure to enflame harsh sentiments within the faithful.

Mattathias led the way along the outer side of the temple courts. Though their view was cut off by the temple annexes that bordered the courts, they could hear signs of activity there. The sounds were not sounds of worship. Coming to the entrance of the temple courts, which opened to the east, they saw a crowd of several hundred men. Everyone was clearly agitated.

Mattathias led his small band around the edges of the crowd, observing and listening so as to ascertain what was happening. On the raised area in front of the temple whereupon sat the bronze altar for burnt sacrifices, there stood thirty to forty Syrian soldiers, each armed with a shield, sword, and *pilum* – the deadly wooden and iron spear that was normally carried only into battle. Every eye of the crowd was focused on what was happening around the altar. Distress could be read in every face.

Mattathias listened closely to what some were saying.

"Look!" exclaimed one man. "That Syrian just came out of the temple."

"He has defiled our most holy place. Surely he should die," another said, to voices of accord from others.

Mattathias looked up to see a Syrian officer escorting a robed figure from the doors of the temple.

"There are women in the priest's quarters," shouted another voice.

Mattathias, along with many others, turned his eyes toward the parvis running beside the temple, the outer side of which held quarters for priests during their times of duty. Mattathias, himself, had spent many nights there in earlier years when he would serve in the temple. Now, standing in the parvis, he saw two women dressed in filmy white material that revealed as much as it covered.

Someone else shouted, "Those are prostitutes, just like in the Greek temples."

A clamor rose in the crowd. A contagious rage began to move them toward the parvis. The women, seeing the edge of the crowd pushing in their direction, quickly disappeared into one of the priests' quarters. The Syrian soldiers rapidly fanned out into a single line so as to intercept anyone who might try to enter the area. They held out razor sharp *pila* ready to thrust them through the heart of anyone who came too near. The crowd stopped its advance, but the clamor did not die.

Above the roar suddenly came the squeal of a pig. Everyone's attention was pulled back to the altar. A robed figured held a modest-sized pig over the altar with one hand and a knife in the other, preparing to offer the pig as a sacrifice. An overwhelming rage seized Mattathias as he watched what was transpiring, for there behind the figure holding the pig, dressed in the sacred robes of the high priest of Israel, stood Menelaus, holding a bowl to capture the blood of the pig.

A cry came up from the crowd. "Blasphemy! Blasphemy!"

A sudden surge pushed through the mass of angry men. Those at the front leapt across the altar just as the knife slid across the pig's throat. Hands wrapped around the throat of the man holding the knife. The pig was jettisoned to the ground as blood spurted from its severed jugular, splattering its crimson message across the front of the high priest's garments.

The soldiers went into action. In a few seconds, thirty Hasidim died as spears were thrust through their bodies. Seeing the death of their brothers did not stop the crowd however. They poured onto the steps of the temple, overwhelming the soldiers by their superior numbers. The scene was the same on every side. As a soldier would fight to extract his pilum from his victim, two or three Hasidim would seize him, commandeering his weapons. Within less than a minute, every soldier was dead, although twice as many Hasidim died in the process.

Menelaus had fled through the doors of the temple, shutting them tightly behind him. As quickly as it had started, it ended. There was a prolonged silence, quiet murmurs running through the crowd, as they began to take stock of what had just happened. Suddenly, there was a cry from the back of the crowd. Everyone turned. There, blocking any way out of the temple courts, stood an entire Syrian *phalanx*.

The phalanx was the battle formation perfected by Alexander the Macedonian. With it, he had conquered the highly trained Persian army. Now, a century and a half later, the same invincible war machine was being employed to annihilate unarmed Jews who just wanted to be free to worship their God. Two hundred fifty-six men, sixteen files of sixteen men so that the overall result was a square formation, held *sarissae* – heavy fifteen-foot spears – lowered to the level of a man's body. Every soldier in the front file had the shafts of four other sarissae extended at varying lengths on either side, those being held by the soldiers in the files behind them. The result was an impenetrable wall of spear points. A skillful phalanx could change directions at any moment, so it was impossible to successfully attack the phalanx from any side.

The phalanx began to move methodically toward the temple, immediately impaling those who had been caught off guard. The men in the crowd frantically backed away, casting anxious glances for avenues of escape but never taking their eyes off the advancing machine of death. Those on the temple steps took up the pila from the soldiers who had been killed, launching them into the midst of the phalanx. Two found their marks, but the rest were deflected by the rimless shields the *phalangites* carried on their shoulders. Once the pila were thrown, there were no more to throw. Some took the swords and shields from the dead soldiers, but it was to no avail. As they tried to fight their way thought the first file of spears, the points of the next file were less than three feet behind, and they were still more than twelve feet away from the soldiers who held the spears. The phalanx continued to advance with deadly results.

Mattathias stared in horror as he watched men die.

"Father, there's no way out!" Judas was shouting in his ear.

Mattathias stood in alarmed amazement as he watched the ground being carpeted with the bodies of Israel's faithful few. "They intend to kill us all."

"Father!" Judas was shouting again above the piercing cries of his countrymen. "Father, you know the temple. Is there a way out?"

Mattathias fought to make himself think rationally. He glanced all around the temple compound, shaking his head in defeat. Suddenly his eyes rested on the temple doors.

"Hezekiah's tunnel," he said, more to himself.

"What?" shouted Judas above the roar.

"Hezekiah's tunnel," shouted back Mattathias.

"Hezekiah's tunnel? That's doesn't come in here. That runs through the City of David, doesn't it?" Judas knew the history of how centuries earlier during the reign of King Hezekiah a tunnel had been carved through solid stone to route a spring from far outside the city walls into the lower city, the City of David, so that there would be water in times of siege by enemy armies.

"Yes," Mattathias answered. "But there were other tunnels dug at about the same time. Nothing so great as the tunnel everyone knows about from the Gihon Spring to the Pool of Siloam, but there were others. Everyone always knew that the temple would be the place of last resistance, so one tunnel was dug as an escape from there. That's why the Babylonians never found the ark. It was taken out through the tunnel."

"Where is this tunnel?"

Mattathias looked again at the doors to the temple and waved his head in that direction. "In there."

"There's a tunnel that comes out *inside* the temple?" Judas couldn't believe what he was hearing.

"Yes. Not many people know about it. If it was known, people could secretly enter the temple. I learned about it as a young man when I used to keep the night watches during my times of duty. Menelaus may not even know about it."

Looking quickly at the devastation going on before them, Judas cried, "Let's go then. It's our only chance."

Mattathias shouted at Simon and Hananiah, "Come with me."

Hananiah was almost to the point of passing out with fear and fatigue. "I can't."

"Simon, pick him up and bring him," Mattathias shouted before rushing toward the doors of the temple. Simon snatched Hananiah up into his arms, amazed at how light he was, and ran behind Mattathias and Judas.

As they ran up the temple steps, they saw the bloody body of one of the prostitutes who had been seen earlier lying on the pavement just in the parvis to the priest's quarters. Someone had bashed her skull against the stone wall of the temple to avenge himself of the certain death that awaited him in the carnage going on in the temple courtyard.

Mattathias tried to open the temple doors. They were obviously barred from the inside. He began to pound and shout, "I am Mattathias ben Hasmoneus, priest of the order Joarib. I demand that you open this door."

He looked back at the advancing phalanx, men continuing to die in its path. Hearing a creak behind him, he turned again and saw that the door had open just a finger's width, eyes peering out through the crack. Judas seized the moment and with lightening movement, reached his fingers into the crack. With already powerful arms feeling a strength that was beyond them, he flung the massive door on its hinges. Mattathias and Judas ran in, followed by Simon with Hananiah in his arms.

Taking a quick look about the interior of the temple, Mattathias was aghast. It hardly resembled the place in which he had at one time served the God of Israel. The things he was familiar with were all missing. Nowhere to be found were the gold lampstand, the table for the showbread, or the altar of incense. Instead, towering in the middle of the room that was known to all Israel as the holy place stood a great stone representation of Zeus. Near the door they had just entered stood Menelaus.

Menelaus shouted at Mattathias. "You can't come in here and defile this place! Get out!"

The gentle priest from Modin suddenly became the silver-haired warrior for Israel. As Moses casting down the tablets given him by God, or Elijah before the Baal prophets, with eyes as of fire, Mattathias advanced menacingly toward Menelaus. "You curse of Israel, you have brought this abomination to us. You stand here in Israel's holy place wearing the most holy clothes in all the nation, covered in the blood of a swine. May hell receive you before this day is over."

Astounded by Mattathias's rage and seeing the powerful young man standing behind him, Menelaus backed away.

Reminded by the screams coming from outside that escape was a more pressing matter than revenge, Mattathias turned to see again the one-sided battle being waged in the temple courts. Just outside the door he saw some men, thirty or forty, who had been attentive to the door's opening. "Come quickly!" he shouted. "Save yourselves."

Some of the men ran in, but others hesitated. One man looked at Mattathias with troubled eyes. "It would be sacrilege for us to enter the house of the Lord."

Looking again at Menelaus, he replied, "There is nothing here left to defile. This is no longer the temple of our God. It's a place of idols." Mattathias pointed to the statue of Zeus.

The men hesitated a further moment then quickly moved inside the door. Mattathias looked outside again then said to Judas, "Judas, close the door and bar it."

Judas faltered. "But Father, there may be others."

"Close it now," shouted Mattathias, "or we all die."

Judas quickly pulled the door shut and dropped the heavy bar into place.

"Watch them. Don't let them move," said Mattathias to those who had entered, pointing to Menelaus and two other priests who cowered behind him. "Judas, come with me."

Judas followed his father along the southern wall of the temple. Mattathias closely examined the stones in the floor. About midway he stopped. "Here it is," he said. "Bring me one of those torches."

"But there's no fire," said Judas.

"Just bring it," said Mattathias. Judas quickly obeyed.

Mattathias used the brass decorative handle of the torch to dig away the built up sediment between the stones. Then, prying with the torch handle, he lifted one end of the large slab. As soon as it was high enough to get his fingers under, Judas grabbed it and lifted it away, revealing a steep stone staircase descending into blackness.

Chapter 8

A thunderous pounding hit the temple doors, replaced after a few moments by a rapid though violent tapping, as if being struck by metal. Mattathias walked partway to the front of the temple, watching the doors and observing the fearful group of Hasidim as they looked questioningly at him.

"The last of our brothers have died," he said almost matter-of-factly. "What you hear now are the points of spears on the door. It won't take them long before they either chop their way through or bring in something larger to break the doors in. We must hurry."

Menelaus, who had been standing open-mouthed at seeing the tunnel revealed in the temple floor, now sneered at them all. "You'll never get away. You may as well give up."

Mattathias turned to Judas. "We must do something about him and the other two. As soon as we are gone they will open the doors and immediately we will be caught."

Judas walked straight to Menelaus. Looking Menelaus in the eye, he said sardonically, "God forbid that I should lift a hand against the Lord's anointed," repeating the words said centuries earlier by David when he had opportunity to kill Saul. Before Menelaus could react, Judas smashed his huge fist into Menelaus's face. Menelaus crumpled into a heap on the floor. Judas looked down at his unconscious body and said bitterly, "You are not the Lord's anointed."

Judas turned to the group of Hasidim as he walked back toward the opening in the floor. "Take care of those two," he said, indicating the other two priests. Without hesitation, the group began pounding on the other two priests. One priest shouted that he was forced to take part in the sacrifice, but his protests gained him nothing. Moments later, both priests lay unconscious, possibly dead.

Mattathias gazed only for a moment at the men lying on the floor. Then, searching with his eyes all around the interior of the temple, he said "Does anyone see any fire of any sort? We need light." Eyes combed every corner. Cold brass torches hung along the wall. There was no need for them during the day. Daylight filtering through high clerestory windows provided what illumination was needed. Nothing else offered even the possibility of fire. The closest fire was in the altar outside the doors, doors that were sounding more fragile by the moment. Some looked questioningly at the massive veil that separated them from the most holy place, the room where the ark had rested in the temple Solomon had built on this same spot. This present temple had never held the ark, which had disappeared during the Babylonian siege. Nevertheless, the most holy place was still the place wherein was encountered the very presence of God. Even with death knocking at the door, no one in this group would dare look behind the veil, not even Mattathias.

Mattathias was beside himself with frustration. "There was always fire in the temple. The lampstand was never allowed to go out. Now even the lampstand is gone." He sighed heavily.

Walking to the opening in the floor he questioned Judas. "When we go down these stairs, do you think you can come down last and pull this slab back in place?"

Judas looked down at the slab. "To not die at the hand of a Syrian, I'm sure of it."

Mattathias turned to everyone else. "My friends, we have no light. We will need to feel our way through darkness much greater than any of us have probably experienced. It has been many years since I entered this tunnel as a curious young priest.

I do not, in fact, know where it comes out. I never had the courage to follow it all the way. Now we either follow it or die. There may be other tunnels connected to it, though I doubt it. I will go down first and lead. Everyone must be very quiet, so that if I run into an obstacle or a dead end, I can be heard to inform everyone else."

Everyone nodded that they understood. Mattathias looked at Hananiah, who was now standing by Simon. "Can you make it Hananiah?" The old man blinked his sunken eyes and nodded affirmatively. "Then you come right behind me," said Mattathias.

Mattathias stepped downward into the blackness. He reached his hands forward and to each side. He was able to feel each wall as he progressed. This tunnel was happily wider than the tunnel of Hezekiah that everyone knew about, which was only about two feet wide and at some points little higher than a man's waist. Obviously, this had been dug with the intention of allowing for the passage of something besides water.

Hananiah shuffled silently behind Mattathias, reaching out his hand to touch his cloak. Simon arrived at the bottom of the steps behind Hananiah. Then, one-by-one, the others slowly and silently descended into the darkness. Last of all, Judas lowered himself onto the steps. Sitting on a step near the top, he lifted his hands above his head and slid the stone slab until it fell into place.

Minutes later, a hole was chopped through the temple door large enough to reach through and throw the bar out of its brackets. Soldiers burst into the room with swords drawn. Seeing the three men unconscious on the floor, an officer ran to Menelaus and sat him up. Menelaus's head lobbed to one side. Judas had done his work well. The high priest would be out of commission for some time.

Several soldiers dashed forward and ripped down the veil in front of the most holy place, expecting to find the men they had seen come in. All that welcomed them was an empty room. They looked around the room, then at each other. Not only were they surprised that no one was there, they were bewildered by the fact that the room was entirely empty. What did these Jews worship? Why have a temple to nothing?

Looking across the room toward the door they had entered and then from side to side, the soldiers were perplexed. There were no other exits from the temple. One solider commented to the others, "This must be the work of the gods. I'm sure I saw many men come into this place, yet where are they?" Mystified, they looked at the officer holding the high priest. Perhaps the high priest had the answers, if only he could talk.

Mattathias groped his way through the nightmarish darkness. Solid rock surrounded them on every side. No longer could the din of fighting be heard. This did not mean it did not linger in the thoughts of each man as they moved along what seemed an endless tomb. Though eyes could not see, minds could not erase the picture of brothers lying dead in the temple courts. A depression as deep as the darkness settled over the troop of survivors, if indeed they were survivors.

Hearing behind him only breathing and the brush of clothing against the stone walls, Mattathias felt his way forward. He whispered so quietly that no one could hear the words of the psalm. "The Lord is my light and my salvation; whom shall I fear?" The God that brought Israel through the sea to escape their enemies could bring them through this darkness.

The air was dank and stale. It had been many years, perhaps centuries, since anyone had walked this dark path. At their slow pace, the tunnel seemed endless. Mattathias wondered as he felt along the walls if the Ark of the Covenant had at one time been carried along this oppressive underground route. Was it still here somewhere, held under cover of darkness until some future age when it would again be brought into the light? The thought both frightened and excited the priest.

After a distance of what seemed well over a furlong descending into the earth, the tunnel took a noticeable upward turn. A short distance further, Mattathias's groping hands suddenly hit against a solid wall in front of him. He felt to either side, expecting to find an opening off to the side. Both sides were solid.

"Stop!" he said, not too loudly. Mattathias puzzled over their situation. Suddenly, they could go no further.

"What is it, Father?" Simon's voice cut through the darkness from behind Hananiah.

"The tunnel has ended," came the surprised reply.

"You mean it just stops?"

Low murmurs echoed up and down the length of the tunnel. Neither Mattathias nor Simon spoke for a long while. Why dig a tunnel with no exit? Their thoughts became as dark as the world in which they found themselves. Only gradually did a light begin to dawn in Simon's mind.

"Father, do the walls feel like stone or earth?"

In the darkness could be heard a brisk rubbing against the wall. In another moment there was a more vigorous rubbing as Mattathias used his sandal to try to dig part of the wall away.

"It's not stone, but it's very hard. My guess is that it's clay that has become very hard. Wait." There was another long moment and more rubbing. Mattathias spoke again, this time with measured jubilation. "On the ceiling, I think I feel roots."

Simon felt above him, feeling nothing. Reaching forward, over the head of Hananiah, he felt the ceiling again. There he felt a difference. There were definitely roots. "You're right!" he exclaimed. "We must be close to the surface. Can we dig straight up?"

Mattathias clawed at the dried earth with his fingers but only managed to fill the air with dust. Simon squeezed by Hananiah and tried his hand at it. He dug until he felt the blood pouring from the ends of his fingers.

They paused and tried to think. Mattathias asked the men standing closest, "Does anyone have a knife or anything of metal? Does someone here happen to have one of the swords taken from the Syrians?"

The question passed along the tunnel. Soon the answer came back. One man close to the front answered for all. "No one has anything. Those that got the swords tried to use them in the fight. They are all dead now."

A gloomy silence fell upon the group. Their brothers were dead, and now they were in a trap that could only end in death, for it was only a matter of time before Menelaus or one of the other two priests told the Syrians where they had disappeared to. Depressed murmurs could again be heard along the passage.

Simon removed his sandal and used its edge to scrape the earth. After several minutes, he felt a clump of roots. "I think I'm making progress," he said. Grabbing the roots, he gave a downward tug. A hard clod fell at his feet, and a shaft of light instantly illuminated his face which was now covered in dust.

A cheer was about to erupt among the men who were close enough to see what had happened, but Mattathias quickly suppressed it. "Be quiet! We don't know where we are. We might still be in danger."

Simon widened the hole carefully. When the hole seemed wide enough for a man's head, he scraped out two shallow holes in the side of the wall into which he could place his feet. All who could see him from their position in the tunnel watched intently as Simon pushed with his hands against the opposite wall while stepping with his feet in the holes he had dug. Slowly he raised his head through the hole.

Suddenly, Simon jerked his head down. His wide eyes told the story almost as well as his words. "We are just outside the outer doors of the citadel, and they are open."

Mattathias dropped his head. Another of David's psalms whispered across his lips. "How long, O Lord, wilt Thou forget me forever? How long wilt Thou hide Thy face from me?"

Chapter 9

Simon slowly raised his head to the opening again, at first taking care not to rise above the level of the ground above, but little by little rising until his eyes were high enough to see around. There were enough weeds and tall grass growing around his position so that he felt safe from being discovered.

The opening was outside the city wall by only a few feet. Looking back in the direction of the tunnel, but looking straight up, Simon could see the wall towering above him. Less than a hundred feet away was the outer entrance of the Acra – the citadel which housed the Syrian garrison. The southeast corner of the city wall was L-shaped. They were just outside the short section of wall which ran east and west, the part that enclosed the southern side of the temple mount's southeast corner. Perpendicular to this was the wall that protected the eastern side of the City of David. Where the walls came together stood the citadel, its outer entrance being part of the city wall itself.

Simon surveyed the area for activity. Since the Syrians were occupied with what was happening within the city, the only soldiers he saw were two guards stationed by the entrance. He looked up at the tower looming above, a tower which oversaw the temple courts. Anyone observing from there would be unlikely to see his present position. In order to do so, one would have to lean over the parapet and look straight down.

To the east he could see the verdant slopes of the Mount of Olives, its base about a furlong away. Simon dropped back into the tunnel and shook the dust from his clothes as he reported what he had seen.

Word moved quickly up the line of men until it reached Judas at the rear. Judas had grown more and more apprehensive each minute they remained in the tunnel. He was in the most precarious position of all. He would be the last out, and if the Syrians found their way into the tunnel through the temple, he would be the first attacked from the rear. He peered back through the darkness of the tunnel as he listened to the anxious thoughts of his countrymen.

Every mind was reliving the events of the past hour, the image of the blood of their brothers running on the pavement of the temple courts still vivid in their thoughts. To be captured meant certain death, only their death would be more cruel than that of their brothers, for the Syrians would make an example of any they captured. They had learned well from Antiochus's seizure of the city two years earlier on his return from Egypt just how cruel a Syrian execution could be. To this day, it was unbelievable to them that their own countrymen had opened the gates to the city and given it over to Antiochus without a fight. Antiochus had at that point systematically proceeded to publicly torture to death any who opposed his rule. Eventually, Antiochus had returned to his palace in Antioch, but his garrison remained in Jerusalem. Things had been relatively calm for the past couple of years, but today everything changed. All understood that any further attempts to lure them peacefully and diplomatically into the Greek world would be abandoned. Now it was either conform or die.

A faint scraping caught Judas's attention. Though the upward curve of the tunnel prevented his seeing Simon – and he could only discern a pale glow from that end of the tunnel – he had heard Simon's digging as it resonated along the tunnel walls. This was a different sound, like stone scraping against stone.

"Shh!" Judas touched the man in front of him, and the man

quit talking to his Hasidim brothers who were in front of him. The cacophony of low murmurs silenced itself along the tunnel. Every ear focused into the silent darkness.

"Stay very quiet," whispered Judas. "I thought I heard something, but I can't be certain."

Judas turned and felt his way along the tunnel, returning in the direction of the temple. In a few steps he was again in pitch blackness. He thought he felt a draft in his face as he felt his way along. This would mean the air was able to circulate, the tunnel now open on both ends. But he wondered if he was imagining it. After some distance, he stopped and listened. He heard nothing but the sound of his own pulse beating heavily in his ears.

He was about to venture further when he distinctly heard a voice. Holding his breath to stop all other sound, he focused all his senses into the darkness. He heard nothing, but a few seconds later, his dilated eyes discerned a diffusion of light far up the tunnel. Though it had been undetectable in the dark, the light made it plain to see that the tunnel had a gradual curve, for Judas was unable to see the light's source. Judas waited. In the distance his eyes suddenly picked up the glow of a torch. He waited just a moment longer, long enough to see that the soldier holding the torch held a sword in his other hand. Menelaus or one of the other two priests had regained consciousness. The way of their escape had been discovered.

Judas backed silently but quickly away. He knew he was far enough away in the darkness so that the soldier would have been unable to see him. Before many steps he could no longer see the torch's glow, only the light disseminated around the curve of the tunnel wall. Staying at a crouch so as not to bump against the ceiling, Judas moved almost at a trot, touching the walls lightly with his hands as he went. A few seconds later he crashed into the Hasidim brother standing at the rear of the line, knocking him into his compatriots.

"Soldiers are coming down the tunnel!" Judas kept his voice low despite the instinct that pressed him to do the opposite. "We have to leave now!"

Within seconds, the message was received at the front. Simon looked out the hole toward the Acra. Only one guard was presently in sight, and he was talking with someone inside the gates of the citadel, probably the other guard.

Simon spoke rapidly to the men in the tunnel. "If we are quiet, we may go undetected, at least for a while. Stay low. The high weeds may help hide us. Run to the Mount of Olives and hide among the trees. It's the only protection."

Simon pulled at his father and pushed him upward through the hole, saying, "I'll push Hananiah up after you. Then I'll take him."

Mattathias crawled out and slid along the ground, mostly hidden by the weeds. He turned around to help Hananiah. Simon almost threw Hananiah's light body out of the hole into the air. Mattathias caught him and dragged him across the ground. An instant later Simon was by their side. The guard had not yet turned in their direction.

Simon ordered Hananiah to climb on his back, an order which found immediate compliance. His frail burden clinging tightly, Simon rose to a crouch and ran silently along the wall toward the Mount of Olives, Mattathias right behind him.

Just as they cleared the corner of the city wall, they heard a shout behind them. "Stop!" They froze for the instant it took to look back and see the guard running out from the citadel gates toward where they stood. Behind them several of their compatriots who had made it out likewise momentarily froze in position. An instant later, everyone broke into a frantic run. There was no longer any reason for caution.

The guard stopped midway to their place of escape, his sword drawn. He was armed, but he was only one, and they were many. He looked back at the other guard who had run from the gates and was staring unbelievingly at what was happening. "Get help! It's the Jews who hid in the temple. Hurry!" The other guard turned and ran into the citadel shouting. The remaining guard advanced nervously to where men were pouring from the opening. If he attacked, he would be outnumbered. If he did nothing, he would be executed for cowardice.

Caught between possible survival and certain death, the Syrian threw himself at a man halfway out the hole, running him through with his sword. The man fell back into the hole. As he pulled his sword from the falling man, the guard felt himself grabbed from behind, his arms bound uselessly behind him. As he fought to get away, another man wrested the sword from his hand and thrust it under the guard's breastplate into his stomach. The guard crumpled to the ground, the sword protruding from both sides of his body. With no thought of the usefulness of the sword, the two Hasidim broke into a run.

In the tunnel, men backed away in fear at the sight of their compatriot falling dead at their feet. Yet the pushing from behind forced the man next in line to step on the dead body and look out the hole. Seeing the dead guard lying in front of him, he launched himself onto the surface and ran. Others followed.

Mattathias looked back as he ran, his aged body resisting the intense activity. He saw the successful killing of the guard, but from his present vantage point he could also see inside the gates of the citadel. At least a dozen soldiers were running toward the entrance, swords drawn. Mattathias turned his face toward the Mount of Olives, tears running down each cheek. There would be no hope of survival for Judas. Why had he brought his sons to Jerusalem? Why had God abandoned them?

Judas watched anxiously behind him. The group in front of him was no longer quiet. The Syrians coming down the tunnel would mentally posture themselves to attack.

"Lord, show me what to do." Judas prayed frantically as his thoughts ran rapidly through the possibilities.

A few seconds later, he discerned the subtle flicker of a torch shining around the distant curve of the stone walls. Glancing back at the only means of escape, Judas knew he could not make it in time. With scarcely a plan formed in his mind, he broke into a crouched run toward the approaching torch light. Once he was able to see the actual fire of the torch, he took a few more steps and dropped to the ground. The flaming torch rapidly approached, the soldier carrying it in a careful run. Judas covered himself in his cloak. Somehow, providence had seen to it that his cloak was dark blue, not immediately visible in the dim light. Judas lay flat with his face covered, praying that the soldier was looking ahead rather than down. There were other soldiers, perhaps three or four, behind the one holding the torch, but all Judas saw was the one torch.

In another moment the soldier with the torch, moving quickly, was only a few feet from where Judas lay. Holding the torch extended in front of him, his sight hampered as he peered beyond the flame, the soldier's next step would have come down on Judas. Too late, the Syrian realized that something lay at his feet.

In a single swift motion, Judas lunged upward with all his might throwing the top of his head into the soldier's groin as he grabbed his arms, throwing them outward against the stone walls. The soldier's helmeted head hit the ceiling in a moment of shock as he felt the skin shredded from the back of his hands by the rough wall. He cried out in pain as his sword and torch clattered to the ground.

Still on his knees, in one fluid motion, Judas reached for the sword with his right hand and the torch with his left. The soldier fell backward, but by the time he hit the ground, Judas had run the sword through his side into his heart. Without pulling out the sword, he used both hands to run the burning torch under the soldier's clothing, pulling up his tunic with his right hand and thrusting the torch with his left. This extinguished the flame, casting the tunnel into darkness, a darkness Judas found safer than the light.

Finding themselves suddenly plunged into darkness took away what little confidence the other soldiers had. They hesitated as Judas warily but quickly pulled the sword from their dead comrade's side. Judas had bought time, though only moments. He was still one against many. His mind raced, searching for his next move.

Making sure he would be understood, Judas blurted out in broken Greek, *"Yoanna, phere moi ten loghen!"* (John, bring me the spear!) Judas hated the very fact that Greek had become widely spoken among his people, but this was one time he was glad he had learned it as a child on the streets of Jerusalem. He prayed his ruse worked.

The soldiers stood frozen. They had seen no one else, but then, they hadn't seen Judas either until he had appeared as a ghost out of the darkness. In these narrow confines, a sword would be no defense against a thrusting spear.

Moments later, Judas heard the soldiers' footsteps rapidly retreating up the tunnel. Working as swiftly as possible in the dark, Judas removed the dead man's helmet and fastened it on his own head. Feeling his away around the soldier's body, he unfastened the cords that held the small square iron plates that served as breast and back plates. Judas's hands were sticky with blood that had soaked through the man's clothing.

Removing his cloak, Judas fastened the plates over his tunic. He pulled his tunic up into his cincture until the lower hem was midway his thighs. Though he could not see himself, he imagined he looked as Greek as he ever would. His beard might give him away, but he hoped the cheek-pieces on the helmet would cover it if he kept his head averted. Seizing the sword in his hand, he ran down the tunnel toward what he prayed would be freedom.

Arriving at the way to the surface, he saw three bodies lying in a heap just under the opening. He wondered if one of them might be the Hasidim he had crashed into earlier. Outside he heard shouts and screams.

Judas looked back up the tunnel before moving further. There would be no way out for him there. Forcing a decision, he stepped upon the bodies and raised his head through the opening. Immediately, two swords were thrust in his face. Seeing the helmet, the two soldiers immediately withdrew their swords.

Hoping his accent would not give him away, Judas shouted as he pointed out across the field, "*Ode ouk esin eti! Sullambanete autous!*" (There are no more here! Catch the others!)

After a moment's hesitation, the soldiers turned and ran, joining their comrades in trying to capture or kill the fleeing Jews. Judas waited another moment. He hoped his words would not result in anyone's death. Probably, those fleeing for their lives, if they had already gotten away, would easily outrun the armed soldiers.

Judas climbed out of the hole and ran toward the Mount of Olives as if in pursuit of the escaping Jews. He noticed seven or eight bodies lying on the ground. One of them appeared to be Syrian.

Almost a half hour later, Judas quit running. He was about three miles from the city. He found a place to hide himself from view and sat looking back toward Jerusalem. No one was in sight. He wondered how many had escaped. He had seen bodies lying by the city wall. What about his father? What about Simon? And what about frail Hananiah, his future father-in-law? Were they among the dead?

Judas remained in his concealed position throughout the afternoon. Once the sun had set, he began walking, taking a southerly course at first so as to walk around the city and enter from the other side. The helmet would be of no further use to him, and might even raise questions if seen, so he left it. The sword he would definitely keep. The breast and back plates might prove useful too. He removed them, then removed his tunic. The cool Kislev evening air bit his skin. He quickly fastened the plates against his body and put the tunic back on over them. The thin tunic helped little against the chill air. How he longed for his cloak now.

Judas made his way around the southern end of Jerusalem, always listening for signs of danger. The night turned frigid. Judas held his hands under his arms to warm them, still clutching the sword, which was becoming an encumbrance. How he wished he had thought to take the sword's sheath off the dead Syrian.

It was well into the third watch of the night, the night more than half over, when Judas passed through the city gates. There was scarcely a sound in the sleeping city, though he wondered if any actually slept in the many homes that were suddenly deprived of husbands, fathers, and sons. Judas stayed to the shadows, lest anyone be watching.

Arriving on the street where Hananiah lived, Judas stopped in a dark doorway for several minutes before proceeding. He listened to every sound. If anyone had seen or was following him, they would move before long and he would know it.

Finally, satisfied that no one was following, he went to the door of Hananiah's house. He tried the latch first, not wanting to make a noise by knocking. As expected, the door was locked. He knocked very quietly then stopped to listen. At first, there was no sound, but then he heard the shuffle of feet. The door opened a crack, just enough for the flame of an oil lamp to shine through.

Simon let out an audible sigh of relief as he opened the door, and Judas entered. The room was dark except for the single lamp. Mattathias, sitting on a mat in the corner wept openly. "You're alive!" he exclaimed. "God be praised! He has brought my son home alive!"

Rebekah leapt to her feet and ran and put her arms around Judas and held him as if never to let him go. Tears streamed down her face. Judas handed the sword he was holding to Simon so he could hold Rebekah. There was nothing else he wanted to do but hold her. Today it had seemed his life had been snatched away from him, but now it was given back.

Judas looked down at Hananiah lying on a mat, Miriam clutching his hand. They were all in the front room. No one had slept. In the dim light of the oil lamp, Judas could see a faint smile flicker across Hananiah's face, but he could see concern in Miriam's eyes. Had the strain been too much for Hananiah?

Not letting go of Judas but backing her body away, Rebekah exclaimed, "You're freezing!" She put her hand against Judas's chest and looked into his face with a befuddled look.

Judas laughed. "It's my breast plate. And it *is* cold. I look forward to removing it. If you will give me just a moment, I'll be right back."

Judas let go of Rebekah and stepped into the other room, just long enough to remove his tunic and remove the breast and back plates. After redressing he returned to the others, handing the plates to Simon, who was still holding the sword with a questioning look in his eyes. Miriam handed him a cup of wine. Judas drank it down and allowed her to fill it again. It tasted good. It was the first of anything he had had to drink since the morning before. After a short while, the alcohol began to have a warming effect upon his body. Finally, the anxiety of the past day, the slaughter in the temple courts, the fight in the tunnel, the flight to escape death, began to fade, if only for this moment.

He told them all how he had escaped, and Simon told how they had managed to get away and return home. Mattathias and Hananiah, knowing the city better, had known other safe ways back into the city. Rebekah sat close beside Judas, holding his hand tightly. No one asked whether it was proper. They were together, and alive. That was all that mattered right now.

When all had been said about their escapes, Judas looked at Hananiah's pale face. "Hananiah, are you all right?"

Hananiah stared back through hollow eyes. A cock crowed outside, the first herald of the morning as Hananiah responded. "I'm all right, Judas," he said feebly. "I just need to rest." But there remained a question from the way Hananiah had said it.

Miriam put out her hand and touched Judas's arm. "It's Shimri," she said softly. "He never came home last night."

Chapter 10

The next day was quiet. There was little movement around the streets of Jerusalem as the population struggled to make sense of the previous day's events.

Mattathias implored Hananiah to leave Jerusalem, but to no avail. Hananiah did not get up from his mat all day, but his weakened condition was not the reason for his refusal to leave. The reason he stayed was Shimri.

Mattathias tried to talk sense into his old friend. "Don't you see, Hananiah? Shimri is dead to you. He has abandoned everything you stand for. He hates everything you are."

Hananiah mournfully countered, "But he might come back. He might wake up and see what is really happening. We need to be here for him."

Miriam did not participate in the conversation but sat somberly in the corner of the room, her eyes downcast. Mattathias knew that Hananiah spoke for both of them.

"Then at least let Rebekah return to Modin with us," Mattathias urged.

Hananiah waited a long while before speaking. He looked at Miriam, their eyes meeting. "It wouldn't be proper."

"But it's dangerous in Jerusalem," said Mattathias. "Think about her safety."

"It may be no safer in Modin," countered Hananiah.

Judas and Rebekah were in the next room, where Rebekah

was preparing the noon-day meal, hearing every word. Judas looked down into Rebekah's eyes. The thought of her coming with them made his heart leap. Rebekah looked back up at him and saw the question in his eyes. For a moment, she looked as though there was nothing in the world that she wanted more, but then she dropped her eyes with an inward sigh.

"I can't leave my parents, not yet, not now," she said dolefully. "Don't you see? They have already lost their son. What would it do to them to lose me, too? What would it be like for them if suddenly neither of us were here? And you heard Father, he won't leave. He still hopes that Shimri will come home."

Judas looked away from Rebekah. "Do you think he'll come home?"

Rebekah didn't answer immediately. Her mind raced back across the years, years in which she had watched Shimri make the choices that had made him what he was today. Finally, looking down at the cakes she was patting in her hands, she said, "No. Shimri will never come home." After a long pause she continued, "He may come to this house, but he will never come home. I love my brother, and I pray for him every day. May God help me, I pray for him, but there is very little faith in my prayers. Shimri is lost to us."

"Then why stay?" Judas urged, not yet willing to give up the idea of Rebekah's coming to Modin.

Rebekah wiped her hands on a cloth and turned to Judas. Putting her arms around him, she looked up into his face. "Judas, I love you more than anything in the world. We belong to each other. I lay in bed at night thinking what it will be like to be your wife. Our day is coming soon. But right now, my place is with my parents. They need me."

Judas looked down into those warm, serious eyes, and he knew there was no point in talking further. What made her the daughter she was also worked to make her the wife and mother she would become. Pulling her tight against himself, he kissed her in a way that, for the moment, set the world aside and spoke of hearts that were able to transcend their immediate circumstances.

In the other room, Simon entered from outside. He had been out picking up what news he could.

"There's very little movement in the streets today," he informed everyone. "Even the market is mostly shut down. Watching the west gate, there does seem to be quite a number leaving the city. Many seem to think there might be an escalation of what started yesterday."

Mattathias looked at Hananiah. Surely these words would move him. But Hananiah just shook his head. Mattathias dropped his eyes. It was no use. Hananiah would not leave Jerusalem, not so long as he held a thread of hope for Shimri.

Before the sun rose the next morning, Mattathias and his two sons left. Judas was wearing a cloak that Rebekah had found that had belonged to Shimri. Shimri would no longer wear it because it looked too Jewish. Judas also had under his tunic the breast and back plates. Tied to his cincture and hidden under his cloak was a homemade sheath he had made the previous afternoon in which he held the sword he had taken off the Syrian soldier.

When they came to the end of the lane before turning into another street, Judas turned back to look at Rebekah standing in the doorway. Her figure was dimly silhouetted in the doorway by the light of an oil lamp. Though some distance away, he could see her lift her hand in a gentle wave as he himself did before stepping out of sight around the corner. He knew she was crying, even as he blinked back tears of his own.

Judas had suggested staying in Jerusalem, but Mattathias had insisted that he come with them to Modin. "We must plan our response to this threat that hangs over our nation," he had said, adding, "while there is still a nation to respond."

Judas was torn. Killing the Syrian in the tunnel had affected him deeply. He had never killed a man before. He still trembled with fear as he thought about it, yet at the same time he realized he had taken great pleasure in it. Was it right to even feel this way? He didn't know, but there was a part of him that wanted the opportunity to do it again. But then his thoughts filled once again with Rebekah. He literally ached for her. He wondered, would one desire exclude the other?

The sun was rising to their backs as they left the city. Others were leaving also, not an extraordinarily great number, but it was unusual to see this many people traveling this early. Syrian troops stationed at the gates seemed content to allow people to leave but were inspecting anyone coming into the city, as Mattathias and his sons saw them doing to a merchant bringing a cart of his wares in to sell in the market.

Mattathias informed his sons that they would stop in Mizpah. Simon was happy about this – his future wife was in Mizpah – though his emotions were more difficult to discern than those of Judas. Mizpah was less than a half hour off the road that led back to Modin. Since the journey home was mostly downhill, it would not take them much longer than the journey to Jerusalem had three days earlier, even with the added detour. Mizpah, being closer to Jerusalem than was Modin, would be an early measure of how the new Syrian policy would affect the other rural areas.

As they walked, Mattathias began to discuss the matters that were upon his heart. "My sons, you have seen everything I have over these past couple of days. We have – all three of us – escaped death together. God has preserved us, and I believe it is for a reason. But now the question is what to do. We have known for a long time that the Syrians are our enemies. What troubles me most is the enemy within, the enemy among our own people."

The men looked straight ahead as they walked along the road. Their minds went to Shimri, and especially to what they had witnessed at the gymnasium with its disgusting display of public nudity. The very existence of such a place, it would seem, would be an offense to any Jew. But Jews were not only participating, they were actually having their circumcisions reversed so they would feel comfortable doing so. There was a conscious decision by many to abandon their heritage and embrace all things Greek.

Mattathias continued. "When I think about what we are up against, I am overwhelmed. The Syrians have garrisons of armed and trained soldiers. We have nothing. Besides this, now we find that many of our own people, not just a few, are siding with them."

There was a long silence as they continued to walk. Simon finally spoke. "Perhaps if there were a champion – a true *Jewish* champion – for our people, then others would rally to him. Those who are going along with the Syrians seem to be doing so because the Syrians are the winning side. If a person wants wealth, he has to do it the Syrian way, or he has nothing. If there is a contest of any sort, whether it's economic, political, or military, who wins? The Syrians. The Syrian way is the way to power and success, at least in the eyes of a lot of people. What if that changed? What if a Jew came along who turned that all upside down? What if a Jew began to exercise power over the Syrians? What if it became dangerous to do things the Syrian way rather than the Jewish way? Wouldn't the people turn?"

Several minutes passed without a further word as they walked along the rough road. Though there were great distances between them, they could see others traveling along the same road in the same direction as themselves. No one appeared to be going in the opposite direction, toward Jerusalem.

"But how can anyone fight such overwhelming odds?" said Mattathias, breaking into the silence.

"Gideon beat the odds." Judas had waited for just the right question before entering the conversation. "With only three hundred he beat the whole Midianite army."

"Gideon also had a visitation from the angel of the Lord," rejoined Mattathias.

"Yes, Father, but think about it," Judas continued, not willing to have his comment suppressed so easily. "Whatever Gideon did, he did secretly or by surprise. The scriptures say the first thing he did was destroy the idols in his home town. He did it by night so no one would know what was happening.

When he fought the Midianites, he did it by surprising them and throwing them into total confusion."

Mattathias could see Judas had been thinking hard upon this, not just in what could be done, but how to do it. "So what are you saying, Son?"

Judas's passion began to show itself. "Father, when I was in the tunnel, I knew there was no way I was going to survive what I was up against. Several armed soldiers were coming in my direction, and I had nothing to fight with, and no way of escape. But I *did* survive, and I killed the Syrian and confused the others because I was able to surprise them. These Syrians are trained for an open battlefield. What if we refuse to follow their rules?"

Mattathias looked over at Judas, then at Simon. He had never wanted his sons to have to shed the blood of others. After all, they were Levites. God had not allowed David to build the temple because he had been a man of bloodshed. Should one whose very purpose was the service of the temple lead in the fight against others? Nevertheless, a glimmer of hope dawned in Mattathias's heart as he reflected upon what each of his sons had said.

It was just before noon when they arrived in Mizpah. As Mizpah was not a large town, it only took a couple of minutes to arrive at the door of Jedaiah ben Haggiah, which was on the town's eastern edge. Jedaiah was delighted at the coming of Mattathias and his sons. He called his wife Naarah and gave quick orders to increase the amount of food for the noon meal. Naarah hurried away to see to the meal as well as to send someone else out to meet their visitors.

A few moments later, Mahlah appeared in the doorway, hanging her head bashfully. Simon just stood and looked at her. Seeing that a word of encouragement might be needed, Jedaiah said to his daughter, though the words were intended more for Simon, "Mahlah, if Simon would like to take you for a short walk while we are waiting for the meal, it will be all right."

An awkward moment followed. Mahlah stood timidly looking at the floor, rolling her eyes up every few seconds to see if Simon was going to move. Simon just stood there, his eyes darting from face to face is if he didn't know what he was suppose to do. Finally he caught Mattathias's grimace as Mattathias shook his head toward him, motioning him out the door. Then he caught the smirk on Judas's face and jumped as if suddenly awakened. He stepped toward the door and quietly said to Mahlah, "Would you like to take a walk?"

"If you would like to," Mahlah replied, still looking down.

The two left and walked slowly across the open field toward the top of a low hill that overlooked the town. The three men in the house stared after them in amusement. Jedaiah laughed, "They will become comfortable with one another soon enough." Mattathias and Judas both voiced agreement.

After another few moments watching the future husband and wife, the men settled on a mat on the floor and began to talk. Judas sat where he could see out the door to where Simon and Mahlah walked on the hillside. How different was their relationship to that of him and Rebekah. Simon and Mahlah hardly knew each other. As he watched, he never once saw Simon reach out and touch Mahlah's hand. They were going to spend their lives together, but right now, there was nothing between them. He couldn't even tell for sure if they were talking to each other.

Mattathias was in the midst of discussing the reason for their visit with Jedaiah, telling him of their personal ordeal two days earlier. Jedaiah was well aware of what had happened in Jerusalem. Mizpah's population had already swelled to no small degree from people fleeing the city in the short time that had passed. Word had gotten around quickly.

As Mattathias questioned Jedaiah about the people of Mizpah, he learned that Mizpah, like Jerusalem and seemingly most other towns, had its Syrian sympathizers. There was arising a genuine animosity between the opposing segments of the population.

Judas asked about the Hasidim.

"I know some of the Hasidim," Jedaiah replied. "In fact, I would probably be considered one of them. But it's not a well defined group, not in any organizational sense. The sole interest of the Hasidim is faithfulness to Torah. To be sure, it is the Hasidim who come in sharpest conflict with the Syrian sympathizers, especially the Sadducees."

Mattathias reentered the conversation. "We can all be thankful for the zeal of the Hasidim, but are there any ideas around of what to do? To be sure, there are strong emotions, but is anyone here proposing any course of action?"

Jedaiah took a deep breath. Then he answered slowly and deliberately. "We would fight if someone would lead us. We are just waiting for God to send us the man."

At just that moment, Naarah entered with a basin of water so the men could wash their hands before the meal. All three men silently washed as Jedaiah's words took root in their hearts. After washing, they still said nothing. Just the knowledge that scattered through towns and villages all over Judea were those who were ready to fight was enough to give pause. What could be accomplished if they were brought together?

Their thoughts were abruptly interrupted, pierced by a scream coming from several streets away. It was a scream that would not stop, a scream of unimaginable pain.

Chapter 11

Judas and Mattathias looked questioningly at each other, then at Jedaiah. Jedaiah looked back at them wide-eyed and open-handed in a gesture to indicate that he knew no more than they. Judas jumped to his feet and ran outside, followed closely by the two older men. The cries of agony continued in the near distance. Simon and Mahlah were soon at their side, out of breath from running.

"What is it?" panted Simon.

"We don't know," said Judas. Then after another moment, he added, "But I'm going to find out."

Judas walked at a fast pace, almost at a run, the others struggling to keep up. The screams ceased for a brief moment, and Judas stopped to listen. A moment later, however, the cries renewed, and Judas broke into a trot.

Rounding a corner, Judas stopped short. Seconds later, the others arrived beside him. Mahlah ran to the side of her father and buried her face in his side. Jedaiah held her tightly with both arms. They were all having difficulty accepting the reality of what they were seeing.

Standing in semicircular fashion so as to enclose access to a house was a contingent of Macedonian mercenaries, their spears pointing into a scattered crowd of townspeople. Judas recognized the soldiers immediately, for standing within the circle of their protection was Apelles, the representative of

Antiochus. Most of the townspeople stood far away, fearing to come closer but unable to leave, their eyes riveted to what was taking place before them.

Looking through the ring of soldiers, Judas saw the source of the cries. Splayed across the doorway of the house was a man who had been crucified on the doorposts. The man writhed in agony, his feet trying to touch the ground, the spikes through his wrists holding him just high enough to put the ground out of reach.

To one side, held tightly on each side by two soldiers stood a young woman, her hair soaked in sweat, her face wet with tears. She seemed to be near collapsing, but the soldiers would not allow it. They held her head, forcing her to look at the man nailed to the doorposts. She kept trying to look away while clutching tightly to her chest a small bundle, a baby.

To the other side, gathered against the front of the house, stood a group of men. A collective arrogance issued from their common demeanor. It was obvious they were in agreement with what was transpiring. Mattathias, taking in the scene, raised a finger and pointed at the group and looked at Jedaiah. Jedaiah responded with more of a snarl than a word under his breath. "Sadducees!"

Apelles shouted to the crowd over the cries of the man in the doorway and the sobs of the woman held by the two soldiers. "You Jews! When will you learn that you are a conquered people? When will you learn that the king's edicts will be obeyed? You have brought this upon yourselves. When I was with you before, I told you, by the king's command that it was absolutely forbidden to circumcise your children. Yet I come here today and find you have carried on as usual. Let this be a lesson to you. You were told there would be consequences for noncompliance with the king's orders. Perhaps after today you will begin to understand that we mean business."

Apelles walked to the young woman and put his hands around the bundle in her arms. Violent sobs came from the woman as she fought to keep the small bundle. However, the Syrian prevailed and ripped the child from her arms, the soldiers holding the woman's arms so she could not move. Apelles yanked away the cloth in which the infant was wrapped and threw it to the ground, holding the crying child in the air with one hand.

"There will be no more of this!" He shouted, pointing to the unhealed marks of the child's circumcision, which had obviously been performed only a few days earlier.

Apelles reached for the cloth belt the young woman wore around her waist and removed it with a vicious tug. Then, in a swiftness that indicated previous similar experiences, he wound the cloth around the infant's neck and gave it a fierce snap, instantly breaking the child's neck. The woman screamed out, as did the already suffering man hanging in the doorway. Gasps came from the crowd. One woman collapsed on the ground. A few ran away, unable to watch any longer. Even some of the Sadducees could be seen to blanch at Apelles's actions, knowing themselves to have been the reason Apelles knew of this particular child.

Judas reached into his cloak for his sword and started forward. Mattathias grabbed him and said quickly but quietly, "No, Judas. Not now, not here. If you die here today, you can kill no more. And you would surely die, along with many others."

Only with difficulty did Judas control the rage inside of him. He would gladly die, if only he could kill Apelles in the process, but he knew his father was right.

Apelles walked to the doorway and hung the dead infant around its father's neck by means of the cloth belt. Looking back at the crowd scornfully as he pointed at the child and his father, he shouted, "Maybe this will be something you will remember, since you can't seem to remember what I say otherwise."

The young woman continued to emit wails of anguish. The soldiers allowed her to drop to the ground. When Apelles saw this he shouted at them, "Pick her up!" They immediately obeyed.

"What else can I do to make my point so that I won't have

to keep coming back here again and again? What will it take for your feeble minds to remember?" he bellowed at the crowd.

He walked over to the young woman and stood in front of her, contempt filling his eyes as he spoke directly to her, though his words were intended for all. "How could a Jew woman have a baby in the first place? Who would want to make love to one? Well, let's see what she has to offer."

Grabbing the top of her tunic in both hands, Apelles ripped it apart. When it did not come off in one tear, he ripped again and again until the weeping woman was held completely naked between the two soldiers. Many of the people in the crowd, men and women alike, turned their faces down to the ground, only rolling their eyes up as to observe in an indirect fashion. Many of the soldiers, though facing the crowd, looked over their shoulders in sinister delight. The woman's bare breasts, full from nursing, warranted examination, even if she was a Jew.

Apelles looked out at the crowd and laughed at those pretending not to look. "Does nudity offend you?" he mocked. "Why, I've been told that you don't like our gymnasium in Jerusalem, all because of the nudity. Well get use to it, people. The gymnasium is here to stay. *We* are here to stay. This is a new world. Become a part of it or prepare to leave it. We will get rid of Judaism one way or the other. Either you will stop this abominable religion of yours, or we will just get rid of all the Jews."

Apelles looked out at the crowd as if expecting some sort of response. After a long pause, and seemingly having nothing else he could do to further offend the watching crowd, he said, more to himself than to anyone else, "Let's be done with this." He pulled out a small dagger and, pulling the young woman's head up by her hair, ran it across her throat. Her eyes rolled back in her head as blood ran down her naked chest. The soldiers held her for a moment then dropped her to the ground.

Looking again at the sobbing man stretched across the doorway, he said to the soldiers who had been holding the woman, "Kill him now, or they'll take him down when we leave." One of the soldiers pulled out his sword and ran it through the man's heart. One last painful gasp erupted from the man before he dropped his head, his chin touching his infant son who hung around his neck. The soldier reached down and picked up a piece of the dead woman's clothing and wiped the blood from his sword before dropping it back into its sheath.

Apelles shouted to the commander of the soldiers to prepare to return to Jerusalem. The commander barked orders, and the soldiers divided into two ranks in front of and behind the litter upon which Apelles rode. Just as Apelles was about to take his place in the litter, he turned to the group of Sadducees. "See to it that no one takes him down or covers her for the rest of the day. I want people to see them long enough for it to make an impression." He paused to look toward the dead bodies before glancing around, frowning at the crowd. He then climbed onto his litter and was carried away by his slaves.

Watching Apelles and the cohort of soldiers pass by, Mattathias turned his head toward Jedaiah. "Jedaiah, you said you would fight if someone would lead you." Jedaiah nodded without taking his eyes off the departing troops. Mattathias then said, "You have your leader. I will kill this Gentile dog myself. When that happens, you will know the war has begun."

No one said anything for a long while. The people began to leave, one by one. When the soldiers were out of sight, Judas turned to the others. "Father, go with Jedaiah and Mahlah to their home. Simon and I will be there directly."

"What do you intend to do, Judas?" Mattathias asked, worried that his son might try something reckless.

Judas motioned toward the dead bodies. "These are Israel's faithful. They will not remain on public display today. I'm going to bury them."

Mattathias looked at the bodies then at his son. He nodded slowly. "Just be careful," he whispered, his emotions causing his voice to break.

"I will, Father. I intend to be at your side when you kill Apelles."

Mattathias had not known whether anyone else had heard

his words to Jedaiah, but he felt assured by Judas's simple statement that this would be done. He turned to Jedaiah and gestured him and his daughter forward, and the three of them left together.

Judas turned to Simon. "Are you with me in this?"

Simon's simple response was, "You know I am."

The two crossed the open space to the house. Simon picked up the woman's clothes that were lying in the dust. Though they were torn, he managed to cover the woman's body with them. Judas lifted the infant from around the man's neck and placed it under the clothing with its mother.

Judas then began to try to wrest the spike binding one of the man's arms out of the mortar by the doorpost as Simon did the other. In no time at all their hands were covered in the man's blood, nevertheless they continued.

One of the Sadducees standing nearby ran beside Judas and snapped at him as if scolding a child. "Didn't you hear what he said? Don't move the bodies for the rest of the day."

Neither Judas nor Simon spoke, but continued to work at loosening the spikes.

The Sadducee repeated himself. "The king's official said to leave them."

Judas continued his work, but said in a voice quivering with rage, "Damn the king's official and damn the king. And damn all of you who had a part in this."

The haughty Sadducee reviled Judas. "Who are you to disobey the king?"

With the speed of a striking serpent, Judas grabbed the Sadducee by the throat and crashed him against the wall, holding him with one hand so that his feet barely touched the ground. All in the same movement, with the other hand Judas had drawn his sword from under his cloak and held it with the tip pointed into the lower part of the man's neck. The man was stiff with fright.

Judas put his face close to the Sadducee's and looked into his terrified eyes. "I will tell you who I am. I am the hammer that will crush you." In that instant, Judas wanted desperately to run the sword through the Saducee's throat, but he suddenly realized that urine was running from under the man's cloak down around his feet. His anger momentarily switched from intense anger to pity. For some reason, the immediate tendency is to pity a coward. But then the anger returned.

Judas threw the man to the ground and ordered him, "Go home!" Judas looked around at some of the others who he recognized as part of the group of Saducees who had been standing by condoning Apelles's actions. Speaking to all of them, he said, "Go home! If any one of you goes after Apelles to bring him back, know this: We know who you are, and you will be the next to die. You cannot escape us all."

After some moments of hesitation, with Judas continuing to watch them, the group of Saducees began to leave. All made sure they did not go in the same direction that Apelles had gone.

The man Judas had held the sword on picked himself from the ground and backed away, confused as to what to do. "My house is that way," he said, pointing in the direction the soldiers had gone.

Judas had no pity this time. "Then you had best go to someone else's house. If you go that way today, you will not see tomorrow."

The frightened man looked around and ran to one of the other Saducees who was walking away. Judas could see the other man shake his head indicating that his fellow Saducee could accompany him.

As Judas put his sword away and returned to his work with the spike through the crucified man's arm, Simon repeated Judas's words to him. "You cannot escape us all." Then he added, "I'm glad they didn't know that the 'us all' is only you and me."

"And me," said a voice from behind them.

Judas and Simon turned to look at the young man who had walked up. The young man grabbed the waist of the crucified man so as to lift the weight from his arms to make Judas and Simon's work easier.

Simon immediately recognized the young man. "You were in the temple with us in Jerusalem. I remember seeing you before we went down into the tunnel."

"That's right," he said. "I owe my life to you. I'm Nethanel."

"Nethanel," Simon repeated. "It will be easy to remember your name." They all understood what Simon meant, for there were ten different Nethanels in the history of Israel as recorded in the Tanakh.

Judas commented, making no effort to hide his discouragement, "Then there are three of us," as they lowered the body to the ground.

"Oh, there are more than three," Nethanel said quickly.

"Then where are they?" said Judas.

"Waiting for someone to lead them. Those who could have led died in Jerusalem. Now we are like sheep without a shepherd. If someone will lead, these sheep will all be rams."

The three men stood looking at the bodies, thinking they would have to manually carry one at a time to the edge of town for burial. After a few moments Nethanel told Judas and Simon to wait. He ran off and came back a few moments later pulling a donkey cart.

As they picked up the bodies and placed them on the cart, Nethanel looked at Judas with a slight smile on his face and said admiringly, "The hammer that will crush you." Judas looked away, embarrassed at the repetition of his own words, but said nothing.

Together they pulled the cart outside of town where there was a cave where the poor were buried. Though there was a stench from another recent burial, they found a place that had been cleared for future burials and laid the bodies there, placing the infant between his parents. When they had come out, taking deep breaths to get the stench from their lungs, they looked back at the cave.

"We don't even know their names," said Judas morosely. "Do you know them?"

Nethanel shook his head. "No. I'm not from Mizpah. I just

came here to get out of Jerusalem. I'm staying with a cousin. I don't really know anyone here."

Simon picked up Judas's lament. "Not even a cloth to wrap their bodies in. Surely they had family here, but no one came out to help. It's as though no one cares. No one will remember."

"I care," said Judas. "I will remember. I will always remember."

Nethanel looked directly at Judas and spoke quietly, hope and respect filling his words. "Judas the hammer. Judas the *Maccabee*."

When they reentered the town, Judas and Simon parted ways with Nethanel, though they knew they would meet again. Judas and Simon returned to the house of Jedaiah where they cleaned up and had a meal. Mattathias and Jedaiah had been in deep discussion regarding the future. No one realized the full impact of their discussion, that this very day the decision had been made to wage a war that would last years and cost many lives.

When they had finished eating, Mattathias and his sons made haste to get back on the road to Modin. As they left the house, Simon took Mahlah's hand and held it for just a moment as their eyes silently said good-bye to each other. It was the first sign of affection anyone had seen between them, the first time they had ever actually touched. Perhaps what they had witnessed this day had made them realize that each moment was precious. Their life together could be cut short, so whatever feelings of love could be stated between them should be expressed, even if their shyness only allowed them to say it with the touch of a hand.

It was dark when they arrived in Modin. It seemed that several days had passed since their departure from Hananiah's house in Jerusalem just that morning. The road had been long and tiring, but the emotional turmoil of the day had been exhausting. They were welcomed home by John and Leah, along with Eleazar and Jonathan. They were eager to hear about everything. It was well past midnight before anyone went to bed. Tired bodies and minds had no problem finding sleep that night, but the dreams that wandered in and out of their minds were dark. Tomorrow they would begin to prepare for war.

Chapter 12

The next couple of weeks saw a great deal of activity, though on the surface life appeared to go on as usual. Mattathias and his sons realized that knowledge of their preparations could lead to disaster. They had seen how the Sadducees served as informants for the Syrians, so they were careful to hide their activities from Matthan and Akim, as well as anyone who held an amiable relationship with them.

They knew that Apelles would probably come with the same cohort of Macedonian mercenaries they had seen on previous occasions. Their greatest weapon in any effort to defeat trained soldiers such as these would be the weapon of surprise. Preparations for their arrival would have to be done in secret. However, everyone in town expected to hear from Mattathias about his time in Jerusalem. Mattathias would have to take great caution as he reported on what they had learned. He wanted to enflame passions, but he also saw the prudence of keeping their plans hidden.

Mattathias sent his sons throughout Modin calling the men to meet at the synagogue the following morning, the day before Sabbath. Mattathias personally visited Eliud and Azariah, two friends he knew he could trust. He told them in detail the events of the past few days and of his own thoughts and plans. Eliud had two sons and Azariah had three. They both assured Mattathias that they, along with their sons, would be committed to any fight against the Syrians. Mattathias then warned them against being vocal about their willingness to fight. They all understood that some of their greatest sources of danger were among their own people.

That evening, Mattathias and his sons discussed how best to fight Apelles and his soldiers. Judas had given the matter the most thought. The obstacle before them seemed almost insurmountable. They presently had no weapons. The only sword any of them knew of in Modin was the one Judas had taken off the Syrian he had killed. They would have to make their own weapons before Apelles arrived. They would also need some idea of how to use them. None of them were soldiers. None had seen battle before. Almost every Jewish young man other than those who had spent their lives in the larger cities had at some time used a bow and arrow. This would prove to be an asset. However, killing an unsuspecting deer or hare was quite different from killing an armored soldier who was trained to protect himself. Mattathias gave Judas the job of preparing for and planning the attack.

Simon brought up the important matter of what they would do if their attack succeeded. Even Mattathias had not thought that far ahead, even though he had assured Jedaiah that he would lead the fight against the Syrians. How would he do it? They were all willing to die, but what if they lived? The fight must continue. Where would they go? They could not remain in Modin. A literal army would come down upon them, not just a few mercenaries. Mattathias gave Simon the task of preparing for the larger war. He would leave immediately following the Sabbath and find where they could hide and how they would be supplied.

The following morning, the men of Modin assembled in the synagogue. Matthan and Akim were not late this time, though Matthan was not able to be there without grumbling. His acrid nature would not allow otherwise.

"Let's get this over with," he complained as others were still arriving. "Some of us have work to do."

Everyone knew that there was little work in the winter, and

there was nothing that couldn't wait till later in the day. A voice from the group commented sarcastically, "What's the matter? Won't your money count itself?"

Matthan's head snapped around. "Who said that?" No one spoke, but quiet snickers reverberated around the room.

Mattathias stood and faced the group. Everyone listened intently as he related the experiences of the last few days. He began with the rapes of the women in Lower Beth-horon then proceeded to telling about the gymnasium in Jerusalem and how young Jewish men were having their circumcisions reversed so as to no longer appear Jewish. Judas noticed that Akim looked uncomfortable at the mention of the circumcision reversal and wondered what would be found if one were to raise Akim's tunic. Akim did spend extended amounts of time in Jerusalem.

When Mattathias told of the events in the temple a contagious anger spread through the synagogue. Mattathias told how they had escaped, though he said nothing of Judas's killing the Syrian soldier. Though there were comments to praise God for their escape, an insuppressible stream of murmurs circled the room. According to his directions prior to the meeting, Mattathias's sons watched closely every man in the room, making mental notes of who would be likely to side with them in the fight and who appeared to be sympathetic to the Syrians.

When Mattathias told of the murders in Mizpah, the rage in the room boiled over. Murmurs turned into shouts. More than one demanded the death of Apelles. Mattathias and his sons observed those who remained silent. They noticed exchanges of glances between them. Matthan was not alone in his loyalties. These must never know of what was being planned.

In the midst of the shouts, Matthan raised his corpulent figure from its seat. He raised his arms to gain the floor and everyone gradually grew quiet. Matthan was about to speak when Eliud interrupted by saying, "Simon and Judas, I want to thank you for giving three of Israel's children the burial they deserved. May God curse those who had any part in this." A buzz of agreement filled the synagogue.

Matthan looked down at Eliud reprovingly as if Eliud had treated him rudely by interrupting. He held up his hands once again, and again the room grew quiet. Though he had allies in the room, he knew as a whole he was not in friendly company, so he chose his words as he spoke. "Mattathias, most here seem to look to you for direction. How do you propose that we respond to these things you have spoken of?"

Mattathias had been thinking upon how to respond to just such a question. He had determined beforehand that his answer would fall short of stating his full intentions yet would leave no question of his position. Looking from face to face around the room, he said, "It is obvious, as I said before I ever went to Jerusalem, that we cannot comply with what is being demanded of us. There would be no more Jews, for there would be no more Judaism."

"But," interrupted Matthan, "if only some measure of compromise was made then perhaps it wouldn't be necessary to give in on everything. Perhaps none of what you have been telling us about would have happened if we had just worked with the Syrians a little."

"And what do you propose?" Mattathias asked the question so that there would be no doubt of where Matthan stood.

"I propose that we sit down and talk with the Syrians. When Apelles comes back here, let's not treat him like an enemy. Let's show him we are reasonable people. We can make a few concessions if we need to."

"And why would we do that?" prompted Mattathias further.

"For our safety, for our survival," said Matthan, condescension filling his words. "We can't possibly fight the Syrians. We have to learn to live with them." Matthan looked around the room to certain faces as he spoke. Mattathias watched the same faces and saw their affirming nods. They were the same ones who had remained silent earlier.

Mattathias surveyed the sea of faces as he spoke in response to Matthan's suggestion. He knew that some would not understand what he was about to say, but they would soon enough. "When Joshua established our people in this land, he gave the people a choice as to whom they would serve. As for himself, he said, 'As for me and my house, we will serve the Lord.'" Quiet words of concurrence were heard around the room. Mattathias continued. "I say the same thing. As for me and my house, we will serve the Lord. Each man must decide for himself. I will not comply with the edicts of this pagan king. As for you, do what you must."

Mattathias walked out. Many in the room were shocked. They had expected more. One man turned to Judas. "Judas, we need to fight these Syrian bastards. Is this it, just every man for himself?"

Judas responded simply, "I will do whatever my father does."

Judas stood up and left, followed by his brothers. Murmurs of discontent circulated among many of those who remained. Matthan and his allies, however, felt they had gained a small victory. The town was divided, and even those who were against Matthan and his friends were unhappy with Mattathias. Little by little, the group dispersed. Some huddled in groups of twos and threes and talked among themselves before leaving.

Mattathias returned to his house, joined shortly by all five of his sons. They sat and waited. Within a few minutes, a knock was heard at the door. It was three of the men who had been in the meeting. They had come to personally express their displeasure with the way Mattathias had conducted the meeting. All three were eager to fight the Syrians.

Mattathias proceeded to tell them his plan to indeed fight the Syrians, explaining to them why he had not taken a stronger stand in the synagogue. It didn't take them long to understand the need for discreetness. Judas described to them what they would have to do to prepare, not just for the initial attack, but for afterwards. All three men voiced a desire to participate in the fight, committing not only themselves but their families as well, since a war never merely involves the one wielding the sword.

They returned to their homes, but within an hour two more

men arrived at Mattathias's door. They too wanted to fight. And so it continued throughout the afternoon. By the end of the day, twenty-eight able-bodied men of Modin had enlisted to fight the Syrians. The army had its first soldiers.

Two days later, when the Sabbath was over, Simon left Modin. If anyone raised any questions as to his whereabouts they were told that word had come of a sick relative, and he was going on behalf of the family.

Judas took Eleazar and Jonathan and met with several others of the younger men out in the hills. They were all careful to leave Modin separately, trying not to be seen. If one was seen, he pretended to be going hunting, for each one came armed with a bow and quiver of arrows.

Judas explained to the men the speed and skill that would be required of them. He showed them the breast and back plates he had, putting it on so they could all see what parts of the body were left unprotected and could be penetrated by an arrow. Though they did not have one on hand, they had all seen the helmets that the soldiers wore. Since Judas had worn one for a short while, he better described for them what parts of the head it covered. All agreed that if they were in a position to shoot with accuracy, they should aim for the neck, a small target but one that would yield the desired results. No soldier could continue the fight with an arrow run through his neck, even if the wound was not immediately fatal. If it were not possible to shoot for the neck, one should aim for the side or lower abdomen, whichever was presented.

From that day forward, Eleazar and Jonathan along with nine others committed to two things, making as many arrows as possible and learning to shoot them quickly and accurately. Jonathan proved to be the most skillful at the use of a bow and became the natural leader of the group. Jonathan had a small bow made with layers of ram's horn that was superior to the larger wooden bows. The bow being less cumbersome, he was able to continually notch and release arrows every three seconds, even while running if necessary. Others had similar bows, but the ones that didn't dedicated their evenings to making their own by the light of an oil lamp. Within a week they all had bows made of ram's horn.

So as not to arouse suspicion, they agreed that they would come to practice their skills in groups of twos or threes. Whenever the possibility presented itself, they killed some game so they could be seen returning to town with it, providing an answer to anyone who would question what they were doing. Day after day they went far into the wilderness to practice their deadly art. Cloth sacks filled with dirt were swung from trees as moving targets. Once they had gained some proficiency in shooting the swinging targets, they began to do it while someone stood at a distance and threw rocks at them. The challenge was great, but they knew they had to be alert to everything happening around them. Within a couple of weeks, they had become adept at dodging attackers while continuing to unleash a spray of arrows with considerable accuracy.

One of the men who had come to the home of Mattathias expressing his desire to fight the Syrians was Obed, the town's smith. His was probably the most essential of any of the preparations for the coming battle. John, the oldest of Mattathias's sons, temporarily became a sort of apprentice to Obed. From morning into the evening hours Obed's hammer rang against his anvil while John tended the forge and kept watch for inquiring eyes. A plow head was kept heated in one side of the forge so that if an untrustworthy person was seen approaching, the sword being hammered could be quickly hidden and the blows of the hammer begin to rain upon the plow head. The swords were nothing to compare to the weapons carried by the troops that occupied their country. In fact, they were little more than flattened pieces of tempered iron that were sharpened on both edges on a mill stone and filed to a point. Leather was bound tightly around the handle to serve as a grip. They were crude in appearance but more than adequate to kill a man.

Not only were swords made, but spears also. The spears were the easiest to make, being about an arm's length of iron rod with a sharpened wedge-shaped head which was fitted into the end of a much longer wooden pole. Though little effort was given to making them uniform in appearance, each spear was almost identical to the *pilum* such as was carried by most of the Syrian and Macedonian field infantry. The pilum as a weapon was effective where other weapons failed. Whereas arrows and swords generally had to find an unprotected part of the body to be effective, a pilum could pierce a shield or breastplate if it hit squarely and with enough force.

Each night, Judas would take whatever weapons had been made by Obed and John to a hiding place outside of town. During the day, Judas would take men to this place where they would practice throwing the spears and try to gain some understanding of how to fight with a sword. They all understood that they would be coming up against trained, seasoned soldiers. Even though none of them had ever fought before, their courage did not fail. They found creative ways to sharpen each other's skills.

They all knew that their only route to success was the element of surprise. This occupied much of their talk, how best to surprise the enemy. Details of their attack filled their thoughts and conversations, so much so that they had to find ways to cover their discussions.

One day several of the men were standing outside Obed's shed where he hammered away at yet another sword. Some men squatted in a rough circle while others stood and watched as Judas sketched on the ground where the archers and spear throwers could hide when Apelles arrived. Suddenly one of the men said loud enough for the others to hear, "Akim!"

Those that were in a position to do so looked and saw Akim and a friend of his approaching the group. In one swift movement, Judas brush away his sketch and another man pulled a *dreidel* from under his cloak and tossed it spinning on the ground. Others had tossed a few coins on the ground. Just as Akim and his friend arrived at the group and looked over the shoulders of the men squatting on the ground, the dreidel fell on one side and Judas shouted, "I won!" and began to pick up the coins.

Akim turned up his nose. "Gambling! Somehow I'm not surprised." No one said a word. His curiosity satisfied, and realizing he was not among friends, Akim walked away and his friend followed. A collective sigh came from the group as Judas returned the coins to their rightful owners.

As they looked toward Akim and the other man walking away they could see out to the edge of town. Someone was coming up the road toward Modin. Judas stood up when he realized it was Simon and started walking to meet him. He wondered as he walked, for Simon was not alone.

Chapter 13

Simon approached with four men at his side. Judas was about to shout out a welcome to Simon when he heard a jubilant voice exclaim, "Judas the Maccabee!"

Judas looked closer and recognized a familiar face in the group. It was Nethanel. When Judas arrived in front of the others he embraced arms with Simon.

"Welcome home, brother."

Simon seemed glad to be back. Releasing Judas's embrace, he turned his head toward the others and said, "I have brought friends who are ready to join the fight."

Judas embraced Nethanel. "Nethanel. I knew we would meet again. Welcome!"

Nethanel was ecstatic as he gripped arms with Judas. He looked Judas in the eyes but spoke to his companions. "This is the one I was telling you about. This is Judas, the hammer, the Maccabee."

The other three men looked at Judas admiringly. Judas was not sure at all that he deserved what they were thinking. Nethanel's description of him to his friends had obviously created more legend than reality in their minds. Nevertheless, the image formed indelibly in the mind of Nethanel at their first encounter was that Judas was the Maccabee. Others, it seemed, were going to hold him with the same regard.

Judas welcomed each of the other three men, learning their

names as he went. He led them back to the small group gathered in the front of Obed's shelter. Obed momentarily stopped hammering on his anvil to come out to meet the new arrivals with the rest of the group.

After several minutes of chatter between the men, learning where the new arrivals were from and what their family connections were, Judas turned to Simon. "So, Simon, what news do you bring us?"

The conversation became serious. Simon began, "The news is both good and bad. The good news is that there are many who are ready to mount a resistance to the Syrians. The bad news is that there are also many of our own people who are loyal to them and are perfectly content to do whatever Antiochus wants.

"Over the past fortnight I have walked across more of Judea than I ever knew existed. Most nights someone gave me a place to stay in one of the towns, but on a couple of nights I slept in the countryside. Fortunately, Nethanel here was with me most of the time, and our other three friends here have been with us for the last couple of days."

"How did you meet up with Nethanel?" asked Judas, looking approvingly at the young Hasidim.

"Well," said Simon, knowing what would be coming next, "I went back to Mizpah."

John, who was listening intently to all that was said while tending the forge, commented, "Isn't that where Mahlah lives?"

A voice from the group jeered, "Oh, had to see his woman."

Laughter broke out among the men. Simon looked down at the ground to hide an embarrassed smile. After a moment, Judas raised his arms, himself smiling, "Okay, that's enough. Let him continue."

Simon continued. "I just happened to meet Nethanel as I was coming into Mizpah. I told him what my mission was, and he volunteered to accompany me. Together we talked with Jedaiah, who gave us names of people he knew would be loyal to our cause in the other towns and villages nearby. Each step of the way, as we progressed from town to town, we would learn from the preceding town who we could likely trust in the next town. And so we visited probably half of the towns and villages between Jerusalem and Samaria.

"What we have found is this: the closer you are to Jerusalem, the more people are loyal to the Syrians. It seems they are influenced by the life of the city, which has grown more and more Greek in its life and politics over the past few years. Of course, the Sadducees are all pro-Syrian, and there are plenty of those. But even those who aren't Sadducees just passively go along with whatever the Syrians want.

"As you travel north, away from Jerusalem, you find people more like ourselves, wanting to hold on to our ways and to be rid of the Syrians. But then as you go further, as you get closer and closer to Samaria, you begin to find more and more that people are not only loyal to Antiochus, but more and more they hate Jews and anything Jewish."

One man standing by spat on the ground and muttered, "Samaritan cowards."

There was no question of the contempt most Jews held for the Samaritans. During the times that the Ptolemies of Egypt had ruled Judea and the kings of Egypt had looked favorably upon the Jews, the Samaritans had claimed to be Jews. However, when the Seleucids had gained control over Judea and Antiochus as king had come out against everything Jewish, they sent a letter to Antiochus saying that they were in fact descendants of the Sidonians and that they desired to embrace the religion of the Greeks and be rid of all the wicked practices of the Jews.

Judas mulled over what Simon had been saying, then he asked, "So where should we go when we leave here?"

"Well," said Simon, "the safest place is exactly halfway between Jerusalem and Samaria, in the Gophna Hills."

Judas had heard of the Gophna Hills but had never been there. He knew from stories he had heard that it was an easy place to lose oneself. It was thickly forested and filled with caves and ravines.

Simon continued. "Not only is it a good place to hide, there are four towns close enough and loyal enough to our cause to provide us support: Tappuah, Lebonah, Shiloh, and Gilgal. Jadon and Oren here are from Lebonah." Simon motioned toward two of the men who had arrived with him, then added as he indicated the third man, "And Joseph here is from Gilgal. They all know the land like you know the back of your hand. There is not a cave they don't seem to know about already."

The one named Oren commented, "We spent a lot of time in those hills growing up. There's plenty of game there, too."

Simon nodded his head and added, "And they are ready to guide us and to fight with us. They have seen enough to know that our only hope of survival as a nation is to fight the Syrians."

Joseph from Gilgal spoke up. "I'll fight them. They killed my great-grandfather."

"Great-grandfather?" queried Judas, putting the emphasis on "great." Not many people had a great-grandfather who was still alive. "He must have been old. Have they gone to killing old men? I shouldn't be surprised. I saw them kill a newborn infant with my own eyes."

Joseph proceeded to tell the story. "My great-grandfather was the most highly respected man in our town. His name was Eleazar, Eleazar ben Nehum. He was ninety years old."

"Ninety years old. One of the elders of Israel," Judas whispered in amazement as Joseph continued.

"They came to our town and set up an altar to their pagan god. They wanted my great-grandfather to offer a sacrifice they had brought along with them – a swine – but they finally saw he was too feeble to do it. So when they had made another man offer the sacrifice, they still tried to make him eat the meat. My great-grandfather refused. Some of the men of our town even took him aside and tried to get him to substitute his own meat. They told him that the Syrians would never know that it wasn't pork he would be eating, but he refused. He said that God had given him ninety years on this earth and that he would not dishonor God now. Because he refused, the Syrians tied him to a post and beat him with a whip until his insides fell out. They made us all watch. I saw it all, and I heard his last words as they were beating him to death. He looked at all of us and said, 'I have great pain in the body, but I have joy in my soul because I have stayed true to God.'" Joseph blinked back tears and added in a cracking voice, "That's the last thing I heard him say."

There was a long silence. Finally someone in the group asked, "Was it Apelles? Was that who came and did this?"

Joseph was unable to speak for emotion but just nodded his head affirmatively.

"There's more," said Nethanel, interrupting the silence. "Simon could tell you what we heard happened in Shiloh. There was a woman there who had seven sons. They tried to get them to eat their cursed pork from the same kind of sacrifice. They all refused, and the Syrians killed the sons one by one, forcing the mother to watch. But they didn't just kill them, they tortured them to death. They first cut out their tongues and then cut off their hands before burning them alive. They say the youngest one was only a child. They did this during a whole day until finally they killed the woman herself. Yet none of these, not even the child, would give in to their demands."

Judas looked at Simon. "Is all this really true?"

Simon shrugged. "I don't know. It's what people in Shiloh told us. I can't imagine all of them standing up to that kind of torture, but it's what they say happened. One thing for sure, though, no one in these towns is loyal to the Syrians any more. If some had loyalties before, they don't any more. As I said before, the towns far from Jerusalem are less loyal to the Syrians anyway, but what little loyalty there was in these particular towns is all but gone."

"Good," said Judas, hardly able to speak for anger. "Then it is where we will go. And we will keep the memories of these people who willingly laid down their lives alive in our hearts. We will avenge their deaths, not only upon the Syrians, but upon any who would give them aid."

There were nods and murmurs among the group and then a choleric silence fell among them, interrupted after a few moments by the sound of Obed's hammer falling upon his anvil. Everyone turned and watched him as he returned to his work, his anger visible in every spark that leapt from the glowing iron under the blows of the hammer.

After watching the end of an iron rod flatten out into the shape of a spearhead, Judas asked Simon, "Do you have any idea where Apelles is?"

"We heard that three days ago he was in Emmaus."

Judas pondered what little he knew of the geography of Judea. "Then he is on this side of the hills. He is probably not far away. Have you heard in the other towns if he has a way he normally goes about this evil business of his? Is there any kind of routine he follows?" In pondering how best to prepare for Apelles's arrival, Judas had realized that any routine of the enemy could work to their advantage. Surprise was most possible when it interrupted a routine.

Simon thought for a moment. "From what we have heard, where we have been, if there is a synagogue, that's where he goes. Of course, the towns closest to Jerusalem mostly don't have synagogues since they have access to the temple, but where there is one, that is where he goes."

"Why?" Judas questioned. "It would make sense if he always arrived on a Sabbath. But he doesn't just show up one day in seven, does he?"

"No. It's the scrolls. He always starts by destroying the scrolls. And they are kept in the synagogues."

"We had better hide ours. What else? What else does he routinely do?"

Simon spoke slowly as he thought out loud. "Well, he sets up a small altar right in front of the synagogue, an altar to their god. That's where they sacrifice the pig, it's always a pig. They know that is the most offensive to us." Simon scratched his head as he searched his thoughts for useful information.

Joseph jumped into the conversation. "He always tries to

get the most highly regarded elder of the town to offer the sacrifice. That's what he would have done with my great-grandfather if he could have. It seems that if he can get the elder of the town to offer the sacrifice, then the rest of the people will go along with it."

Judas and Simon looked at each other and said almost in unison, "That will be Father." Mattathias would have no trouble getting close to Apelles with a knife in his hand.

Judas thought for a moment then said to everyone, "When you go home today, make your preparations to travel. Pack whatever provisions you can carry. Apelles will be here in the next few days, and we need to be ready to leave quickly.

"Everyone meet at our house at the beginning of the second watch tonight. Make sure you are not seen. Pass this word along to everyone else. Tonight we make our final plans."

As soon as Judas had finished speaking, the men broke up and went in different directions, most of them headed for their homes. Soon all that could be heard was the ring of the smith's hammer against his anvil.

That night, the home of Mattathias ben Hasmoneus was filled with talk of war. There were moments of great emotion, but mostly there was just careful instruction. A schedule was made for the men to keep watch for the arrival of Apelles. At all times someone would be watching two miles outside of town. As soon as Apelles and his troops were sighted, the watchman would run to town with the news. A network was formed so that all the fighters would be quickly informed.

Once everyone was informed they would take their secret positions and wait silently for the signal. A person from each position was made to repeat out loud the plan of attack. This drama would play itself out many times in their minds, sleeping and waking, before the actual fight took place.

It was almost midnight when they finally went to bed. Because of the extra room needed for the guests that had arrived with Simon, Simon and Judas opted to sleep in the stable.

Lying on a cushion of hay in the dark corner of the stable, their senses filled with the odors of the animals in a stall nearby, Judas ended the day by keeping Simon from the sleep that had almost overtaken him. "By the way Simon, how is Mahlah?"

"Oh, she's okay, I guess" came what seemed at first a noncommittal reply. But then he added, "At least she didn't run away when I kissed her. Now go to sleep."

One could almost feel the smiles in the darkness.

Chapter 14

Apelles arrived the day after Sabbath. Diligent in his sinister task, he showed up exactly one month after his first visit to Modin, just as he had promised.

One of the young archers who had trained with Eleazar and Jonathan was watching from two miles outside of town. It was about midmorning on a sunny day when his eye caught the glint of sunlight reflecting off helmets on a rise in the distance. It did not take long for him to discern that this was indeed a uniformed group and marching in ranks. He waited just long enough to see the decorative fabric top of the litter upon which rode Apelles. Descending from the tree in which he sat, the young man hastened toward town, careful to stay among the rocks and trees so as not to be spotted by the soldiers, lest they perceive it for what it was, a warning to prepare for battle. They were still at least a mile from where he had been watching, but no chances could be taken.

Several minutes later the breathless young man arrived in front of the house of Mattathias. Simon was coming from the stable and saw him. The young archer panted the words, "They're here! The Syrians!"

"How far?" said Simon, setting down the bucket of milk he was carrying, the pastoral feeling of just having milked a cow instantly displaced by a surge of nervous energy.

"About three miles." The young man thought a moment

then said, "Maybe two miles by now."

Simon said to the young man, hardly more than a boy but who would possibly kill his first man in the next hour, "Good work. Now go to your contacts and inform them. Tell John and Obed first. Do it quickly, but do not run or draw attention to yourself. Then take your position."

As the young man walked swiftly away, trying to steady his breathing, Simon opened the door to the house. "Apelles is here. He's about two miles outside of town."

Seconds later, Eleazar and Jonathan left the house in separate directions, clutching their weapons discreetly under their cloaks. Inside remained Mattathias, Judas, and Simon. Leah stood in the corner by the stone oven, her eyes revealing a barely controllable trepidation.

Mattathias watched philosophically from where he sat as Judas and Simon fastened the sheaths for their swords to their belts. "Our people have always seen God move on our behalf when we have fought for what is right. May it be no different today."

As Judas pulled his cloak on over his tunic, hiding his sword, he said to his father, "Father, do you not need a sword?"

A weak smile crossed Mattathias's face. "From what I hear, the sword will be provided for me in due time. I will kill Apelles with his own knife."

Judas was about to comment but then stopped himself, accepting what his father had said. He knew that Mattathias saw the day as not belonging to them, but to God. In the end, whether they succeeded or failed was up to God, not them. He turned and looked at Leah. "When we leave, you stay here and get everything ready. We will come back just long enough to get what is needed."

Leah looked at him with a troubled expression. She had heard all the plans, but up to this day that was all they had been, plans. Suddenly the realization was pouring in that this was not just men talking of what they would like to do. This was for real. It was really happening. Her thoughts made her shudder.

Would she still have a husband after today? Would this family of men that she had so come to love all live through the day? She tried to trust God with these questions, but at this moment, the fear left her with nothing but uncertainty.

To an outsider, the activities in town over the next few minutes hardly seemed anything out of the ordinary. However, there were things happening in almost every corner that were far from ordinary. Many were attaching homemade scabbards under their cloaks in which were sheathed the swords made by Obed. Others walked casually toward the synagogue but disappeared one by one into neighboring houses before arriving at the synagogue.

The synagogue stood alone as a building at the end of a street, such that if one were walking up the street one would be looking directly at it. On either side of the street were dwellings, all attached one to the other. As typical of many houses of the day, some of these had flat roofs upon which much of daily life was lived out, especially in the warmer months. Such a roof was generally accessible by an outside staircase. The house on the end had such a roof. Within the next few minutes, this roof became filled with archers. One by one each archer would arrive. Once on the roof, he would take his bow and sheath filled with arrows out from under his cloak and lie down close to the edge of the roof just above the street, holding his weapons close to him. Only Jonathan was allowed to look over the edge, and that only in furtive glances. They did not know how long they would need to lie there, but they would remain hidden as long as needed, no matter how uncomfortable it became. No one would move until the signal was given.

On the opposite side of the street, men ducked one by one into three doorways, two men to each house. Upon entering, they removed from their secret places the spears that had already been hidden in the houses and leaned them against the wall by the door. Eight spears were in each house, three for each man to throw and one for defensive purposes if necessary. Once in the houses, the doors remained closed by Judas's strict order. If a soldier were to notice a door cracked open even slightly he might suspect an ambush and warn the others. They would have to depend entirely on what they heard to know when to join the attack.

It was just over a half hour from the time the young watchman had brought the warning to when a knock came at the door of Mattathias. Simon opened the door. A coarse looking soldier stood at the door with three more behind him, their spears held in upright positions showing they were not expecting anything out of the ordinary. "Is this the home of the man they call Mattathias?"

Simon fought to hide his quaking nerves. He opened the door and motioned. "He is here."

Mattathias did not give the appearance of being shaken in any way. Looking up from where he sat but in no way implying politeness, he said to the soldier, "Yes? What do you want?"

The soldier stated his business. "The king's officer, the honorable Apelles, has said that you are to come with me to your synagogue." Then he looked at Simon and Judas. "You are to be there too. There is a sacrifice about to take place of which all the men of the town are to take part."

Without saying a word, Mattathias rose and walked to the door. Stepping outside, he motioned the soldier forward and said, "Lead the way."

The soldier looked at the other soldiers and nodded. By prearrangement two of them began marching in the direction of the synagogue. "Follow them," the first soldier commanded Mattathias and his sons. Mattathias, Simon, and Judas fell in behind the two mercenaries. The first soldier and the remaining one fell in behind them as if to prevent any attempt of escape.

Upon their arrival at the synagogue, Mattathias and his sons quickly took in the situation. Erected a few feet in front of the synagogue was a small brazen altar with a figurine representing Zeus on one edge. The altar was only about waist high but was large enough to build a fire in. One of the slaves that carried Apelles's litter was in the process of building a fire in its midst.

Facing the altar but standing about twenty feet away stood the Macedonian mercenaries in four ranks, ten to a rank. Some of the ranks were shorter, but these would quickly grow to ten when the soldiers who had accompanied Mattathias and his sons joined their number, along with two more who were presently in the synagogue. There were forty soldiers in all.

Behind the soldiers sat Apelles's litter, attended by the slaves who had the chore of carrying it all over Judea. They held their heads down, having grown accustomed to the unwritten rule of never making eye contact.

Gathered in no particular fashion on either side of the contingent of mercenaries were citizens of Modin, mostly men, though there were a few women present. They kept some distance from the soldiers, not from fear, but because even in the chill winter air, to the Jewish senses the soldiers reeked. They had probably not bathed since summer.

Judas looked around upon arrival, taking special note of everyone that was there. He was careful not to look up to the roof or to the doors behind which he knew men stood ready with spears in hand. He met eyes with several men who he knew had swords under their cloaks. Matthan and Akim stood at the front, apart from the townspeople, not willing to just be a part of the crowd.

When the soldiers had accompanied Mattathias to a place just in front of the altar, they left him and took their position with the other mercenaries. In a few seconds, Apelles appeared in the doorway of the synagogue, coming out behind two soldiers who also rejoined their ranks.

Without calling him by name, Apelles looked at Mattathias and demanded, "Where are the books?"

"Your orders were to destroy them," said the old man, not exhibiting the least sense of fear.

"And did you?" said Apelles as if talking to a child.

"I assure you, sir," responded Mattathias, "that these books that you so despise no longer exist in Modin." Were it not for the emotions of the moment, Judas would have found humor in his father's words as he thought of the cave outside of town in which the scrolls were hidden in earthen jars.

Apelles started to question Mattathias further but suddenly changed his tone. "Well, perhaps someone is finally being reasonable." Apelles looked around the crowd. "Are your sons here? I am told you have five."

Mattathias replied, "Two of them are out in the countryside hunting. If they had known you were coming they would have been here. But three of my sons are here." Mattathias pointed to each one as he called their names, ending with John who was standing by Obed to one side.

Apelles eyed John for a moment, noticing his blackened face and hands from the smith's forge. "Why is he so dirty?"

"He's been working with Obed there. Obed is a smith."

"Yours isn't a family of smiths," said Apelles suspiciously. "You're the religious leader in this town. Isn't blacksmithing the sort of thing that stays in a family? Why would your son be working with a smith?"

"Because he is a friend. There's much work to be done to make and repair plows for spring planting."

Apelles seemed satisfied with the answer. Turning to the business at hand, he said to Mattathias, calling him by name for the first time. "Mattathias, I can see that I have chosen the right person. I called you here today because you are the respected elder of these people. I can see that you are also their friend, as is even seen in your sons." Apelles glanced at John with this last comment.

A line from one of the psalms of David crossed Mattathias's mind as he listened to Apelles's flattery: "With flattering lip, and with a double heart, do they talk." Mattathias silently prayed the next line of the psalm. "May the Lord cut off all flattering lips, the tongue that speaketh proud things!"

Matthan, envious that Mattathias was being recognized as the leader and desirous that the flattery be spoken of himself, wanted to say something but feared interrupting the king's officer.

Apelles continued. "Because I know the people will follow

you, I am asking you to take the lead today. I want you to lead them into this new world, a better world than any of them have known before." Looking at the crowd he said, "You can all become part of this new prosperity. All you have to do is embrace it."

Apelles turned to the slave by the altar. "Is it ready?"

The slave gave a quick nod of the head. Then Apelles commanded, "Then bring the sacrifice."

The slave ran past the soldiers to a crate sitting behind the litter from which he extracted a squealing pig. The slave wrestled with the pig, which although small and its legs tied together, was intent on getting away. Returning to the front of the altar, the slave took up a position between Apelles and Mattathias.

Apelles spoke again to Mattathias, but loudly as if making an announcement to the people. "Mattathias, you can honor the people you lead by honoring the king Antiochus Epiphanes. Embrace his god, his chief god. Sacrifice to the great Zeus."

Apelles backed away from the side of the altar to watch the sacrifice and to avoid any splatter of blood. The crowd was silent. All that could be heard was the periodic squeal of the writhing pig. The slave held the pig by its tied feet above the smoking altar as he had done in other towns. When Mattathias did not immediately reach forward to slit the pig's throat, the slave looked at him questioningly.

"I do not have a knife," said Mattathias simply.

The slave looked at Apelles for direction. Apelles unsheathed his dagger and motioned the slave to come to him. Carrying the pig the few feet with him, the slave received the dagger from Apelles and returned to the altar, handing the dagger to Mattathias.

The situation was not as Mattathias had envisioned as he had mentally prepared for this day. Apelles stood too far away, and the slave was in the way. By the time he would be able to cross the ground to the Syrian officer, a mercenary's spear would already be through his heart. He held the blade out as he stared at the pig.

"I cannot do this," he finally said. "I cannot dishonor my God by sacrificing to another. Though all the nations around us follow these false gods, I will not, though it cost me my life."

"Then it will cost you your life," shouted a suddenly irate Apelles. "But first, you will watch this sacrifice and know that you have lost." Apelles looked at the crowd. "Who will offer this sacrifice? Who will honor the king?"

Without hesitation, Matthan stepped forward. "I will offer the sacrifice. Honorable Apelles, I want you to know that not all of us are as obstinate as this man you have thought to be a leader of his people. He is no leader. He is a relic of the past. There are those of us who are ready to embrace the new ways. I would be honored if you would allow me to offer this sacrifice."

Apelles was surprised but pleased to find this kind of support. "And what is your name, sir?"

"My name is Matthan, of the party of the Sadducees."

"Ah, a Sadducee. At last, a voice of reason. Fine then, Matthan, take the knife from this man and honor your king." Matthan stepped forward and took the dagger from Mattathias's hands. Mattathias stood very still, unable to decide his next move.

"Mattathias," shouted Apelles, "you come stand by me. You will watch all of this and you will know that it is one of your own, a Jew like yourself, who is offering this sacrifice to the king. Before you die, you will know that you have died in vain. Yours is a lost cause. Now come stand by me."

Mattathias stared straight ahead, stone-faced, as he walked to Apelles's side. He glanced at Judas but gave no indication with his eyes as to what he would do. The slave again held out the squealing pig. Matthan, with sinister glee, slid the knife across its throat and the squeals stopped. The slave laid the now still body onto the grill of the altar and backed away.

Matthan drew a cloth from inside the sleeve of his cloak with which he wiped the blood from the dagger. As he walked pompously toward Apelles to return the knife, he said, "You see, Most Honorable Apelles, there are those of us who welcome the friendship you bring us. We are quite willing to be subject to the great Antiochus Epiphanes."

Matthan held the dagger by its blade and handed it, handle first, to Apelles. In the next instant, the future history of Israel changed.

Mattathias screamed out, "You enemy of all that is holy, die with the pig on the altar!" As he spoke, the visible character of the old priest changed. Suddenly more warrior than priest, Mattathias grabbed the handle of the dagger being extended in front of him as Apelles was reaching to receive it from the hand of the Sadducee. With one fluid motion he swept the blade across Matthan's throat and then swung his arm around to plunge it into the heart of Apelles. Matthan grabbed at his throat as he sunk to his knees. His eyes rolled back as he fell on his face dead at Mattathias's feet.

Apelles stood for a moment, too stunned at first to feel the pain of the knife in his chest, but then realizing what had transpired, he grabbed for it. He turned his head in a frantic look to the captain of his troops, looking for a source of salvation, but it was too late. As the soldiers who had been momentarily frozen in disbelief sprung forward, Apelles crumpled into a lifeless heap.

What happened next took little more than a minute, though time seemed to stand still. Soldiers from the front row of troops sprung forward with their spears poised to thrust into Mattathias. Hardly had they taken a step when three of them fell to the ground and began thrashing about, arrows extending from each side of their necks. Four others fell from arrows in less vital locations but would die directly from repeated attacks. In less that three seconds, another spray of arrows caused soldiers from the other ranks to fall. All heads turned in search of the source of the missiles that were raining upon them.

Two soldiers were still lunging toward Mattathias who now stood defenseless. Judas was immediately upon one of them, his sword drawn. With a quick and powerful thrust, he caught the mercenary mid torso in the side. With a second sharp upward thrust, he assured the man would be no further threat.

The other soldier was upon Mattathias, his arms pulled back to ram his spear through Mattathias's body when suddenly a choking pain ran from his neck into his chest. Grabbing at his neck on the right side he felt the base of an arrow. It had entered at his neck and angled downward into his chest cavity. Almost the entire shaft of the arrow was buried in his chest. In a seizure of pain he went suddenly stiff before collapsing to the ground.

Judas, helplessly frantic at seeing the soldier ready to thrust the spear into his father, looked in wonder as he saw the soldier drop. Looking up at the top of the wall he got a fleeting glance of Jonathan, bow in hand. Their eyes met for just a moment before both re-entered the fray.

Realizing the source of death coming from above, the mercenaries who were still standing ran for the staircase on the side of the house in order to gain access to the roof. As they turned, three suddenly fell hard to the ground, spears in their backs. The ones closest to them turned and saw that the doors on the opposite side of the street had opened and men were launching spears rapidly at them. Several of the mercenaries turned and charged the open doors, holding their shields in front of them for protection. Rather than fight the seasoned soldiers, those who had been throwing the spears ducked inside the doors and barred them shut. The soldiers pushed against the doors and struck them with their spears, but two of their number dropped to the ground with arrows in their backs. Facing the threat of the spears had left their backs exposed to the archers. They turned and defended themselves with their shields.

The first two soldiers charging up the staircase of the house were met by instant death as Jonathan and three others released a constant volley of arrows down toward them. Their bodies rolled down the steps into those behind them.

Realizing they faced death from both sides of the street as well as from above, one of the soldiers shouted out an order they all understood. The captain had already died so no one was truly in command. Nevertheless, every soldier ran to the middle of the blood-soaked street and huddled in a tight turtle formation such as used by a phalanx when defending against missiles while attacking. Facing outward on every side, they locked shields together over their heads. Arrows continued to fall over them, some shallowly piercing the shields but most bouncing off. For a few moments they were protected from the fire raining upon them from above.

For one moment, time seemed to stop. The soldiers looked about them as they protected themselves with their shields. Half their number lay dead around them. Facing them on every side were about a dozen Jewish men, not soldiers, but each held a sword. Their eyes met, Gentile to Jew for that one brief moment. Then the moment was over.

Oddly enough, it was Akim who ended the short-lived standoff. In an act of utter foolishness, he ran toward the mercenaries shouting, "I'm not part of this! I'm not part of this! It was my father who made the sacrifice. I'm with you!" The mercenaries heard but understood nothing of what he said. All they saw was a Jew running toward them. As soon as he was close enough, a soldier thrust a spear through his chest.

Seizing that brief moment of their distraction, Jonathan launched himself from the bottom step of the staircase into the street, releasing an arrow into a soldier who was still holding his shield over his head. Jonathan was stringing another arrow even as the soldier fell. The doors across the street opened just long enough for spears to be thrown into the other side of the formation.

The soldiers burst forth upon their sword-wielding foes about them. Those that were on the side toward the open street made quick jabs with their spears and then fled up the street away from the battle. Two of these were killed by arrows as they fled. The others, the ones facing the synagogue, had no such means of escape. They leapt forward to do battle, for their lives depended upon it.

Though this final phase of the attack was launched by the mercenaries, the men of Modin showed themselves clearly to take the offense, especially Judas. As if hungering for his next kill, Judas met the largest of the Macedonians, parrying the soldier's spear with his sword as he rammed his own body against the Gentile, knocking him to the ground. As if the whole movement had been choreographed, Judas raised his arm up and thrust the tip of his sword into the man under him. The sword found tender flesh, despite the fact that the soldier's shield was sandwiched between them and the soldier wore a breastplate.

Taking no time to watch the man die, certain in himself that his weapon had found its place, Judas ripped his sword from the body and swung it around to another soldier who was already upon him. Rolling from the man he had just killed, Judas thrust the sword under the breastplate of the other soldier.

The archers on the roof were unable to continue to fire into the chaos below. They just watched in awe, mostly at the catlike movements of Judas, though equally inspired by the strength of others.

The last kill of the day almost cost John his life. In the last futile thrust by the mercenaries, John found himself hand to hand with a soldier who had thrown down his spear and drawn his sword for quicker movement. John made a wide swing with his homemade sword and the sword flew out of its leather grip. The Macedonian, sure of his kill, moved quickly into John as John backed away defenseless. John tripped and fell onto his back, looking up at what he believed to be certain death as his enemy raised his sword to run him through. Just as the man's hand was about to bring the sword down, the man suddenly rose off his feet. His eyes bulged in horror as he struggled for breath. Suddenly, a dull cracking sound came from the soldier's body as blood spurted from his mouth. It was only then that John saw the huge burly arms that were wrapped around the soldier's body from behind.

Having crushed his rib cage, Obed threw the dead soldier down like a limp piece of cloth. The smith held out his massive arms from his tank-like chest. Looking down at John he said through his thick beard, "Nobody messes with my apprentice."

Almost as soon as it had begun, the attack was over.

Almost thirty professional soldiers had died at the hands of the townspeople of Modin. Because of the utter surprise and planning of the attack, not one of the men of Modin had been killed, though there were some injuries, some serious but not life threatening.

Mattathias posed himself behind the pagan altar. Raising his foot against it, he kicked it over and the slaughtered pig rolled across the ground as burning coals spilt out into the dirt behind it. Every eye turned in his direction at the crash of the altar. The warrior-priest shouted out for all to hear, "If anyone is zealous for the God of our fathers and for the laws he gave them, let him follow me. We will submit no longer to this tyranny. Decide this day which side you are on. If you are not with us, you are against us. Those who are with us, gather your belongings and return to this place within the hour. Those who are not with us, return to your homes and lock your doors. Do not open them for the rest of the day. It is no longer the Syrians you have to fear, but those of us that you have betrayed. Now go!"

Everyone left except for Mattathias's sons and Nethanel and his friends. Some ran to their homes, others walked. Some left in fear, others left in victory. Some spent a few moments before leaving, congratulating one another on their victory. Others backed silently away from the scene. Mattathias stood erect like a statue and watched. No one escaped his notice.

Judas drew his attention to the carnage in the street. "Father, what should we do with the dead bodies?"

"Leave them," Mattathias replied grimly. "Let those who have so favored them bury them. Then they will perhaps realize that this new world they so want to be a part of isn't as sure a thing as they think it is. Even the powerful die."

Jonathan, who was now out in the street holding his bow by his side, suddenly pointed a short distance down the street. "Look! They are not all dead."

Everyone followed his gaze to where they saw four trembling men lying with their faces to the ground, slaves that had carried Apelles's litter.

Chapter 15

Mattathias stood looking down at the four slaves lying prostrate on the ground. None dared to look up, but one said shakily in Greek as he continued to face the ground, "Please don't kill us. We will do whatever you ask."

Mattathias turned to Jonathan. "Jonathan, you and Eleazar go see what you can of the others, soldiers as well as slaves. Be sure they really have fled and are not lying in wait somewhere." As they started to leave, he added loudly, "And be alert!"

Mattathias returned his attention to the four slaves who had remained. Speaking to them in Greek, he ordered them gently, "Stand up. You have nothing to fear from us."

Slowly, their faces still filled with apprehension, the four slaves rose to their feet. The one who had spoken earlier continued to look at the ground as he spoke again. "We will do whatever you want. We will become your slaves."

A gentle smile crossed Mattathias's face. "We have no slaves here. In our nation we at times have slaves, but it is only for people that are unable to pay their debts, and then it is only temporary. On every seventh year, every slave goes free and all debts are canceled. You owe no debt to us. As far as we are concerned, you are free men."

The slaves looked at each other. The day's turn of events had put them in a position they had never thought possible.

Now they dared to look at Mattathias, though only fleetingly, still finding it difficult to make eye contact.

"What should we do?" asked the man who seemed to be the spokesman for the others.

Mattathias thought for a moment before speaking. "Well, being free men, you are certainly free to leave."

One of the other slaves spoke up in a language that Mattathias thought to be a Persian dialect, though he was unable to follow it. The four slaves conversed animatedly among themselves for a few moments before the spokesman turned back to Mattathias. "If we leave, we will probably be captured by the soldiers that got away. They would mistreat us. They did that anyway, but now it would be worse since our master is dead. They like to use us like women. Can we stay here with you?"

Mattathias was disgusted by this reminder of some of the heathen sexual practices of not just the Syrians, but of all the nations that had embraced the Greek ways. He answered the group, who he realized all understood his Greek though they had failed to understand the directions he had shouted out to the citizens in Modin earlier since he had spoken in Aramaic at that point. "We will not be staying here. After today we all must go into hiding."

"Then can we come with you?"

Mattathias thought for a long moment. He looked around at his three sons who were standing close by before answering. "You would have to become one of us."

"What does that mean? What would we have to do?" The one who spoke for the rest seemed more than ready to adopt the ways of a people who did not have slaves.

"It means," said Mattathias slowly, "that you would serve our God. You would obey his laws." Mattathias paused before continuing, for he knew his next statement would be the hardest thing for them to understand. "It means you would have to be circumcised."

One of the four appeared to ask a question in the strange language. A response came from the spokesman and the other three looked down toward where their genitals were hidden under their clothes before looking up again with wide eyes.

"Why would we have to do this?" asked the spokesman.

"It is a sign that God commanded that every Jewish male have in his flesh as a sign that he will live by God's covenant."

"And you have all had this done to you?" said the slave, looking around at the Jewish men.

Mattathias's sons and the others nodded, slight smirks appearing on the faces of some. So that they wouldn't be misinformed, Mattathias said, "Most Jewish boys have it done when they are infants, but for anyone who has not been circumcised who wants to become one of us, it must be done even as an adult."

"And we would have to do this right away?"

"No. Not today," said the old priest. "Today we must travel. When we get where we are going, then it would be done."

A collective sigh of relief came from the four slaves. At least they had time to prepare themselves. After a few more words were exchanged among the group, the spokesman said to Mattathias, "Then we will become as you. We just need time to get courage for this new thing."

Mattathias nodded, but then added with a serious tone, "You must be certain, for if you come with us you must stay with us. We will be going to a place of hiding that no one else can know of. If you come to that place and leave us because you fear this circumcision, for our own safety we would have to find you and kill you."

The slave thought for a moment and then said, "Even this circumcision, no matter how painful it is, will be better than the life we have known with the Syrians. It is better to be a man than an animal." The other three nodded in agreement.

Mattathias nodded sympathetically, as did the other men standing by. "Very well then, you will come with us. Now we must prepare to leave. You can be a great help. You can start by helping to gather all the weapons from these soldiers as well as their provisions of food."

The four slaves went immediately to work, jabbering with

each other in their own language as they worked. Weapons and body armor were collected from each dead soldier and piled on the litter. They also picked up every arrow and spear they could find that had been used by the men of Modin. There was little food to be found. Normally troops going into a military campaign would take enough food for several days, usually in the form of sacks of barley groats that each carried on his back. However, this particular contingent was not planning on much time in the field. Rather, they were moving from town to town, where they would appropriate whatever they wanted from the citizens who were helpless before their demands. All that could be found was a sack of fruit on the litter along with a skin of wine, obviously delicacies for Apelles as he traveled.

John and Simon went back to their house to get Leah and the supplies for their family. Nethanel and his friends went to help. In a short while Jonathan and Eleazar returned.

"We went far enough up the road to where we could see some distance," said Jonathan to Mattathias and Judas. "We could see them in the distance. They are getting as far from here as they can."

The slave who had spoken for the others, though not really understanding what Jonathan had said since it was said in Aramaic, thought he could discern from the pleased expression on Jonathan's face what he had reported. He asked, "Did you see any of the other slaves?"

Jonathan replied, "They are with the soldiers."

The four slaves exchanged glances and shook their heads. They knew these men would suffer greatly. Even Apelles tempered the lusts of the Macedonians for the simple reason that they were his property. Now Apelles was gone. There would be no limit to what the Macedonians would do to the slaves to placate their own frustrations.

In less than a half hour the street leading toward the synagogue was filled with men, women, and children, most carrying loads on their backs. They gathered down the street from the synagogue such that the bodies of the Macedonian soldiers lay between them and the synagogue. The women gasped at their first glimpse of the result of the battle their husbands had been a part of. Many covered the eyes of their children. Some just told them not to look. Others took the philosophy that the children might as well get hardened to it, for they would no doubt see more of the same.

The men who had sustained injuries in the fight had tightly bound up their wounds and prepared to travel. Judas ordered the two most severely wounded, having leg injuries, to ride in the litter. They reluctantly complied, settling themselves among the weaponry that had been piled there.

Three brought donkey carts, two pulled by donkeys and one pulled by its owner. The one pulling his own cart was Obed. On his cart was his anvil and forge. "If we don't kill Syrians fast enough, I may have to start making swords again," he explained.

The other carts were filled with sacks of grain. A small girl was perched on the top of a large sack on one of the carts. A few goats were brought along for milk and meat. The goats bleated noisily, their sound echoing off the walls of the houses on either side of the street.

Mattathias surveyed the group. In a small sense, it led him to wonder if this was just a little of what it was like when Moses led Israel out of Egypt. Of course, counting the women and children, he only had about fifty people that he was leading into the wilderness. Moses had a nation. But they had both seen the deliverance of the Lord. How amazing, he thought, as he looked up the street littered in dead bodies, that no Jew had died this day. Then he looked at the body of Matthan lying next to Apelles, and then at Akim, lying in a contorted position with a dead mercenary lying across him. That's right, he thought again, no Jew died this day.

No one needed directions as to what they were doing. All had been planned well in advance. Mattathias shouted to Nethanel's three friends, calling them all by name, "Oren. Jadon. Joseph. You know the way. We are trusting you to get us there. Now lead us out." Several men joined the four former slaves carrying the litter, throwing the bundles they had brought with them on the litter around the two injured men among the other baggage. All were in good spirits.

The new warriors, who would be called rebels by some but patriots by others, left behind them their homes and everything they owned except what they could carry with them. None had any idea when or if they would be back. Other than this crowd moving nosily down the street, the town lay silent, for the majority of the people, whether out of fear of identifying themselves with the freedom fighters or out of sympathy to the Syrians, had done as Mattathias had said and locked themselves in their houses. This was as Mattathias and his sons had planned, for they wanted no one to see the direction of their departure.

The small throng moved out of the town and headed north, opposite the direction the surviving soldiers had gone. They would enter the Gophna Hills from the west, a difficult way to go but the least visible and rarely traveled.

Judas, Jonathan, and Eleazar remained on the edge of town until the band of travelers was out of sight. They watched for anyone who might try to follow at a distance and then go inform the enemy of their whereabouts. Twice they saw men venture from their homes, and twice they appeared from around a corner with drawn swords. It had the desired effect. The doors slammed shut.

When darkness had fully fallen, the three brothers left Modin and headed north. Eventually a quarter moon rose to light the countryside well enough for them to travel without danger. The vegetation was low on the gentle hills this close to the coastal plain, and they could see any nearby obstacles. It would be more difficult when they cut inland into the Gophna Hills. They knew that the three of them would travel much faster than the larger group, even though traveling by night. If they stayed due north, they would eventually see campfires that would be burning as the group made camp for the night. They could see the Pleiades well up in the east. Orion would be rising above the horizon soon. Keeping these to their right, they would not lose their direction.

There was no sense of fatigue. The battle was still very much alive in their minds, and they talked of it as they walked, each telling it as he had experienced it. There was a satisfaction they had received in the fight that none would openly admit. But each one knew he wanted more.

After a couple of hours of reliving the fight they fell silent. The night was growing colder, and they were ready to be with the others. Judas began to think less of the battle and more about Rebekah. The picture engraved upon his mind was that of her standing in the doorway, tears running down her face, almost a month earlier as they had left Jerusalem. Jerusalem seemed a world away now, but thoughts of Rebekah were a constant presence. When would he see her again? What was it like for her right now? Was she well? What was life like for her in Jerusalem now? Had Shimri come home? Was Hananiah better? Judas resolved that as soon as they established their base in the Gophna Hills, he would find a way to get to Jerusalem.

The three men walked quietly, only sharing the occasional word, all absorbed in their thoughts. They had just come down a gentle slope when they noticed some distance up a defile to the east a small but brightly blazing fire. They stopped and stared at it for a long moment. A single small fire would certainly not be what one would expect in a camp of fifty people.

"Do you suppose it's them?" Eleazar expressed out loud what they were all asking themselves.

"I don't know. It's not what I was expecting. Not one small fire," answered Judas.

"It could be a trap," said Jonathan.

Judas thought for a moment, then started leading the other two forward cautiously. "Keep your eyes open to everything around. Don't look at the fire. If you do you won't be able to see what may be hiding in the dark."

They moved slowly, careful that every step came down softly and silently. There were no signs of life around them. Coming closer to the fire revealed nothing more. For all they could see, there was nothing here but this one small fire. All that could be heard was the crackle of the flames.

Jonathan and Eleazar stopped at the edge of the encampment, if such it could be called. Judas walked warily around the fire so as to see beyond it. He was puzzled. Someone had to have made the fire, but who? He turned to his brothers and gave a shrug when suddenly a voice out of the darkness pierced the silence.

"Don't take another step, you Jewish dogs!"

Chapter 16

Before the voice ended its sentence, Judas had his sword in his hand. He spun in the direction from which the voice had come but saw no one. There were some low-lying shrubs nearby, but nothing large enough to hide a man.

Jonathan and Eleazar started backing away into the darkness.

"I said don't move!" ordered the voice. They froze and looked all around, seeing no one. The voice spoke again. "You can't go anywhere unless you know the password."

Jonathan and Eleazar looked at one another in the flickering light of the fire. Both were at a complete loss for words. In the few moments that had passed, though, the reality of what was happening had dawned upon Judas.

"There can only be one password if I know what I think I know," said Judas. "It has to be 'Maccabee.'"

Laughter erupted as a figure rose up as if a ghost coming out of the ground. Covered in straw from head to foot, Nethanel stood holding his sides. "What gave me away?"

A huge grin broke across Judas's face as he put his sword back its sheath. "Well, for starters, if you're going to call someone a Jewish dog, it's probably better not to speak in Aramaic. Secondly, I caught your voice."

Jonathan and Eleazar came by the fire where Judas and Nethanel were. They feigned beating up Nethanel, but just for a moment. The warmth of the fire was too enticing to stay away from it long.

As they warmed themselves by the fire, Judas asked, "Where are the others?"

"Not far. Just over the next rise actually. There's a ravine that makes a good hiding place for the night. I just stayed back to watch for you and leave you a signal in case I missed you. We're only about a half hour from Timnah-serah. Your father figured it would be best if no one knew we were here. We don't know what the people of Timnah-serah are like or if they would be sympathetic to our cause. Oren and Jadon say that we can get into the Gophna Hills from here if we just follow the course of ravines as they go east, so we decided to head inland here."

"Then let's get going," said Judas. "It's been a long day."

They were all reluctant to leave the warmth of the fire, but they were eager to be with the others. Nethanel kicked dirt over the fire until it was not only extinguished, but covered over so that no smoke would rise from it.

As Nethanel led the way for the others, Judas said from behind him, "By the way, Nethanel, that was pretty good the way you hid from us back there. You were only a few feet away and I couldn't see you. You'll probably get to do that again. Only next time, the dogs won't be Jewish. They'll be Syrian."

"I'm planning on it," came Nethanel's cheerful reply.

It was just after midnight when Nethanel and the three brothers arrived at the encampment. Silence enfolded the sleeping camp. There were four low burning fires scattered around an open area toward one side of the ravine, some little more than glowing embers. Lying on the ground at varying distances from the fires were outstretched bodies wrapped in their cloaks. Some lay alone, some lay in pairs, husbands and wives huddled together for warmth. In a couple of places, whole families lay tightly together. The unforgiving ground was cold and hard. Occasionally someone would rise and throw an extra log on one of the fires in an effort to fight off the chill. All this was but a prelude to the discomfort of the months to come. The leftover adrenalin rush of battle quickly died when one was fighting to stay warm through a seemingly interminable night. War quickly lost its romance. The only thing that would carry them through would be the resolve of their leaders.

Sitting behind a fire that burned brighter than the others, its flames crackling from fresh fuel, Mattathias peered into the darkness at the four men as they arrived. Sleep had fled from his eyes. He was the only one in the camp who was not at least trying to sleep. The four drew close to the fire, holding out their icy hands before its flames.

Mattathias greeted them in a low voice. "How was it when you left Modin?"

Judas answered. "The streets were deserted when we left. We left after it was dark, so no one saw which way we went. Even if someone did try to follow, they would certainly not find us here, at least not tonight. This is too far off the way that anyone would travel."

"Have you eaten anything?" asked the father.

It was only now that any of them realized that they had not eaten anything since breakfast. Suddenly the very thought of food made them ravenously hungry. Mattathias gave them some barley cakes that had been baked in a pan over the open fire. It wasn't a meal in the way of variety, but there was enough so that they would not go to bed hungry. Once they got settled in the Gophna Hills, their first job would be to procure a steady supply of food. Surviving on grain was sufficient for a while. In fact, most armies went on a campaign with nothing more than a twenty-day supply of grain. However, eventually they would need a source of meat. Oren and Jadon had assured them there was plenty of game in the hills, but that was always an uncertain source, especially if their numbers grew and more was needed. Much of their success would depend on the relationship they built with the people in the towns nearby.

As the men sat chewing on their simple meal, washing it down with an occasional sip of water from a skin, they all stared into the fire. The chill was gradually leaving them. Occasionally each one would turn and warm the other side for a moment before returning to face the fire.

Mattathias looked at each of his sons. "Do you have any regrets?"

"Regrets?" said Judas. "About today?"

"Yes," the old man replied. "We have embarked upon a course of no return. Either we continue to fight and win, or we will die. This is not something we can simply stop because we no longer want to fight." Mattathias paused and then asked the question again. "Any regrets?"

"No," said Judas resolutely. "Not at all. We all knew what we were getting into." Jonathan, Eleazar, and Nethanel, who had remained at the fire with them, all nodded their heads in agreement.

"What about my killing Matthan?" said Mattathias, a far away look taking over his demeanor as he relived the moment.

"You didn't plan on that, Father," came Judas's quick rejoinder. "Who knew that Matthan would do anything so foolish as to so openly side with those Syrian devils?"

Mattathias shook his head, but the distant look in his eyes did not leave. "Nevertheless, as I've sat by this fire for the last hour, I've had very troubling thoughts. Did I do right?" There was a long pause as he opened his mouth as if to say more but could not seem to find the words. Finally, letting out a sigh, he withdrew from the distant place in his mind and looked around at the others. "I guess it's always in the quiet moments of the night that we most wrestle with our thoughts, isn't it?"

Everyone considered what he said and shook their heads in shallow nods of agreement as they continued to gaze into the fire. They were all familiar with the doubts that often arise in the night watches. After a long lull in the conversation, Judas spoke up. He felt strange giving his father spiritual advice, but he said what was on his heart. "Father, it was you who taught us Torah. You know it better than anyone. Do you remember what Moses said to the Levites after the matter with the golden calf?" Mattathias looked at his son's face across the flickering flames as Judas continued. "Moses had come down from the mountain, and the people were worshiping a golden calf they had made. He said, 'Whoso is on the Lord's side, let him come unto me.' It was the Levites who rallied to him. Moses told them to strap on their swords and to go through the camp, killing their brothers, friends, and neighbors. And they did. They killed three thousand of their own people because they had abandoned the Lord. Because of what those Levites did, God preserved our nation. And do you remember what Moses said to the Levites that day?"

Mattathias shook his head in the affirmative as if realizing something for the first time, citing the Scriptures he knew so well. "Consecrate yourselves today to the Lord, for every man hath been against his son and against his brother; that He may also bestow upon you a blessing this day." The old man looked into the fire and allowed the truth to dawn upon him. He slowly put that truth into words of his own. "God's blessing comes upon those who choose Him above all else. It was because the Levites obeyed God, even though it meant having to kill some of their own people, that God set them apart as special to Himself."

When Mattathias had finished, Judas said simply, "Father, we too are Levites, not just in name, but in our hearts."

Mattathias found new life in the words of his son. He lay to rest the doubts that had risen in his heart during the stillness of the night.

After several more minutes, the others found a place away from the fire and lay down to sleep. Judas remained by the fire with his father, a restlessness not yet allowing him to sleep even now.

When he felt sure the others were asleep, Mattathias spoke quietly to his son. "Judas, there is something else I've been thinking about this evening, something that relates to what we were just talking about."

Judas leaned over to hear his father's quiet voice.

"I've heard the others calling you the Maccabee, the hammer."

Judas looked embarrassed. "That's just Nethanel. I wish he would stop."

"No, no. It's a good name. I hope it catches on so people will know they are dealing with someone who is strong. And it's not just Nethanel. I heard some of the others call you that as we walked on the road today, especially from the archers who watched you from the roof. I have to admit that I, myself, was amazed to watch you fight. You are a strong person, and it is you who will inspire people to follow the good cause.

"But Judas, you need to understand something of what it means to be the Maccabee. It doesn't just mean killing Syrians, and that's the hard part. A while ago, I told you how I was troubled over killing Matthan. It didn't bother me to kill that Syrian officer or watch all of his soldiers die with him, but Matthan was a different story. Your words helped me to think rightly again."

Mattathias paused as he considered his next words. "Judas, you remember the story of how Solomon built the first temple?"

Judas nodded but was confused by the question. "I think I do. Why?"

"You will remember that all the stones for the temple were dressed at the quarry so that no hammer would be heard at the temple site while it was being built." Judas nodded again, indicating that he remembered the history. "Judas, the temple that must be built is Israel. The stones are the people. Not all of the stones will fit, and the hammer must be used on them before we can become a nation again. This will be much harder than fighting the Syrians, because it means fighting our own people, people like Matthan."

"And like those Sadducees we saw in Mizpah," added Judas, remembering the one he had collared while taking down the body of the man Apelles had crucified.

Mattathias looked into the fire. "That's right. These are people that will not fit into the nation, not unless they change. The kind of nation we are supposed to be has been shown to us by God. That will never change because God never changes.

Those who would try to change God's design are as much enemies of Israel as are the Syrians." Mattathias paused for a long while before adding with hesitation, "The Maccabee can be a hero, . . . but some of his own people will see him as an enemy because they will not understand. But you must stay the course. This is God's fight."

The father and son sat silently by the fire without further conversation, lost in their thoughts. After a few more minutes, Mattathias stretched out on the ground and pulled his cloak tightly around him. Judas sat for almost another hour, watching the flames die. His father's words lingered in his mind. Not only would the Syrians have to be defeated, Israel would have to be purified. It would do no good to eliminate the enemy without if they ended up being destroyed by the enemy within. He finally lay down, turning his back to what were now just glowing embers. Sleep finally came, but even in his sleep he found no real rest. The fire within him was burning a vision in his mind, a vision of an Israel that was not only free of Syrians, but that was also pure from their ways.

The next day the new company of warriors and their families arrived at the place they would call their home for months to come. It took most of the day, trudging up and down uneven terrain as the hills became higher and higher and low scrubland turned into a thick forest. The donkey carts had to be abandoned, most of the goods being loaded on the donkeys' backs. Obed hid his cart with its cargo of anvil and forge in a thicket, trusting the assurances of Oren and Jadon that they would be able to find the place again later.

The new home for the weary travelers was partway up the northern side of a valley about an hour away from Lebonah. There were two sizeable caves that would provide immediate shelter situated about five minutes apart on the mountainside. Other forms of shelter would be built in the days to come. Fuel was quickly rounded up and fires built so that a meal could be prepared before nightfall. They had contented themselves with leftover barley cakes from the evening before for lunch, not wanting to stop with the end of their journey in sight.

While the others were making their first preparations for where they would be living for the next few months, Judas and Simon accompanied Oren and Jadon the rest of the way to Lebonah. Just as the way by which they had come from the west, there was no road the rest of the way through the winding valley to Lebonah. They followed deer trails along the sides of the mountains. Oren and Jadon seemed to be able to follow them as well as any road and knew where they were going. They saw no sign of human activity along the way. Eventually the valley opened to a much wider expanse on the edge of which was situated Lebonah. The road running directly from Samaria to Jerusalem ran on the eastern side of the town.

The four men entered the town discreetly, staying close to the buildings and in the shadows. Eventually they came to the home of Oren's uncle, a man both Oren and Jadon had described as a trusted elder of the town. They would have stayed the night with him, but it was the news he gave them that kept them from staying.

Just as the sun was setting, the four men, already tired from two days travel, left Lebonah to return to their camp. They had stayed with Oren's uncle less than a half hour. Darkness fell quickly, but that did not deter them. Oren and Jadon seemed to know the mountains in the dark almost as well as in the light. Even though there was no moonlight, for the waning moon would not rise till later, they managed to follow a path, though Judas and Simon were not always certain that it was the same path that had brought them there. Jadon assured them that since they were following a valley, they could not go too far off the trail. Eventually they would see the fires of the camp.

Despite the assurances of their guides, Judas and Simon later confessed to some doubts. Their doubts were quickly dispelled by sighs of relief, though, when they finally saw the distant flicker of a campfire. A few minutes later as they walked into camp they were greeted by a welcoming aroma. While the others were setting up camp, two of the men had managed to kill two sizeable deer.

John's wife, Leah, cut appetizing chunks of meat off the animal roasting on the spit over the fire and handed it to each of the four men along with a piece of bread. They ate voraciously as they told the latest news. Others gathered around to listen.

Judas waved a savory rib with his right hand as he talked between bites. "Word of our attack is already headed to Apollonius, the governor in Samaria."

Simon interrupted. "He probably knows by now."

Judas explained. "In Lebonah, Oren's uncle told us that today about noontime a unit of ten Syrian cavalry stopped there and demanded to be fed. He told us that while they were there someone heard them talking about a Syrian officer being killed in a town called Modin. Evidently those soldiers that got away yesterday made it all the way back to Jerusalem and told their story. This unit that came through Lebonah today must be part of the cavalry stationed at the Acra. They were wasting no time getting the word to Apollonius."

Mattathias, sitting a few feet away from the fire, voiced his interpretation of this news. "Apollonius will demand immediate action. He will probably give the responsibility to the garrison in Jerusalem. That is what they are there for, to deal with us Jews." There was a note of humor in his last statement and caused some nervous laughter among the group. "The best thing we can do at this point is to stop all communication between Jerusalem and Samaria. We must not allow ourselves to rest. Starting tomorrow, we must begin working to gain support in every town between here and Jerusalem, and we must set up ambushes to stop any Syrian or Syrian sympathizer from traveling that road."

Judas took a bite of venison as his mind echoed the words "or any Syrian sympathizer" as he recalled his midnight conversation with his father. The purification of Israel would begin tomorrow.

Chapter 17

Apollonius slapped the goblet of wine from the extended hand of the elderly Jewish slave, splashing the wine down the front of the slave's white tunic. The slave bent down and picked up the goblet then crouched to wipe up the wine with the hem of his garment.

As if the slave embodied the entirety of the Jewish race, Apollonius shouted at the white-haired old man crouched on the floor, "Damn you Jews! Why can't you just accept the way things are? You are all fools! You can't change anything, yet you never quit trying."

The old man raised up and backed away from where Apollonius sat, fearful that his master's wrath might become more than it already was. The governor's narrowed brows and pursed lips spoke nothing but contempt as his eyes followed the slave. An awkward silence reigned in the room. Standing before Apollonius was a cavalry officer from the Jerusalem garrison. The news he had brought with him had aroused both fear and anger in the governor. At this moment, his anger burned toward every living Jew, but underneath it was a dread fear of the king who held him personally responsible for anything the Jews might do. A full minute passed without a word being said.

Apollonius turned his gaze to the officer. "When did you say this happened?"

"Yesterday morning."

"And where are these rebels now?"

"I don't know, Sir. I was sent directly here to inform you as soon as we received word. Troops are combing the countryside and searching every village even as we speak."

Apollonius did not know how to proceed at the moment but did not want to appear incompetent in front of the officer, so he directed his attention to the elderly slave once again, who by now had found a position out of the governor's line of sight. Seeing no need to explain himself for what had occurred a few moments earlier, Apollonius looked over his shoulder and snapped, "Don't just stand there, Lucas. Pour me some more wine."

The slave, Lucas, poured wine from a decanter on a stand by the wall and brought the goblet again to Apollonius. When the slave held the cup out, Apollonius deliberately made a quick gesture so as to frighten the slave. Lucas almost dropped the cup but thankfully did not. When the governor had taken the cup from his hand, he again backed to the side of the room.

Apollonius again directed his attention to the officer. "What do we know of the people who did this?"

"From what we could learn from the soldiers who were with Apelles, the leader of the rebels is a man named Mattathias. He has five sons who are all in it with him. They knew this much, but none could remember their names, at least not well enough to be certain about it. But there were more than the man and his sons. The soldiers said it was a well orchestrated attack that involved a great number of the men in the town."

"At least that's what the soldiers say," commented Apollonius.

"Yes, Sir."

"Probably trying to save their own skin."

The officer made some attempt at defending the mercenaries. "I'm not so sure, Governor. After all, the rebels did manage to kill three fourths of a contingent of forty. Besides that, the slaves that came back, the ones that transported Apelles, gave us the same story when we interrogated them."

"Slaves!" Apollonius laughed, making a quick glance over his shoulder at Lucas. "What do you expect? Of course they will say whatever they think you want to hear. You can't trust the word of a slave." Then more seriously, he inquired, "Did all the slaves come back?"

"All but four, Sir."

"What happened to these?"

"Either they were killed, or they joined the rebels. No one seems to know."

Apollonius stared at the floor as if trying to read something that wasn't there. An awkward silence again overtook the room. Several minutes passed. The cavalry officer wondered if he should speak but then thought better of it. This was a time to only speak when spoken to.

After several more minutes, the governor raised his dark countenance toward the officer. "Execute the soldiers and the slaves, and do it publicly. Lest anyone else think they can run from this Jewish riffraff, they need to understand what the consequences will be. A soldier's duty is to fight, not run. As for the slaves, they are just so much livestock anyway. Other slaves need to know that the only reason they are kept alive is to serve their masters."

The officer was not pleased at the thought of executing the surviving soldiers, for he too was Macedonian. "Governor, Sir, um . . . might this not have a negative effect? Might not the troops become less loyal if . . ."

Apollonius rose from his seat in a rage, sloshing wine from his cup as he waved his hand toward the officer. "How dare you question me?" To Apollonius, rescinding an order was an indication of error, which itself would demonstrate weakness. "You will do as you are told, or you will share their fate!"

The officer dropped his head and said quietly, "Yes, Sir. Forgive me for being so presumptuous."

Apollonius glared long and hard at the officer. After what seemed an eternity to the officer, the governor again seated himself and, as if the vicious interchange that had just taken place had never occurred, said, "How many of these rebels were there?"

"Probably thirty or forty. Really just a group of thugs, Sir." The officer was relieved that the focus had turned once again to the Jewish rebels. He had no qualms about killing Jews. Being part of the Jerusalem garrison, he had been forced to tolerate these obstinate people for the last two years. He had found it entertaining a month earlier as he had leaned against the parapet of the Acra watching part of the infantry wing of his own garrison march in phalanx formation across the temple courtyard leaving behind them hundreds of dead Jews. Perhaps with this open rebellion, there would be no more need to tolerate the Jews or even to try to change them. They could just purify this cursed land by killing them all.

"Surely this can't be much of a challenge for our garrison there in Jerusalem." Apollonius was trying to minimize the situation in his own mind, for he was with difficulty suppressing the fear that was quietly gnawing in his stomach. If he could stop this uprising before word got to Antiochus, later when it did come to the knowledge of the king he would be commended for having handled it well.

"This is certainly something we can handle, Sir," said the officer, wishing to portray efficiency. "This attack on Apelles just came out of nowhere. No one in Judea can stand up to our troops if we meet head-to-head. They have all been on a battlefield more than once. It's just that they were totally surprised. Now that we know the rebels are there, they will have to fight like soldiers are supposed to fight, face-to-face in open combat. There will be no more surprises, no more of this criminal behavior."

The governor thought as he listened to the officer's assuring words. His mind calculated the strength of the garrison in Jerusalem. "Very well. I charge the Jerusalem garrison with the task of eliminating these troublemakers and anyone else who might join them . . ." Then after a slight pause, he added before continuing, ". . . or help them. We can show no mercy to such as these. Come back in an hour for written orders to take back to Jerusalem. You will return there tomorrow."

The cavalry officer bent stiffly at the waist and clasped his right fist to his chest in a gesture of subservience before turning and walking out. When he was gone, Apollonius stood and held out the goblet in his hand toward his side without looking back. The elderly slave took the cup from his hand. As the governor walked away, he motioned toward the small puddles of wine on the floor without looking back and commanded, "Clean up this mess."

Lucas, the elderly slave, went in search of a towel and a basin of water. When he returned, he crouched down on stiff knees and began wiping the wine from the floor. Under his breath so that only he could hear, he spoke to himself as he worked. "I have been a slave my whole life. But soon, I will be no man's slave. Soon, I will bow to no one."

Chapter 18

The first rays of light were filtering through the valley as Judas belted his sword to his side. He looked up at the smoke rising from the cook fires into the trees and thought about it for a moment. Smoke could give away their position. Unlike the light of a fire that needed a direct line of sight to be seen, smoke could be seen from miles away. Though they were an hour away from the closest settlement, and the trees would disperse most of the rising smoke, there was no use taking chances. He gave a quick order to one of the women tending the fire closest to him. "Tell all the other women to keep the fires hot and make sure the wood is dry so there is no smoke. We can't risk being found." The woman threw some sticks on the fire she was tending and trotted off to relay to message to others.

Despite the fatigue, Judas had lain awake much of the night. It wasn't because of the discomfort of sleeping on the ground. A bed of leaves was not very different from sleeping in the stable back in Modin, something he had done many times. What had chased sleep from his eyes was anticipation of the coming day, and of days after that. People would look to him for direction. It was he who had planned the details of the attack in Modin, and it was he who would plan every subsequent attack. His plans must always succeed. If they did not, his friends, and possibly his family, would die.

Going on the fleeting glance he had had of it the day before, he formed an image in his mind of the terrain around Lebonah. It was different from the land that lay around Modin. Trees were more plentiful, and there were more places to hide. This would work in their favor. However, the increased vegetation also made it more difficult to see an approaching enemy. He would depend greatly on Oren, Jadon, and Joseph for their knowledge of the area.

Judas calculated their resources and laid out a plan in his mind. He divided the men into groups according to their abilities. He ordered five of the men, two of these being those with leg injuries, to remain in the camp with the women and children. They could hunt as needed and prepare a more permanent camp. Not all of these were happy with the idea of being left out of the fight, but Judas assured them the effort was best served if they remained behind. They would spend whatever spare time they had cutting and trimming shafts for arrows. The women would help with this also. After the skirmish in Modin, Judas envisioned archers playing a major role in future battles.

Obed was among the five who would remain in the camp. It was determined the night before that his skills would indeed be needed. Feeling quite certain that he could retrace their steps, he and another would go back along the trail to retrieve his anvil and forge. No one envied Obed's having to tote an anvil across miles of mountainous terrain, but they figured that anyone who could break a man's ribcage with his bare hands was up to the task.

Besides the five that Judas had ordered to stay, there were the four slaves who had carried Apelles's litter. Mattathias circumcised the four men and put them in a camp away from the others until they healed. Though expressing some measure of fear before the circumcision, they showed no regret afterward. This was a new life. They gladly endured the temporary pain if it meant permanent freedom.

Though weary from the previous two days, Mattathias deemed it necessary to immediately visit the four nearest towns –

Lebonah, Tappuah, Shiloh, and Gilgal. He chose Joseph to accompany him since Joseph was from the area. If what Joseph and the two men from Lebonah, Oren and Jadon, had told them was true, he would have no trouble soliciting support from these towns, both in men and supplies.

Within the next hour, the small ragtag army moved out. Tearful wives stood by the fires, watching their husbands disappear through the trees, not knowing for sure that they would see them again. Children huddled close to their mothers, some not understanding what was happening, still seeing everything as one great adventure.

Each man carried his own supplies. Because they expected to procure food from fellow patriots in towns along the way, they only carried enough grain for about three days. Some carried skins for water which would be shared. There was usually a source of water somewhere in the mountains so they could be filled often. They also went well armed. Every man carried two spears, some being those that had been made by Obed, some the *pila* that were taken off the dead soldiers in Modin. Every man had a sword. The archers all carried their bows and a full quiver of arrows. A few had put on the breast and back plates that had been taken off the soldiers in Modin, but some of these soon complained about the extra weight.

When they came near the road south of Lebonah, Judas held the band of warriors back in the trees. Mattathias and Joseph left the others to go the rest of the distance into the town. Talking to Oren and Jadon who were by his side, Judas asked, "What is the best way to see the greatest distance up and down the road?"

The two men from Lebonah both looked out through the trees seeing how far they could see. "Let's walk out to the road," said Jadon.

The others held back while Judas walked with Oren and Jadon through the scattered trees until they arrived at the road. They were about a mile south of Lebonah. Standing in the middle of the way from Samaria to Jerusalem that had been beaten clear by marching armies, merchants, and simple travelers of every sort over the centuries, the three men looked one way then the other. The dusty, pebble-strewn road was wide, but because it was not particularly straight, taking turns and curves due to boulders and rising hills, it was impossible to see a great distance in either direction. Mattathias and Joseph, who had just started up the road a couple of minutes earlier, were already out of sight. All three pondered the situation.

"You could see from up there," Oren finally said. Judas and Jadon followed his gaze. From where they stood, they saw the summit of a low mountain.

"That's right," said Jadon. "That hill rises just north of Lebonah."

Judas saw the possibilities. "So from up there, would you be able to see the road both north and south of town?"

"Sure," they both said together. Then Oren continued. "We've been up there countless times. You can see Lebonah. You can see the whole valley from up there, as far as Gilgal."

"Then we have no time to lose." Judas was speaking even as his plan was forming in his mind. "Oren, you go as quickly as you can into Lebonah. Try not to be seen. Go to your uncle. He will help us. Get two large pieces of cloth, two different colors but bright enough to be seen from a distance. Also, get some rope. We will be with the others where we left them. Be quick. If I guess correctly, that cavalry unit that came through yesterday will be returning today taking orders to Jerusalem. They will probably stop for food again in Lebonah, since it's about midway. We need to be ready." Oren handed his weapons to the others and took off at a fast trot toward town as Judas and Jadon disappeared among the trees.

Almost an hour later Oren came through the trees to where the others were waiting, cloth held under one arm and a coil of rope draped over the opposite shoulder. Oren proudly presented his goods to Judas. Judas looked at the cloth as he held it in his hands. Both pieces were damp. One piece was a pale blue, elegantly embroidered linen tunic. The other was an expensive looking gold-colored cloak with narrow burgundy stripes. Judas looked at Oren with suspicion. "Where did you get these?"

"I found them drying stretched across a bush beside the house of the only Sadducee in Lebonah," Oren replied, his face beaming with delight. "He won't be needing them much longer, not if he stays a Sadducee." Laughter broke out among the men.

"And the rope?" ask Judas. "Did you steal that too?"

"No. My uncle gave me that. He said he would get more if you needed it, but he wanted to keep some because he's hoping someday to hang that Sadducee." More laughter erupted around them.

Judas held up his hand for quiet and the laughter died away, though smiles remained. "Well done, Oren. Now everyone listen closely." Judas laid out the plan that was in his head. When he had finished, there were a couple of suggestions from others which were adopted after a brief discussion. One thing that endeared Judas to the hearts of those who followed him was that he was always willing to listen to what they had to say. There was no question of who was in command, but it was clear that he truly valued those who were with him.

After a short while, Oren and Jadon disappeared through the trees with the stolen cloak and tunic as well as a bronze breastplate, which was gladly relinquished by one of the men who had complained of the extra weight. The rest of the group went out to the road and began making preparations for their ambush. About a half hour later Judas saw a bright flash of light near the crest of the mountain they had looked at earlier. Oren, with Jadon on the mountain, was catching the morning sun on the polished breastplate he had carried with him. Judas returned the signal with a breastplate of his own. Jadon raised the pale blue tunic extended on a long pole that he had cut from a tree with his sword. A moment later, Oren raised a pole holding the gold and burgundy cloak. Judas flashed with the breastplate again, signaling that he was able to see them. From that point on, there would be no more flashes with the breastplates. Such flashes could quickly attract the attention of an enemy. The simple raising of a flag, though, was only likely to be noticed by someone who was looking for it, especially since it would not be in the normal line of sight of someone traveling north or south on the road. Even so, signals with the flags would be made then immediately taken out of sight.

Simon took the monotonous task of watching for the signals from Oren and Jadon while the others refined their preparations. If the pale blue tunic was raised, it would mean someone had been seen approaching from north of Lebonah. If the gold and burgundy cloak was raised, someone was approaching from south of their position on the road. They were not expecting an enemy to pass from this direction, but they wanted to be ready in any case. If someone passed who was not an enemy, they would remain hidden. If someone left Lebonah headed south toward their position, both flags would be raised. In all cases, if whoever was approaching appeared to be military, the flags would be briefly waved from side to side.

When there was no more to be done in way of preparation, the men sat around talking. Judas came over and sat beside Simon, who never took his eyes from the side of the mountain.

"Do you think that Sadducee in Lebonah might see his clothes waving on the side of the mountain?" said Judas, trying to lighten the moment.

Simon smiled. "It is rather ironic, isn't it, that a Sadducee's clothes are helping us fight Syrians?"

"It is, at that."

"There it is!" said Simon, suddenly raising his head higher.

Judas looked toward the mountain. It took a moment for his eyes to spot the pale blue flag against the trees. Then he saw clearly that it was waving back and forth. Judas turned and shouted to the others and every eye turned toward the mountain. A minute later the flag was no longer in sight.

Judas suddenly felt overcome by doubts, but he let only Simon hear him. "What if we are not ready? I didn't think this through well enough. We don't even know how many are coming. Apollonius may have sent more back with the cavalry. He may have sent a whole army. I should have told Oren to give some sort of signal telling us how many there are."

Without turning his head, Simon said calmly, "Brother, we

are all learning as we go. If we are way outnumbered, we just won't attack. Besides, they will probably stop in Lebonah. It's almost noon. Send someone to check things out."

Judas shouted out to Eleazar, who came instantly to his side. "Eleazar, run to Lebonah. Stay in the trees as you get close to town, out of sight. See if you can tell how many are coming this way. Even if you don't make it back, don't risk being seen."

Eleazar dropped his weapons on the ground and took off at a dead run. Watching him leave, Judas said to Simon, "I'm seeing how important it is for us to know everything we can about what the enemy is doing. We need to establish spies in every town and village."

Simon nodded. Few generals commanded an army without previous training, without having ever been a soldier. But that was the situation they were in. They were just simple Levites whose life was to have been one of serving in the temple, and now they were being called upon to mobilize a whole country for war. Simon put his hand on Judas's shoulder and said simply, "God will help us."

It wasn't long before Eleazar was back. He talked through long gasps for air. "I saw ten horses and a couple of soldiers standing by them. I think the others were inside a house eating."

"Is that all?" asked Judas, already relieved that he had guessed well.

"That's all I saw. Lebonah is not a very big town, and it didn't take long," replied Eleazar, still trying to catch his breath. Then he said with a smile, "There was a man talking to one of the soldiers I could see. He was telling them that someone stole his clothes this morning. He wanted them to do something about it, but they didn't seem too interested in helping out."

"Our supplier of flags," Judas smiled back.

"They're coming!" shouted Simon. Every head turned toward the mountain. Both flags were waving from side to side. In less than a minute, the road was empty. Any traveler could easily have passed by and never known that armed men lay all around.

In a few minutes the rapid clop of hooves could be heard against the hard ground. As the sound grew louder, hearts began to race to match their cadence. The cavalry unit came into sight at a moderate gallop. The horses and their riders ran in pairs. By training, the two riders in front combed the road with their eyes from side to side, but they saw nothing.

Judas had chosen the first action as his own. This would be the signal for the others to attack. By silently throwing themselves into the battle without the expected shouts, they expected to disorient their enemy a second longer.

At just the right point in the road, the riders sitting high in their saddles, a rope sprang suddenly from the dust and drew taut at the height of a rider's neck. Judas pulled with all his might on the rope which was tied at the other end to a stout tree. The first two riders were pulled immediately over the backs of their horses and fell onto the ground as the horses continued their gallop as though nothing had happened.

In the same instant, both sides of the road seemed to come to life. What had earlier appeared to be clumps of weeds, suddenly sat up. Each one let go an arrow. In the first few seconds, five of the cavalrymen lay dead on the ground.

Judas dropped the rope and leapt into the fray with a spear in his hand. One of those he had pulled from his horse with the rope was rising to his feet with his hand on his sword. Judas planted his spear in the man's chest, piercing his breastplate, before the other man's sword left its scabbard. The other man who had fallen to the ground had already been brought down by an arrow.

Realizing the hopelessness of their situation, the remaining four horsemen shouted and kicked their horses. The steeds bolted forward. A hail of arrows and spears followed them as they raced down the road in the direction of Jerusalem. Just as they thought they had escaped, another rope suddenly cut across the riders' necks, throwing all four to the ground. A few seconds later, the four men lay dead upon the ground, the handiwork of spears and arrows that had come from yet more invisible enemies hidden in the brush.

Judas looked down the road at the four fallen men. "Nobody expects the same trick twice," he said with satisfaction.

A moment later a horse trotted up beside Judas. Nethanel proudly sat astride the finely bred Arabian. "Hey, Judas! We now have our own cavalry." A couple of others came holding the reins of other horses, though having no experience with horses, they had not mounted them.

Judas shouted to everyone as he looked up at Nethanel, who still had grass and weeds sticking to his clothing and in his hair from having hidden himself before the attack. "Catch all the horses!" Several ran after the remaining Arabians. Most had stopped close by, but a couple had continued at a gallop down the road.

Nethanel saw the situation and kicked his horse, which bounded forward. "I'll get them!" he shouted over his shoulder. It was obvious that this wasn't the first time Nethanel had been on the back of a horse.

Judas turned to look at the bodies of the Syrians lying in the road. It was only then that he noticed Simon slumped on the ground, propped against the large rock he had spent most of the morning sitting upon watching for the signal from the mountain.

Chapter 19

All the blood was drained from Simon's face, but he had a sheepish smile. Judas ran to his side. "What is it? Are you hurt?"

Simon seemed embarrassed. "I think I broke my leg."

"Broke your leg? But how?"

Simon looked at the ground, not wanting to make eye contact. "I jumped up on this rock to throw a spear and . . ." He was reluctant to say more.

Judas repeated what Simon had said. "You jumped up on the rock to throw a spear and . . ."

After a long pause, Simon finished, "I fell off. I broke my leg."

Simon pulled up his cloak and everyone close by gathered around. The lower part of Simon's shin held a slight bow shape.

Judas shook his head. "We fight trained Syrian cavalry, and you get hurt by falling off a rock."

Though in obvious pain, Simon couldn't help but laugh.

As the others gathered around, some holding horses by their reins, Judas looked away from Simon for a moment to give orders. "Remove everything that seems useful from the bodies and then drag them well off the road, well out of sight. Cover them with rocks or whatever you can find."

Everyone went to work. While most of the men were in the trees hiding the dead, Judas and Eleazar lifted Simon to the back of one of the gentler seeming horses. Eleazar led the horse into the forest to the place they planned to camp that night. When they were gone, Judas walked along the road covering up signs of the short battle. Primarily this meant kicking sand over splotches where blood had soaked into the ground. An hour later, anyone coming along the road would never have suspected that ten men had died there an hour earlier.

The Jewish fighters watched the road for the rest of the day. Except for a couple of merchants, no one passed by. People did not generally travel much during the winter. The passing merchants never suspected that just a few feet away were men ready to swoop upon them with swords and spears had they shown signs of being in any way allied with the Syrians.

That night, the fledgling army gathered in a clearing in the forest. Not far away, tied to a line strung between two trees, were the ten Arabian steeds. Now rejoined by Oren and Jadon from the mountain, the men sat around a hotly blazing fire trying to ward off the chill, some of them munching on raw grain from their food pouches.

Simon leaned against a tree with his legs stretched out in front of him. Amidst grunts of pain, Judas with the help of two other men had pulled the bone straight before binding it with splints. Simon would be out of commission for a few weeks. The next day, he would be carried back to the encampment on a makeshift litter.

In the light of the dancing flames, Judas led a discussion of their next move. When it was all over, it was decided that most of the men would remain close to Lebonah to hinder any movement by Syrians up and down the road. They would operate much as they had this day, watching from the mountain for any Syrian movement.

Judas designated six men, dividing them into two groups of three, to go to all the towns between Lebonah and Jerusalem. Their job would be a twofold recruitment: fighters who would join them in the Gophna Hills and spies who would remain in the towns. John would lead one group, Nethanel the other.

Despite Nethanel's pleas to the contrary, Judas refused to allow them to go on horseback. Judas insisted that it would be difficult to explain how three Jewish men had come to be riding horses that were so obviously cavalry horses. Even though their Scriptures recorded that Solomon had at least 12,000 horses in his army, the Jews had mostly adhered to the injunction given them by Moses in Deuteronomy that the king "shall not multiply horses to himself." The warriors of Israel had fought most of their battles standing on their own two feet. The horses would be kept and used when needed, but at the moment, Judas saw no great advantage in them. After all, that very day, amateur fighters had killed ten professional cavalry in less than a minute.

During the next two days, there was little activity along the road. Judas gave much thought to what future battles would entail. He devised a training schedule for the small army. While some watched the road, others practiced with the various types of weapons. They made blunt wooden swords for the sake of practice. Most found it to their advantage not to wear a breastplate. Judas gave them permission to fight without a breastplate as he too had found it cumbersome. Though most were complete novices with horses, they all spent some time riding the Arabians. More than anything else, Judas was adamant that everyone run several miles each day excepting the Sabbath. The key to victory, he insisted, might be simply one of endurance.

On the second day, Joseph appeared along the road. He would have walked right past those lying in wait, so well were they hidden, had not someone recognized him and called out to him. Joseph had come looking for them. He and Mattathias had recruited a number from the towns they had visited. Some of those were on the way with Mattathias back to the encampment carrying food supplies. According to the numbers Joseph gave them, their small army had now more than doubled in size. Mattathias had requested that Judas return to their camp in the hills to train the men he had brought with him and to discuss how to deal with the Jews who were supporting the Syrians.

Judas left that same morning, leaving Jonathan in charge of those watching the road. Jonathan had proved himself popular with the other men, especially as they saw his unequaled abilities with a bow.

Just over an hour later, Judas and Joseph arrived at the encampment in the hills. The camp was bustling with activity. Mattathias and thirty-two men had arrived just a short while earlier. Some of the men had brought sacks of grain which the women were now busy storing away in dry corners of the caves. A number of chickens and goats had been brought as well, adding to the noise of the camp.

Judas saw Mattathias bending over the figure of Simon who was sitting in the entrance of one of the caves. Mattathias stood up as he saw Judas approach. He extended his arms and hugged his son in as powerful an embrace as he could muster. Judas could tell from his father's grasp that Mattathias was weak from the past few days. It wasn't physical strength that kept a man Mattathias's age going, it was raw conviction. Judas tried to encourage his father to sit down and rest, but Mattathias pushed him aside, saying, "First let me introduce you to our new friends." Mattathias shouted across the hillside, summoning the men to come closer.

A few moments later, the group of unfamiliar faces surrounded them as Mattathias spoke. "This is my son, Judas. Judas, for lack of a better word, is the general of our small but growing army. He led the planning of the attack in Modin that you have already heard about. I have just learned a moment ago from my son Simon, who you see here with a broken leg, that just two days ago our men attacked a small unit of cavalry just south of Lebonah, wiping them out without any casualties to our side, except of course Simon's broken leg."

Scattered grunts of approval resonated through the group. One of the men was heard commenting to another, "They were the ones we saw in town a couple of days ago, the ones old Jada was going out of his way to help."

Judas looked inquiringly at the man who had spoken. The

man understood Judas's unvoiced question and responded by simply saying, "A Sadducee." Judas nodded and looked back at his father, who was continuing to speak.

"Judas will show each of you how you can best serve the cause. Remember, this is not the cause of just a few people. This is the cause of God, who gave us the laws that have preserved our nation through the centuries. If we abandon those laws, our nation will be lost. So serve with all your heart, because God is on your side."

When Mattathias had finished speaking, he returned to the entrance of the cave and sat beside Simon, weariness etched in every line of his face. Judas knew it was his father's simple way of transferring the authority over the men to him. Judas immediately took charge and began learning what he could about their new warriors. He divided the men into two groups, appointing a captain of each group. One group was composed of men from Tappuah and Lebonah, the other group being of the men from Shiloh and Gilgal. He selected two men from each town to return to their towns as spies. While appearing to involve themselves in the everyday affairs of the town, they would serve as informants of any Syrian sympathizers. They would also work at keeping a steady stream of supplies and new recruits coming into the hills.

During the afternoon, Judas outlined for his new troops their method of fighting. Though their techniques were unorthodox by military standards, it had worked for them so far. Training began that very afternoon using what few weapons they had. They had a few remaining weapons won from the Syrians but most of those weapons were presently in use by the men Judas had left on the road below Lebonah. Obed was at work at his forge again but had not had time to make the number of weapons that was now needed. The matter of supplies, both in weaponry and food, would become as crucial in the fight as the men who fought it. One of the men from Gilgal had experience as a smith, so despite his personal craving to shed Syrian blood, Judas put him to work alongside Obed.

Late that night, as most of the camp slept, Judas sat huddled by the fire with his father and Simon. Mattathias turned the conversation again toward the subject that Judas had tried not to think about. "Judas, Israel must be purged of the poison in its midst." Judas knew his father was referring to the Jews who supported the Syrians. "It cannot wait," Mattathias added.

"But how will we know who they are?" Judas asked.

"They are not difficult to find," said Mattathias. "During these past couple of days, as we have gained support in each town, God has enabled me to speak his laws again to the people. I have called upon them to return to the ways of our fathers. I have told them to circumcise their children and to obey all the laws Moses gave us. I have also told them to pay no more taxes to Antiochus. When I told them this, it became obvious who was against us. Whether they are all Sadducees or not, I do not know. Maybe some do not belong to that party, but it is obvious that they do not belong to us. These are as great a danger to our nation as any foreign army."

"So how should I go about dealing with them?" Judas found it easy to fight an enemy in a Syrian uniform armed with a sword. It was the enemy that looked much like his own friends and relatives that he had trouble knowing how to fight.

Simon had been thinking as he listened to the conversation. His calculating mind provided the answer. "It must be done in the dark."

"What do you mean?" Judas did not immediately pick up Simon's meaning.

Simon explained his thoughts. "One reason most of our people so hate the Syrians is because they have been such an open challenge. When the Ptolemies of Egypt occupied our country, we paid them taxes just like we do to the Syrians now, but the people accepted it because they did not challenge us or denigrate us, at least not openly. But the Syrians have openly scorned us from the beginning. You remember that day in Mizpah. Apelles made a point of holding a public execution and in the vilest way imaginable. This enflamed our hearts to the point that all of us were ready to fight. Many hated the Syrians before, but they weren't ready to fight. If we are not careful, we could accomplish the opposite of what we intend. The open killing of other Jews could draw sympathy toward them. We must go about this in a manner so as not to let that happen."

Judas shook his head slowly, showing that he understood Simon's reasoning. "So how do you propose that we go about it?"

Simon laid out a plan. "You have appointed spies in each town. These spies will tell you who is siding with the Syrians. Then primarily by night, but also by whatever covert means presents itself, simply make these people disappear. Eliminate them but leave the populace ignorant as to what has happened to them. Most people will assume they just became fearful of all that was happening and fled to one of the Samaritan towns to the north, or maybe went to Jerusalem to seek protection there."

Judas stared into the fire. "It still won't be easy."

Mattathias looked across the leaping flames at his middle son. With no great emphasis but simply as a statement of fact, he said quietly, "Judas, this must be done."

"And one thing is very important," added Simon. "You must use people you know you can trust. They must never speak of what they do."

Judas drew a deep breath as he stared into the fire. Without looking up, he asked his father, "Do you think Joseph would be good for this?"

Mattathias was quick to reply. "Yes. We've had some good talks over the past couple of days. He is a man to be trusted, and he knows what is at stake."

"Good," said Judas. "Then we will start when the sun sets on the Sabbath. We will begin in Lebonah with this Sadducee I have been hearing of. What was his name?

"Jada," replied Mattathias. "A good place to begin. I have been told of the damage he has already done to our people. Eliminate him. Then Lebonah will be clean again. We will claim one town at a time. Then one day, Jerusalem will again be ours."

Chapter 20

Judas spent most of the next day instructing the new troops. In a couple of days he would send those who seemed most able to serve with those who were already stationed along the road to Jerusalem. Jonathan would see to their training even as they remained ready for battle.

The men Judas had selected as spies returned to their towns. Before leaving, they received thorough instructions for the coming days. They would live in the towns but would help Judas and Joseph in the covert elimination of Syrian loyalists.

No word had come from John or Nethanel and their companions who were making their way through the towns from Lebonah to Jerusalem. This was not surprising as there were many towns, and great care would have to be taken the closer they came to Jerusalem. As Simon had discovered some weeks earlier, Syrian support increased the closer one came to Jerusalem or to Samaria.

All was quiet in the camp the following day. It was the Sabbath. Mattathias led in prayers and in the reading of Torah. As he prayed, Mattathias purposely faced south, toward the temple in Jerusalem, the place chosen by God to hear the prayers of his people.

When the sun set, Judas and Joseph quietly left the camp. Traveling through the wooded valley by night was slow. There was no moon, but they had little fear of getting lost. If at any time they felt themselves rising to higher ground, they knew they were straying from the path, a lesson they had learned from Oren and Jadon. It took them over two hours to finally arrive in Lebonah. They immediately went to a home where they found both of the spies that had returned there two days earlier.

The wife of one of the spies served them supper and then quietly stationed herself on a mat in the corner of the one-room dwelling. In the flickering light of a single oil lamp, the spies shared with Judas and Joseph about another group of cavalry that had come through that morning.

"How many were there? Which way were they going?" Judas immediately probed for more information.

"There were ten, just like the ones who came through last week. They were headed to Jerusalem," one of the spies answered.

Judas sighed relief. "Jonathan should have handled them without too much trouble. Probably some of Apollonius's cavalry."

The other spy shook his head. "I overheard one of them talking to Jada, that Sadducee that we will be seeing tonight. They had been traveling for several days. They weren't from Samaria. They were from Antioch. The best I could understand, they came directly from Lysias."

Judas felt a knot grow in his stomach. "Lysias. He is second only to Antiochus. How would they know so soon?"

"I don't know," said the spy, "unless maybe they were coming from Lysias anyway to oversee how Apollonius is managing affairs in Judea. The commander of this group seemed to be more than just a mere cavalry captain. He may have authority to act on his own without having to wait for Apollonius."

Judas could not dispel the disquiet that rose in his spirit. "Whoever this was, surely Jonathan stopped him. For tonight, anyway, we will have to believe that is so. We have enough to think about without worrying about that now."

The others agreed. As the hours passed, the conversation

turned in many directions. Mostly, the other men wanted to hear from Judas what it was like to be in battle. Judas told them of the anxious moments in the tunnel under the temple mount and how he had discovered the weapon of surprise. He told how it was this great weapon that had given them success in the two skirmishes they had fought thus far. It was a weapon he would continue to use, for it was something the Syrians did not seem to be equipped for.

The men wanted every detail, not just from interest in what they would all eventually face, but also as a distraction from where their thoughts kept taking them. It was one thing to kill in battle. It was quite another to kill as an executioner. None of them looked forward to what they would do this night, though no one questioned its necessity.

When it was well past midnight, Joseph looked at Judas. "It's time." Judas didn't say a word but simply rose to his feet and pulled his cloak tightly around him. Though the others would accompany him, this first time Judas would do what had to be done. He would never ask someone else to do something that he was not willing to do himself.

Judas opened the door and stepped out into the night. There was a full ceiling of stars, but they provided no comfort. All he could feel was darkness looming in his spirit. Led by one of the men from Lebonah, they moved silently through the streets. In a couple of minutes they arrived at the door of the man called Jada. Judas had never laid eyes on this man. He was putting his full trust in those he had selected that this was indeed an enemy that had to be dealt with, an enemy as deadly as any he would confront on a field of battle.

Judas put his hand on the door and stood for a moment as if trying to visualize what lay on the other side. He knew an oil lamp would be burning, as was the case in most Jewish homes throughout the night. Jada would probably be lying on a mat on the floor. Judas's one point of relief was in having learned that Jada would be by himself. Though still claiming to hold to the teachings of Torah, Sadducees were much more open to divorce for any and every reason, something Jada had done not just once, but twice. There would be no woman to deal with. Judas had not yet brought himself to the place of believing he could kill a woman, though he knew from the biblical accounts of women such as Jezebel and Athaliah that there were times when women had to be put to death because of their own sinister deeds.

Judas pulled up on the latch gently in hopes that the door would open readily. People in small towns were less prone to lock their doors at night. Jada, however, was not one of those people. Judas pushed and pulled the door just enough for it to rattle as the wind would rattle it. He could tell that though the door was locked, the latch was not strong.

Joseph silently gestured to him, asking if he wanted him to break the door open. Judas shook his head. He knew that bursting the door open himself would bring the surge of energy that would help him complete what he had to do. Just as in battle, once the first blow was struck, the rest came without further deliberation.

Judas motioned for the other men to back away from the door. He took a moment to draw a deep breath before lunging hard against the door with his shoulder. A sharp crack resonated as the latch snapped under his weight. Following his own momentum, Judas fell upon Jada who had just had time to raise his head, startled at the sound that had suddenly awoken him. Jada tried to scream out, but it was too late. Judas had both hands around Jada's throat. Judas had considered using a weapon, but he had not wanted to leave any sign of blood. What he needed to do, he knew he could do with his bare hands.

Jada's eyes bulged as he clawed at Judas. Judas tried to turn his head away as Jada frantically tried to gouge his eyes. Joseph leapt into the struggle, pulling Jada's arms behind him. The other two men quickly came inside and closed the door. Judas did not cease crushing the Sadducee's windpipe for what seemed to be several minutes. Jada's body fell limp, and still Judas continued his death grip upon his neck. Another minute passed. Judas felt a tug on his shoulder. Joseph pulled at his arm. "It's enough, Judas, it's enough! He's dead!"

Judas released his grip and Jada fell to the mat on which he had been sleeping moments earlier, a death stare fixed upon his face. Despite the chill in the room, Judas was pouring sweat. He slid to the wall and propped himself against it as he gasped for air. Looking at the Sadducee's body, almost in tears he said, "There's no glory in this. This feels more like murder than war."

The other three men looked down at the body in silence. Still shaking inside, Judas looked at Joseph. "Joseph, can you do this? Can you lead others to do this?"

Joseph waited a long while before answering. He gave himself time for his heart to quit racing, then he turned his mind to the day in Gilgal he had watched a Syrian beat his ninety-year-old great-grandfather until his intestines had fallen out on the ground. He saw in his mind a particular Sadducee who had stood to one side watching the whole thing with a sneer on his face. Joseph's nerves became as ice, and he said through clenched teeth, "I can do this in every town in Judea if need be."

In the dim light of the oil lamp sitting on a shelf, Judas's eyes met Joseph's cold stare. This was the man who would lead forces that most of the others would never know about.

After some more quiet moments, Judas looked up at the other men, both of whom were standing by the door. "Do you think we were heard?" One of them had occasionally cracked the door open a breadth to see if there was any activity outside. "I don't think so," he said.

"How about that lock?" asked Judas. "It needs to look like Jada just left during the night. We don't want it to look like someone broke in."

The other man from Lebonah took the oil lamp from the shelf and examined the latch. "I can fix this in a few minutes. I will just need to get some things from my house."

"Good," said Judas, rising to his feet. He bent over Jada's body and lined it up square with the mat he was lying upon. Then, looking around the room, he spied a chest in the corner.

Going to the chest he took out several folded garments and dropped them on the Sadducee's body and then rolled the body and clothes all up together in the mat. The others all had puzzled looks on their faces. Judas caught their expressions and said simply, "If a man's going to travel, he will need clothes." They understood. This was all part of the ruse. Judas added, "But we aren't going to leave the clothes with him. I'm sure we have someone who can use them."

His strength now returned, Judas picked up the rolled up mat and threw it over his shoulder. After a cautious look up and down the street, he stepped out into the night air. He and Joseph headed in one direction. The other two headed in the other. They would be back in a few minutes to repair the latch and return home before the sun came up. Judas and Joseph silently but quickly moved through the darkness beyond the edge of town and into the forested hills.

Just as the sky was starting to show some light in the east, they finished disposing of the body. A gully running into a shallow ravine had provided a place to cover the body with rocks. It was in a place where the only possible person who could find it would be a hunter.

Keeping the mat and the clothes, Judas and Joseph began making their way back toward Lebonah. They did not intend to go into Lebonah, but that was the direction in which the road lay. There was no point trying to find their way through the forest if the road would get them to where they wanted to be sooner. Their plan was to hook up with Jonathan and the others.

As the sky brightened in the east, they heard the first cock of the morning. It had been a full twenty-four hours since either had slept. The crow of the cock made them suddenly realize how tired they were. They planned to rest some once they found Jonathan and the others, but for now they had to keep pushing.

Joseph suddenly stopped short, putting out his hand to stop Judas. Something in front of them was moving. In the dim light, seeing through bleary eyes, he wasn't sure he wasn't seeing things. But that wasn't possible, for Judas now saw it too. They were within sight of the town, but just outside the town there appeared to be someone moving from tree to tree. It was as if he were spying, studying the town from behind a tree and then moving to a closer position to study the town again.

Judas and Joseph came quietly up behind the figure who was crouched behind yet another tree only a stone's throw from the nearest dwelling. "What are you doing?" said Judas. Turning to see two men, one with a sword drawn, the white-haired old man pressed himself against the tree, his eyes wide with fright and his breath suddenly having left him.

Chapter 21

Judas spoke to the old man again. "Who are you? What are you doing here?"

Still pressing his back against the tree, the old man's eyes darted from Judas to Joseph, then to the sword in Judas's hand. Judas studied the frightened creature before him for a moment. While the elderly man showed no immediate signs of being weak or ill, fatigue was written all over his face, the kind of fatigue Judas had begun to see in the eyes of his father. Knowing the man would be no match for him and Joseph, and seeing the apprehension in the eyes that kept returning to the sword in Judas's hand, Judas slowly sheathed the sword and asked again, "Who are you?"

Willing himself to speak, the old man said through trembling lips, "My name is Lucas."

Judas's hand dropped instantly to the handle of his sword again. "Lucas! Are you Syrian?" Judas's voice was harsh now. "What are you doing here?"

The old man dropped down with his face to the ground. "No! I'm a Jew! I'm a Jew!" Sobs came from the pitiful figure whose face lay inches from the ground.

Judas and Joseph looked at each other, trying to understand. It was Joseph who spoke next. "How does a Jew, especially one your age, have a name like Lucas?"

The old man raised his head, tears running down both

cheeks. "Because all my life, from my earliest recollection, I have been a slave of Gentiles. I have belonged to Carthaginians, Romans, and Macedonians. The name I have is what pleases them, not me."

Judas's hand left his sword, and he crouched down in front of the old man. Speaking gently now, he said, "Sit up, Lucas." Lucas raised himself to a sitting position and pulled his cloak around him. The perspiration from anxiety had begun to chill upon his body in the cold air. Judas looked into Lucas's face in the pale glow of the steadily lightening sky. "What are you doing here? Why are you here hiding behind trees looking at the town?"

A small measure of comfort began to grow within Lucas, though he did not know with whom he was talking. Whoever this was that was interrogating him, they held no love for Syrians, for the large man had been ready to draw his sword again at the thought that Lucas might be Syrian. "I don't know where to go or who to trust. Perhaps I have acted foolishly in even thinking I could find who I am looking for."

"Who are you looking for?" Judas queried.

"I'm trying to find a man named Mattathias. In Samaria I heard that a man named Mattathias is leading a fight against the Syrians. I want to join him."

Judas and Joseph looked at one another in wonder. The old man looked from one to the other, puzzled at their expressions. Judas put his hand on the old man's shoulder. "Lucas, God has led you here. Mattathias is my father. His camp is only about an hour from where we stand."

Lucas broke down and wept as he lifted his eyes upward. "Thank you, God of my father! Thank you for guiding my steps!"

Judas breathed a prayer of thanks along with Lucas. At the end of a night that had sunk him into a dark depression despite his knowing what he had done to be a necessary aspect of the war, here he found a glimmer of light. An elderly Jewish slave who had been in bondage all his life had found a place to run to for freedom. The camp of Mattathias in the Gophna Hills would be a pocket of hope to oppressed Jews everywhere.

Judas urged Lucas to stand and told him that he could accompany them to Jonathan's camp along the road below town. After that, before the day was up, he would take him to see Mattathias. Despite the encouragement that they thought Lucas's escape from slavery would bring to others, neither Judas nor Joseph imagined that an old man would be of much practical use in their resistance against the Syrians. However, as they walked south along the road together in the cool morning air, they learned that quite the opposite was true. This old slave would become one of their greatest assets, not so much for what he could do, but for what he knew. Knowledge was a powerful weapon. Lucas told his story as they walked.

"My father was a merchant in Alexandria. He was a good man. So was my mother. They taught me the ways of God. We spoke the old language in our home, though as I'm sure you can tell from the way I speak now, it has been many, many years since I have used it. I have tried to keep it alive in my mind even when there was no one around that I could speak it with.

"When I was still very young, my father became deeply indebted to a man from Carthage named Haminar. Because Haminar insisted that the debt be paid, my father had no choice but to deliver his whole family into Haminar's service as slaves. I have been a slave from that day until today."

Lucas stopped and breathed in deeply the cool fresh air. Upon releasing the breath, he said with satisfaction, "But today I am free."

Judas and Joseph stopped long enough to allow the old man this emotional moment. Lucas then began walking again and continued his story, Judas and Joseph on each side taking in every word.

"And so, our whole family, my parents, my two sisters, and me, were moved to Carthage. Our slavery was just to be enough years to satisfy my father's debt, but things have a way of changing.

"Just after my twelfth birthday, Haminar was called along

with most of the other landowners of Carthage to serve Hannibal in his conquest of Spain. As you well know, soldiers who have the means to do so often take their slaves to war with them in order to carry their supplies and serve them along the way. Despite the protests of my family, Haminar forced me to go to Spain with him, assuring my father that if he ran the household well in his absence that upon our return, we would all be freed. We never returned.

"I will never forget how afraid I was. Though I didn't like him at all, I stayed very close to my master because I knew he did not want to lose me and so would protect me. We had only been in Spain a few days when Hannibal started the siege of Saguntum. I tried to stay hidden most of the time. It was awful. I remember especially the way the people of Saguntum fought back. They had a special type of spear called a *falarica* that is a lot like the *pilum* that the Greeks use. The iron head of the weapon was as long as a man's arm and was fastened into a stout shaft of fir. The Saguntines would bind the shaft with tow and smear it with pitch. As Hannibal's forces would approach the wall they would light fire to the pitch and throw the *falaricae* down upon the troops. The amazing thing was that even though the iron head of a *falarica* was capable of piercing a man's body, armor and all, this wasn't what caused the most damage. It was the flaming pitch. The spears would pierce the shields the troops were holding over their heads and the pitch would splatter fire in every direction. The troops would throw down their shields to keep from being burned only to die from the archers' arrows. They would then collapse into the flames that were all around them. I can still see the mounds of charred corpses. But Hannibal would not stop. He just used the mounting pile of corpses to bring him closer to the top of the wall. In the end, the Saguntines were no match for Hannibal."

Judas looked across to Joseph. Their eyes met as they realized the same thought. What they had just been hearing was information that would prove useful in coming days. Lucas continued.

"There were many other battles in Spain after that, but

what Hannibal really wanted was Rome. The only way to Rome was across the mountains." Lucas feigned a shiver. "I never want to be that cold again. And the elephants, those cursed elephants. Hannibal valued those elephants more than he did any of his men. They would trudge up the slopes and pack the snow tight as they went until it was a solid sheet of ice. Then an elephant would slip on the ice and come sliding down the side of the mountain, killing or maiming everything in its path. More men died just going over the Alps than in most of the battles, mainly because of the elephants.

"But it wasn't the Alps that finally defeated Hannibal. It was the Romans. It looked as though Hannibal would outdo the Romans at first, but the Romans were too smart for him. They even knew how to defeat his elephants.

"Everything changed at Zama. Hannibal charged eighty war elephants at the Roman lines. The Romans did two things. First they blew trumpets. Most of the beasts were so frightened that they turned back and trampled their own troops. The ones that did keep charging were given free passage. The Roman lines just opened up and let them run through. There's no point trying to stop one of the beasts. Just let it go its way. The men on top can't do much if they are not around very long. Once the Carthaginian infantry was in disarray because of the elephants, the Roman cavalry came in and took the day. Hannibal fled with a small unit of his own cavalry.

"I never saw my master Haminar after that day. I assume he died in the battle. I was taken as a slave by the Romans. Now I know the Greeks would call it fate, but I must believe it was the hand of God for reasons I can't begin to imagine. I became the slave of Scipio, the Roman consul who had defeated Hannibal at Zama. Life was not uncomfortable during the years I spent in the household of Scipio, but I must confess that there were times I would have preferred the cruelty of Hannibal to the debauchery of the Romans. If you understand my meaning, the Romans are much like the Greeks and the Syrians as to what they think is acceptable."

Lucas looked from side to side and saw the affirmative

nods from both Judas and Joseph.

"Well, like I said though, life could have been worse. I was well cared for, even though my life was not my own. They even educated me in both the languages of the Romans and the Greeks. I served in the presence of dignitaries from many different places. This would not last, though. If I count the years correctly, it was seventeen years ago that my master, Scipio, died. In Rome, when an owner of slaves dies, the slaves are traditionally executed, especially if the owner was someone important. I'm not sure why this is other than as a final act of homage. For whatever reason, I did not find this prospect very appealing. As soon as I learned of my master's death, I fled. This was easy at the time because we were at his country villa when he died.

"My education had given me an understanding of the world and how to get from place to place, so I determined that I would make my way to Judea. However, it is difficult to hide the brand of a slave when the weather is hot."

Lucas pulled up the sleeve of his cloak and showed them the brand burned into his upper arm.

"I tried to keep it hidden by keeping a bandage around it as if I had been injured, but I let the bandage slip one day while trying to make passage on a ship from Macedonia. They would have killed me were it not for where I had been in the past. Once they learned that I had lived in the household of Scipio, they brought me to Philip, their king. I served Philip, who despite his previous efforts against Rome, towed the Roman line.

"When Philip died, however, his son Perseus had other ideas. Perseus wanted to be another Alexander, the great hero of the Macedonians. His problem, though, was that he tried to use Alexander's techniques, techniques that had long been studied by the Romans. And for this reason, last year, I watched his phalanxes get crushed by the Roman legions at Pydna."

Judas stopped short. "You were at Pydna?" Even in Modin they had heard the stories of what had happened at Pydna.

Merchants arriving on ships at Joppa would often stop for the night on their way to Jerusalem. The stories they brought of the great battle of Pydna had filled many a discussion during the past year.

Lucas and Joseph, having walked a couple of steps further before realizing that Judas had stopped, turned around. "Yes, I was there," said the old man. "I watched it all, standing right in front of the king's tent. The ground in Pydna is very uneven, so the king had his tent pitched on a rise where everything could be seen. It's the kind place that is great for *watching* a battle, but a terrible place to *fight* one, at least if you plan on fighting with a phalanx. The ground was the undoing of the Macedonians."

Judas recalled the horror of the Syrian garrison moving their phalanx across the temple court. It seemed to him at the time to be an invincible machine. "So a phalanx can be defeated," he said, both as a statement and a question.

"In more ways than one," replied Lucas, shaking his head with a smile on his face, realizing for the first time that he would indeed have something to contribute to the fight for freedom.

"So how are you here now?" said Judas, starting forward again.

"Well, after Pydna, Perseus wanted nothing that would remind him of the Romans. I seemed to do that to him. He gave me as gift to Antiochus, his ally in Syria. Antiochus did not want a Jew in his palace, so he gave me to Apollonius, the governor in Samaria. That is where I have been for the past several months."

Judas slowed his pace. "You have been serving Apollonius?"

"Yes. I have been in his service since last summer. That's where I escaped from. A few days ago a cavalry officer came telling of how your father is leading a revolt. I was standing there as he told the governor. It was then I knew I could find my freedom. You see, I have tried to be free before, but if the only place you can run to is a place that will just enslave you again, it is to no purpose. But if you run to people who are themselves trying to be free, you can be free together."

Judas stopped and looked the old man in the face for a long moment. "Then, my friend, we will be free together."

Lucas pursed his lips into a satisfying smile and then repeated the words. "We will be free together."

As if part of the conversation, a loud voice came seemingly from out of the air. "Or die trying!"

Chapter 22

Lucas jerked his head in surprise, but Judas and Joseph just stood and smiled. Knowing where they were, they had already spotted the men lying in ambush. Jonathan stepped from behind a tree. Three others stepped into the open from other positions. Judas introduced everyone to Lucas, who was relieved to see he was among friends.

"Where is everyone else?" Judas asked, looking around to see if there were others in hiding.

"They will be here shortly," replied Jonathan. "They are still at our camp in the woods. They are rather discouraged. I'm glad you're here."

"Why? What has happened?" Judas noticed the dejected look on Jonathan's face.

Jonathan looked down at the ground, occasionally glancing up at Judas as he talked. "A couple of days ago, late in the afternoon, just an hour or so before the start of Sabbath, a small unit of Syrians came along traveling north toward Lebonah. They were accompanying a chariot that, the best we could tell, was carrying one of Menelaus's agents with taxes he had collected to Samaria, or maybe Antioch. Anyway, there was a box filled with money, so we figure it must have been tax money.

"We attacked and killed them all in a matter seconds. We took the chariot, horses, money, and weapons as we always do." Jonathan stopped and let out a sigh as he looked at the ground.

"That sounds great," said Judas, not finding a connection between the message and the sentiment with which it was being given. "So what's wrong?"

Jonathan raised his eyes to look into Judas's face. "One of the Syrians did not die fast enough, and he was very quick with a spear. He killed Ezra."

Judas's mouth dropped open. "Eliud's son?"

Jonathan gave a couple of short nods, dropping his eyes to the ground again. Judas raised his head and looked up at the sky, then at the mountains on either side. He pursed his lips to keep them from trembling. "There had to be a first," he said. Halting between sentences, the reality still taking hold of his senses, he continued, "God has protected us so far, but we knew this would come. Do they know yet, I mean, the people at the camp back in the hills?"

"No. Sabbath began, so no one could travel to tell them. All we could do was bury the body before the sun set. We planned on someone going this morning."

Judas put his hand on Jonathan's shoulder, still overcome with emotion himself. "I will be returning to the camp later today. I will take the news. You and the men have done well. Ezra did well. He died well, standing for what was right."

Jonathan blinked back tears for a moment as he thought of his longtime friend, now gone. Then he thought again of seeing the Syrian spear through his body and his jaw tightened. "His death will not be in vain."

Judas watched his brother steel himself against what he was feeling. He knew they would all do the same many times in days to come. Many others would die, but the fight would continue. They could not stop to mourn. Their grief would have to accompany them into the fight.

Judas was about to turn to go to the camp for some rest but suddenly remembered. "I nearly forgot. There was another cavalry unit that came through yesterday. What happened with them?"

Jonathan waved his hand as if the question made little sense. "We saw them come through, but there was nothing we could do."

Judas stared at Jonathan in disbelief. "Nothing you could do?"

"It was the Sabbath."

"But . . . but . . . ," Judas stammered. For the first time, he realized they had a problem for which he did not have the answer.

"We can't fight on the Sabbath, can we?"

Judas did not answer Jonathan's question. Instead, he stated the problem, allowing his frustration to surface. "That cavalry unit is probably in the Acra now. They will find out from the commander of the garrison there that the unit that came through last week never got there. That will be news to them all, for only then will the commander know for sure that Apollonius had sent them back when he did. Then, no doubt, someone will ask about this tax shipment that came through two days ago, and the cavalry will have never seen it, even though they would be bound to pass each other on the road somewhere between Jerusalem and Samaria."

"But what could we do, Judas?" defended Jonathan. "It's God's law. We can't even kindle a new fire on the Sabbath. How can we possibly engage in war?"

Judas had no answer. It had never dawned upon him that the law he was fighting for could itself be a hindrance to the fight. After a long and meditative pause, he said in a calmer tone, "I have no answer for this. God forbid that we would break his law, the very thing we are fighting for. I will talk with Father about this. He has not led us wrong yet. He will know what is right."

Jonathan, seeing that Judas felt the same struggle as himself, nodded his head. Judas had not intended that Jonathan feel reprimanded by anything he may have said. He put his hand on Jonathan's shoulder again and said, "You have done well, Brother. You have done well. That tax money you captured will serve to feed our army rather than the Syrians this winter. If we can't kill them all out right, maybe we can starve some to death."

Jonathan put his hand over Judas's as it rested on Jonathan's shoulder. Judas continued. "I will send you some help tomorrow. No doubt, whatever Syrian units come through from now on will be larger, and you will need more men. Now, let Joseph and the old man and me get some food and rest by your fire, then we will go back to the camp in the hills. We have been up all night and are very tired."

Jonathan looked at his older brother. "What have you been doing?"

Judas didn't answer immediately. He wanted as few to know about the kind of activities they had been engaged in that night as possible. Finally he answered, "Let's just say that the Syrians have no more eyes in Lebonah. If you find it necessary to go to Lebonah for food, you should now be able to do so without fear of being discovered by the enemy. Lebonah is clean." Then he added, "Be watchful, all the same."

"We will," said Jonathan, patting his brother's hand which still rested on his shoulder. "Now go get some rest. I have to watch this road."

Several minutes later Judas, Joseph, and Lucas were sitting by the warm blaze of a fire eating venison they pulled off a spit one of the men had made. It was dry from having roasted on the spit most of the night, but the hot meat warmed and relaxed them. As the other men drifted out of the camp for another day of waiting, watching, and possibly dying, they lay down close by the fire and pulled their cloaks tightly around them. Sleep came quickly, but sleep is not always rest, and it certainly wasn't for Judas. A restless spirit haunted his dreams. His mind ran through many dark places. He saw Jada's bulging eyes as he made his final grasp at life. Then he saw a vision of a tearful Eliud learning of his youngest son's death. Along with these visions, his mind found its own covert place to wrestle with the question of how to fight and kill on the Sabbath and still remain faithful to God's law.

Chapter 23

Seron, military commander of Coele-Syria, had no intention of being trifled with by the likes of Lysimachus, commander of the Jerusalem garrison. Though of comparable rank, Seron considered Lysimachus his inferior. Seron answered only to Lysias and the king. Lysimachus was the subordinate of Apollonius, a man that both Seron and Lysias secretly looked upon as a weakling and a fool. Were it not for previous favors Apollonius had won with King Antiochus, Apollonius would probably be a *hoplite* in Seron's army rather than governor of Judea. In time, Seron thought, Apollonius would make a mistake, and then Seron would be elevated to his position. Perhaps that mistake was already in progress.

Seron had ridden for four days after meeting with Lysias in Antioch, only stopping for a day in Samaria for an uncomfortable audience with Apollonius – more uncomfortable for Apollonius than for Seron. Apollonius had taken offense in what he considered to be interference in the affairs of Judea, but he dared not speak too boldly against any order coming from Lysias. It was apparent to Apollonius that Lysias neither trusted his handling of Judea nor believed that Apollonius would send accurate communication of the true state of affairs there. Apollonius well knew that Seron was jealous for his position, so much so that he had doubled the guard at his chambers the night Seron had stayed in Samaria for fear of assassination. Seron clearly had the support of Lysias, so Apollonius measured every word he uttered in his presence. He had hoped his assurances would turn Seron back toward Antioch, but his words were not enough. Only one thing would make Lysias and the king happy with Judea, a steady flow of taxes. Despite his guarantees that tax revenues would be received from Jerusalem within the week, Seron had not been deterred from continuing his journey to Jerusalem.

Now Seron stood outside the chambers of Lysimachus, clearly annoyed at being kept waiting. He had sought a meeting with Lysimachus upon his arrival the evening before, but the garrison commander had sent word that he had more pressing affairs and that the meeting would have to wait until the next day. What, wondered Seron, could be more pressing than meeting with the special envoy of Lysias himself?

Finally, the door opened and Seron was ushered by a guard into a room where he saw a low stone table on which was a plentiful spread of meats and fruits. Despite the effort for comfort, the room was nothing like what he had experienced four days earlier as he had met with Lysias. Despite the braziers burning in each corner, the gray stone walls left the room dank and dark. The mood of the room seemed to find its way into the spirits of the two men who rose to meet him. One, he recognized immediately as Lysimachus. The other, he had never seen before.

Lysimachus stepped forward and gave Seron the traditional embrace, cordial in form only. "Seron, commander of Coele-Syria, welcome to Jerusalem," he said formally. "We are honored at your presence."

Seron returned the traditional greetings. "On behalf of Lysias, supreme governor of all Syria, I greet you. And I bring you the greetings of Apollonius, governor of Judea in Samaria, whom I left just yesterday morning."

Continuing with the formalities, Lysimachus motioned toward the other man in the room. "I present to you Menelaus, high priest of the Jewish people."

Seron looked at Menelaus and gave nothing more than a

shallow nod. He knew this to be an important man in the eyes of many, and who had been empowered by the king as tax collector in Judea, but he personally did not trust a man who would sell out his own people. Such a man might be useful in the necessary political machinations of running an empire, but he was not to be trusted. A man like this would just as readily turn and serve another were he to find it in his own self-interest to do so.

Lysimachus motioned for them all to recline at the table. Seron sat, but did not recline as did the other two. As Lysimachus and Menelaus began to finger the food in front of them, Seron went straight to the point. "Commander, I have been sent directly from Lysias to learn of affairs in Judea. In case you are wondering why I did not simply talk with Apollonius and return to Lysias, let me simply say that Lysias ordered me to see the situation first-hand. That I cannot do in Samaria, so I have come to Jerusalem, to the heart of this nation."

Lysimachus stared at Seron without commenting. Seron was aware that the garrison commander considered his behavior rude and not according to protocol. Polite conversation over a meal was expected before any discussion of official matters. Seron, however, had no interest in politeness or protocol. His sole interest was the exercise of power, so caring little whom he offended, he continued to address Lysimachus. "Before leaving Antioch, the governor informed me of the steps being taken to bring the Jews under control." Seron looked at Menelaus for a brief moment but continued to direct his words toward Lysimachus. "I have learned from Apollonius that this has led to a revolt among some of the people, a revolt in which the rebels have met with some success."

"I assure you, Commander Seron, that their successes, if that is what they may be called, have been greatly exaggerated in the minds of those reporting them." Lysimachus wanted to appear in control, but was clearly intimidated by Seron. He had delayed meeting with Seron upon learning of his arrival for the simple reason that he might prepare himself for whatever questions Seron might ask. It was for that reason that he had brought in Menelaus. Being directly appointed by the king, the presence of Menelaus would perhaps temper what Seron might say, or so Lysimachus hoped.

Lysimachus continued his response. "Essentially, what has happened is that a small group of thugs in a very insignificant town halfway between here and the coast was able to ambush a handful of our troops and kill one of our officials. But it should be noted that all the rebels immediately fled and have not been heard from since. They know they are no real match for us when it comes to an open confrontation."

"What have you been doing to bring these rebels to justice?"

Lysimachus had anticipated the question but was nonetheless irritated by it. "I immediately sent out patrols. We will find them, eventually, and they will be punished. I sent word to Governor Apollonius informing him of the event but have not yet received word from him concerning what further steps I should take. I would assume he will demand something further, some form of reprisal upon someone – anyone – as an example of what will happen to those who resist the will of the king. We must do something to prevent any who may have similar ideas as these rebels in the future, but I await his orders for that."

A baleful glee hid itself behind Seron's dark eyes. Here was another sign of failure by Apollonius. "The cavalry unit you sent to Samaria last week has not returned?"

Lysimachus did not answer immediately. The look in Seron's eyes told him that the unit had been dispatched from Samaria days ago. Realizing the truth, he said slowly, "When did the governor send them?"

"The day after you sent them to him. Have you not wondered why they were almost a week in returning?"

Lysimachus could think of no proper response. "I have had my hands full with matters here in Jerusalem. I knew the governor would send them back in good time."

"He did send them back." Seron spoke as if scolding a child. "It appears that these thugs, as you call them, have been more active than you think."

"You don't know if it's the same group," defended the garrison commander.

"Well, if it isn't the same group, you have a bigger problem than you thought," retorted Seron. "If it isn't the same group, then this rebellion is rising up in other places. And it would appear that they are quite capable of doing what they set out to do. They have made ten of your best cavalry completely disappear. We rode all the way from Samaria yesterday and saw no sign of them anywhere."

Menelaus had quietly listened to the exchange between the two commanders up to this point. He raised his hand slightly for recognition and caught Seron's eye. "What?" barked Seron, already annoyed and having no desire to hear from this Jewish traitor.

Menelaus was timid in his tone. "Do you know whether a shipment of tax revenues arrived in Samaria in the last few days?"

"No. There was no shipment," said Seron bluntly. "Apollonius said he was expecting something this week, so clearly nothing had arrived, or he would have said as much."

Menelaus became hesitant in his speech. "And you did not encounter an infantry unit between here and Samaria that was escorting a chariot that would be carrying the taxes?" Menelaus and Lysimachus exchanged troubled glances.

"No," said Seron again, his pleasure deepening. Their loss would be his gain, even if it cost the king a few tax revenues. The blame would be laid at someone else's feet. Seron looked from face to face. After a long pause he put the situation into words. "So, somewhere between here and Samaria, you have not only lost a unit of cavalry, you have managed to lose the king's tax revenues. I'm beginning to think you have severely underestimated your little band of thugs."

Both Lysimachus and Menelaus realized the gravity of the situation. Antiochus did not care how many Jews died. His concern for his own troops that occupied Judea was not much greater. Most were mercenaries, and he could just as easily hire more. The Greek states seemed to have an endless stream of men who were willing to wield a spear and sword for a profit. What Antiochus could not do without, however, was taxes. Without a steady stream of tax revenue, he would be unable to raise or support an army. And without an army, even a king who called himself Epiphanes would perish at the hands one of his neighbors, whether that neighbor be Persia, Rome, or Egypt. If Menelaus failed to raise taxes, and if Lysimachus failed to protect those taxes, they were no longer of any use to Antiochus. They would be quickly replaced with someone the king felt could serve him better.

Struggling to maintain his composure, Lysimachus searched for a way to reassert his authority. "There have been some setbacks that we had not realized. But that does not mean the situation has gotten out of hand. From what you have just told us, we now have a better idea of where to look for the rebels. To be sure, the way from here to Samaria is a vast area, but we now know to pull our troops back from the area east of here and begin searching town by town to the north. These rebels will be found and killed, even if it means destroying every town along the way. They will not find a place to hide. You can tell Lysias that this present trouble will be dealt with swiftly and another tribute from Judea will be on its way within a fortnight."

Menelaus grimaced. "But we can't raise taxes that quickly, not this time of year. There's no . . . "

Lysimachus shouted at Menelaus, cutting his words short. "We *will* raise more taxes. We will do it even if we have to rob some of your damned Sadducees. They always seem to have plenty."

Menelaus started to protest but thought better of it. He had no illusions about his true position, and that of his fellow Sadducees. Though they openly supported and received special treatment from the Syrian occupiers, they were still mere pawns. Their value depended totally upon their usefulness to the king.

Seron stood up to leave. "I think I have learned what I can here. Those were my orders. I will leave today to return to Antioch."

"Leave today?" said Lysimachus. "You rode four days to meet for a few minutes? Stay and rest." The garrison commander wanted some time to prove himself to Seron, and to perhaps soften the report he would take to Lysias. "Stay and see some of the good things that are happening here in Jerusalem. I fear all you have seen is the negative. Menelaus here will show you how many in Jerusalem have taken to our ways. There are good things happening. Don't let this band of rebels presently roaming the countryside give you the impression that all is bad."

Seron said simply, "I have seen what I came to see." He had no interest in seeing any of the things of which Lysimachus spoke. If he did not see it, he would not be obligated to report it. If nothing good was happening in Judea, then Apollonius was clearly failing in his governance. That was the way Seron wanted it. Apollonius's failure would be his own rise in power. One day, he would succeed where Apollonius failed.

That afternoon, after a brief ride through the city with his small band of cavalrymen, Seron left Jerusalem. They did not take the road to Samaria, however. Seron considered what had already disappeared along that road and wondered how they had traveled the same road without incident. He chose, instead to take the road toward the coast. He would study the way well as he went, for in the near future he envisioned marching an army in from that direction. Let the Jews have their little war, Seron thought. Even let them succeed against Apollonius. They would serve his purposes well, for they would provide him opportunity to show what real power was. He would succeed where Apollonius failed. He would do it all for the glory of the king. He would wipe out this nation of Jews if need be. Then Antiochus would deny him nothing.

Chapter 24

Judas warmed himself by the fire near the front of the cave. It had snowed during the night and most of the morning. The gray sky gave outward expression to the spirit that had hung over the camp ever since he had returned a week earlier bearing news of Ezra's death. Few words were spoken, but those of the camp who came from Modin and had known the young man mourned silently.

Mattathias did what he could to raise their spirits, but strangely enough, everyone's greatest distraction turned out to be the old slave, Lucas. While the thoughts of others turned toward the missed comforts of home, Lucas reveled in his new life living in a cave, for at least he was free. Besides this, Lucas was filled with stories. Each night, everyone gathered around to listen to his tales of Hannibal crossing the Alps and of battles of men fighting from atop elephants.

The day following their return to the camp, Joseph had left again, taking with him three other men. Only Judas, Simon, and Mattathias knew what their specific task was. Besides searching out traitors in each town, Joseph proved proficient in recruiting others to the cause. Within two days of his departure, more than a dozen men found their way to the camp saying they were from Chusi. Judas was surprised, for Chusi was north of Lebonah and much closer to Samaria. Nevertheless, Joseph had managed to find some there who stood for the law of God and were eager to join the fight. Judas immediately began forming a plan to use them as scouts in the north, for he knew that eventually Apollonius would send more than just a few small patrols into Judea. The more warning he could have, the better.

Simon's leg was mending well, though he would always walk with a limp. Though Simon felt useless sitting in the mouth of the cave watching the daily activities, his true value was in the workings of his mind. When Judas came to Mattathias with questions about fighting on the Sabbath, Mattathias came to Simon. It was Simon who could examine every perspective of a matter and come up with a solution. Mattathias would be the spokesman, for he was respected as the elder, but the words he voiced often originated with Simon. Simon did not mind this, for this was as it should be. The fight they were in transcended any thought of personal glory.

Judas's mind suddenly snapped to attention. The snow was having a numbing effect. What had Simon just said? He turned to look at Simon in the cave. Simon was trying to raise himself on one leg. "There's someone coming!"

Judas followed Simon eyes. Men on horseback coming through the trees. How was it no one had heard them? The snow. The beat of hoofs were dampened in the snow. But why hadn't the guard posted at that side of camp cried out? Had they killed him? Judas's hand went to his ever-present sword. Simon spoke again. "It's John and Nethanel!"

Judas immediately recognized the shape of his brother on one of the horses. There, too, was Nethanel. Leave it to Nethanel to arrive on a horse. The two riders rode their horses to within a few feet of the fire before dismounting. Both immediately took a position so close to the fire that everyone feared they would be burned. Icicles hung from their beards and clothing. "Make that fire bigger!" said Nethanel. Judas threw on some extra wood and stood looking at Nethanel and his brother curiously as others began to gather around.

Mattathias came out of the cave. "You have traveled through the snow? What is so urgent that you nearly freeze yourselves to death?" Leah came out of the cave behind Mattathias. She saw her husband and ran and put her arm around him. He squeezed her tightly to himself while still trying to gather warmth from the fire.

Rubbing his hands together over the fire, Nethanel answered Mattathias through teeth he could barely keep from chattering, "What we have to tell you could not wait. You need to know what's happening."

"What is it?" said Judas.

Nethanel took the lead as John interjected comments from time to time. "The first few days we were out, we did not run into many Syrians. It seems, from what we can tell, that they sent patrols mostly toward the coast, from the Way of Bethhoron on down. We managed to garner a lot of support, but there are also quite of few siding with the Syrians, especially as you get closer to Jerusalem."

John interrupted. "The Hasidim are all ready to fight with us."

"How many?" asked Judas.

"Hundreds. Perhaps as many as a thousand. They have been ready ever since the massacre in Jerusalem."

Nethanel took over again. "But everything changed last week. We had arranged to meet at Gibeon three days ago and come back together."

Judas stopped Nethanel. "Where are the men that were with you?"

"They're safe," said Nethanel. "They are camped in a ravine east of Mizpah with about fifty other men, all Hasidim."

"Good," said Judas.

Nethanel continued. "We met in Gibeon, as I said, and began making our way back. We stayed off the road because we saw there was a lot of movement of Syrian troops on the road. It wasn't that way when we went. When we got to Ramah, we found out from the ones we had recruited there that the Syrians were beginning to search every town, and would do so from Jerusalem to Samaria. They come in and beat our people, trying to get information about where the rebels are."

"We've brought more suffering to our people," someone from the group around the fire lamented."

"Wait. There's more," said Nethanel. "And I wouldn't worry about the people suffering. They are more than ready to fight. When a patrol arrived in Mizpah, some of our people ambushed them and killed most of them. Our people in Mizpah were supported by a large group of Hasidim that had gathered there. Then they fled into the hills north of the town."

John interrupted again. "They were pretty much doing the same thing that we had told them we have done."

"What you must know about, though," said Nethanel, "is what happened yesterday." Nethanel drew a deep breath and released it, sending a blast of vapor into the cold air. "We were camped some distance from the town for the Sabbath, waiting for the Sabbath to break to continue our journey back here. From where we were camped, we saw a large contingent of Syrian infantry along with some cavalry march into Mizpah. We followed them from a distance to see what they would do.

"They went straight through the town into the hills. It seemed like they knew exactly where to go. They went directly to where our people were hiding. The people were in caves just like we are here. The commander of the Syrians ordered them to surrender, but they would not surrender. So the commander called them to come out and fight, but they would not fight, because it was the Sabbath."

Nethanel choked on his words momentarily. John was clearly blinking back tears. Nethanel blurted out, "They killed them all in the caves. The Syrians built fires at the mouths of the caves and stood guard until the smoke killed them all. I expected some to run out only to die at the end of a spear, but they all just sat there and died."

"How many?" asked Mattathias, clearly distressed from what he was hearing.

"I don't know," answered Nethanel. "Maybe two hundred. Maybe more."

John echoed his words. "Maybe more. We stayed hidden until the Syrians left, then we entered the caves to see if anyone was still alive. They were all dead, every one of them. Some were women and children."

"During the night we found that a cavalry unit was staying in Mizpah," said Nethanel. "They were all getting drunk at the home of a Sadducee. I think it was that same one you nearly choked the day we met, Judas. Too bad you didn't kill him." Judas tightened his lips as he remembered the man. "Anyway," Nethanel continued, "John and I managed to steal two of the cavalry horses. We've been riding since about the fourth watch. God be praised for the snow. He has covered our tracks."

No one spoke for several long moments. Only the crackling of the fire interrupted the silence. John's eyes fell upon Simon, leaning to one side on a crutch he had fashioned from a limb. John pulled Leah's arm from around him and walked over to his brother. Their eyes met, the message already spoken, but John said the words. "Mahlah was in the cave." He paused and then answered the further unspoken question. "The whole family."

Simon said nothing. Leaning on his crutch, he hobbled past the group and walked toward a place he could be alone. Judas started to go after him, but Mattathias put out his hand and said quietly, "Let him be alone. He doesn't need words right now."

Judas stopped. His father was right. Words were not always needed. In fact, sometimes words tended to cloud the grim reality, a reality that had to be realized in the quiet place of a man's thoughts. Judas watched him leave through the snow-laden trees. Simon had hardly known Mahlah, but they would have spent their lives together. Judas's thoughts were suddenly filled with Rebekah. What if it had been Rebekah in that cave? Images of her corpse covered in soot filled his mind. His emotions raced between depression and rage.

Slowly and deliberately, Judas spoke. "This must be avenged. For every man that died, a Syrian will die. For every woman, five Syrians will die. And for every child . . ." Tears came to Judas's eyes as the image played itself through his mind. ". . . ten Syrian soldiers will die at the ends of our swords."

Judas raised his voice as he changed his tone from that of an impassioned brother and friend to that of a commanding general. "Every man in the camp who is able to fight, gather the food you will need for several days along with whatever weapons you can take." Judas looked at Obed, who was standing by the fire along with the others. "Obed, we will take whatever extra weapons you have made. These fifty Hasidim that John and Nethanel spoke of who are camped with our men will need them. Tomorrow, we will leave for Mizpah. We will no longer hide in the hills like frightened animals. The Syrians chose Mizpah as the place to bring death to our people. We will make Mizpah a fortress that they cannot defeat. Now go make preparations."

Everyone began walking away from the fire, talking noisily to each other as they went. Some were excited, others were uncertain. Either way, they were preparing to enter the fight.

Judas turned to his father and said quietly. "After Mizpah, I'm going to Jerusalem."

Mattathias raised his eyebrows. "You can't take Jerusalem, not yet. You do not have anything near what will be needed."

"I'm not going to Jerusalem to fight. I'm going to get Rebekah."

Mattathias started to speak, but Judas stopped him before he could utter a word. "Don't you see, she's not safe there, neither she nor her parents. It is only right that I get them out of the city. I will do it discreetly. I will do it alone. No Syrian will ever know I was there."

Somehow, Mattathias feared the thought of his son trying to slip in and out of Jerusalem more than he did his engaging in open battle. In battle, there were others to watch his back. He knew from watching Judas plan every fight during the past weeks that Judas always created an advantage for himself. How would he create such an advantage alone in a city guarded by a whole garrison, a garrison now on the alert? Nevertheless, Mattathias knew his son's heart, and he knew there was no talking him out of it. "Very well," he said, resigning himself to Judas's determined will. "God will be with you as he has been with us thus far. Bring our friends to safety. We do not need to lose any more." Mattathias looked through the trees to where he could see Simon sitting in the snow leaning against a boulder. Simon was staring upward into the gray sky. Mattathias knew he was asking God the hard questions, questions for which logical answers were seldom provided. He whispered again under his breath, "We do not need to lose any more."

Late that afternoon, Mattathias called the entire camp together. A couple of the men added fuel to the fire around which they all stood so everyone could feel its warmth. Weary in his eyes but forceful in his words, the old man looked from face to face as he spoke.

"Tomorrow morning, most of you will be going out to meet the enemy of God's people, at least the present enemy. God has promised to be with us so long as we are faithful to him and live according to the law he gave us. We just learned this morning that some of our brothers, many of them along with their wives and children, died at the hands of our enemies because they determined to live according to one of God's laws, the law of the Sabbath. I have called you together because I want to speak of this, and because I want you to take this message to our brothers everywhere who are engaged in this fight with us.

"It is not an infraction of the Sabbath law when we fight to defend our lives. If we refuse to fight on the Sabbath, the Syrians will choose that day to attack, and they will destroy us. We must be prepared to meet the enemy of God's people at all times.

"The scriptures tell us that God treats the fight of his people against their enemies different from the affairs of everyday life. There is another law that says, 'Thou shalt not kill,' yet even Moses through whom God gave the law prayed for Joshua as he fought the Amalekites. When Joshua led the people into the land that is now ours, God who had given that same law ordered the people to kill and destroy the nations that were the enemies of God.

"You know also that when David was fleeing from Saul, the king, that David entered the house of God, and he and his companions ate the bread there that was only lawful for the priests to eat. Yet God blessed David and made him king in the place of Saul, even though he had violated the law. There was a greater good to come.

"I will tell you also, that when I served as a priest in the temple in Jerusalem, I served on the Sabbath. It has been this way through the generations, from Moses to the present. The priests carry on their work even on the Sabbath.

"There are laws that are greater than the law of the Sabbath. One is the law of justice. This is the very heart of God. Those who kill the servants of the Lord must not go unpunished. Another is the law of God's holiness. Our God stands unique and above all. There is to be no other God before him. Yet the enemy in our land has erected a graven image in the temple we built to worship the God of Abraham, Isaac, and Jacob. Every time this enemy kills our people, he is saying that his god is greater than ours. If we allow this to happen, then we are also allowing his god to be before our God, and we are breaking the first and greatest of all the commandments.

"Let us never again allow our God to be maligned and belittled because we refused to fight on the Sabbath. Our God is a great God and is to be given glory in the face of our enemies at all times at all places. The Sabbath is no exception.

"Let this message be proclaimed in every town and village in Judea. Israel will never again just lay down and die."

When Mattathias had finished, he turned and walked back into the cave where he was staying. This was a signal to everyone that there was to be no discussion. This was not merely an opinion being expressed. Far from it, most of the ones standing there felt they had heard an oracle from a prophet. They would communicate it as such, wherever they went.

Chapter 25

The next morning Judas led almost all the men in the camp down the valley toward Lebonah. Only Simon remained, along with the two elderly men from Modin, Eliud and Azariah, and Lucas, the former slave. Lucas only agreed to remain behind after Judas promised to one day personally escort him to the temple in Jerusalem. Simon longed to go with the others, but Judas persuaded him to remain and train any new recruits Joseph might send their way.

Though Judas urged Mattathias to remain in the camp, Mattathias insisted that he go once again to the towns close by to – in his words – "call the people back to God." This time, John would be at his side. While Judas was taking Mizpah from the Syrians, Mattathias would be taking other smaller towns from apostate Jews. Rather than doing it with a sword, however, he would do it with the power of his preaching. In every place, he ordered the people to expel the idol worshippers and to return to the God of their fathers. When he saw he had an ample following in a town, he demolished the idols and altars that he often found there, altars much like the one Apelles had set up in Modin. He ordered the people to return to circumcising their children. Whenever he found someone who resisted his orders, he ordered them to leave Judea. If they refused to leave, Mattathias aroused the faithful to stone them to death. There were few of these, however, for

Joseph had already been meticulously carrying out his work in the towns of the area.

As Judas neared Lebonah, he took an easterly direction that brought him to Jonathan's camp. He exchanged some of the men who were with him with some of the more experienced men who had been with Jonathan. The four slaves who had once carried Apelles's litter remained with Jonathan. Judas would depend on Jonathan to train them and the others. It would be up to Jonathan's small band to protect or warn them of anyone coming behind them from Samaria.

Taking the advice Lucas had given him the night before, Judas took six of the ten horses Jonathan had. Though not yet convinced of their usefulness in battle, he saw how they might prove useful for reconnaissance. Nethanel and another young man who was experienced with horses rode far ahead of the main group to scout out what might lie ahead. The other four horses were used to carry the baggage.

A southwesterly breeze brought in warmer air and melted the snow from the previous day. Though thankful for the warmer air, they could not say the same for the now muddy road. Spring was but weeks away, thoughts of which prompted visions of Passover in Judas's mind. He wondered when they would again celebrate Passover in Jerusalem. Thinking of Jerusalem filled his mind with Rebekah. The only thing that induced fear in Judas was the thought of something happening to her. The anticipation of battle only made his heart race, anxious to engage the enemy. He never gave thought to losing. But when he thought of Rebekah, a silent dread lurked in the recesses of his mind, a fear that he might actually lose her. Judas whispered a prayer as he slogged along the muddy road with the others. "God, watch over her until I get there."

Toward mid-afternoon, the two scouts on horseback appeared along the road ahead of them. When they pulled up in front of the group, Nethanel dismounted.

"What have you seen?" asked Judas, expecting him to be reporting a considerable enemy movement.

"Very little actually," came the reply. "We went almost all

the way to Mizpah, to the ravine where our men are camped. It was very enlightening. They have been keeping abreast of what is happening in Mizpah. Most of the Syrians have left."

"Left?" queried Judas. "Where did they go? Other towns?"

"It appears that most of them have returned to Jerusalem. There is only a group of twenty infantry still in the town. They have remained at the request of the Sadducees who are afraid there may be some sort of retaliation against them. It's the Sadducees in Mizpah that led the Syrians to the people hidden in the caves. So naturally, they are afraid."

Judas's forehead creased with anger. "They are right. There *will* be retaliation. But I thought the Syrians would continue their march, from town to town. I don't understand why most have returned to Jerusalem."

"It seems," said Nethanel, "that they think they've killed us, the ones from Modin. I think it is because of the Hasidim that had come into the town from elsewhere. The Sadducees who were helping the Syrians did not know who they were, so it has been assumed that it was us. So they think they've won."

Judas pondered what Nethanel had said. Eleazar had been hearing everything. He came up beside Judas with a smile on his face. "Brother, that won't even be a fight. Twenty infantry? I was ready for a lot more."

Judas looked at the faces of the men who were with him. Some appeared relieved. Others seemed disappointed. He looked away from their various expressions to the road ahead. "You're right. It's not much of a fight. It's not enough." He paused before speaking again. "It's not enough to send the Syrians the message they need to hear. They need to know that they can't cross us without paying dearly."

Judas said nothing more for a long while, prompting Nethanel to inquire, "What do you intend to do, Judas Maccabee?"

Judas met eyes with Nethanel and allowed a glimmer of a smile to show through. "I have an idea, but I need to think on it." He looked down at his feet. "Is there a good place ahead for us to camp for the night? This mud has slowed us up. We won't try to go the whole way today."

"Ophni is less than an hour up the road. There are a number of Hasidim there. They will take care of you. I will go tell them you are coming."

"Tell them to just find a safe place for us to camp for the night, a place we won't be seen."

Nethanel mounted his horse again as he spoke. "Someone will meet you on the road."

"Good," said Judas. "Oh, one more thing. The fifty Hasidim that were hidden with our men close to Mizpah, are they still there?"

"Oh, they're there," grinned Nethanel, "But now it's more like a hundred and fifty. Ever since what happened day before yesterday, they have been finding their way to us."

"Do they have weapons?"

"Not many. Mostly bows, but some swords."

Judas's mind was calculating all the possibilities with what he had to work with. "Tell them we will be there tomorrow. We have some extra weapons, and we know where the weapons of twenty Syrian infantry can be found. We will have those soon."

Nethanel smiled down from his horse. "The Syrian army is our best supplier. I don't know what we would do without them."

Judas grinned back as Nethanel kicked his heels into the side of the horse and bolted away. The other young man with him kicked his horse and raced to keep up. Clods of mud flew from the horses' hoofs as they galloped away.

Less than an hour later two men, a father and son, met Judas's band of ragtag soldiers on the road. They led them into the woods just out of sight of the village of Ophni. Some other men from the village had already built a fire and begun to cook some cuttings from a side of beef for them. The melting snow had produced a flowing stream near the camp. All the men were glad to wash the mud from their feet. Though most wore the ankle-high leather shoes that were typical for winter, the mud had seeped in and left their feet wet and dirty. They were all glad for the meal which was much better than they had expected. When night had completely fallen, other men came from the village. There were over twenty in all, most of them Hasidim. They all wanted to join in the fight. Judas welcomed them all, but questioned them until he felt sure that they could all be trusted. If the Syrians gained knowledge of the plan he was forming, it could prove disastrous.

About noon the next day, they arrived in the camp near Mizpah. Judas wasted no time organizing the men according to their fighting skills. He outlined the plan for them, a plan that would cover the next four days, all except the last part. Not everyone needed to know that part. Some did wonder, though, when he asked for four men who spoke excellent Greek. Judas gave no explanation.

Two days later, toward the middle of the afternoon, men began to arrive in ones and twos in Mizpah, arriving from different directions. One man led a sheep tied to the end of a cord. Another pulled a cart loaded with a large sack of grain. But mostly, they just tried not to be seen. By the time the sun began to cast long shadows, thirty men had hidden themselves in groups of five in six different homes along one street. They were not welcome in two of the homes, but they cared little about it. The Sadducee owners were quickly tied and gagged or knocked unconscious. Three of the other homes were vacant, their former owners' bodies now lying cold in a cave north of town. The remaining home belonged to an elderly man who was glad for his visitors and would have helped them had he the strength to fight. In each home, swords, bows, and sheaths of arrows were removed from underneath clothing.

Judas allowed Eleazar to start the fight since he had battle experience and was well practiced with a bow. Eleazar peered around a corner up a street perpendicular to the one they were on. The day before, Judas, Nethanel, and he had come into the town to see where the Syrians were staying, whom they had learned were actually mercenaries. They had found the fact that it was a unit of mercenaries to be in their favor. Mercenaries were never as conscientious in their duties. They cared nothing for a cause, only for what they could profit. The mercenaries were boarding in two adjoining houses, houses that were vacant because their owners now lay dead in the forest. Next to these houses was the home of the Sadducee that Nethanel said had boarded some Syrian cavalry a few days before.

Eleazar watched the doors of the houses. The few days of inactivity had lulled the mercenaries into a sense of security. No one regularly patrolled the streets. The weather was just cool enough to keep them from wanting to remain outside. One would exit only occasionally so as to give the appearance of following orders, orders to protect the interests of the Syrian sympathizers in the town. Eleazar could hear talking coming from within the houses. Occasionally, there was a burst of laughter. He heard such a burst as one of the doors opened. A soldier stepped out and looked up and down the street. He had no helmet or breastplate. He was wearing a sword but did not seem to have any idea that he would need it. The soldier began walking down the street, leaving the door to the house hanging open. A shout came from inside and the soldier laughed as he shouted something back. From what Eleazar could tell, the man was going to relieve himself, and related vulgarities were being shouted back and forth between him and the man inside who was unhappy about the door being left open. Now was the time.

Eleazar stepped out, his bow fully drawn. The soldier had only seen Eleazar from the corner of his eye when the arrow planted itself solidly into his chest. The man gurgled a scream as he fell. Eleazar already had another arrow strung. He released it just as another man appeared in the doorway. This arrow only found its mark in the man's upper thigh, but it had the desired effect. In an instant, amidst chaotic shouts, soldiers poured from both houses, some carrying swords, some with spears. Eleazar released one more arrow before breaking into a sprint up the street. He had no idea whether the arrow hit its target, but it didn't matter.

The full unit of soldiers ran from the two houses after Eleazar. When they rounded the corner, all they could see was a lone archer fleeing for his life. They would just maim this one and then entertain themselves with the way they would slowly kill him. They continued their pursuit unhindered. They had to give it to this crazy Jew, he had guts. He suddenly turned with another drawn arrow and let it go at his nearest pursuer. The man it was aimed at dodged and grinned as he heard the arrow whiz past his ear. He pulled back his arm to thrust his *pilum*, aiming for the Jew's thighs. He relished the idea of torturing this man to death. Before he could release the pilum, an arrow from nowhere sunk itself into his side under his raised thrusting arm. He turned, unable to speak, to see doors opened up and down the street behind him before collapsing to the ground. Men poured out of each door, releasing arrows from already drawn bows.

The mercenaries were now spread from one end of the street to the other, the slower ones just rounding the corner into the unexpected fracas. None of them carried shields or wore any body armor. Several of the mercenaries fell from the arrows before others could reach their attackers with drawn swords and spears. As one mercenary lunged toward an archer who was stringing another arrow, Judas leapt in front of the archer, his own sword slicing the air and opening the soldier's throat. Two other soldiers hesitated as they saw the speed with which Judas had dropped their comrade. Their hesitation was fatal, for the arrows had not ceased to fly. Within moments, the last four enemy soldiers fled from the town. They could easily have been chased down and killed, but Judas stopped the pursuit. It was his hope that they would reach Jerusalem before midnight.

Judas looked up and down the street as Eleazar and the others removed the weapons from the bodies. He could see eyes peering through doors held slightly ajar.

"Judas, two of these are still alive," shouted one of the men.

"Leave them," Judas shouted back. "Let their Sadducee friends take care of them."

A few minutes later, Judas and the band of thirty moved out the north side of town. They made no effort at hiding the direction of their departure. The sky was growing dark. A little over an hour later they were deep in the hills, about a mile away from the caves that still held the bodies of their countrymen. They made a blazing fire in front of a cave they had found earlier in the day and sat talking loudly about their small victory.

They were well into the second watch of the night when Judas looked up and saw eyes peering at them from out of the darkness.

Chapter 26

Nethanel stepped out of the darkness into the light of the fire. He looked at Judas. "You were right, my friend," he said quietly. "You were followed. Now they know where you are."

Judas smiled. He thanked God for helping him to see into the minds of their enemies. He also thanked God for Nethanel's skills at stealth. Many a deer had no doubt met its end because of Nethanel's willingness to endure silence and discomfort. Nethanel had lain buried under the leaves at the edge of the forest as Judas and the others had passed by. They never knew he was there. Neither did the Sadducee that nearly stepped on him as he followed them through the darkness from a distance. Nethanel had followed the Sadducee until he saw the fire, then he hid himself behind a tree and watched. A few moments later, the Sadducee had passed him again on the way back to Mizpah. Judas's plan was working.

While the other men slept in the cave that night, Judas and Nethanel found a semi-dry spot out in the darkness away from the camp to bed down. They did not expect anyone to come during the night, but they chose the side of caution. It was unlikely that anyone would get to the cave without passing them first.

Before the sun rose, Nethanel left. Judas found a location within sight of the cave and hid himself under leaves and small branches. He lay the entire morning on the damp ground, watching and listening. His thoughts ran in many directions. His mind bounced from plans for battle to thoughts of when he would see Rebekah again.

It was early afternoon. He must have dozed off, but he was suddenly alert to a movement through the trees. He listened. Moving as little as possible, he turned his head slightly toward the sound. A few seconds later, two men stood only a few feet from where he lay. They both hid behind trees and looked toward the cave where men sat gathered around a fire. Judas listened to what the two were saying. One was a Jew, but he was speaking in Greek. The other was a Syrian soldier. When the Jew turned his head so that Judas could see his face, Judas's blood ran hot. It was the Sadducee, the one whose betrayal of his people Judas had witnessed on their return from Jerusalem. Had Judas known the extent of his betrayal, he would have killed him then. Judas had learned his name the day before when Eleazar, Nethanel and he had scouted the town. The man's name was Zabad, a name that would prove hateful to him for the rest of his life. He hoped to meet no one else by that name, for he knew that it would affect his impression of the person who bore it.

Judas did not move. He hardly breathed. He just listened. After a few minutes, the two men turned and slipped away. He waited until he was sure they were gone, then he rose up out of the leaves and returned to the cave with the others to await the arrival of Sabbath.

About an hour after night had fully fallen and Sabbath had come, Nethanel showed up at the cave again. He sat down with the others by the fire. The rustling of leaves could be heard in the forest around them. Nethanel's face showed the weariness they were all beginning to feel. "We need the weapons you took off the Syrians yesterday, as many as you can spare," he said.

Judas motioned to the others around the fire who retrieved the weapons from the cave. He peered out into the forest and could faintly see faces reflected in the light of the fire. "How many do we have?" he asked.

"Almost everyone, almost two hundred. There were a few who still refused to fight on the Sabbath, but the words of your father that you gave them a couple of nights ago did it for most of them."

The men came from the cave carrying swords and spears. Judas directed them. "Give these weapons to whoever doesn't have one and lead them to the places I showed you this afternoon. Make sure the captain of each group of twenty understands the plan. As soon as the first light is seen in the sky, everyone is to be completely hidden from sight, the way Nethanel showed them night before last."

The men left the light of the fire and faded into the darkness. For a while, there was considerable noise as scores of men felt their way through the forest, but in a few minutes, that too faded.

"So what are we up against?" asked Judas.

"Almost a hundred," Nethanel answered. "I rode toward Jerusalem until I could see them coming in the distance. Then I hid until they passed. You figured right. They must have left early this morning. They didn't want to miss the opportunity to attack on the Sabbath. Will they be surprised this time!"

"And they only think there are about thirty of us." Judas considered just how surprised the Syrians would be. "Where are they camped?"

"They're just on the outskirts of town. The captain of the unit set up a large command tent that should serve your purposes well later."

"So now we wait," said Judas. "Now get some rest. You look tired."

"I'm okay," said Nethanel.

"But will you be tomorrow? Go into the cave and sleep. When the others come back, we will set up a watch through the night so that we all get to sleep at least a little."

Nethanel did not have to be told a third time. He lifted himself from the ground and disappeared into the cave.

Sleep was fitful for all that night. Most of the men lying on the ground in the forest had never seen battle. They well knew that some of them would die in the hours to come. But no one would run, for if they ran, where would they run to? A coward was as bad as a Sadducee, and it would be better to be dead than to be ranked with the Sadducees.

It was mid-morning when the Syrians arrived. Judas had stationed archers at intervals far from the camp. When the archer farthest from camp saw the Syrians in the distance, he released an arrow at a pre-selected tree. When the arrow hit, another archer a few feet away let go another arrow. And so it continued until the message reached the camp. Arrows could fly much faster and quieter than a runner could run. Within a few seconds, the camp was warned of the approaching enemy. The archers hid themselves until the enemy passed.

Judas and some of the others stood by the fire watching the forest in front of and around them. Others hid in the depths of the cave to keep their eyes accustomed to the darkness. From all appearances, the forest was empty and peaceful. Judas heard the movement through the trees before he saw the approaching troops. When they appeared, he was momentarily overwhelmed at how much more a hundred troops appeared to be than the tens and twenties he had fought previously. He had fought up to forty in Modin, but that seemed long ago.

When the Syrians had come well within sight of the cave, the captain called the ranks to a halt. He glanced around at the forest about him, but mostly he looked at the dozen or so unarmed men standing at the entrance to the cave. "These foolish Jews," he sneered as he spoke to the soldier beside him. "Why do they bother to fight if they only lay down and die every time they have one of these Sabbath days? We could wipe out the whole race by fighting one day in seven."

The captain moved slowly forward. His troops, marching in a square formation ten wide and ten deep, matched his progress as they broke file from time to time to go around trees in their path. When he knew he could be heard, the captain shouted to the men watching his approach from the mouth of the cave. "You Jews killed some of my men two days ago. For this you must die. You can surrender, and you will meet your death swiftly. If you resist, we will choose the method by which you will die, and I assure you that we can be quite inventive with that." Some snickers came from the soldiers behind him.

Judas shouted out a response. "We will not surrender!"

According to arrangement, Eleazar spoke up, making sure he was loud enough for the Syrians to hear. "But Brother, it's the Sabbath. What can we do?"

The captain turned and looked at his troops, his lip curled up at the side in a sinister grin. From the looks on the faces of the soldiers, their sentiments were mutual. The captain ordered the troops to advance. When they did, Judas and the others ran into the cave. "Okay men," said the captain. "You know what to do." He then ordered the first three ranks to the cave.

The first rank laid down their shields and began using their spears to push the logs of the already burning fire to the cave entrance. The twenty soldiers of the other two ranks stood behind them with spears lowered. Hardly had a burning log been rolled into the cave entrance when the soldier pushing it dropped his spear and grabbed his throat. The others did not realize what was happening at first until he spun around and they saw the protruding arrow. In another second, screams were heard from others as arrows pierced their bodies.

The captain shouted to the ranks who were standing momentarily frozen, spears still lowered in front of them. "Get them!" They immediately charged into the cave amidst the flying arrows, leaping over the bodies of their fallen comrades. Having just stepped out of the light, they could see nothing in the black depths of the cave. Nevertheless, they charged forward, for to retreat would be equally suicidal. Their captain, they knew by reputation, was very unforgiving to any who fled in the midst of battle.

Judas and those with him had run past those already in the cave, allowing them the first strike at their enemy since their eyes were already adjusted to the darkness. They had the equal advantage of looking outward into the light while the Syrians had only darkness to look into. The Syrians charged, their shields raised, but the men in the cave could easily see every vulnerable spot on the Syrians while the Syrians could not see them at all. The Syrians thrashed around in the darkness, hoping their spears would find a mark. Judas's men had positioned themselves at the farthest recesses of the cave. Some continued to shoot arrows, but others picked up the few spears they had kept in the cave. Using the full advantage of the weight of a pilum, they threw with all their might. The pila easily found their marks, piercing both shields and soldiers. Yet the Syrians charged unrelentingly. Spears gone and arrows of little use as the Syrians came upon them, the men in the back of the cave drew out their swords and charged into the Syrians. Having yet the advantage in the darkness, they slashed at any vulnerable body part they could find.

Suddenly, all fell quiet. Judas surveyed the cave as best he could, his eyes having adjusted better to the darkness. Syrian bodies littered the ground, easily recognized by the glint of their helmets. But among the Syrian dead lay two bodies without helmets. Judas and the others immediately understood that two of their own were among the dead. Judas glanced around and recognized Eleazar's perspiring face in the dim light from the mouth of the cave. He breathed a short sigh of relief but quickly returned to the matter at hand. "Quick, gather the shields and spears. This isn't over."

Outside the cave, the captain stood still with the remaining seventy troops. He was bewildered by the sudden silence. He watched the entrance to the cave. In another moment his eye caught some movement. He watched intently as one of his own soldiers slid painfully along the cave wall out into the open air and collapsed, a pilum hanging from his abdomen. The captain turned crimson with rage. He ordered four ranks to stand with spears ready on either side of the cave entrance as the other three found all the dry wood they could to throw into a pile in the entrance. He warned them as they worked to stay out of direct line of fire from the entrance of the cave. The soldiers piling the wood laid down their shields and spears as they gathered wood. Some considered how their comrades had worked unshielded and died for it. Now, however, they knew exactly what the enemy was capable of. The enemy was in the cave and could only attack what crossed the entrance. They would start the fire from the side, out of the line of fire, and increase it until the smoke overcame all those inside. If they ran out, they would be attacked from both sides. If they stayed, they would die from the smoke, as the ones had a week earlier.

The Syrian captain was privately commending himself for his new strategy when the very ground seemed to suddenly come to life around him. The captain was the first to die. Those who had been piling the wood fell next due to their lack of protection. Arrows and spears flew from the hands and bows of men covered in dirt and leaves.

A few of the Syrians who had been guarding the cave entrance acted by reflex but made the fatal mistake of leaping just inside the entrance of the cave for protection from the onslaught outside. They died instantly from the spears and arrows that came out of the darkness of the cave.

When only about twenty Syrians remained, they fled through the woods back toward Mizpah. They had no sooner reached a point where they began to feel some measure of safety than the woods around them again came to life. They were attacked on every side, first by arrows, then by spears. Some fell upon them with swords and yet others who had nothing more than wooden clubs.

No Syrian survived. The ferocity of the fighting was such that if one were struck down by one arrow or one spear, another soon followed. No chance was taken that a man might rise to strike another blow.

Four Jews died in the fight, one man from Modin and three Hasidim. Judas ordered them buried in the cave. The bodies of the Syrians, after being stripped of their weapons, were left for the wolves and the vultures. Judas also ordered that the caves where their countrymen had died a week earlier be closed up. They would be a constant memorial to Israel's faithful. Judas's last order before leaving the men under the command of Eleazar for the next several hours was that no one would approach Mizpah until the sun had gone down. There was a task yet to be done.

Late that afternoon, four Syrian soldiers approached the door of a house in Mizpah. One of the soldiers knocked on the door. When the door opened a crack and a pair of eyes peered out, he said, "Are you Zabad?"

The door opened wider. "Yes. I'm Zabad."

"Are you the one who showed our captain where the rebels were camped?"

The Sadducee looked at the four soldiers proudly shouldering their shields and spears, their helmets reflecting the afternoon sun. They represented the power of the new world. In the Sadducee's mind, the simple fact of their shaven faces spoke of progress. The few words the soldier had said revealed a certain eloquence. His Greek sounded nothing like what most of his fellow Jews spoke. They insisted on hanging on to their archaic language, only learning this superior language that joined them to the world when they had to. "I'm the one," he replied to the soldier.

"Our captain would like you to join him if you could," said the soldier. "He was so pleased with your help in the victory he won this morning that he wanted to reward you."

"The victory?"

"Yes. We managed to wipe out the rebels with not a single casualty on our side."

A smile crept across the Sadducee's face. "And he wants to reward me?"

"That's right. Commander Lysimachus of the Jerusalem garrison has provided the captain with ample means to reward those who provide services to the king."

Zabad's eyes grew wide with delight. "Let me just get my cloak." He ducked back into the house but was back in a few short moments wearing an elegantly embroidered dark blue cloak.

"One more thing," said the soldier as Zabad locked the door to his house. "The captain thought you might want to bring some of your friends along. It's always nice to be rewarded in the presence of your peers. Besides, there will be plenty of food and wine that they can enjoy as well. This is a victory celebration. I'm sure they will want to be a part of it."

The Sadducee's delight visibly deepened at the thought of recognition before others. This would more than make up for the humiliating experience he had endured before them when that horrid man had made him pee on himself after Apelles had left town. "Yes. I'm sure they would like to come. Let me show you where they live and we can all go together."

Over the next several minutes, the four soldiers and Zabad went to six different houses. When they had visited the last house, the four soldiers marched with seven strutting Sadducees through the streets of Mizpah to the camp on the outskirts of town. As they walked, the soldiers talked with the seven men. The Sadducees wanted to know what the battle was like. The soldiers, one and then another, told about the total victory they had accomplished and how all the rebels were now dead. One of the Sadducees exclaimed how glad he was after those vile rebels had bound and gagged him in his own home two days earlier. They all agreed that the world was better off without such as these.

The seven Sadducees, blinded by their own pride, did not seem to notice that the Syrian camp was empty of any human presence as they approached the captain's tent. Two of the soldiers stepped in front of the group to open the flaps to give them entrance. They stepped inside with large smiles, but those smiles quickly vanished. They tried to turn to retreat through the door of the tent, but the four soldiers were now behind them and the tent flaps had been drawn.

Judas, with three men holding drawn swords on either side of him, said to the soldiers, "Are they all guilty?"

"Yes," said the one who had first spoken at Zabad's door, now reverting into Aramaic. "They had much to say on the way here, and they have all condemned themselves with their own words."

Judas looked inquiringly at the other three soldiers, and

they all nodded agreement. He then turned his gaze to each of the Sadducees, one by one. He spoke slowly and deliberately. "You came expecting a celebration for the slaughter of our people. This is not a celebration. This is an execution. You have betrayed Israel for the last time."

The blood drained from Zabad's face. He was unable to speak, but one of the other traitors spoke up defensively. "If you kill us, then how are you different from the Syrians that you think are so bad?"

"The difference," said Judas, looking the man in the eye, "is that we will not enjoy it. As Elijah killed the prophets of Baal, we purge Israel of its evil because we must."

Despite other protests, Judas said nothing more. Moments later, the seven Sadducees lay dead on the ground. Judas and the others dug a deep hole inside the tent and buried the bodies. They would leave the tent standing where it was until there was a need for it elsewhere. Others would wonder what happened to the seven Sadducees of Mizpah, but no one would know for certain what had become of them. No one had seen them die. The last anyone saw of them, they were being led away in the company of four Syrian soldiers.

That night Judas slept in the same tent, on the cot of a Syrian captain over the bodies of traitors to Israel. He would give orders to his men the next morning concerning the future of Mizpah. Mizpah would become the new base from which he would build his army, the army that would liberate his people. The men would begin work immediately, preparing fortifications and training more troops. As for himself, tomorrow he would go to Jerusalem.

Chapter 27

The next day, Nethanel, Eleazar, and others tried to dissuade Judas from going to Jerusalem. When they found they could not discourage him from what he had set his mind to do, they offered to go with him, but Judas insisted on going alone. In the end, he agreed that someone could accompany him partway.

Just as when facing an approaching battle, Judas had used the hours of wakefulness during the night to plan his strategy for the day. As soon as the day broke, he set about preparing his departure. It did not take much asking around to discover that one of the Sadducees had been an olive oil merchant. Finding the Sadducee's storehouse, Judas used the help of two other men to load large earthen jars of the oil onto a donkey cart. Travel with a donkey cart would take most of the day, but fewer questions would be asked if he arrived at the gates of Jerusalem posing as an olive oil merchant.

Judas gave up his sword for the journey, exchanging it for a small dagger that he could keep hidden on his body. He did not plan on a fight, but he did not want to be totally unprepared. His intention was to go to Jerusalem, find Rebekah's family, and leave.

Nethanel and Eleazar walked with Judas most of the day. This seemed prudent as robbers were always a possibility along the roads. Though recent events had produced frequent military patrols along this particular road, those patrols could not be depended on to protect a Jew.

The morning carried a warm breeze as the three men walked alongside the slow moving donkey pulling its charge. As they made slow progress toward Jerusalem, they discussed the days to come. Eleazar would return to the camp in the Gophna Hills to report on the events in Mizpah. Though Mizpah would become a base of operations, the camp in the hills would continue to hold a strategic position in the fight. Stopping all Syrian movement between Mizpah and Lebonah would not only hinder communications between Jerusalem and Samaria, it would enable them to draw from all the towns in between for men and supplies.

Nethanel would direct the building of fortifications in Mizpah and training new recruits until Judas returned in a couple of days. Once news of their previous day's victory reached other towns, they expected many more to join them, especially from the Hasidim. Once Mizpah was strong enough, they could cut off all Syrian movement not only from Jerusalem to Samaria, but along the Way of Beth-horon as well.

When they came within sight of the walls of Jerusalem, now orange in the glow of the soon setting sun, both Nethanel and Eleazar tried once again to persuade Judas to allow them to accompany him all the way, but Judas refused. This time he took the tact of a commander, reminding them that they both had jobs to do. Embracing them both before they left him, Judas then waited until he saw them disappear over a low rise in the road on their way back to Mizpah before again prodding the donkey forward.

The sky was growing dim when Judas reached the city gates. He saw four Syrian guards at the gate. He followed the course around the city to enter by the next gate to the south but found it to be guarded as well. Less than two months earlier, guards had been stationed only at the citadel, though there were always roaming patrols. Now, it seemed, there was fear that the insurrection spreading through the countryside might enter the city as well. Everyone entering the city was checked and interrogated.

Judas resigned himself to the interrogation. He began leading the donkey through the arches.

"You there! Stop!" came the sharply spoken words.

Judas looked at the guard without allowing their eyes to meet. Though he was sure it would be no great challenge to kill at least two of the guards with their own weapons before they knew what had happened, his purpose would be better served if he appeared somewhat fearful and submitted to their demands. Judas stopped the donkey's progress.

"What's in the jars?" the guard demanded.

"Olive oil," said Judas. "I've brought it to sell in the market tomorrow."

Another guard walked up and looked in the cart. "You wouldn't have swords hidden in this oil, would you?" he said snidely. He removed the leather cover that was tied over the opening of one of the jars and peered inside but could see nothing in the dim light. The first guard gave a glance in the jar before nodding to the guard who had removed the covering. The latter guard, following the unvoiced instructions, turned the jar on its side in the cart, allowing most of the oil to pour out on the ground.

Judas was not surprised at the guard's actions, but played the part expected of him in the small drama. He jumped forward, reaching for the jar, protesting loudly. The first guard thrust a spear in his face and forced him back. Judas showed fear and surprise in his eyes, though inside he was fighting the urge to kill them both. He backed against the side of the stone archway and froze.

"That's better," said the guard, still menacing him with the spear.

The guard who had tipped over the jar said nonchalantly, "There's nothing here. Let him go."

The first guard lowered his spear and said to Judas crossly with a quick snap of his head toward the city, "Go on!"

Judas stepped gingerly from the wall and righted the jar in the back of the cart, oil now coating the cart's bottom and steadily dripping onto the ground underneath. He protested mildly so as to give the impression that the loss of the oil was of great concern to him. "How am I going to replace the oil you've poured out?"

"Just call it taxes!" barked the guard. "Now get on to where you are staying the night. No one is to be on the streets."

Judas frowned and pulled the donkey forward, through the gate and away from the guards. He felt their eyes on his back as he made haste along the street. The donkey resisted his tugs, but Judas pulled him onward until they had rounded a corner out of sight of the guards. Only then did he slow his pace.

Night had quickly fallen, and Judas was finding his way through the streets with difficulty. The moon would not rise for another hour, and the usual street torches he remembered were not lit. It was as though the city had died.

A short distance further Judas came upon a sheepfold. There were no sheep in it, which was unusual with Passover only a few weeks away, but there were two donkeys someone had left there. Judas unharnessed his own donkey and put it in the fold with the others. He left the cart by the entrance. Judas figured the oil would probably be stolen by noon the next day, but he didn't care. He only hoped whoever took it would leave the cart. If Hananiah was still as feeble as the last time he had seen him, the cart would be needed to take him to Mizpah.

Judas wondered at the quietness of the streets as he made his way deeper into the city. Usually there would be a continuous din of mealtime conversation up and down the streets at this time of night, especially on an evening that was still quite warm like this one despite it being winter. One would have expected to see doors standing open to allow the air to blow through, but all the houses were tightly closed. Some were completely dark, but Judas could make out a dim rim of light around the doors and shutters of most of the dwellings.

Judas was only a street away from Rebekah's house, his heart already leaping with anticipation of holding her in his arms when he saw the light of a torch approaching. He ducked under a cart propped on end against a wall to watch. Two Syrian soldiers made their way up the street, stopping at each house. One would rap on the door while the other held his spear leveled as if expecting an enemy to leap from the house once the door opened. Judas watched as one door after another opened. The soldiers would peer in, say a few words to the occupants, then proceed to the next house. When they came to a house that was completely dark, they knocked in the usual manner. When no one came to the door, one of the soldiers kicked hard against the door where the latch was. The lock splintered and the door swung violently on its hinges. The other soldier held his torch into the room and cautiously leaned in after it. He commented to his comrade that the room was empty.

Judas remained squatted behind the cart watching the slow progress of the two Syrians. Evidently the garrison commander had invoked a curfew upon the city and every house was being checked to make sure there were no gatherings of any kind. Judas imagined there were pairs of soldiers such as these in every quarter of Jerusalem. Though he had not cared for it a few minutes earlier, he was now glad that there was no moon. It made hiding easier than it would have been otherwise.

The two soldiers turned the corner in the direction of Hananiah's house. As soon as the light of the single torch disappeared, Judas walked cautiously to the corner where he could see it again. When they were most of the way up the street, they kicked in another door where no one was at home before continuing down the street. As soon as he was certain the torchlight would not reveal his movement, Judas made quiet haste to the house with the kicked-in door. The door still hung open, so he had no fear of being exposed by the creak of a squeaking hinge.

Judas watched from the darkness of the house. The routine of the soldiers continued to be the same. After another sharp rap, a door opened. Judas could see beyond the torchlight into the house and make out that there was a man, a woman and at least two small children in the room. A moment later, the door closed.

Judas leaned out the doorway in which he stood as the two soldiers came near to the house at the end of the street. His heart turned over as he expected to see Rebekah's face in the light of the torch in the next moment. The soldier with the torch approached the door but the other stopped short.

"Wait!" said the one who had stopped as he looked up and down the street. Judas ducked back into the doorway, fearing that somehow he had been found out.

"What is it?" The other man stopped and held his torch high, looking around for whatever it was his companion was searching.

After another moment of looking up and down the street, the first man said, "Yes, this is it. No need to check that house."

"Why?"

"That's the place that belongs to that Jew they call Antigonus. Nobody is there, but the captain says we are to leave his place intact."

Judas cocked his head to one side as he strained to hear every word. He recalled the day in the gymnasium when he had heard Rebekah's brother, Shimri, called by the name the Syrian had just used.

The soldier holding the torch held out his arm so as to cast a better light on the other man. "Antigonus? I know him. He's a Jew? I didn't even know he was a Jew. I thought he was one of us. I've wrestled with him in the gymnasium." The Syrian stood thinking for a moment then spoke as if having made a sudden discovery. "Wait a minute. He's no Jew."

The other soldier burst out in laughter. "Oh yes, he is. Born and raised."

"But . . . I've seen . . . I mean . . . how?" the man with the torch stammered.

"He got an operation," came the simple explanation.

The torchlight flickered across the man's puzzled expression as he tried to piece it all together in his mind. "Well, who would have thought it possible." After another long while he ventured to ask, "But does that mean he's not a Jew any more?"

"Well," said the other man as he motioned his friend toward the next house, "the Jews won't accept him any more, not the fanatical ones. But I'm not sure we will either. We can sure use him though. At least, the captain thinks so."

The two soldiers continued from door to door up the street. Judas slumped down in the doorway. A weight seemed to press all the air out of him. He did not know what lay behind the door to the house he had spent so many wonderful hours in as a boy, but he did not expect to find anything there but emptiness. Where was Rebekah?

He waited a good while in the darkness, long enough for the two Syrians to be out of sight. A nearly full moon had just begun to rise. Long shadows continued to leave large pockets of darkness, but he could see that the street was completely empty. Judas rose to his feet and cautiously approached the door to Hananiah's house. There was no evidence of life inside, no rim of light around the door or shutter as there was from other homes along the street. Judas knocked, but no one came. He tried the latch, but it was tightly locked. He considered breaking the door open as he had seen the soldiers do but reconsidered.

Judas walked to the house where he had seen the man and woman and two children. He knocked quietly on the door. The door opened a crack and a man's timid voice spoke. "Who is it?"

Judas kept his voice low. "I'm a friend of Hananiah ben Zachariah, your neighbor. I was wondering if . . ."

The door swung open and the man pulled Judas inside. He leaned out and looked quickly up and down the street before closing the door. Judas looked around the room in the dim light of a single oil lamp. Seated on a mat on the floor was a young woman. She hugged two small boys against her sides. All three looked at Judas with wide uncertain eyes.

The man took the oil lamp from its shelf and held it in front of Judas to see him better. "Yes," he said slowly, continuing to examine Judas, "I've seen you before." The man searched his own thoughts for a moment. "Wait. You were here the day the Syrians killed all those people in the temple court. I remember it because you and some others walked by the house, and Hananiah was with you. I remember it because it was so unusual to see Hananiah leave his house."

Judas started to speak. "Yes, I was here with my father and . . ."

"Wait!" the man interrupted again, his eyes growing wide. "Are you the one they call the Maccabee?"

"What . . . how did you . . . where did . . ." All Judas could do was stammer.

The man holding the lamp smiled. "You are, aren't you? You're the Maccabee." He looked down at his wife and smiled a broad smile. "This is the Maccabee."

A thousand questions raced through Judas's mind. How did this man know who he was? "I am Judas ben Mattathias. It was my father and brother and I who were with Hananiah that day, the day of the slaughter at the temple."

"Then it *is* you." The man returned the lamp to the shelf. "Sit down. We don't have much, but what we have is yours."

Judas sat down on the mat, still puzzled that the man knew him as the Maccabee. The man handed Judas a piece of bread as he introduced himself as Elon and his wife as Esther.

"How do you know who I am, I mean, where did you hear that name, Maccabee?" Judas asked as he chewed on the bread.

Though he kept his voice low, Elon was jubilant in his speech. "I imagine your name is known all over Judea. Everybody heard about how you fought the Syrians in Modin. Word got around that it was started by a man named Mattathias and his sons. Then we heard that they were getting up an army, sending people into all the towns and villages to recruit. Somehow word got around that the army is led by the son named Judas and that they call him the Maccabee. It's talked about in the streets, the marketplace, everywhere you go. Some are thinking you might be the messiah we have been awaiting for so long." Elon paused for just a moment than asked, "Are you the messiah?"

"Nethanel," Judas said under his breath, now understanding. Legends could be made out of thin air if the right person was promoting it. Judas saw the questioning looks coming from both Elon and his wife. "No, I'm not the messiah." When the man did not seem ready to accept Judas's simple answer, Judas stopped the direction the conversation had taken by saying plainly, "I'm a Levite." Every Jew with the most basic religious education knew the messiah would come from the tribe of Judah. A wave of disappointment swept across Elon's face. Judas looked at him for a moment then said, "But Gideon wasn't the messiah either. I guess I'm more like him." Elon's face brightened.

Seeing hope restored in his host, Judas proceeded to get his own questions answered. "How did you know that I was Judas ben Mattathias? How did you know that the men you had seen with Hananiah that day were the same as the ones from Modin?"

Elon looked at his wife. Esther spoke, but her voice did not communicate the same hope that her husband's had. "It was only last week that we found out that you are engaged to Rebekah. I was over at their house trying to help her and Miriam, and she was talking about how she wished you were here. Hananiah's dying has been so hard on both of them."

Judas's mouth fell open. Esther read his expression. "You didn't know?"

"When?" said Judas, shaking his head in response.

Esther looked at her husband, who counted on his fingers before answering. "It was eleven days ago. He just grew so weak, and he grieved so over their son. I suppose you already know about him."

Judas nodded affirmatively, his eyes focused on an imaginary spot on the floor. "Where is Rebekah now, and Miriam? Are they with other family?"

"No," said Elon without hesitation. "Shimri came for them two days ago. He has taken them into the Acra."

Judas felt as if the wind had been knocked out of him. He

struggled to speak. "The Acra? Are you sure?"

"Yes. Shimri had Syrian soldiers with him when he came. I'm fairly certain that he was already in the Acra. They say there are over a thousand of the Greek Jews who have taken refuge there ever since word has gotten around about your activities. It seems that some of their comrades in towns north of here have been mysteriously disappearing, so they asked the garrison commander for protection."

"Greek Jews?"

Elon explained. "That's what they are calling the Jews who support the Syrians. Most of them are Sadducees. They act like Greeks. They look like Greeks. They only speak Greek. Frankly, I can't see calling them Jews, but that is the term that is used."

"Were Miriam and Rebekah forced to go with Shimri?"

Elon paused a moment as if to replay what they had witnessed two days earlier. "I wouldn't say they were forced, but I don't think they went by choice either. I can't imagine them wanting to leave their home, not to move in with the Syrian garrison."

Judas tightened his jaw as tears welled in his eyes. He was at once both angry and afraid. "They know," he said through clenched teeth.

"What?" asked Elon, not following Judas's thoughts. "What do they know? What does *who* know?"

"Don't you see," blurted Judas, trying to hold back the panic that was fighting to take him. "You knew who I was. You knew about me and Rebekah. Don't you see? The Syrians know too. Shimri has told them. They are holding Miriam and Rebekah prisoner in the citadel. Or . . . worse." Judas could not allow himself to articulate the thoughts that lodged in his mind. "Shimri doesn't care about them. He never cared about his father. He let him die a broken old man. But he will use them if he thinks he can gain some prestige with those Syrian bastards."

No one spoke for several minutes. A contagious depression settled over the room. Esther held out another piece of bread for Judas, but he refused it. The two children nestled their mother's side. One had fallen asleep.

Elon finally broke the silence. "What will you do?"

Judas swallowed hard. "I don't know. The one thing I really feared has taken place, and I'm to blame. Rebekah is in danger, if not dead, because of me."

Esther timidly put out her hand and touched Judas's arm. "No, Judas," she said quietly. "You mustn't think that. When Rebekah heard what you and your father and brothers had done, she was proud. And God will watch over her, just as he has watched over you."

Judas bit his lips and nodded, thankful for her gentle words, but tears in his eyes revealed his inner struggle. After a few minutes he stood up and went to the door. Despite Elon and Esther's urging that he stay the night, Judas insisted on spending the night alone. He thanked them for their brief hospitality. Before opening the door, he told Elon where he could find a donkey cart filled with jars of olive oil that were free for the taking if he went as soon as it was safe to be seen outside. Elon was grateful for this unexpected economic boon to their subsistence lifestyle.

Judas opened the door and looked up and down the street. The gentle breeze that had blown most of the day had now settled. All he could hear was the bray of a donkey in the distance. He turned briefly and thanked Elon and Esther once again. Then he stepped out into the night, pulling the door shut behind him.

Chapter 28

The moon had risen high enough to make movement along the streets easier. It also made it easier to be seen by a roving Syrian patrol. Judas moved warily from shadow to shadow, not knowing exactly where he was going. His thoughts were in such disarray that he felt himself bordering on madness. By instinct more than rational thought, he knew continuing to move aimlessly about the dark streets with no plan in mind would lead to disaster.

With no conscious purpose in mind, Judas moved steadily toward the western access to the temple mount. On the low embankment along the western wall Judas spotted a cluster of juniper trees. Even in the light of the nearly full moon, the area in the midst of the trees was blanketed in darkness. He mounted the embankment and sat down in the midst of the trees.

From the blackness in which he sat, he could look out upon much of the city. His mind was a confusion of thoughts, taking no particular direction other than leading him into a deeper depression. After about an hour he noticed the light of two torches coming up the same street by which he had arrived. As they grew closer, he could see that there were four soldiers. He assumed it was two pairs of the soldiers that were enforcing the curfew. They turned south and continued just a few feet from the wall. Though already well hidden in the shadows, Judas pulled himself behind the low branches of one of the junipers. They passed within a few feet of him. A couple of hours earlier he would have felt like springing out and killing all four soldiers. Now he felt as if all strength had been drained from his body along with the will to fight.

It was only as the four Syrians passed and his eyes followed them that he looked up at the western towers of the Acra, their destination. Judas had not seen the fortresses other cities held, but he could not imagine any being more impregnable than the Acra. When Antiochus had built the Acra, it had been with the intention that it be a reminder to Jews everywhere of his invincibility. Judas recalled the times he had heard his father teach from the prophet Daniel about a future king who would exalt himself above God and would honor a god of fortresses. Was Daniel speaking of Antiochus? Judas tried to remember what else the prophecy said. Everything was a blur in his mind.

Daniel's prophecies had told how the king would go about destroying. That sounded like Antiochus, except for one thing. The prophecy had also said he would conquer Egypt. The Romans had stopped Antiochus cold in his quest for Egypt. The simple knowledge that Antiochus could be stopped had brought courage to every Jew who had endured his brutality. If only the Romans had kicked him out of Judea as well. Perhaps it would have made little difference. According to Lucas, the Romans were no better than the Syrians. This was a fight the Jews would have to make for themselves.

Judas stared at the citadel as the four soldiers neared its entrance. The woman he loved was behind those walls. Surely the garrison commander knew who she was. Shimri would have told him. Otherwise, what would be his purpose for bringing her into the citadel?

Judas tried to penetrate his rampant emotions with rational thoughts. He struggled to assess the situation. It was possible that Rebekah was dead, but Judas doubted that. Judas did not take the Syrians for fools. They would know that this would increase the sentiment against them and add fuel to the insurgency. Judas was also fairly certain that Shimri's actions were not out of concern for his mother and sister. He was using them for his own preferment. Rebekah and her mother were hostages, held as leverage against him.

Judas's thoughts became clearer as he considered the events of the past couple of days. Elon and Esther had said that Miriam and Rebekah had been taken two days earlier. That would have been the day before Sabbath. Judas had launched the initial attack in Mizpah the day before that, sending the surviving soldiers fleeing to Jerusalem where they would have informed the garrison commander. The commander had sent the contingent of a hundred to Mizpah on the same day Miriam and Rebekah had been taken into the citadel. How did this fit together? According to Nethanel, the Syrians had thought they had killed all the initial insurgents in the Sabbath massacre a week earlier. They had thought the rebellion ended, or at least depleted of its leadership. The attack three days ago had proven them wrong. They now knew the leaders to be alive and active. Beyond this, they knew who the leaders were. It was inevitable that they would. Nethanel's and John's recruitment efforts had no doubt reached some of the wrong ears. The Syrians now knew about Judas the Maccabee. They would use any tool in their arsenal to crush him. They would use Rebekah.

Judas continued to stare blankly at the towers of the Acra. There was no fortress built by the hands of men that men could not conquer. The woman he loved more than his own life was behind those walls. He had to be stronger than the fortress. He had to be stronger than anything Antiochus could build, be it fortress or army. So long as he never failed, Rebekah would be safe. If he ever gave any indication of weakness, her life would be forfeit. They must fear him. He must become the phantom that haunted their dreams. He would be the Maccabee. They would willingly return Rebekah to him, not because he surrendered to them, but because they feared him.

Judas heard voices. The moonlight revealed two more soldiers coming from the city, one holding a burnt out torch. Now was the time to put fear and uncertainty behind him. Fear was what his enemies needed to feel. Judas pulled the small dagger from the sheath hidden under his cloak and clutched it tightly in his right hand. Silently rising to a crouching position, he studied the size and bearing of each of the two soldiers as they approached. He listened to their voices. The larger one was dominating the conversation. This would be the one to die. The one having the most confidence in himself would be the most dangerous. He would be the target. Judas uttered a silent prayer for help.

The two Syrians were returning from their duties, looking forward to a hot meal. Though they had met with mean looks during the evening, there had not been any overt resistance. Many had fled the city, and those who were left had seemingly resigned themselves to their present situation. They had passed in and out of shadows all night and had encountered no danger. The cluster of juniper trees by the side of the road did not strike them as threatening.

Life can change, or end, in an instant. Judas appeared as a ghost in the moonlight, materializing from the shadows. Before the awareness had even dawned that someone was there, the large Syrian was grappling with the dagger lodged in his throat. He looked up at the moon. It was the last thing he saw before permanently sinking from consciousness.

The other soldier dropped the burnt out torch and was trying to level his spear, but Judas lifted him off the ground with a kick to the groin. The man writhed upon the ground, clutching his groin. Judas wasted no time. He dragged the dead soldier into the shadows and pulled out the soldier's sword.

Judas returned to the other soldier who struggled to pull out his own sword as he lay bent double on the ground. Judas stomped the man's arm to the ground and held the other man's sword to his throat. "I need your help," he said.

"Help you!" the struggling man gasped, pain filling each word. "They will kill you for this."

Judas pressed the tip of the sword into the Syrian's skin until it brought a trickle of blood. "I don't think you are in a position to be talking about who will die tonight. If you can't help me, I have no reason to let you live."

Still in pain, the man examined Judas's face in the pale moonlight. In another moment he shook his head, indicating he would submit.

"Roll over on your stomach and put your hands behind you!" Judas commanded. The soldier complied. Judas cut away the strap holding the scabbard to the soldier's sword and bound his hands behind him.

"Now stand up!"

The Syrian stood facing his captor.

"Now listen very closely. If you utter a sound other than what I ask of you, you will die instantly. Do you understand?"

The soldier nodded.

"Tell me where I can find a horse." Judas neither knew nor cared much about horses, but necessity had a way of creating interest where none had been before.

"A horse?" questioned the soldier.

Judas pressed the sword to the man's throat and spoke condescendingly to him. "A horse."

"The stables for the cavalry are one street over from the Acra."

"You lead the way," said Judas, turning the man with his hand and jabbing the sword lightly into his back. "And remember what I said."

They walked almost to the citadel before cutting into a side street that curved around to where the stables were. When they came within sight of the stables, Judas pulled the soldier into the shadows and stood assessing the situation. All seemed quiet except for the periodic kicks, snorts, and other related sounds that more than a hundred horses make.

Judas pulled the Syrian in front of him and pushed him toward the closest stable. Coming to the entrance, they peered inside. Flames flickered in a single iron brazier as the sole source of light. Torches could be lit from this as needed by the stable keepers. At the moment, the keepers were nowhere to be seen. Judas knew they were probably somewhere eating their supper and would return shortly.

Judas took no chances with the Syrian. He backed the man against a post and wrapped the leather strap of a harness around his neck and the post before tying a tight knot in it. The soldier could not sit or move without choking himself. All he could do was watch as Judas searched in the darkness for a bridle.

Despite the little experience he had with horses, Judas did know how to put a bridle on one. Four horses were in the enclosure closest to the stable entrance. Judas put the bridle on the first horse he could grab by the mane. Satisfied that the bridle was well secured, he pulled his sword from where he had temporarily stuck it in the ground as he worked. Grabbing the horse's mane with one hand as he held the sword with the other, he swung himself onto the horse's bare back.

Judas walked the horse to where the soldier stood tied to the post. With a quick chop with the sword against the post, he cut the strap binding the soldier. The Syrian made a quick lunge to get away, but it was a move Judas had anticipated. Judas grabbed the top of the quilted linen cuirass the man was wearing and yanked him into the air, dropping him onto the horse's back in front of him. The horse was startled but quickly calmed. Had it not been trained for battle it would have probably thrown both of them off since Judas had released the reins to grab the soldier. Holding the soldier lying on his stomach across the horse's back in front him, Judas said calmly but firmly, "You have a choice. You can die now, or you can live to tell others how you rode on the same horse with Judas the Maccabee."

The Syrian lifted his head toward Judas and looked at him sideways. "You're the Maccabee?" Both fear and respect could be heard in his voice.

Judas said no more. He lifted the now submissive Syrian into a sitting position straddling the horse and prodded the horse from the stable. He followed the street away from the stables and, as soon as they came to the next street, put more distance between them and the citadel. All that could be heard as they moved through the streets was the clop of the horse's hoofs.

Judas led them to the same city gate he had entered hours earlier. In the light of their torches, he recognized the four guards to be the same as had been there earlier. He considered just making the horse run past them, but he was more interested in sending a message than he was in how easily he got away.

All four guards turned their heads in his direction at the sound of the approaching hoof-beats. Judas pulled the sword around to the front of his hostage and aimed it upward into his throat. All four guards raised their spears.

Judas continued to advance. "Lower your spears, or your friend dies."

No one moved.

"Do what he says!" shouted the man with the sword in his throat. "He's the Mac . . ."

Judas cut him short with a slight jab with the point of the sword. "Not yet. You'll get your chance," he said quietly into the soldier's ear.

The four guards lowered their spears slowly.

"Now lay them on the ground and back against the wall."

They reluctantly laid down the spears and backed to either side of the archway. Judas advanced the horse past them, looking from side to side to make sure they remained still. When he was beyond them and outside the gate he turned the horse around. Still holding the sword to his captive's throat, he spoke to all of them in a voice that demanded their attention.

"Do you men know the name Judas ben Mattathias?"

There was a pause and then one of the guards exclaimed, "You're the Maccabee!"

The eyes of the others grew wide. They looked from one to the other. The soldier on the horse with Judas tried to shake his head to tell them they were right, but the sword in his throat limited his movement.

Judas knew they were taking him seriously now. He spoke so all could hear. "Listen to every word I say. What part one of you forgets, another will remember. I have a message for your commander. Tell Lysimachus that Judas ben Mattathias freely walked the streets of Jerusalem tonight, and I will do so again. He does not have the power to stop me. If he thinks he can, then tell him to go into the hills beyond Mizpah and look upon the rotting bodies of the hundred soldiers he sent after us three days ago. They are only a sample of things to come if he persists.

"Tell him that the two women he is holding must be brought to me at Mizpah. If a hair on the head of either is harmed, every person in the Acra will die. There will be no opportunity of surrender. He will learn why the people of Israel call me the Maccabee."

With these last words, Judas threw the soldier mounted in front of him from the horse. The Syrian thrashed his legs as he fell through the air, his hands still bound behind him. His head struck the ground at the same time as his body, but only enough to daze him. Judas swung the horse around and kicked his knees into it. He heard spears hitting the stones behind him, but he did not look back.

Judas ran the horse along the moonlit road toward Mizpah for almost an hour. At first he had trouble staying on, but after a while he discovered how to move with the horse's stride. When he came to a rise that allowed him to see some distance behind him he stopped and looked back toward Jerusalem. Seeing nothing, he walked and led the horse for the next hour, stopping to look back and listen. Still seeing nothing, he mounted the horse once again and continued in a gentle trot until he had come near the town of Ramah, which was less than an hour's walk from Mizpah.

The approach to Ramah was not hilly as was the land closer to Jerusalem, though the elevation was about the same. He could see a considerable distance across the plain. Judas tied the horse's reins to a tree and perched on a large rock to watch the road. Toward the end of the third watch, he saw what he had been expecting. In the distance he could see repeated glints of moonlight on the road from Jerusalem. The cause, he already knew, was the reflection of the moon on helmets and breastplates. God had again blessed him with anticipating his enemy's moves. They seemed to be moving at a rapid pace, but Judas knew they would not be able to run their horses all the way from Jerusalem to Mizpah. He estimated that, all things considered, they were about an hour and a half behind him.

Feeling encouraged that God was again with him, Judas mounted his horse and raced toward Mizpah. When he was within a half mile of the town, three men ran out brandishing spears in front of him. He pulled the horse to a halt.

"Who goes there?" one of the three Hasidim shouted.

"It's the Maccabee!" one of the others exclaimed before Judas could speak.

Judas spoke rapidly from astride the horse. "Are all our brothers still here?"

"Yes," came the response. "Some more even came in just yesterday."

"Awake them all," Judas commanded. "Syrian cavalry will be here by time the sun is up. We must meet them with everything we have."

Judas kicked the horse and raced ahead, looking back to see the three Hasidim running behind him. When he arrived in the town he was met by more watchmen. "Awaken the town," he ordered. "Syrian cavalry are close behind."

Judas found Nethanel and explained the situation. Nethanel quickly took command of four groups of twenty. Sending the four groups armed with bows just outside the town, he stationed them out of sight on either side of the road. Judas took command of those remaining in the town. He estimated there to be between eighty and a hundred men. About half of these had bows. The rest armed themselves with the *pila* they had taken off the hundred Syrians that had attacked them in the forest. Judas prayed that it would be enough, for when the pila were thrown, they would be forced to fight with swords, something Judas was not yet sure many of these men were ready for.

The sky had just begun to give some light when the Syrians came into view. Judas tried to count them. There couldn't be more than fifty. They had, no doubt, thought to capture him along the road, but they had come prepared for a battle along the way. Though he had nothing that could be considered an army, he wanted to give the Syrians the impression that he did. These fifty cavalry had to be overwhelmed by the size of the force against them. Some would get away. The ones who lived would serve him better than the ones who died, for they would take back the message of the impenetrable force holding Mizpah. Judas hoped that an attack from three sides in the pale light of the morning would give the impression he hoped for.

The cavalry approached at a rapid pace, riding in ten ranks of five. When Judas saw that the last rank had passed the farthest of Nethanel's men, he shouted to four men who blew shofars as archers came to life from both sides. Some arrows immediately found their marks. The cavalry broke their charge into the town, splitting to both sides to stop the source of the arrows raining upon them. This was the mistake Judas had hoped they would make. Had they continued their charge forward they could have inflicted many casualties. Judas shouted again and led the charge from the town. The men screamed as if released from hell while shofars continued to pierce the air with their blast.

The cavalrymen, now divided and in disarray, turned to face the hail of pila that met them. Breastplates were no protection against the weight of a pilum, and more Syrians fell. When they turned to face the new threat, the archers on each side shot them without resistance. In less than a minute, the surviving troops realized the futility of the fight and fled. Over half of them had died, and some that had gotten away had left wounded.

Judas stopped anyone from pursuing them. He knew that Lysimachus would receive the message. He prayed that message would save Rebekah.

Chapter 29

Lysimachus sat down hard upon a cushioned couch at the end of the stone table after the two cavalrymen had left the room. A servant approached him with a pitcher and cup. "Not now!" Lysimachus said irritably, waving the servant away. The servant quietly backed away and left the room by a side door.

Menelaus sat at the other end of the table. Lysimachus had sent for him in the middle of the night and forced him to remain up all night until the troops returned. It had been the intention of Lysimachus that when the troops returned with Judas, the one everyone called the Maccabee, that Menelaus would publicly pronounce the judgment and subsequent execution of Judas so that everyone would know that the highest Jewish official in the land was taking a stand against the rebellion.

A thick silence filled the room for several minutes. Finally, Menelaus ventured to speak. "You know where he is now. He's in Mizpah. If you were to send a much larger contingent from your garrison you could take him."

"Larger contingent!" the garrison commander shouted. "How large? You just heard what the man said. Those were fifty of my best cavalry. They said they were outnumbered ten to one."

"Perhaps the man exaggerated to cover their own failure."

"Is it an exaggeration that not a single one of the hundred men I sent to Mizpah last week has come back?" Lysimachus stared stonily at Menelaus, offended that the Jewish high priest would even attempt to offer him advice. "Now this brazen Jew roams our streets during the night and brags how they have wiped out our whole unit." The fact that Menelaus was a Jew did not temper Lysimachus's slanderous use of the word.

"You don't know for sure that they are all dead." Menelaus did not want to admit, even to himself, the dangerous turn things had taken.

"Then where are they? That many troops don't just disappear. If things keep going like this, we won't have any left. Besides, this is a garrison put in place to hold this city and the surrounding area. This is not an army equipped to fight a full scale war. I'm beginning to think that is what we have on our hands. If I send too many of our forces out to meet this devil in the hills I will leave the city vulnerable."

"So what are you going to do?"

Lysimachus dropped his head and stared at the floor. "I don't see I have any choice. I must send word to the governor. This has escalated beyond our control." Lysimachus recalled the sharp interchange he had had with Seron, the commander from Coele-Syria, and only with great pain reconciled himself to the present state of affairs. "My job is to hold Jerusalem. Apollonius will have to raise an army to fight this Maccabee." Lysimachus's lips turned down in a frown as he uttered that last hateful word.

The door opened and a guard stepped in. "Antigonus is here as you ordered, Sir."

Lysimachus looked up. "Good. Send him in."

The guard stood to one side as Shimri entered the room. Shimri gave a stiff shallow bow and addressed the commander. "You sent for me, Sir."

"Yes. Antigonus. You have proven yourself to be a friend of the king."

A smile crossed Shimri's face. He had been uncertain as to why the commander had summoned him. Now he felt much more at ease. "I am grateful for the new way of life that our king has worked so hard to bring us. I only regret that some of my people have made his task more difficult by refusing to give up their archaic ways. I want you to know that I will render whatever services are needed by the great Antiochus Epiphanes."

Lysimachus exchanged glances with Menelaus. Both recognized a man who was hungry for power and willing to do whatever it took to acquire it, even if it meant betraying his own flesh and blood. "You have done well in bringing your mother and sister to us, and only in the nick of time. Your friend, Judas, was in this city only last night."

Shimri was quick to respond. "I assure you, Sir, that he is no friend of mine. I have already heard some of the talk around the citadel this morning from the troops that went out to Mizpah last night and how so many were mercilessly slaughtered. Judas ben Mattathias and all his family are a blight upon this nation. I will do whatever it takes to rid both my family and the nation of him."

"Just as I had expected," said Lysimachus. "I do have a task for you, a very important task. I want you to go to Samaria, to Governor Apollonius."

"Governor Apollonius, Sir? I'm honored."

"I will give you a letter to take to the governor. In the letter I will be requesting his help against Judas and his fellow rebels. I feel quite certain that he will raise an army as quickly as possible to bring against Judas from the north. I am going to suggest that he give you the authority to create a cohort from among the Jews who live in the area. I have seen how influential you are among the Jews loyal to the king here, and I don't think you will find what I am suggesting overly difficult. The Jews who live in Samaria are generally loyal to the king." Lysimachus paused and studied the face of the young Jew standing before him before adding. "A cohort of your own to command, how does that sound?"

Pride glowed through Shimri's demeanor. "It is what I was made for," he said arrogantly. "You will not be disappointed, Sir."

"Good," said the garrison commander. "Now go make preparations to leave. You will leave in a couple of hours. You will be accompanied by a unit of twenty cavalry, and it will take you at least two days to get to Samaria."

"Two days, Sir?" Shimri was well educated in the geography of Judea and knew that on horseback Samaria was no more than a day's travel from Jerusalem.

"You will not be traveling the usual route to Samaria," explained the commander. "We know the rebels are in possession of Mizpah, and we think they may be in control of some of the territory north of there also, though we don't know how much. You will travel south to Beth-zur and then out to the coast before turning north to go to Samaria. I regret that it will not be a comfortable journey for you, for I am ordering the cavalry captain to avoid towns along the way. You will have to sleep on the ground for a night or two."

"A small price for the privilege of serving my king." Shimri made a shallow yet formal bow.

"Now go see the captain of the cavalry. He will help you with what you will need for the journey. Come back just before you leave for the letter to the governor."

Shimri bowed again, then turned to leave. Just as he reached the door, he turned back to the commander. "Oh, Sir, about my mother and sister . . ."

Lysimachus waved his hand. "You need not concern yourself over your mother and sister. They will be well taken care of. I would not let anything happen to them. They may be quite useful to us in the future. Thank you, again, for bringing them to us."

Shimri nodded and left. Menelaus waited until the guard had closed the door behind Shimri before speaking. "What *will* you do with them?"

"Exactly as I said," responded Lysimachus. "I will take good care of them until the proper time. If I find it expedient to me that they live, they will live. If it proves more beneficial that they die, they will die. It's as simple as that."

Lysimachus did not give voice to all his thoughts, for he

knew Menelaus would betray him just as easily as he had betrayed his own people. Lysimachus had watched the machinations of ambitious people all his professional life and knew that political expediency often led to strange ends. Though nothing would have pleased him more than to give the head of this Judas the Maccabee to the king on a platter, he took seriously Judas's threat that had been communicated to him by his guards during the night. This Judas was a force to be reckoned with. No one yet had any means of measuring just how great a force. Today, the commander had to answer to Apollonius. Tomorrow, he may be answering to Judas the Maccabee. In the meantime, he would keep these two women who were so important to Judas under constant guard. To kill them would only enflame passions more than they already were. To release them would show weakness. He would wait until he knew for sure how they would prove the most useful.

Lysimachus clapped his hands and the servant with the cup and pitcher returned and poured him a drink. The commander ordered the servant to bring writing materials. While waiting for the servant to return so that Lysimachus could write his letter to the governor, Menelaus raised a question about what he had heard Lysimachus say would be part of the letter's content. "A cohort of Jews?"

"Yes," replied the commander caustically, again irritated that the high priest would question him in such matters. "I think Apollonius will see the wisdom of it. The more we can turn this into a civil war rather than it just being Syria against Judea, the better off we will be. Besides, even if they don't fight very well, we will have eliminated more Jews, who are the problem in the first place."

Menelaus grew red in the face, though Lysimachus did not look at him to see how his deliberate offense had affected him. The servant brought the writing materials and Lysimachus set to writing his message for Apollonius. Menelaus cleared his throat for attention, but Lysimachus made no further acknowledgement of his presence. After a long while Menelaus stood and walked loudly from the room, slamming the door behind him. Lysimachus looked up only for a moment at the closed door before returning to his writing.

Within the confines of the same stone walls in which the garrison commander sat writing his missive to Apollonius, Rebekah strained to see out the narrow slit of a window looking out onto the central courtyard. She could see a small area of the stone pavement and make out the voices of some of the soldiers. The gate from the citadel into the city was open and she could hear the unmistakable sounds of horses. She had also heard them during the night. The sounds had returned later in the morning. Along with the sounds of horses, she had heard much loud and excited talking among the soldiers echoing across the pavement.

Miriam, her mother, sat back away from the window on one of the hard, narrow beds that had been provided for them. It was not comfortable, but it was not overly uncomfortable either. They realized they were hostages, but they were not mistreated. Their door was locked, and a guard was permanently stationed just outside. Nevertheless, their basic needs were seen to.

Miriam's mind was black with depression. She had lost her husband. Now her own son had given them into the hands of the Syrians. He had tried to tell her and Rebekah that it was for their own safety, but a locked door with a permanent guard indicated something more. "Have you heard any more?" she said to her daughter, no real emotion conveyed in her voice.

"Nothing more than what we heard earlier," replied Rebekah. "But Mother, think about it. Judas was in Jerusalem last night. I heard them say 'the Maccabee.' That's what we've heard people calling Judas. I'm sure he had come for us. If only he had come sooner."

Miriam put her face in her hands. She would have cried, but she had no more tears to shed. "What's going to become of us?" she said dejectedly. "What's going to happen to you, my daughter? We should have sent you with Mattathias and his sons when they returned to Modin. We knew it wasn't safe in

Jerusalem. If we had sent you with them, at least you would be safe now. Can you forgive us?"

Rebekah left the window and sat beside her mother on the bed. She put her arm around her and hugged her to her side. "Mother, this is not your fault. Don't blame yourself. I wouldn't have gone if you had asked me. I needed to be close to you and Father. We'll get through this. God will take care of us. You'll see."

Miriam looked up at her daughter. A hidden reserve of tears had been found, for now her face was moist with them. They looked into each other's eyes and then suddenly embraced and held each other tightly.

After a long while, a familiar voice was heard from outside the window. Rebekah abruptly pulled away and ran to the window. She leaned from one side to the other to see as much of the courtyard as she could. Suddenly she exclaimed, "Mother, it's Shimri. I see him."

Miriam rose and ran to the window. "See there, Mother," said Rebekah, pointing to where she saw Shimri walking across the courtyard. Shimri was wearing the clothing of a Syrian officer and was carrying a bundle such as soldiers in the field carry to provide their bedding and several days ration of grain.

Rebekah shouted from the window. "Shimri! Shimri! Up here!"

Miriam joined Rebekah in trying to get Shimri's attention. "Shimri! Son!"

Shimri stopped for a moment and looked up at the window. A loud voice was heard, though neither Rebekah nor Miriam could see who it was that was speaking from their vantage point. "Antigonus," the voice was heard to say. "Do you have everything you need for the journey?"

Shimri lowered his head from looking at the window and resumed walking in the direction of the voice. "Yes, Malchus," Shimri said in response to the unseen man who had spoken.

"Then the captain says we need to be on our way," the voice said.

A moment later, Shimri could no longer be seen from the window. The two women continued to peer out, hoping to see more, but a minute later they heard the clopping sound of many hoofs on the stone pavement outside the citadel gate. In a short while, the sounds faded in the distance and all that could be heard were the voices of soldiers and civilians going about their tasks in the courtyard.

Miriam returned to her place on the bed while Rebekah continued to look out the window. Miriam stared at the wall opposite her for a long while. Then, turning her eyes toward the window, she said, "Come away from the window, Rebekah. There's nothing more to see."

Rebekah turned and lamented loudly to her mother. "He saw us, Mother. Shimri saw us. But he didn't even acknowledge that we were here."

Miriam lowered her eyes to the floor. "Speak his name no more, Rebekah. Your brother is dead. I gave birth to him. I nursed him on my breast. I held him and cared for him when he was sick. I saw him grow into manhood. But now he is dead. I must accept this, and so must you."

Miriam lay on her side on the hard bed and closed her eyes. Perhaps sleep would remove the pain, if only for a while.

Chapter 30

During the next several weeks, every Syrian authority from Jerusalem to Samaria to Antioch became maddeningly aware that the countryside of Judea had turned against them. Lysimachus saw his garrison whittled away man by man every time he attempted the slightest move against the insurgents. The situation continued to deteriorate until he feared allowing his troops outside the city. He began stationing ten guards at every gate of the city instead of the usual four, and at night he ordered the city gates closed.

Apollonius set to raising an army after receiving the communication from Lysimachus by way of Shimri, known to them as Antigonus. More than once he sent messages to Lysimachus demanding further action but never received a reply. Either the message was intercepted on its way to Jerusalem, or the couriers bringing the reply were killed along the way. Not only was communication cut off, but all tax revenue from Judea as well. This proved a great frustration for the governor as he struggled to raise an army with very limited resources. He feared incurring the displeasure of Antiochus, who had moved his army beyond the Euphrates to exact tribute from the Persians, by turning to him for funds. In the end, he fell upon the scheme of building his army primarily from the populace of Samaria by promising them the plunder from the cities and towns of Judea. Many joined the ranks with thoughts of gold and slaves taken from among the Jews. The young man Antigonus that Lysimachus had sent proved useful to Apollonius. At his prompting, the Jews who had settled in Samaria took readily to the idea of helping themselves to the property of their former countrymen.

Though remaining in Antioch, Lysias stayed abreast of events in Judea. He was angered by the failure of both Apollonius and Lysimachus to send a much larger force against the rebels during the first days of the rebellion. He was convinced that, had they not delayed, the rebellion could have been crushed before it had time to grow. His greatest concern was the loss of revenue from Judea. Antiochus had an army in the field. Lysias kept a standing army outside Antioch under the command of his two generals, Nicanor and Gorgias. Besides this, Seron maintained an army composed primarily of infantry in Coele-Syria. Such a massive war machine required revenues to match. Lysias was probably the only man in Syria who did not fear Antiochus. If the gods produced the favorable conditions necessary, he would willingly replace this arrogant king who called himself a god. However, he did fear a deserting army. Even the great Alexander had been stopped on the other side of the Punjab because his army threatened desertion if he went any farther.

The only one who seemed to find any pleasure in the turn of events in Judea was Seron. Seron sent spies into Judea as well as into Samaria to remain current on Apollonius's plans and activities. Whenever a report came that denigrated Apollonius, he made sure it reached the ears of Lysias. One day, said Seron to himself, Judea would be his. Let this man they call the Maccabee have his way for now. Once Apollonius was out of the way, Seron would crush the Maccabee and all who followed him.

Judas remained in Mizpah fortifying the town and training new recruits. Before long, Mizpah was an armed camp, the new home to several hundred troops, a number that increased daily. When the town became overcrowded, Judas sent large blocks of men back to their home towns to await his call to battle. With his troops stationed in more and more towns, most of Judea began to fall under Judas's control. All the Syrians really held was Jerusalem. But to a Jew, Jerusalem was everything. Their temple, their heart, was in Jerusalem.

Judas's heart focused on Jerusalem for another reason as well. Never a day went by that his thoughts didn't turn to Rebekah. He imagined her held in a dark dungeon, deprived of food and warmth. His love for her fueled his hatred of the Syrians. No Syrian would be safe so long as Rebekah and her mother remained within the Acra.

After a couple of weeks, Joseph showed up in Mizpah with about a dozen men. In the group was a young man named Azarias who had gained some notoriety among the others. Judging from stories that circulated, Azarias could be foolhardy at times, but the man feared nothing. It was obvious to Judas that the men Joseph had recruited looked equally to Azarias as their leader Together, Joseph and Azarias had managed to virtually eliminate all Syrian sympathy between Lebonah and Mizpah. Sometimes they did it discreetly, as Joseph preferred, causing the Syrian loyalists to simply disappear during the night. But more recently they had become quite bold about it, as Azarias preferred, removing those who sided with the Syrians from their towns in broad daylight.

Judas put another fifty men under the command of Joseph and Azarias and sent them out as raiding parties wherever they could find Syrian activity in the region around Jerusalem. It became virtually impossible for a Syrian unit of any size to leave the city without suffering casualties from one of their attacks. If a Syrian unit seemed too large for them to handle, Joseph and Azarias would attack anyway. Their men would suddenly appear out of nowhere filling the air with arrows then flee in all directions. The Syrians had learned the foolishness of attempting any pursuit. They had learned from their comrades that a fleeing Jew was often the setup for an ambush.

After several weeks, it was rare to see a Syrian soldier leave the city. Azarias grew bored by the inactivity and convinced Joseph to attack the guards at one of the city gates. During the night, Azarias and twenty of his men took positions tight against the wall on either side of the gate. When the guards opened the massive gate in the morning they were suddenly met by a hail of arrows and the sight of fleeing Jews. Four guards died and one was critically wounded. By the time troops could be mustered to pursue the fleeing Jews, they were nowhere to be found.

It was early summer when Eleazar charged into the center of Mizpah astride a frothing horse one morning. Eleazar was the only one of his brothers that Judas had seen for almost four months. Simon, having recovered from his broken leg, along with John and Jonathan, had successfully built a larger force in the north. Time and again they stopped Syrian patrols coming from Samaria trying to reach Jerusalem. Eleazar had periodically gone back and forth as the liaison between the two camps, reporting on intelligence gathered by their spies. Usually, the news he carried related to the army they had watched Apollonius build against them over the months. This particular day, however, the news related to only one man.

Eleazar jumped from the horse and ran to the house where Judas lived when he himself was not out plundering Syrian interests. Not finding Judas in the house he asked a young Hasidim he found there where he was. The Hasidim indicated a watchtower on the southern edge of town. Eleazar sprinted to the tower. He recognized Judas's profile standing against the blue sky at the top of the tall structure.

Struggling to catch his breath, Eleazar shouted up to the tower, "Judas, come down."

Judas leaned over and looked at Eleazar's perspiring face. "What is it?"

"It's Father. He's sick. I think he's dying. Simon said you need to come."

Judas disappeared from the edge of the tower. In another instant he was seen descending the rough ladder inside the four tall legs made from the trunks of trees. When he was about ten feet from the ground, he leapt the rest of the way.

Eleazar was speaking again before Judas hit the ground. "He got sick several days ago. He just got worse and worse. Simon said for you to come. He doesn't think Father has much time."

Judas walked briskly into the town. Eleazar, already winded, struggled to keep up. Two men were standing outside the first house as they entered the town. Judas pointed to one. "You, get me two fresh horses and bring them to where I'm staying." Pointing to the other man he said, "You, go find Nethanel and bring him to me." Both men scurried off.

Eleazar gave Judas a more detailed account of Mattathias's decline as they continued walking to the house. Judas listened without speaking. Finally he said simply, "An old man shouldn't have to die in a cave in the woods."

Once at the house, Judas went in and strapped on his sword and found a skin that he gave to a young boy playing outside to fill with water. The boy ran off and was back with the filled skin in a short time. A man arrived holding the reins of two horses. He handed the reins to Eleazar and took the reins of the heavily perspiring horse that Eleazar had arrived on and led it away.

Judas was standing outside when Nethanel arrived. Judas explained to him the situation. "You are in command," Judas said. "I will send word of what happens and of anything new I learn of what's happening farther north."

Judas turned to Eleazar. "Is there any new information coming out of Samaria?"

"Nothing," said Eleazar. "Just that there is a lot of training going on. One of our men saw a full phalanx practicing in a field outside the city. But things like that have been going on for several weeks. It may be months before they do anything. It's just hard tell."

Judas returned his attention to Nethanel. "If Apollonius makes his move before I return, you will need to send riders to all the towns to gather everyone here and then proceed north to Lebonah. Send somebody out now to find Joseph and Azarias and bring them into Mizpah. They will need to hold Mizpah and bar the way so that nothing can come behind you that might come out of Jerusalem. We do not need to be facing Apollonius in front of us and have Lysimachus coming up behind us."

Nethanel assured Judas, "I will see to it that all you have said is done. Now you go be with Mattathias." Nethanel's voice broke as he spoke. "Your father is what Israel is supposed to be. He is a true father to this nation. He gave us back hope."

Judas, moved by Nethanel's words, searched for a reply but could say nothing. All he could do was blink back tears and nod his head as a motion of gratitude to his warrior friend. He took the reins of one of the horses from Eleazar and swung himself to the horse's back. Eleazar mounted and they raced away together.

It was early afternoon when they arrived at the camp in the hills. They had run the horses hard all the way to where they left the road just below Lebonah. From that point onward they had moved at a slower pace as they guided their horses through the forest.

The camp was crowded with new recruits. Some distance before they arrived at the caves they found a group of men noisily practicing on each other with wooden swords. As they came closer, the atmosphere changed. Judas and Eleazar prodded the horses up the side of the mountain to the mouth of the cave where Mattathias stayed. Several men as well as women were gathered outside the cave. No one spoke. They just watched silently as Judas and Eleazar dismounted. A man took the reins to the horses and led them away. Judas and Eleazar walked into the cave.

All the brothers and Leah were there. Simon knelt by the low platform they had built for Mattathias that served as a bed. John and Leah stood at the old man's feet. Eleazar went and stood with Jonathan by the opposite wall and looked on.

Simon moved to one side so Judas could sit down by his father. Judas knelt down on the ground and looked into

Mattathias's ashen face. Seeing the old man's sunken cheeks made him think of Hananiah the last time he had seen him, the day they had left Jerusalem after the massacre in the temple court. He had not realized how close Hananiah had been to death at the time. Hananiah died from a broken heart. Illness found its way into Mattathias's body because he had worn it out for the love of his people and his God.

Judas took his father's left hand lying limp on the bed and clasped it between his own two strong hands. Feeling Judas's grip, Mattathias opened his eyes slowly and looked into Judas's face. "Judas!" he said in a weak, raspy voice.

"Don't try to talk, Father." Judas fought back tears. His father had always been a fighter. Even when weak and old, he had stood before others as a voice of strength. Now it seemed he had little left with which to fight.

"No. I must talk," said the withered figure lying on the hard bed made from split branches. "I know I have very little time left, and what I don't say now, I may not be able to say tomorrow."

"Okay, Father." Judas squeezed the old man's hand. "I'm listening."

"Judas, you must keep fighting. This is not what I would have chosen for my children, but it is what God has chosen. You must keep fighting. Israel has found hope in you. They call you the Maccabee. You're their hero." Mattathias paused as if searching for his next words then added, "You're their Gideon."

Mattathias rolled his eyes toward Simon as he continued to speak to Judas. "Always listen to Simon. Simon is a wise man and has a deep understanding of God's laws. Simon will lead the nation when once again Israel knows peace, but you, Judas, are God's chosen one to lead the nation in war. Lead them, Judas."

Mattathias looked slowly around the cave, from the eyes of one son to other. "All of you, follow your brother. He is the leader of your army. Stand behind him. Force the Gentiles from our land. Return Judea to those who honor God and obey his laws."

Low comments came from around the cave agreeing to Mattathias's wishes. Simon said it most eloquently. "We are all as one, Father. Judas will lead us until one day we offer burnt offerings at God's holy temple."

A distant stare came into the old man's eyes. For a moment, they wondered if he had died, but then they heard the quiet words, "If only I could have seen the temple again at Passover." Mattathias closed his eyes and said no more.

No one said anything. Each of the brothers found refuge in his own thoughts and silent prayers. They stayed by their father's bed the rest of the day. Later that evening, Mattathias died. The man who had stood against the tide of the culture and had called Israel back to the God of their fathers, not just in words but in action, was gone. In the moment he realized his father was dead, Judas quietly said, "This was the real hero of Israel."

The next morning, they carried the body of Mattathias wrapped in linen cloth to Lebonah where they found a proper cart. They laid the body in the cart and harnessed it behind a mule. Judas would not allow that it be pulled by a horse captured from the Syrians. "We can use the horses to kill Syrians," he said, "but the hero of Israel will not follow anything that has been tainted by a Gentile."

Judas left Oren in command of the camp in the forest and Jadon in charge of the group that remained stationed in and around Lebonah, giving thorough instructions of what to do at the first indication of activity in Samaria. They were to send two of their fastest riders to Mizpah to inform Nethanel. If something happened to one along the way, the other would make it through. Judas took no chance of the war being lost because a rider was accidentally thrown from his horse. They were to then gather all the forces scattered in the villages nearby to a position south of Lebonah.

Judas sent riders ahead to every town from Lebonah to Mizpah, then down the Way of Beth-horon all the way to Modin to inform the people in the towns that they would be passing by with the body of Mattathias. All five of Mattathias's sons walked behind the cart. Leah walked alongside her husband, John. In every town and village, people came out to honor him. Some wailed loudly. Others mourned quietly. In each town there were men that had trained to fight in either Mizpah or at the camp in the Gophna Hills. Judas recognized many of them. The ones that had swords drew them and held them across their hearts, touching their left shoulders, as a sign that the fight begun by Mattathias was the fight they had made their own.

They spent the night in Mizpah before turning west down the Way of Beth-horon the next morning. Mattathias was honored in every town all the way to Modin. In Modin, the sons laid their father in the same carved out tomb where lay the bones of their mother. Many of the people of Modin feared approaching the brothers because they had not supported them in the beginning. Most, however, had had a change of heart when they had received news of the continued successes against the Syrians. Some had even come and trained at Mizpah. These came to the tomb to honor Mattathias as his sons rolled the great stone across its entrance. The body may be sealed away, some said, but his memory would live in their hearts forever.

After spending the evening in Mattathias's home in Modin, they followed the route back toward Mizpah. They made no attempt to hurry, but stopped in each town along the way to talk with the people. Simon had suggested that some people would be wondering what would happen now that Mattathias was gone. They told everyone of Mattathias's last words. People were encouraged and emboldened by what they heard.

They had just left Upper Beth-horon, when they saw two riders rapidly approaching. Judas recognized the men as two who were staying in Mizpah. When they pulled up their horses in front of them, Judas looked up at them. "What is it? What's happened?"

One of the young men said to Judas, "Nethanel sent me to find you, Sir, and to call out the men from the towns. Word just came down the valley. A lot of troops are assembling outside Samaria. It looks like they are getting ready to move this way."

"How many?" said Judas.

"I don't know, Sir. A lot. Nethanel says you need to come." The young man jumped from his horse. "Here, take my horse. I can go tell the men in Upper Beth-horon on foot, and Jachin here can go to the villages farther away, unless you need his horse too. We can do it all on foot if need be."

"No," said Judas. "We need every man we can get in Mizpah as quickly as possible." He looked at Jachin as he mounted the horse. "Go. Go now. Tell everyone you can find to come. Don't wait until tomorrow. They must come today, tonight."

Judas looked down at his brothers and Leah. "You will be in Mizpah in a couple of hours. Spend the night there and come to Lebonah tomorrow. If there are horses left in Mizpah, I will leave orders that they furnish you with them. Come quickly."

Judas kicked his knees into the horse. Soon all the others could see was a small cloud of dust in the distance. Judas stopped in Mizpah only long enough to make sure Nethanel understood what he was supposed to do. Nethanel had already sent riders and runners all over Judea to call the men to battle.

Joseph and Azarias had arrived in Mizpah just that morning. They regretted not having been there to pay respects to Mattathias as his body had passed through. Judas ordered that one hundred fifty troops were to remain in Mizpah under their command. It would not be many if Lysimachus led out most of the Jerusalem garrison. Judas hoped they had been as successful as they thought they had at stopping communication between Samaria and Jerusalem. If they had, there would be no reason that an attack would come from Jerusalem at the same time the one was coming from the north.

It was well into the second watch of the night when Judas arrived in Lebonah. He had pushed the horse faster than he should have along the dark, uneven road. He had a special sense that God was keeping the horse from stumbling in the darkness. He thought of the words David had written in the psalm: Even the darkness is not too dark for Thee, but the night shineth as the day; the darkness is even as the light.

Lebonah had been transformed into an armed camp in the last few hours. Oren had led the troops out of the hills and Jadon had sent runners to every nearby village. Judas was annoyed that his orders to deploy the men south of Lebonah rather than in the town had been ignored, but he said nothing. He called Oren and Jadon together along with those designated as captains of each group of a hundred. He listened to all that was known of activities in Samaria then ordered the captains to redeploy their men to locations in the forest so that the enemy would find it more difficult to assess how many of them there were. He then gave them a time they were to meet back the next morning.

After they had broken up, Judas asked Oren, "Where's Lucas, the old man that was a slave of Apollonius?"

Oren was confused. "He's still in the hills. Judas, he can't fight. He's too old."

"No," said Judas, "he can't fight, but don't underestimate what he can do for us. Send someone with a horse back to the camp tonight. Bring him to me in the morning."

Oren did not argue, though he did not understand what help an old man like Lucas could be. He had been stationed out along the road below town the evenings Lucas had told his stories each night around the fire at the camp in the hills. He would soon learn that no one with a fervent heart outlives their usefulness.

Chapter 31

The spirited Arabian jostled Apollonius as he observed the phalanx moving rapidly across the field in a simulated attack. The governor pulled back on the reins to still the horse that seemed intent on joining the charge.

"The Jews don't have anything that can stand up to that," Apollonius boasted, pointing to the front of the phalanx where the first six ranks of sixteen men each had their long *sarissae* leveled, creating a wall of spear points. "Anyone trying to penetrate that will be run through several times before he even gets close to our men."

The field commander mounted on the horse beside Apollonius was less enthusiastic than the governor. "It didn't stop the Romans at Pydna, Sir."

Apollonius snorted. "Pydna! Pydna was a fluke." Apollonius again waved his hand toward the formation of men in the field. "This is how Alexander conquered the world. Besides, the Macedonians were fighting Roman legions at Pydna. We're going after a bunch of Jews using homemade swords. There's hardly a comparison."

The commander waited before speaking, knowing it wise that he at least appear to have considered the governor's remarks before voicing thoughts to the contrary. "You may be right, Governor, but I still don't think our men are ready. Drilling on a practice field is one thing. Fighting where men around you are dying is quite another. Most of these men have never experienced battle. I suggest we give them a few more weeks."

"We cannot wait!" Apollonius said sharply. "If we do, our present advantage will be gone. We have just gotten word that the leader of the rebellion has died. Don't you see it? The rebellion has had its head cut off. If we wait, we may be giving it time to grow another head. We must attack now."

The commander kept his eyes on the activity in the field as he questioned the governor, careful not to make his remarks sound challenging. "Where did you get this news, Sir? It was my understanding that we have been basically cut off from Jerusalem."

Apollonius smiled. "We have our spies. The rebels think they are eliminating the progressive Jews from their towns, but they aren't able to get rid of everyone. One of these men of ours made his way to us yesterday afternoon. He is from a little village somewhere between here and Jerusalem. He said that two days ago all five of the sons of this rebel leader that died are accompanying his body all the way to his home town, a little place out toward the coastal plain called Modin. They are making a big thing out of it, stopping in every town so people can pay their respects. That's why it is so urgent that we move now.

"The leader is dead, and the sons are away burying him. Even the son the people call the Maccabee – the one they've turned into some kind of a legend – even he is away mourning the death of his father. I tell you, this old man's death has dealt a blow to their cause. The gods have certainly smiled on us. They are not prepared to face an army. But we must move quickly."

"I pray to the gods that you are right, Governor," said the commander.

"Of course, I'm right," laughed Apollonius. "We have an army of five thousand men that we will move out in the morning against a bunch of farmers who have been hiding in the hills for the last few months. They may do well with their little skirmishes when they attack like a bunch of highway bandits, but they will melt like wax in front of an army like this." Apollonius motioned toward the phalanx that was leaving the field as another came behind it in another demonstration.

Apollonius squinted as he watched the new unit taking the field. "Is that the young man Antigonus? Is that his unit?"

"Yes, Governor," replied the commander. "All Jews, all two hundred and fifty-six of them. I had thought they would serve better in another capacity, with the baggage or even as light-armed troops, but you said to give him freedom to form the kind of unit he wanted. He wanted to command a phalanx, so that is what you see."

Shimri spied the governor from his position on the wing of the phalanx. He shouted orders to halt the phalanx. With sarissae raised straight up, following Shimri's orders, the entire unit turned in unison and faced the governor and his commander. In a uniform motion, each man clasped his right fist to his chest and saluted the two men on horseback. Apollonius and the commander returned the salute. At Shimri's order, the phalanx turned again and the front ranks lowered their sarissae to simulate an attack.

As the phalanx charged across the field, Apollonius said to the commander, "Put them at the front of the army in the morning."

"At the front, Sir?" The commander was surprised and puzzled. "Why? Because they are Jews? You know the rebels will not hesitate to attack other Jews."

"Exactly," said Apollonius. "Why lose our own people when Jews can die in their place? Let them go down first. After all, they are only Jews."

Apollonius pulled his horse around and galloped across the field back into the city. The commander waited a few moments, watching the unit of Jews charging across the field, before pulling his own horse around and trotting to where the supply lines were being organized. Everything had to be in order. Tomorrow, prepared or not, the army would move south.

That same day, later in the afternoon, Judas, Oren and the old man, Lucas, rode on horseback to the top of a mountain north of Tappuah. Tappuah was the farthest town to the north that they were confident was on their side. Beyond that, the towns fell more and more under Syrian influence.

Oren knew the country well and guided them to a place where they could look out across the land without being seen. From the mountain looking northward, they could see how the land broadened out, providing level ground to a traveling army. They were certain this would be the way Apollonius would come.

That night, the three men camped without a fire lest they be spotted. It mattered little, for the night was warm. They ate bread cakes they had brought along as their sole food for the evening while they looked across the moonlit countryside and talked of the coming confrontation.

Simon, John, and Leah had arrived in Lebonah just before noon. Jonathan and Eleazar stayed back with Nethanel to bring the army that gathered at Mizpah north. According to the word brought by Simon and John, Nethanel and Eleazar would arrive later in the evening with almost two thousand men. Jonathan would wait in Mizpah for others who would yet come from other parts of Judea. He expected to bring several hundred more the next day. Judas calculated that altogether, the troops coming from the south along with those already gathered around Lebonah, they would have just over three thousand men. He had no idea what size force was coming against them.

The next day they spent the morning watching from their high vantage point. Toward midmorning they saw two riders in the distance. As they came closer it was obvious from their clothing that they were military. "Scouts," said Lucas to the others. "The army is moving. They will be several hours behind. The scouts will find a safe place for the army to make camp for the night then they will return. That will give an indication of how far they will march today. An army never moves far the first day out. It's a test of their organization. If they have forgotten needed supplies, they are not far from home. After that, they can travel considerable distances. If unhindered, I would imagine they could march all the way to Jerusalem tomorrow."

The two riders passed below the position from where the three men watched. In a short while they had passed out of sight as they followed the road around to the south side of the mountain. Within an hour, the same two riders were seen riding north again. "They've found their place," said Lucas.

"Tappuah?" queried Judas.

"I would imagine," the old man replied. "They always look for a place where there is a source of water. Towns always have wells or cisterns. An army requires a lot of water."

"Tappuah has a good well," commented Oren. "It's been there for generations."

The men watched the two riders for a few moments before Lucas spoke again. "Someone needs to warn the people of Tappuah. If this army is mostly mercenaries, they will plunder the town. That's essentially the pay they receive, whatever they can take."

Judas looked at Oren who received the message before Judas even had the chance to speak. "I will go," Oren said. "I'll tell them to evacuate the town."

Oren rose to leave. As he was untying his horse, Judas shouted after him. "Oren, tell the people to cave in the well. If they can't do that, tell them to dump all the salt they can find in it."

As he mounted his horse, Oren shouted back, "Someone may not like the idea too much. What is the town to do without a well?"

"Tell them we will dig them a new one," came Judas's response.

"Okay. I hope they understand why." Oren disappeared around the side of the mountain.

"Very smart," said Lucas, commenting on Judas's plan to deprive the enemy of water. "The more difficult their march south is, the less ready they will be to fight. That is ultimately what defeated Hannibal in the end, sheer exhaustion. The men just gave up the will to fight."

"I am glad you are with me, my friend. You can help me think of other ways to make life hard for the Syrians," Judas responded. During the next couple of hours, the two discussed various possibilities of how to aggravate their enemy.

Oren returned after having warned the people of Tappuah. "The people are leaving, heading south," he said, "and nobody will care much for the water in Tappuah. It now tastes like the sea, only saltier."

"Good," said Judas. "Now I have another mission for you. Go back to Lebonah and find three hundred of our best archers. Tell them to gather an ample supply of arrows and jars of pitch. Then tell them to rest all afternoon, because they will be up all night."

When Judas had fully explained the plan, Oren left again.

It was the middle of the afternoon when Judas and Lucas got the first glimpse of the army advancing in the distance. Judas had never seen an army marching into a campaign before. To him, it appeared as a swarm of locusts that covered the countryside. Uncertainty rose up in him.

Lucas noticed his expression and placed his hand on Judas's arm. "Don't be afraid of this army, Judas. An army is only as good as the man who leads it. Apollonius is a fool. I learned some things about the man during the time I was his slave. The main thing is that Apollonius will insist on being in charge. He may have other men that know much more about fighting than he does, but he will not let them lead. He is afraid of anyone else getting any of the glory. As such, he will be much more interested in how his army appears than in what it can really do. He will make a show of power, but whether there is really any power in the show . . . well, we will see."

They watched over the next hour as the army slowly advanced. From their high vantage point they were unable to make out individual faces, otherwise Judas would have recognized Shimri commanding a phalanx made entirely of

Jews. Shimri's phalanx led the army. The only men in front of the phalanx were a unit of ten cavalry, two of which were carrying signal banners.

"Apollonius is the fool I thought he was," commented Lucas as the advanced ranks were passing underneath them.

Judas looked at his elderly friend. "Why do you say that? What are you seeing?"

Lucas began to explain. "His first mistake is leading the army with a phalanx in full square formation. He is obviously more interested in making a show than in strategically placing his troops. Whenever they pass through a defile, the men are pressed into each other. If they are attacked from any direction but the front, they are practically helpless. It is difficult enough for a phalanx to change direction because of the length of a sarissa, but put them in a narrow space and it's all but impossible. Alexander's phalanxes were masters at changing directions, but they were fighting on the plains of Persia. At Pydna, the Macedonians were on an entirely different kind of terrain, and the Romans destroyed them. Besides, look closely at the difference between the front ranks of that leading phalanx and the ranks in the rear."

Judas peered over the edge of the rock shelf they were lying on. "The last four ranks don't have . . . what do you call those long spears?"

"Sarissae," said Lucas. "This is not an unusual practice, but it tells us something. They anticipate fighting an enemy who will attack them head on. The last ranks in a Greek phalanx are often more lightly armed than the men in front of them. If things go badly for the front ranks, the men in the rear can always avail themselves of the sarissae of their fallen comrades. These last ranks only have a sword and a wicker shield, though none of the men of a phalanx is usually well trained in the use of a sword."

Judas was weighing out everything that Lucas was telling him.

"Judas," Lucas continued. "This phalanx is no great threat to your fighting abilities, but you must choose the place of attack, and make them fight on your terms, not theirs."

"I already know the place," Judas said. "South of Lebonah."

"Good," replied the old man. "Now, look at what else you will need to deal with."

The two men examined the army that followed the leading phalanx. Behind the phalanx were what appeared to be over three hundred men that Lucas called *hypaspists*. Each of these appeared to be armed with a *pilum* and shield as well as a short sword. Lucas explained that hypaspists were positioned so as to protect the flank of the phalanx, which, as they had already seen, was quite vulnerable.

Behind the hypaspists was about eighty cavalry. From what Judas and Lucas could tell, Apollonius was riding in the middle of the front rank of cavalry. Riders on either side carried banners, one for signaling, the other being the standard under which the army marched. "That will be my personal target," said Judas.

"I wish I was young enough to join this fight," said Lucas with a deep sigh. "I would love to look Apollonius in the face just before he dies."

Judas looked over at his friend for just a moment before returning his attention to the scene passing below them. Behind the cavalry were several hundred archers who were followed by another hundred or so hypaspists. Coming on their heels, covering a considerable distance, was the baggage train. Lightly armed troops, *hoplites*, were interspersed in small ranks among various sizes and shapes of wagons being pulled by both men and animals. Judas knew enough to know that all the food, cooking utensils, tents that housed the officers in the field, and various kinds of tools and weaponry were in this train of wagons. The troops interspersed among the wagons were attached to different units within the army, as each unit was responsible for its own supplies. On either side of the baggage train, along its whole length, were two columns of infantry troops.

"Those men have sarissae just like in the phalanx at the

front," commented Judas, pointing to the columns of troops guarding the baggage train.

"They are actually another phalanx," replied Lucas. "Judging from their number, I would say it's actually two phalanxes, maybe more. On the field of battle they would form up in ranks just like the one we saw. They often march like this to guard the baggage." Lucas paused a moment before adding, "Just remember, a sarissa is useless once you get close to the man. If you get within arm's length of a man with a sarissa, his weapon is too long to help him much. Normally, from what I've seen, hypaspists take this duty guarding the baggage. It just lets you know that Apollonius is more impressed with the length of a spear than he is with what can be done with it. It also lets you know that Apollonius fully expects to pull up battle lines before the fight begins."

"I'm afraid we'll have to disappoint him," Judas commented wryly.

They continued to watch as the rest of the army passed by. Following the baggage train, bringing up the army's flank, was another phalanx in full square formation. Being at the very rear of the advancing army, there was no thought of guarding the flank of the phalanx, something that did not go unnoticed by Judas and Lucas. Though calculations were difficult, Judas and Lucas estimated there to be between four and five thousand in the army moving into their country, though several hundred of these attended the baggage.

As the army's flank was passing below them, Judas and Lucas walked their horses through the trees a distance before mounting. Once on horseback, they worked their way around the far side of the mountain back toward Lebonah. When they came close to Tappuah, they heard the blast of a trumpet. They ventured through the trees just enough to gain a vantage point to see into the valley. The army was halting. The baggage train was grouping in a tight formation surrounded on all sides by troops who were making camp for the night. There was about an hour of daylight left, so Judas and Lucas continued finding their way around the hills to Lebonah.

There was work to be done. By the next afternoon, the strength of Judas's men would be put to the test. Before then, however, something had to be done to rob Apollonius's army of some of its strength.

Chapter 32

A spirit of discontent fell over the camp once news got around that their water would be rationed. It seemed that these cursed Jews had salted the only well in the town which their brilliant officers had chosen as the place where they would make camp for the night. Although assurances had come that there would be plenty of water from the wells of other towns the next day, a negative mindset had already taken over among many of the troops who were used to a much softer life. The day had been one of the hottest of the year, and they had marched most of the day in full gear.

The camp was spread for over half a mile on the north side of Tappuah. Though the town had been deserted by its inhabitants, Apollonius and his officers had set up their tents in the midst of the camp rather than avail themselves of the empty dwellings. The evening was warm, so spending the night in an open tent would be much cooler. Besides this, in a display of vanity, Apollonius had his decorative command tent set up in the center of the camp with the army's standards and his own personal crest raised high on a pole for all to see.

The second watch of the night had just begun when the first arrows fell. A group from a larger unit of *hypaspists* was gathered around a small fire in the southwest corner of the camp. It was a scene that was being duplicated over much of the camp. No one sat particularly close to the fire because of the warm evening, but having the glow in their midst so as to see one another's faces seemed to add to the camaraderie. Conversation passed around the fire. A burst of laughter erupted as one man expressed a vulgarity. For a few moments after that, a jovial animation filled the air before things quieted to the previous level.

The man who had spoken so vulgarly moments earlier suddenly cried out in pain. Everyone looked his way. Some started to laugh, thinking he was playing a joke, but were quickly silenced by what they saw in the flickering light of the fire. The shaft of an arrow protruded from his thigh as he grabbed his leg and rolled on his side in pain. Everyone stared in disbelief. Some peered out into the darkness. They knew there were pairs of guards spaced at intervals around the circumference of the camp, yet no alarm had been raised. A thud suddenly drew their attention to another arrow sticking vertically from the ground only a few feet from the fire.

"Where did it come from?" one man shouted.

"Grab your shields," shouted someone else.

Another voice barked out, "Put out the fire!"

A few seconds later, a mound of dirt stood where the fire had burned only moments earlier. The men listened as they peered out into the countryside, hoping to see their invisible enemy by the pale light of the moon. Most of them held their shields over their heads. The man with the arrow in his leg continued to moan and struggle with the wooden shaft that was bringing him so much pain. Some distance away, on the other side of the camp, they heard shouting. Then, a few seconds later, sounds of chaos started pouring from other quarters. A scene similar to what they had known was being re-enacted all over the camp.

The camp grew dark as fires were extinguished in every corner. The previous drone of scores of conversations throughout the camp of five thousand men was replaced with an uneasy silence. An officer stepped among the group of hypaspists. "Have any of you men been able to tell where these arrows are coming from?"

One young man exclaimed, "They just seem to fall straight down out of the sky! They are coming from straight above. Maybe it's the gods. Perhaps we shouldn't even be here." Low murmurs broke out among the group.

"Silence!" shouted the officer. The men could barely make out the officer's face in the pale moonlight, but his tone disclosed his anger. They quickly grew quiet. "I want to hear no such nonsense," stated the officer firmly. "We are here in service of Antiochus Epiphanes, who is himself a god. We are obviously being attacked by the members of this rebellion we have come to quell. Now what we need to do is to find out where they are."

"Sir," one of the other soldiers called to the officer, "I think I see something."

Together, they all looked out into the countryside. A faint glow shown against some bushes some distance away.

"It's their camp," shouted the officer. "Every man, come with me."

No sooner had the words left the officer's mouth but the sky was lit by over a dozen streaks of fire rising from the ground right where the glow had been seen. Every head rose as they followed the streaks with their eyes. As the flaming missiles reached their apex, someone shouted, "Look! There are more coming from over there!" Sure enough, another dozen flaming missiles were being fired from the other side of the camp. Someone else shouted, "Look! There's more!" Before any of them hit the ground, they saw four barrages of the flaming arrows streaking into their camp, all fired from different locations.

"Quick! After them!" screamed the officer. Similar orders were heard around other quarters of the camp. The men picked up *pila* and shields and raced toward the position where they had seen the pale glow against the bushes. Behind them, the flaming streaks burst apart into a spread of flame upon the wagons carrying the baggage and the ground around them. As each arrow hit its target, the flaming pitch caked in the tow around its tip splattered in every direction, spreading the fire for several feet. Within moments, the camp appeared to be ablaze. Soldiers beat down the flames with anything they could find.

Apollonius stood outside his tent watching the debacle. "Damn these Jews!" He shouted at the officers who were standing close by. "Put a stop to this!" A moment later, he stood alone, except for his two personal attendants who cowered behind him, fearful that his wrath might somehow be vented on them.

The officer led the unit that was first attacked in a reckless charge toward the position from which they had seen the flaming missiles rise. They were about halfway there when the officer's feet suddenly hit something lying across his path. He stumbled and rolled across the ground. In the darkness, he could just make out that he had tripped over one of the perimeter guards. A few feet away lay the body of his companion. Both had their throats cut.

The officer rose to his feet and proceeded more cautiously. His men walked silently along behind him. Each one paused at the bodies of the two dead guards. The officer knew that for these men who had such limited training, war was already losing its sense of glory.

A few moments later they were at the spot where they thought they had seen the glow on the bushes. "This is where they were. I'm certain of it," said the officer in a low voice.

"There's no one here," said one of the men. "It's like they're ghosts."

"Maybe they are," said another. "Unless it's the gods."

"If you say that again," rebuked the officer sharply, "I'll kill you myself." The man said nothing more.

The officer ordered the men to crouch down so as not to be easy targets. They sat for several minutes and listened to the darkness. They looked back at the camp. The fires in the baggage had been quickly extinguished. The night carried nothing but silence. The sounds of the camp that were so prevalent earlier were now gone. Syrians, Macedonian settlers turned mercenaries, and Jews who preferred the Greek ways, were gathered in small groups surrounding the vast camp.

Toward midnight a trumpet blew from within the camp, a call to regroup within the camp confines. Everyone drifted back into the camp, leaving guards stationed around the perimeter. The officers gathered outside the tent of Apollonius, the only place where torches had been relit.

"They appear to be gone, Sir," volunteered the captain of one of the phalanxes. "I don't think we need to fear a full fledged attack tonight. I think it is just to throw us off balance. These people are skirmishers, not real fighters."

Apollonius was about to respond when suddenly arrows thudded all around them. All but one of the arrows stuck into the ground. The one arrow that found a human target struck an officer square on top of his unprotected head. It pierced the officer's skull the length of a man's thumb. The man stood for a moment staring straight ahead before collapsing to the ground. Less than three seconds later, arrows fell again.

"Put out those torches," shouted Apollonius, but it made little difference, for the sky was again ablaze with missiles streaking toward the precious baggage at the middle of the camp. Apollonius could hardly speak for anger. "Station all the men from two full phalanxes around the perimeter of the camp an arrow's shot away. Tell them not to come in until the sun rises. We must protect the baggage."

Apollonius called an officer to himself. "Place an archer beside every phalangite. Have them fire an arrow every few minutes."

"But, Sir," said the officer. "What are they firing at?"

"The people who are firing at us, you fool!" Apollonius responded angrily.

"But, Sir," the officer tried again, "they are not likely to hit anyone they can't see."

"Just do it," shouted the irate governor. "If it keeps them away from the camp, that's enough. Tomorrow we will see them in the light, and then we will kill them all."

The officer said no more, but walked quickly away to pass along the orders. Apollonius looked only for a moment at the dead officer who lay on the ground with the arrow sticking from the top of his head. "Get rid of him," he said to his attendants. Then he turned and went into his tent, taking a shield with him.

Oren looked at the men gathered around him. He could hear them more than see them. All were panting to catch their breath. They had launched their arrows until they had seen the enemy soldiers pass the edge of the camp in search of them. Then they had turned and run as hard as they could to a prearranged meeting place almost out of sight of the camp. They made no apology for fleeing. It was part of the strategy.

Every man was equipped with a bow. Two held clay jars still partially filled with pitch. Another held a jar with oil and a knot of tow in the bottom that served as a discreet torch for lighting the arrows that were saturated with the pitch.

"My fire went out the last time I ran," said the man with the jar of oil.

"There come the others. They'll have fire," someone else said.

Other men could be heard coming through the trees and shrubs from the north of where they stood. "That's okay," said Oren to the first man who had spoken. "We won't need any more fire tonight."

A similar scene was taking place far on the other side of the Syrian camp. Oren had stationed several groups on both the eastern and western sides of the camp. Some groups had as many as twenty, others as few as a dozen. Four of the groups had carried the pitch and were responsible for sending the flaming arrows onto the baggage train.

Oren gave orders. "We've done most of what we came to do tonight. Our purpose has been to tire our enemy. I don't think they will be doing much sleeping for the rest of the night. However, we need to rest, because tomorrow the real fight comes. I need about thirty men to stay here until the fourth watch and shoot volleys of arrows as you find opportunity. Don't take any chances. It doesn't even matter if you hit anyone. They just need to know you are still here. The rest of us will leave now. You follow at the fourth watch."

Oren had no problem getting volunteers. All the men he had chosen were younger men since they needed to be able to run fast. Being younger, and having discovered by now that there was only limited danger in what they were doing, some had come to regard the evening's activities as a game.

As the sun began to rise the next morning, bleary-eyed phalangites and archers stumbled back into the camp. Those that had remained within the camp looked no less fatigued. All during the night there had been the periodic thud of arrows finding their way into the camp despite Apollonius's orders that the phalangites form a perimeter outside arrow shot.

Those of Oren's men who had remained during the night had not ceased their activity right up to the time they left to return to their own camp south of Lebonah. Occasionally they launched their missiles at the phalangites, not allowing them to rest during their watch. At other times, they ventured to within only a few feet of the phalangites and released arrows into the camp. The Syrian archers released arrows into the darkness during the night but to no avail. Oren's men simply became a part of the wilderness into which they fired.

In the end, only about thirty Syrians died during the night, most of those being the perimeter guards who had been in position at the beginning of the evening. Despite appearances to the contrary, very little of the baggage had been destroyed by the flaming arrows that had rained upon them. But one thing was certain, no one in the Syrian camp had slept. When they would meet the Maccabee, they would meet him with much of their strength having evaporated into the Judean night.

Chapter 33

Upon returning to Lebonah with Lucas, Judas had met with all the leaders including the captains of hundreds and fifties. His foremost order was that the men eat well that evening and sleep as best they could, though he knew sleep would be fitful for most. Final orders were given concerning positioning and battle plans before the captains returned to be with their troops.

Judas ordered some men to draw as much water as needed from the well in Lebonah then to find a way of stopping up the well without destroying it. There was more time than had been available for the people of Tappuah, so the men constructed a heavy platform that they lowered into the well about an arm's length onto long stakes that had been driven horizontally deep into the well's earthen sides. They then poured dirt on top of the platform, filling in the opening to ground level. The low stone edge that had been erected around the mouth of the well was broken up and removed. In the end, the men walked over the area, kicking dust and pebbles as they went, until the area appeared as level ground. If anyone in Apollonius's army had any knowledge of Lebonah, they would assume the well had been filled in. Apollonius's troops would be deprived of replenishing their water supply a while longer. Little would they know that just under the surface of the ground was an abundance of clear water in a well that was being kept perpetually full by an underground spring running from the mountains nearby.

It was midmorning the next day when the signal was relayed to Judas that Apollonius's army was again moving. Signals were given by flags, the first being on the mountainside where Oren and Jadon had waved Jada the Sadducee's clothing months earlier to signal the coming of a Syrian cavalry unit. The signal was relayed down the valley to the defile along which Judas had positioned his troops several miles south of Lebonah.

Judas divided his army into two nearly equal halves, each half positioning itself along either side of the long defile. Judas had chosen the location for the narrowness of the way by which Apollonius's army would have to pass and for the ample places in which he could hide his own army. On the eastern side of the passage, where Judas was stationed with several hundred men wielding swords and spears, the land rose sharply but not too steep to climb. The hill crested about a stone's throw from the road. An entire army could hide on the other side of this ridge and the troops passing below would be unaware of it. The western side of the passage rose more gently, but the forest ran almost to the road. Nethanel commanded several hundred men on this side, some of whom waited deeper in the forest with horses.

Stretching for some distance on both sides, north of where Judas and Nethanel held their troops, were over a thousand archers. Jonathan and Oren commanded the eastern side, Eleazar and John were on the west. There was also a unit of fifty spearmen with Jonathan on the eastern side. These had been selected for their speed and throwing abilities. In the farthest position north, ready to flank the passing army, were Simon and Jadon with men ready for face-to-face fighting, though they also had about seventy archers who would initiate their part of the attack.

Judas had chosen his field of battle and tried to anticipate the enemy's every move. All during the night, he had fought Apollonius's army in his dreams. Early the next morning, he moved from captain to captain assuring himself that they understood the plan of battle. Time and again he emphasized the importance that no one move before the command to attack was given. Their victory, as in every skirmish they had been in so far, depended greatly upon the element of surprise. With each captain, as other men gathered around, Judas would end by saying, "Take courage. This is for Israel, that we may serve God as he has called us to. He will be with us as he was with our fathers. Remember how he used to fight for Israel before Israel went the way of the nations. Keep your hearts pure. Remember what you are fighting for. God will fight for us again."

Less than an hour after the initial signal had been given from the mountain, another signal was given of men approaching. Judas was confused at first, knowing it was early for Apollonius's army to have moved this far. Nevertheless, the entire army took their positions.

Shortly, two riders were seen coming down the valley. It was scouts, probably the same two they had seen the day before. Now Judas understood. They had not set up signals for what size group would be coming, so the man he had stationed on the mountain had had no choice but to signal as if the army were coming. It was just as well. If the scouts had seen men along the rode, they would have turned around and taken word to Apollonius. As it was, this was a good test of whether Judas's men could remain unseen where they awaited the approaching enemy.

Peering over the ridge, Judas considered quickly what to do about the two riders who were rapidly approaching. He sent a runner with a quick message to Jonathan.

The two riders held their horses to a slow gallop. One watched the countryside toward the west while the other one's eyes combed the ridge on the east. Nothing caused the horses to break stride. Suddenly, the air was filled with arrows. The scouts had no time to react. Both were pierced through several times and fell from their mounts. The horses broke into a faster gallop, one with an arrow protruding from its back, leaving their masters lying dead on the road.

Jonathan came out of his place of hiding with the rest of the men who had fired upon the scouts. They quickly pulled the bodies from the road and collected any stray arrows they could find. A few minutes later, there was no sign that anything had occurred.

Sometime later, the signals indicated that Apollonius's army had halted. "They've had just enough time to reach Lebonah," commented Judas to the captain of a hundred who sat on the ground beside him. "I can imagine how frustrated Apollonius will be when he finds the town deserted and with no water. He will have no choice but to keep moving."

Nearly an hour later the signal came that the army was moving again. Judas called out, "Pass the word all the way up the line. From this point on, no one is to be seen from the road. Remain in your positions and make no unnecessary sounds. The next time you move will be to kill the Gentiles who have invaded your land."

The next hour and a half seemed an eternity. The sun beat down upon the three thousand men who quietly waited, listening for the sound of the approaching army. Occasionally a man would take out a water skin and take a sip, passing it to those around him. Judas knew Apollonius's troops were not able to be as free with what little water they would have left among them.

Finally, a young man came up behind Judas and said quietly, "The signal just came down from your brother Simon that the front of the army has just passed their position."

Judas nodded, confirming reception of the young man's message. Simon was almost a half mile to the north. From behind the ridge, he looked back at his own signal man who stood ready with a flag. The signalman stood far enough back so that he could signal the troops on the eastern side of the ridge without enemy troops in the defile below seeing. A short distance away, Jonathan made sure he had clear sight of Judas's signalman.

A few minutes later Judas heard the sound of the army. It

began as a faint, distant thunder, but then the earth rumbled from the movement of five thousand human feet, horse hoofs, and baggage wagons. As they grew closer, Judas noticed that there was little talking among the Syrian troops. The spirit of this army had changed from what it was the day before. Even from their vantage point on the mountain, farther away from the passing army, Judas had been able to hear the voices of men who reveled at the thought of plundering the Jews. Now every expression was sullen. They had been more than a day without sleep, and the lack of water was obviously taking a toll as well.

Judas was startled when he realized that the first voice he clearly heard was a voice he recognized. He raised his head just high enough to see the man who had spoken. Immediately below him, he clearly recognized Shimri in the front left corner of the leading phalanx. Shimri was in the full dress of a phalangite calling orders for the ranks not to break despite the tight confines of the defile through which they were marching. Shimri's face was not clearly visible because of his helmet, but Judas knew it was him. Judas noticed that the men in the phalanx were marching so closely together that their shoulders were almost touching. They held their *sarissae* in the vertical position typical for a marching army.

Judas heard another voice that spoke above the steady roar of the moving army. He looked back and saw immediately that the owner was in the same position he had been in the day before. It was Apollonius, sitting midway the front rank of the cavalry. The cavalry was in a narrower file than what Judas had seen the day before. The gorge through which they were marching had forced them into ranks of six. Apollonius was in a foul mood and was shouting to the ranks in front of him not to slow their march.

Turning to the captain beside him, Judas said, "Our time has come. Tell your men to be ready." The captain looked around at the troops beside and in back of him and the word was passed with simple gestures. Judas looked at the young man behind him who was holding his signal flag at the ready.

Judas made a quick chopping motion with his hand, the prearranged sign that the signal was to be given. The flag raised and waved from side to side. What happened after that became a mark in history to oppressed people everywhere.

The fifty men charging down the hill with spears in their hands were first seen by the ranks of archers marching behind the cavalry. No trumpet had been sounded and no cry had been raised by the attackers, so no sound above the rumble of the advancing army caused the men on horseback to turn to their attackers. When the archers cried out, the men on the slope let go their spears into the backs of the cavalrymen, some of whom were still looking about trying to understand the cry raised by the archers. Several of the cavalrymen fell, pierced through by pila that had been captured from their compatriots in other smaller battles.

The archers in ranks behind the cavalry immediately readied arrows to shoot down the group of men that was small compared to their hundreds, but their effort was thwarted by their own general. When Apollonius turned and saw the Jewish men who were now quickly retreating up the slope down which they had come, he swung his horse around and called out to the horsemen around him, "After them! Don't let any of them get away!"

The cavalry on the side toward the slope turned and charged up the hill after their attackers, cutting off the line of fire for their own archers. As they charged, the few horses that were now riderless were startled and bolted in whatever direction would take them from the chaos. Some leapt into the ranks of hypaspists in front of the cavalry, some into the tight ranks of the archers behind.

The Jewish spearmen disappeared over the ridge. The cavalry horses struggled to dig their hoofs into the hard earth on the slope, but only for a moment. The top of the ridge suddenly came to life with archers for nearly the length of the entire Syrian army. In the same instant, the deafening blast of many shofars resounded along the length of the ridge.

Judas bolted over the ridge as he shouted above the blast of the shofars, "For the God of Israel!" He charged down the slope clenching two pila in his right hand. On his heels were more than a hundred other men, each man similarly armed. Judas threw one pilum into his left hand so he could launch the other with his right hand. His powerful arm hurled the spear into the hypaspist on the end of the front rank behind the leading phalanx. The man had begun to raise his own spear as he held up his shield for protection, but Judas's spear stopped him cold as it pierced his shield and pinned it into his chest. Judas tossed the other pilum into his right hand and hurled it at the man closest by the one he had just killed. The spear hit the man's shield at an angle and glanced off into the leg of the man beside him. His hands now empty, Judas drew his sword and threw himself into the ranks of hypaspists, slicing the air and any Syrian who was breathing it.

Those who charged with Judas threw their spears and followed him into the fray, attacking the hypaspists and the flank of the phalanx. Because of the tightness of the ranks in the defile, most of the three hundred hypaspists were of little help to their comrades on the front edge of the fighting. During this time, the five hundred archers on the eastern ridge rained death upon the phalangites who were guarding the eastern side of the baggage train as well as upon the cavalry who were trying to make it up the hill. One of the horses that had nearly crested the hill lost its footing in the mayhem and fell to its side and rolled to the bottom of the slope, thrashing its massive body as it went, not only crushing its rider but knocking the feet from under the horses below it on the slope.

Seeing his flank was being attacked, in an act of desperation, Shimri tried to reverse the direction of his phalanx. No sooner had the men turned and begun lowering their spears but another hundred of Judas's men bounded over the ridge attacking them from what had been their front just moments earlier. The unit of cavalry that had led the army jumped into the fray amidst the men pouring over the ridge, their swords slashing into them. In a few seconds, another hundred men poured over the hill. The men of the phalanx realized immediately that if they continued to try to maneuver the cumbersome sarissae in such tight confines they would be slaughtered. Some tried to throw the heavy spears, but most just dropped them and drew their swords.

The commander of the Syrian archers inflicted the greatest harm upon their attackers. As the mayhem continued on the eastern side of the army, he got the attention of his captains, and they began to shout out orders together. The Syrian archers released a volley of several hundred arrows upon the ridge above them. Jewish archers, unable to protect themselves from such a hail of missiles, fell under the volley. The Syrians strung arrows for another volley, the commander turning them to the slope just above the leading phalanx where an endless stream of spearmen continued to pour over the ridge.

Nethanel had held his troops back in the trees watching. All the attention of the Syrian forces was turned to the eastern ridge. As soon as the attack had begun, the horses had been brought up. Nethanel waited with a spear in his hand on one of the horses. The men under his command watched for his move.

As soon as Nethanel saw the Syrian archers release their first volley, he kicked his horse and charged toward the middle rank of archers. He threw his spear as he went then drew his sword as the horse bolted into the midst of the startled archers. Thirty more horsemen were soon trampling them as swords were swinging over their heads.

The surprised cavalry on the western side, who were struggling to find a way through their own hypaspists to fight Judas's men, turned when they saw the horsemen bound into the midst of the archers. As they turned, several hundred spear wielding men ran from the trees, stopping the Syrian challenge to their own horsemen.

The entire western side came to life. Eleazar and John shouted commands along the long line and arrows rained upon the troops guarding the baggage. Many of the Syrian troops hid behind the wagons for cover.

The captain of the rear phalanx saw the chaos. Cut off by the baggage train from the rest of the army, he made quick calculations of how to best handle the situation. In a quick decision, he split the phalanx into two sections in an attempt to charge it down each side of the army despite the unevenness of the ground they would have to negotiate. No sooner had the phalanx begun to separate and charge with sarissae lowered than cries came from the rear. He turned to see archers on the hills on both sides at his flank, their arrows having already taken out several of his rear guard. He shouted orders to turn the attack against this new threat. Each half of the phalanx raised spears and lowered them in the new direction of attack. They began to advance up the hills on each side. As they crested the hill, the archers fled. In the meantime, Simon and Jadon had charged their men in between the two halves of the now divided phalanx. As had happened at the front, the men of the rear phalanx dropped their sarissae and began fighting hand-to-hand.

The battle raged for about twenty minutes. For the last ten minutes, all the archers on the hillsides could do was to take potshots at the Syrians hiding among the baggage train. The survivors of the phalanx in the rear broke and ran first, a fourth of their number depleted. Their position had left them cut off from the rest of the fighting force, and they saw no alternative but to flee.

The battle was fiercest in the midst of the hypaspists where Judas had led his men. These seemed to be the best trained troops of the Syrians, besides being supported on one side by the Jewish phalanx and the cavalry on the other. This was the greatest concentration of the Syrian forces, and Apollonius was right in the middle.

Judas saw a sudden opening as a hypaspist fell under the thrust of his sword and leapt into the midst of the cavalry. One rider swung his sword down at Judas, but Judas leapt out of the way and swung down with a rapid slice onto the rider's leg just above the *greave* protecting the cavalryman's leg from the knee down. Judas felt his sword hit bone as it sliced across the man's thigh. Blood spurted out onto the ground that was already red from the blood of others. Judas could see the man's face going white, his senses dulling as the blood drained from him. Judas made a rapid thrust upward that buried his sword in the rider's side.

As Judas struggled to extract his weapon from the Syrian's side, he felt a slice down the back of his arm. He winced with pain and jumped quickly to the side, leaving his sword in the body of the Syrian. He turned to see who had struck him. It was Apollonius. Apollonius would have easily killed Judas as he had swung down into the side of Judas's neck, but his horse had jumped just as he had swung and had pulled him away. Before Apollonius could raise his sword again, Judas grabbed his leg with both hands and spun with his hands over his head, wrenching Apollonius's leg and catapulting him from his horse. Holding tightly to his sword as he landed on his back, Apollonius rolled and spun onto his feet. Judas stood with his hands extended on either side ready to counter whatever move Apollonius made. Blood poured from Judas's arm, not the only wound he had from the fighting but definitely the most serious.

Another Syrian cavalryman saw the governor on the ground in front of the Jew and attempted to cut the contest short. He charged his horse toward Judas, but Nethanel, who had been cutting his way through the archers to the cavalry bolted his horse into the charging Syrian and impaled him on his sword.

Three times, Apollonius swung his sword at Judas. Each time Judas jumped just out of reach. On the fourth time, Judas smashed his fist into Apollonius's face, cutting his hand on the cheek guard of Apollonius's helmet. Apollonius lost his bearings just long enough for Judas to wrap his hands around the hand with which Apollonius gripped the sword. Now it became entirely a contest of strength. With his free hand, Apollonius would alternate between grabbing Judas's hands and smashing Judas in the face. But Judas did not let go. Inch by inch, Judas turned the tip of the sword to the Syrian governor's neck. Apollonius frantically struck Judas and tried to kick him in the groin, but Judas seemed to feel no pain. When the tip of the sword came under Apollonius's neck, frantic fear filling his eyes, Apollonius asked with strained words through clenched teeth, "Who are you?"

Judas looked him in the eyes, "I'm Judas, the Maccabee, best friend of a slave named Lucas. This is for all the abuse you gave him and those like him." Fear had so seized the Syrian that the death stare seemed to have already taken command of his eyes. In one powerful lunge, Judas thrust upward, pushing the sword into Apollonius's brain, killing him with his own sword.

Judas withdrew the sword and let Apollonius drop to the ground. He stood over the body for a moment. The cavalrymen close by realized the impact of what had happened and were pulling their horses back away from the fallen governor while protecting themselves from the battle still raging on every side. Nethanel pranced his horse around Judas, threatening any who came near with his sword in his outstretched hand. Judas looked up at Nethanel and shouted through the melee. "Sound the shofars!"

Nethanel shouted until his message was relayed to the men still on the ridge. Suddenly, the air filled with the blast of the shofars. For just a moment, the noise of the battle stilled. Judas seized the moment. Before any other sound could be made, he shouted, "I have killed Apollonius! I have killed him with his own sword!" At the sound of these words, all fighting completely stopped. All that could be heard was the moans and heavy breathing of exhausted and wounded men.

Judas continued in a strong voice. "Leave our land. God gave this land to us. Return to your country and leave us in peace. If you come here, trying to force your Gentile ways on us, you too will die. You are not welcome here." Judas held the sword high above his head. "With this sword, I will lead the armies of Israel, and we will drive you from our land. With this sword, Jerusalem will again be ours, and you cannot stop us. Tell this to your king. Whomever he sends against us, we will crush. And if he comes himself, we will drown him in the blood of his own army."

Silence seized the air for several long moments. Suddenly,

one of the Syrian cavalrymen kicked his horse and bolted across his own archers out of the field of battle and raced northward. Moments later, enemy soldiers of every sort fled, most to the north, but some toward the south, toward Jerusalem. A few minutes later, any member of the Syrian force still able to leave by his own strength was gone. The Syrians made no effort to take their wounded with them.

Judas looked up the defile in the direction of Lebonah then toward the south where Shimri had commanded a phalanx against his own people. The bodies of almost a third of the phalanx lay dead or wounded on the blood-soaked ground. The others had fled toward Jerusalem. Judas wondered if Shimri lay among the dead but did not think long upon it.

Judas looked around at the faces of the men who were gathering around him. Some were wounded and bleeding. All were splattered with blood. Judas looked again across the field and knew that many of the bodies that lay across the field were his own men. His thoughts about those who had died and the sheer exhaustion from the battle was about to take over his spirit when Nethanel said quietly in a tone that spoke reverence, "Maccabee."

Another soldier, still holding a bloody sword in his hand, repeated the word as he looked at Judas. "Maccabee!" Others began to repeat the word as they encircled Judas. Within a few moments the cry had taken the entire field of battle, from the archers who still lined the eastern ridge to the units that had fought the Syrian army's flank and were now making their way along the baggage train to the front. Three thousand men chanted the word over and over. "Maccabee! Maccabee! Maccabee!" For that moment, they no longer saw the death that lay around them. They saw hope. They saw victory. They had defeated the army of the Syrian governor of Judea, and at the moment, they felt invincible. The Maccabee would lead them.

Judas raised his sword high in the air. Voices quieted. He shouted out, "Today, we defeated the army of Apollonius. Tomorrow, we take Jerusalem!"

A shout erupted among the army of Jews that shook the ground. The fleeing survivors of Apollonius's army, now some distance away, heard the roar and sped their flight. How could Apollonius have been so wrong? Surely the king would not allow this to stand. He would send another army, only this time, they would be better prepared for this beast they had awakened.

Chapter 34

Shimri had difficulty focusing on Lysimachus in the flickering light of the torches. He tried to remember when he had last slept. Excitement had robbed him of sleep the night before they marched out of Samaria. His heart had been bursting with pride, knowing that the phalanx he commanded would march at the head of the army. There had been no sleep the next night because of the continuous harassment of the camp by a handful of the rebels. Thankfully, Apollonius had called upon two other phalanxes to set up a guard around the perimeter through the night, but still there had been little sleep for those who had remained in the camp. About the time one would doze off, a shout would come from someone close by because an arrow had suddenly hit the ground beside where he lay, or worse, someone had actually been struck by an arrow.

Finally, there was the humiliating defeat just that afternoon. Shimri had fled with the survivors of his phalanx. One of his men had captured a horse he had found along the road south of where the battle had been fought, evidently the horse of one of the scouts that always preceded the Syrian army. Shimri had ordered the man to relinquish the horse to him. When the man had refused, Shimri had pointed his sword at the phalangite's throat before the man could react and threatened him with his life. The terrified and exhausted phalangite had surrendered the horse and Shimri had charged away on horseback toward

Jerusalem, leaving the exhausted men of his unit to fend for themselves as they too made their way toward the city.

Lysimachus eyed the bedraggled Jewish traitor. "Let me see if I understand what you are saying, Antigonus. You want me to send my troops to Mizpah, where fifty of my best cavalry have already been humiliated, not to mention the hundred infantry whose corpses the vultures have already picked clean in the hills outside Mizpah, while there is an army of thousands, no doubt, coming this way. And you want me to do this to rescue a hundred or so Jews that you yourself abandoned."

"I did not abandon them!" Shimri retorted sharply, reserves of anger rising in a mind almost too tired to feel emotion. "I came ahead on horseback to procure your help. When I came close to Mizpah, even from a distance I saw that it was an armed camp. When my men pass close to there, they will be spotted from one of the rebels' towers, and they will be slaughtered."

"Why did you not turn your horse around and go tell your men to avoid Mizpah?" the garrison commander challenged. "Instead, you continued on to Jerusalem where you knew you would be safe."

Shimri flushed at the accusation of cowardice. "Sir, I watched hundreds of men die today. I have blood on my own sword." Shimri drew his sword and threw it clanking across the stone floor. "I demand that you send someone to the aid of these men who have fought on the side of your king."

"Antigonus!" shouted Lysimachus. He refused to be challenged so blatantly by this traitorous Jew. "Do not presume to give me orders. I am the one in command here, not you."

Even though his mind was clouded by fatigue, Shimri knew he had crossed the line. He looked down at the floor and spoke in a quieter tone. "Then just send someone to warn them. That's all I ask. If they make it here, they can join your garrison. They are trained soldiers. You may need them in days to come."

Lysimachus stared at the young Jew for a long while.

When he spoke again, he, too, spoke in a softer tone. "What you say may be true. I may need these men." Lysimachus walked to a window and, for a few moments, stared down into the torch lit central courtyard of the citadel where a captain was dispatching guards to their posts around the city for the night. "I will send riders out to meet your men, to steer them around Mizpah. I will only send two, and I hope they find them in time. If they are spending the night in the forest, they may be difficult to find."

Shimri welcomed the commander's new tone as well as his words. His guilt over having left his men was somewhat assuaged. "The men were so tired, I feel certain they are already sleeping in the woods somewhere. But if someone can be on the road above Mizpah by morning, they should meet them as they continue toward Jerusalem."

"And what about this army that is behind them?"

Shimri had no answer for this question. "What do armies do when they have won a victory?"

Lysimachus continued to stare out the window. "They celebrate, I suppose. Perhaps that will hold them where they are for a day." Lysimachus felt a heaviness come over his spirit as if the air had suddenly grown more dense. "Are you sure Apollonius is dead?"

"Yes, Sir. I saw it myself. I saw Judas standing over Apollonius's body, holding the governor's sword in his hand. Judas boasted that he had killed Apollonius with his own sword."

"Judas?" Lysimachus turned from the window and looked at Shimri. "Judas the Maccabee?"

Shimri hated the name. More than that, he hated the fact that another was getting glory that he so desperately wanted. "Yes," he replied in disgust. "The Maccabee."

Lysimachus said nothing for a long while. He turned again to stare out the window. His thoughts troubled him as he thought on the future. He was holding the woman that belonged to this one the people called the Maccabee. Though they had never looked upon one another's face, this Maccabee no doubt regarded Lysimachus as his greatest enemy. Now the Maccabee had defeated a Syrian army.

"Sir," said Shimri, interrupting the silence. "There is one more thing."

"And what is that, Antigonus?" The commander did not turn from the window.

"The last thing I heard Judas say, before we made our escape, was that he would come to Jerusalem, he and his army."

There was again a long silence. Finally Lysimachus spoke. "You are not telling me anything I had not already anticipated. If I were him, I would do the same thing."

"What will you do, Sir?"

"I will hold this city. That is why I am here. I will close up Jerusalem so tightly that a mouse will not be able to find a way in. From this moment, Jerusalem will be considered a city under siege."

Shimri stood for a moment longer, his mind so tired he could hardly carry on the conversation further. Lysimachus had little sympathy for the young man's exhausted state, but he turned from the window and said in his usual brusque manner, "Leave me now. I have much to attend to."

Though offended by the manner in which he was dismissed, Shimri welcomed the opportunity to seek out a place to sleep. Perhaps, he told himself, he would awake and all this would have only been a bad dream.

Judas could hardly believe what he was witnessing across the moonlit battlefield. After the battle, Lucas had walked the field with Judas. From one end to the other of the field upon which there had been such fierce fighting less than an hour before, injured men were now binding each other's wounds. Many of those without injury went about the task of burying the dead. Others took up the task of collecting weapons from the enemy dead and loading it on the baggage train. Just as the sun was setting, they led the Syrian baggage train, now loaded down with spoils from the

Syrians as well as many of their own wounded, away toward Mizpah. Most of Judas's army went as well. They would stop to camp a few miles down the road, but most wanted to be away from this place where they had seen the deaths of many of their friends. Judas left a sizeable contingent in Lebonah under the command of John, Oren, and Jadon to watch the northern front.

As they had walked the field together, Judas pulled at the bandage that had been wrapped to close the deep wound in his arm as he questioned Lucas. "What do the Greeks and Romans do with the enemy wounded?"

Lucas looked up at the man he regarded as a hero, always amazed that Judas would seek his advice. "Oh, you needn't worry about these wounded here. I believe most of these men are mercenaries. Once you have left the field, their friends will come back and take care of them. That's the way it is always done."

Judas did not understand the touch of sarcasm in Lucas's voice. Not wanting the burden of the many men who had fought for Apollonius who now lay wounded across the field, Judas ordered his men to clear the battlefield as quickly as possible and to make way for members of the enemy army to come take care of their own.

In the second watch of the night, Judas sat with Lucas on a ridge some distance from the defile in which the enemy wounded yet lay. He had a clear view of the field, even though the dim light made it difficult to make out much detail. Some other men sat with them. Behind the ridge, horses were tied to a line in case they needed to quickly leave. Judas did not plan on a fight this night. He simply wanted to see what part of the enemy army returned.

They had been talking quietly about the events of the day when suddenly Lucas pulled at Judas's arm and pointed. Judas peered through the darkness. Coming through the trees from the western side of the defile were what may have been as many as fifty men. The men on the ridge watched closely as they saw the group scatter themselves around the battlefield. Suddenly, a cry pierced the night. Everyone looked in the direction of the cry. Before they could discover where the cry had come from, they heard another choking scream from another direction. Then they heard another and another.

Judas looked incredulously at Lucas. "They're killing their own men."

Lucas just stared across the field. It was something he had seen many times before. "It's the way of mercenaries, especially those who come from the Greek states."

"But why?" queried Judas, still not believing what he was seeing and hearing. "Why would they do that?"

"Two reasons," replied Lucas in an emotionless tone. "Mercenaries fight for profit. You don't have to share the profit with a dead man. They didn't profit anything today, but there will be other battles. To them it's just business. Secondly, mercenaries fight for whoever hires them. They don't fight because they have any particular loyalty to a king or to a cause. They know that these same men they are killing now, if they were to be taken by you, may wind up hiring out their services to you. Whoever they kill now may be one less person to fight in the future."

Judas continued to stare across the field. "I never cease to be amazed at the things these Gentiles do. First you see them exercising naked, not caring who sees them, then you see them killing their own men. And it's all just business. That's just the way they do things. Indeed, they worship a different god." Judas looked a moment longer then stood up. "Let's go. I've seen enough."

Judas, Lucas, and the others with them mounted their horses and rode to the camp, leaving the killing field behind them. At the camp, Judas gave orders to the captain of a group of fifty to return to the battlefield the next day to clear the road and bury the enemy dead. He and the remaining army would travel the rest of the way to Mizpah. From there, with an army already intoxicated with its own success and enriched by the spoils of the Syrian army, he would stage his assault on

Jerusalem. Surely the Jerusalem garrison would be no match for him. He would return Jerusalem to the people to whom it rightfully belonged, and he would return Rebekah to the one to whom she belonged – himself.

Chapter 35

Judas waited five days in Mizpah to allow the men to rest and recover from their wounds before continuing the march to Jerusalem. He later realized this to be a mistake. His army was already reduced in size by the contingent he had left in Lebonah. Some of the wounded he had in Mizpah would need longer to recover before they would be able to fight again. But the greatest toll was taken by the simple passage of time. During the five day delay, the fire in the spirits of many of the men simply died. Had they not waited, but gone straight to Jerusalem, nothing could have stopped them.

During the five days in Mizpah, some of the men began to think about their families. They thought upon their brothers who had fallen in the fight against Apollonius, many of them leaving behind wives and children. Their minds turned to crops that needed tending or other work that required their attention. The garrison in Jerusalem was not the same threat to their towns and villages as an invading army had been. They had already seen that with Judas controlling the countryside, the garrison seldom left the city.

By the end of the five days of rest, a major portion of Judas's army had simply gone home. The Hasidim remained as zealous as ever and remained with Judas, but when the army marched out of Mizpah to Jerusalem, there were less than a thousand men. Though the Hasidim would willingly die for the privilege to once again worship in the temple court, Judas did not want them to die in vain. He had learned to weigh the odds, and the odds were less and less in favor of their taking Jerusalem.

Judas's heart was heavy. Would he ever see Rebekah again? Was she well? Was she even alive? How quickly things could turn. After such an overwhelming victory only five days earlier, now he felt nothing but defeat. Most of his army seemed to have evaporated.

"Are we foolish to try?" Judas said to Simon, who was on a horse beside him at the head of the army. "Most of our army has disappeared. Their hearts turn so quickly to other things."

"Now you know how Moses felt," commented Simon.

Judas knew well the history of which Simon spoke. Time and again Israel had experienced miraculous deliverance under the leadership of Moses, but time and again the people's loyalties would stray.

"God will do everything in his time," continued Simon. "Perhaps there are a few more battles to fight before we actually take Jerusalem, but we must never rest until Jerusalem is ours. We will never be free so long as the Syrians hold the heart of our country. And the Hasidim will never leave you, so long as they know your goal is Jerusalem. The others, the ones that left, will only fight when they fear they might suffer some personal loss. Just like the pagans, their god is really themselves. It's always been that way. It's always the minority who have a true zeal for God. Our history tells it all. It's the holy remnant that is the preservation of the nation. It's no different now. But they will come when they see it is in their self interest. They just haven't seen it yet."

Judas looked up the road to see Joseph and Azarias approaching them on horseback. They had so bemoaned being left out of the battle once they had received word of the victory that Judas had put them out front in the campaign for Jerusalem. The two men pulled their horses up in front of Judas and Simon.

"The city is locked up tight and guards are watching from

the top of the walls," said Joseph.

Azarias, anxious to be in a major battle, interjected before Judas could respond, "But you know that a couple of sections of the wall haven't been built all the way up ever since Antiochus cut breaches in it on his return from Egypt. It wouldn't take much for us to cross over in those places. With ladders or some sort of siege platform, we could do it."

"Of course, those are the most heavily guarded sections of the wall," added Joseph, more prone to weigh the dangers than was Azarias.

Judas looked in the direction of Jerusalem. The moving army slowed to a halt behind him. The city was not yet in sight, but they all knew it was not far away. Judas knew well the sections of the city wall that were still in the process of being rebuilt. Though Antiochus had entered the city without a fight on his return from Egypt over two years earlier, he had cut two breaches in the wall so the city would be defenseless against him in the immediate future. Only when the citadel that housed his garrison within the city had been built did he allow the reparation of the wall. Though the breaches were now closed, the building of the wall to its previous height was still a work in progress.

Judas stared into the distance as he pondered what Joseph and Azarias had been saying. Azarias, true to his restless nature, started to say something to induce immediate action on Judas's part. "We can cross the wall if we just . . . " Joseph quickly reached across from where he sat astride his mount and put his hand on Azarias's shoulder. When Azarias looked to see why Joseph had touched him, Joseph simply shook his head, indicating to his anxious friend not to speak. It was not his place to try to persuade the Maccabee. Besides this, Joseph knew from previous experience that Judas was in the process of painting a picture in his mind of how the battle for Jerusalem would be fought. When he completed that mental picture, he would give the orders that would make it a reality.

Dropping his gaze from the distant horizon, Judas looked at the men around him and spoke decisively. "We will divide the army into six parts. We will remain out of sight of the city until it begins to get dark. Once darkness falls, we will set up six separate camps surrounding the city. We will set up far enough out so that no one on the wall will be able to tell how many of us there are, but at night we will light enough fires so it will appear as if we have many more men than we actually do. The people in the city can last several months under siege, but eventually, they will have to come out against us. Only in the open field will we have the advantage."

Judas could see on the men's faces that they weren't sure of the plan. "We must be the ones to set the terms of battle," he reminded them.

Azarias, not to be silenced any longer, blurted out, "But if we build a siege tower, we can cross the wall."

Judas looked at the headstrong young man. "Very well, build your tower. There will be plenty of time for it. But understand that we have no element of surprise here as we have always had before. In coming weeks, we may actually use your tower. So build it. In the meantime, we will make sure the Syrian garrison does not forget that they are prisoners in the city they think to keep from us.

"Tomorrow, I will ride to the wall and challenge Lysimachus to surrender Jerusalem to us. He won't do it, of course, but he will know we are here, and he will know he is alone, cut off from all outside help. In time, Jerusalem will be ours."

Seron had sought an audience with Lysias as soon as word of Apollonius's death had reached his ears. Now he stood across a heavy wooden table from the man who was second only to the king. Maps were rolled open on the table, maps that showed all the territory under the supreme governor's authority, from the Euphrates to the borders of Egypt.

Lysias looked from one map to another as he questioned Seron. Seron tried to answer Lysias's questions with just the right measure of confidence, fearing that any appearance of overconfidence would lessen him in his superior's eyes.

"I have an army ready to field," he said to the governor. "We will defeat this renegade who has time and again insulted our king. All I seek is your permission to do so."

Lysias looked at the ambitious young general through narrowed eyes. "Everyone who has come up against this Maccabee so far has underestimated him. What makes you think you will do any better?"

"I have an army of trained men," Seron replied proudly, "not a citizens' army like Apollonius put together. He was doomed from the start with the ragtag bunch he had."

"I admit," said Lysias, "Apollonius was perhaps hasty and led out his army before it was ready, but he also had some good men with him. I have spoken with some of them. Some are men I have led in battle myself. From what they have told me, this Maccabee that everyone is talking about is no ignorant peasant. The men with whom I have spoken told me about the way he fought. It seems he was in command of the battle from the very beginning. He chose the terrain. He managed to bring our army to the point of exhaustion before they even had a chance to fight. He deprived them of water. He set the terms, and Apollonius was helpless to counter him."

"You have made my point for me, Governor Lysias." Seron weighed every word of Lysias in formulating his reply. "Apollonius entered Judea exactly the way Judas knew he would. It's because Judas anticipated his every move that he was able to control the outcome. I intend to come at Judas from another direction. I intend to descend by the coastal plain and then cut inland." Seron ran his finger down the appropriate area of one of the maps Lysias had spread before him. "There are no valleys and ravines for the rebels to hide in along the coastal plain. Then we will come up by the Way of Beth-horon. I've studied the land and the history. In past generations, the Way of Beth-horon was the way by which enemies of the Jews were most successful in attacking them. The Jewish kings, centuries ago, built fortified cities along this passage because it was such a threat to Jerusalem. The walls of those cities are in ruins now, but the way past them is still the most ready entrance into Judea. Whoever controls that passage controls Judea."

Lysias looked intently at the map as he watched Seron trace a path from Syria to Jerusalem. "I can see that you have given this some thought," he said.

"I have studied it from the first day this insolent rebel insulted our king," came Seron's quick response. "Give me your permission, Sir, and I will rid Judea of him."

Lysias continued to study the map as he ruminated on Seron's words. After a long while, he looked up. "Very well. Go after this man and his army. But do not be hasty, as was Apollonius. Take no chances. Every time we suffer a defeat, we embolden the Jews a little more. We cannot afford to lose again."

Seron struggled to hide his inward satisfaction and maintain a serious composure. "Thank you, Governor. You will not be disappointed. And your advice is welcomed and will not go unheeded. We will begin preparations immediately. The army will be ready to move within a month."

Despite his words to the contrary, Lysias could see that the determined young general had not understood him. If something did not slow him down, Seron would fall into the same trap as had Apollonius. Haste had defeated many otherwise great men. But there was more than one way to accomplish what was needed. "How many men can you field?" Lysias asked Seron, who was now anxious to escape his presence since he had gotten what he wanted.

"About five thousand, Sir."

"You need two thousand more," said Lysias.

Seron understood immediately from the governor's tone that this was no mere suggestion. "Two thousand more? But that will take at least another two months to get ready," he protested.

"Then take another two months," Lysias replied sharply.

Seron stared at the king's number two man. "Where am I to get these two thousand? You know as well as I that the funds are only sufficient for the army I am presently maintaining."

"Get them from these runagate Jews who are filling all our cities. Make them the same promises Apollonius did. Maybe they will wind up staying in Judea and leave us alone."

"But, Sir, don't you think these Jews may be more of a liability than an asset? I mean, Apollonius used them and look . . ."

Lysias held up his hand to cut off Seron. "Look, General. I'm not saying you have to use them to fight. Use them for support. Put them to handling the baggage. That will free up men who would otherwise not be part of your fighting force. But I am telling you to increase the size of your force. Now when you have done this, launch your campaign. And may the gods give you success."

Seron stood for another moment then clasped his fist to his chest and made a slight bow. He turned and left. He had what he wanted, but not entirely on his own terms. Very well, he would do it the governor's way for now. Once he achieved this victory, the king himself would reward him. There would be no more having to answer to the king's second in command.

Chapter 36

During the next three months, Judas's men settled into a routine of waiting, harassing, and deceiving. Most of the time was spent simply waiting out the time in the camps scattered around Jerusalem. The camps were pitched far enough away from the city so that the watchmen on the city walls were able to discern little about the army that held them prisoner in the city. At night, however, the watchmen saw hundreds of small fires, around which they assumed groups of men were talking and eating their evening meal together. In reality, most of the fires had no one sitting by them.

Though most of the army maintained its distance from the city, there were always men stationed close in who watched every gate. At the first sign of one of the city gates opening, a signal was relayed throughout the camps. Within seconds, units of archers dropped whatever they were doing and advanced within range of the city. Four times during the three months, one of the times being at night, small units of cavalry attempted to leave the city to seek help from Samaria or Antioch. Each time, the horsemen were forced back through the gates by a hail of arrows.

Each night, archers moved close enough to the city to pick off guards standing atop the walls. After the first week, this only worked when there was sufficient light from the moon. The Syrian guards quickly learned the danger of carrying torches as they made their patrols along the walls.

Azarias completed the construction of a massive siege tower in the camp closest to one of the low sections of the city wall. The construction itself kept a considerable number of men busy for over two months. Lucas, who had insisted on traveling with the army, helped Azarias in the building of the tower with information he had gathered during his years with the Carthaginians and the Romans. The tower had the appearance of a tall, narrow, wooden house with a height matching that of the city wall. It was mounted on huge wooden wheels. The inside had five floors, all connected by ladders. More than a dozen men could stand ready for battle on each level as the tower would be pushed to the city wall with long wooden beams by men who would be protected by the mass of the tower. On each level, there were narrow openings from which the men inside could fire arrows upon those resisting them from atop the city wall. Once at the wall, the men inside would stream up the ladders to the top level from which they would jump onto the top of the wall amidst the defending soldiers.

To assure that the tower was high enough Azarias had seen to it that the uncompleted section of the wall remained in its unfinished state. Each day he sent out archers whose sole duty was to harass the workers who were working to build up the wall. After several of the arrows of the sharp-eyed archers found their marks among the workers, all further work on the wall was abandoned. A heavy guard was maintained there by the Syrians, but they, too, endured constant harassment.

Though Azarias was anxious to see the now completed siege tower put to use, Judas held the men back from attacking the city. The spring harvest had been good over most of the countryside, but Judas knew that a very limited amount of this had made it into the city due to the influence he was already holding over most of the towns. By now, after three months of siege, food in Jerusalem was becoming a scarcity. He was convinced that the garrison commander would have to make a move soon, either to surrender or to come out to meet him in battle. Either way, it would be according to Judas's terms.

The heaviest burden weighing on Judas, however, was his daily reminder that Rebekah and her mother remained captive in the Acra. One day he voiced the complaint he had been secretly harboring against God to his brother, Simon, as they sat watching the afternoon rays of the sun reflect off the western wall of the city. "Why is it that God gives me the power to kill a Gentile governor and defeat his army, but he withholds from me the thing I cherish most?"

Simon looked across the city. From where they sat, he could just make out the tops of the towers of the citadel. Simon was well aware of what constantly pulled at his brother's heart. He admired him for the self-control not to launch a foolhardy attack against the city in an effort to rescue Rebekah. Through all the emotional turmoil he had endured, Judas had maintained the ability to calculate the possibility of success for each move he made.

Simon answered Judas's question with a question of his own. "If she weren't there, would Jerusalem be that important to you?"

Judas stared at his brother for a moment. "Are you saying that God allowed the Syrians to capture Rebekah just so I would fight to take Jerusalem?"

Simon continued to stare across the expanse between them and the city glowing in the afternoon sun. "You remember how Father taught us Solomon's proverbs when we were children? Do you remember the one that says, 'The king's heart is in the hand of the Lord, as the watercourses: he turneth it whithersoever he will?' God has many ways to turn a heart."

"I'm no king. How can that apply to me?"

"You're the closest thing to a king Israel has right now. You're the one God has chosen to lead his people. But understand this, it's still God who is in charge. He will turn your heart to accomplish his ends."

Judas turned his eyes back toward the city, to the citadel towers. "Maybe you're right. But why would God choose me in the first place? Why not you? Father knew well that you are the one who has what it takes to rule. He said so."

"Listen, Judas," said Simon. "The men follow you because you have a passion that other men do not have. There is a strength about you that refuses compromise. Even with Azarias and his men pushing so hard to attack the city with that tower of his, you won't let it happen, not yet, because you know you can't win with the number you presently have. Every day I hear you stand up to their complaints, even their accusations that you are growing soft. But you have determined that when you fight a battle, you will win it. I believe that determination, that passion, that resolve in your heart, is somehow directly connected to the woman that is in one of those towers we see over the wall there."

Judas set his gaze on one of the towers. After a long while, he said quietly, "You're right. You're absolutely right. It's because of her we must never lose. God may have reasons far loftier than that, but my reason is there." Judas nodded his head in a gesture toward the city.

Simon put his hand on Judas's shoulder and said, "Just remember, there may never have been twelve tribes of Israel if Jacob had not been madly in love with a beautiful woman named Rachel. God had bigger plans, but he started it with a man's love for a woman."

Judas looked at his brother with a slight smile. His father had been right about Simon. He was a wise man.

Another month passed. Judas was amazed at how the garrison commander continued to hold out. His own men were growing more and more restless and would have been difficult to hold back had it not been for the approach of Yom Kippur, the Day of Atonement.

Yom Kippur was by far the most important of Israel's holy days. It was the only day of the year on which the high priest entered the most holy place of the temple. Following the strict commands of Torah, he would carry the blood of a sacrifice before the presence of God to atone for the sins of the nation for the previous year. Judas and all those with him knew that no such sacrifice would be offered this year. The corrupt Menelaus had allowed the Syrians to desecrate the temple and had abandoned the holy institutions of the religion.

That did not mean that the day was without impact, however. Yom Kippur, for the rest of the population, was a day of fasting and repentance. The Hasidim, who now composed the greater part of Judas's army, not only took to heart the Levitical command that "ye shall afflict your souls" during this particular day, they enlarged upon it. In constant sight of the holy city, the seat of the holy temple that remained inaccessible to them, they decided among themselves to observe a week-long fast instead of the one-day fast which was according to the traditional interpretation of the scriptures.

Seven days before Yom Kippur, the Hasidim and others who joined with them began fasting and praying together. Each day, they recited the prayers of the prophet Daniel:

> O the Lord, to us belongeth confusion of face, to our kings, to our princes, and to our fathers, because we have sinned against thee. To the Lord our God belong compassions and forgivenesses; for we have rebelled against him; neither have we hearkened to the voice of the Lord our God, to walk in his laws, which he set before us by his servants the prophets. Yea, all Israel have transgressed thy law, and have turned aside, so as not to hearken thy voice; and so there hath been poured out on us the curse and the oath that is written in the Law of Moses the servant of God; for we have sinned against him. And he hath confirmed his word, which he spoke against us, and against the judges that judged us, by bringing upon us a great evil; so that under the whole heaven hath not been done as hath been done upon Jerusalem.
>
> Now therefore, O our God, hearken unto the prayer of thy servant, and to his supplications, and cause thy face to shine upon thy sanctuary that is desolate, for the Lord's sake. O my God, incline thine ear, and hear; open thine eyes, and behold our desolations, and the city upon which

thy name is called; for we do not present our supplications before thee because of our righteousness, but because of thy great compassions. O Lord, hear, O Lord, forgive, O Lord, attend and do, defer not; for thine own sake, O my God, because Thy name is called upon thy city and thy people.

Very little work was done during the days of fasting. Though not bound by Torah to do so, each day was treated with the strictness of a Sabbath. Some were not inclined to agree with the enlarged observance of Yom Kippur instituted by the Hasidim, but because the Hasidim held the majority, no one spoke against it. Judas allowed things to go as they did, though he worried what would happen if Lysimachus chose this time to come out against him. He needn't have worried about the enemy in the city, however, for a much greater threat was moving in his direction along the coastal plain.

Chapter 37

It was midmorning on the sixth day of the fast when Judas heard the call that two riders were approaching from the north. Judas and a few others walked out to where they could see the rapidly approaching horsemen. Within a few minutes he recognized the figure of Nethanel on one of the horses. The other was a young man he recognized but whose name he did not know. The speed with which the two men pushed their horses let Judas know that something was wrong. When they came closer, Judas stepped out and waved them down.

Pulling his horse to an abrupt stop, Nethanel jumped to the ground. Out of breath from miles of hanging on to the galloping horse, Nethanel blurted out, "Judas, you must bring everyone to Mizpah!"

Judas grabbed the reins of the panting horse to steady it before passing them to a man next to him. "Why? What's happening?"

"An army has moved down the coast. At first we thought they might be heading toward Egypt. But this morning, when they broke camp, they set a course into the Way of Beth-horon. They are coming this way."

Judas considered this news for a moment. "How large an army is it?"

"Thousands!" exclaimed the young man with Nethanel.

"It's much larger than Apollonius's army, Judas," added

Nethanel solemnly.

Judas felt his heart sink. "We have less men than we did when we met Apollonius, and most of the men here now have been fasting for six days," he said more to himself than to those around him. Judas turned his eyes toward the city and lost himself momentarily in his thoughts while others continued to question Nethanel.

When most questions seemed to have been answered, Nethanel turned again to Judas. "What do you want us to do, Judas?"

Judas did not answer immediately, his mind still lost in the calculations of men, weapons, and visualizing the terrain along which the enemy army was advancing toward them. Finally he gave Nethanel the response he was seeking. "We must meet them before they make it to the top of the Way of Beth-horon. If they make it any further, they will surely manage to get word to Jerusalem, and then their ranks will be increased by the garrison there."

The decision made, Judas began giving orders to the men standing around him. He selected certain ones to inform the captains in the other five camps around Jerusalem of the looming threat and to pass along orders to break camp and march immediately to Mizpah. One of the men registered a mild protest. "But, Sir, the men have been fasting for almost a week. They are weak."

Judas quickly stifled the protest with a sharp rebuke. "We are at war, Sir! The army advancing on us does not care that we may be hungry. They will kill us all, fasting or not. I suggest you tell the men to eat something and march to Mizpah." Judas received no further argument.

Turning again to Nethanel, Judas asked, "How many men are in Mizpah?"

"We have about four hundred men who can fight, plus there are a lot of women and children there now."

The puzzled look was apparent on Judas's face. Judas knew that less than a hundred men had been stationed in Mizpah until recently. Nethanel quickly explained. "People are fleeing the towns along the way from the coast. Most of the populations of Upper and Lower Beth-horon have come into Mizpah during the last few hours."

"Good," said Judas. "Return there immediately and put them to work. Put the women to cooking for our entire army. As you've heard, most have been fasting all week. They will need strength to fight this battle. Send riders to every town close by to call out whatever men will come. We will be there by the middle of the afternoon. Then we will see how we must fight this army we are up against."

Nethanel wasted no time in following Judas's orders. He sent the young man who had come with him to specific towns while he himself took a direct course back to Mizpah.

Azarias was torn. He was one of the few men who harbored an inward glee at the thought of a fight, yet he was reluctant to leave the siege tower he had spent two months building. "Judas," he said. "If we leave this siege tower unguarded, the garrison in Jerusalem will come out and destroy it."

Judas looked up at the looming height of the tower. "If we don't meet this army approaching us with every available man, it won't matter. We have no choice." Judas could tell that his words did not sit well with Azarias, so he added, "Perhaps God will give us a quick victory, and you can come back before anybody in Jerusalem realizes the tower is unguarded."

Azarias stood for a moment staring up at his beloved tower. Finally resigning himself to the possibility that two months' work may have been in vain, he walked off shouting orders to the men under his immediate command.

By mid-afternoon, all the army that had spent four months encamped around Jerusalem was gathered outside Mizpah with others who had come in from nearby towns and villages. Though these same men had fought with zeal and a taste for victory against Apollonius, a fatalistic spirit had overtaken the army. Six days of fasting had sapped the strength of most, and they were reluctant to enter into a new fight. One of Judas's captains, himself a Hasidim, said to Judas, "The men do not see this as a good time to engage the enemy."

Judas was sardonic in his response. "Perhaps we can send the Syrians a letter asking them to wait until we are ready."

About two hours before sunset, Judas and all his captains along with a few other select men descended the Way of Beth-horon on horseback. As soon as they came near Upper Beth-horon, they saw that the Syrian army had stopped for the night. Hiding their horses behind a ridge, they moved closer on foot to examine the encamped army. Judas studied the terrain closely and called attention to certain features of the land – the downward incline toward the west, certain ridges and dips, and where the valley narrowed.

Judas studied possibilities, but some of the men with him saw only insurmountable difficulties. "They outnumber us at least four to one," said one of the captains. Judas did not try to convince the captain of their ability to fight the army they were seeing. He simply responded, "The greater the glory."

When they returned to Mizpah, word quickly spread throughout the camp about the size army they were up against. In less than a half hour of their return to Mizpah, Nethanel came to Judas. "Judas, there's lots of murmuring among the men. I'm afraid they may be unwilling to fight. They say we can't possibly win against an army this size. And some have refused to break their fast, even though we have more than enough food for them. They say they can't break their fast until the sun sets on Yom Kippur. That's tomorrow. If they go out without eating, they won't last, not after a full week with no food."

Judas said to himself, but loud enough for those around him to hear, "The Hasidim are zealous for God, but adding to his laws at their own whims will cost them the land God gave them if not their very lives."

Nethanel, though himself Hasidim, was not offended by Judas's words, for he also had not been in agreement with the lengthening of the fast for Yom Kippur. He stood staring at Judas, trying to understand his thoughts. Judas suddenly said to him, "Get a shofar and come with me." Judas left the town and walked in long strides to the tower that had been erected on the southern edge of the town. The tower rose in the midst of where most of the army was encamped. Nethanel found a shofar and caught up with Judas. Judas took the shofar from Nethanel and climbed to the top of the tower. Once standing on the platform on top, he put the shofar to his lips and sounded a long blast. Every eye in the camp turned to the top of the tower. Judas dropped the shofar to the platform and waited until he had everyone's attention.

Illuminated by the last rays of the afternoon sun, Judas stood looking out over the sea of almost two thousand men that gathered below him. As he began to speak, a hush fell over the crowd. "Men, servants of the God of Israel, tomorrow we will go out to meet yet again an army of Gentiles that have invaded our land. I have been told that some of you don't think we can meet this army, that this army is too large for us, too strong for us. But let me ask you this: Was the army of Egypt too strong for Moses? Were the walls of Jericho too strong for Joshua? Was Goliath too strong for David? Victory does not depend on the size of the army. Victory depends on the source of its strength."

A voice from the crowd below challenged Judas. "But how can we fight when we have been fasting and praying all week? We are too weak to fight."

Judas was irritated by the challenge and issued a heated retort. "Why do you not believe in God?"

Judas could see from the way heads turned who his challenger had been. The man had a puzzled look on his face. "You have fasted and prayed for six days," Judas shouted down to the man who was now growing red in the face, "but you do not believe God will answer your prayers. Why do you pray if you do not believe God will answer? I say to you that God wants to answer your prayers, but he has called you to be part of that answer. If you believe the scriptures, you must believe that God marches before the army that fights in his name."

"But tomorrow is Yom Kippur," a question rose from another part of the crowd. "the day in which our nation is atoned of its sins. Dare we fight on that day?"

"Yom Kippur is the day we *must* fight," came Judas's strong reply. "There will be no atoning sacrifice offered in the temple tomorrow. The temple courts are trodden under foot by Gentiles. The man who usurps the position of high priest has been bought and paid for by a pagan king. How can we even pretend to ask God's forgiveness of our sins and continue to allow the merchants of sin to hold our land? If there is to be any atonement for our nation, the country must be purged of this Gentile blight that has brought desolation to our most holy place and has led the hearts of our people astray."

Judas saw from the looks on the men's faces that his words were beginning to connect with their hearts. He drew out his sword, the sword that had once belonged to Apollonius, and held it up. "I took this sword from the Gentile who brought an army against us four months ago, and I slew him with it. We defeated his army even though they were many more than we were. God gave us this victory, and God will give us victory tomorrow. Now I call upon you to break your fast. Take food tonight that you may have strength tomorrow. Not only will we defeat this army that has come against us, we will pursue them into the sea. They have come here presuming to destroy us, but they will be the ones who are destroyed. Now eat your meal tonight in celebration before God for the victory that will be ours tomorrow. Before the sun rises in the morning, we march!"

As Judas thrust his sword high into the air, a cheer rose from the crowd below. Judas breathed a prayer of thanks. The hearts of almost two thousand men had been turned, and he knew this to be beyond the power of a man.

That night Judas drew up plans with all his captains for the coming day. Nothing more was said of their being outnumbered. Instead, a fire began to build in their spirits as they looked at the battle plan Judas laid out before them. It was not the detailed plan that had been formed for fighting Apollonius, but it was a plan that had as its foundation a courage built on the faith that God would turn the battle in their favor.

Before the sun rose, the army of Jewish patriots descended the Way of Beth-horon. Guards from the Syrian camp heard the two thousand man army approaching and alerted the camp. As Judas advanced on foot at the head of troops armed with swords and *pila*, two hundred archers, commanded by Jonathan and Eleazar, went to either side and took up hidden positions within arrow's reach of the camp. Judas's entire army was on foot except for forty men that Nethanel held at the back of the army on horseback. The day before, they had seen very few horses and knew that the Syrians did not have the advantage of a sizeable cavalry.

Just as the sun was rising, the Syrian army put itself in full battle array in front of its camp. Judas held his troops quiet and still across the Way of Beth-horon, allowing the Syrians ample time to assemble. He did not want the battle to begin too soon. Instead of the element of surprise, the sun would be his ally this day.

The front of the Syrian army was a formation of two phalanxes combined as one, over five hundred men in a single formation. Galloping at a slow gait across the front of the enlarged phalanx was a horse carrying a finely armored man that Judas immediately recognized to be a general, no doubt the leader of this expedition, though Judas had not yet learned his name. Judas turned to a young man standing behind him. "Quick, take a message to my brother Jonathan who is commanding the archers on our right wing. They already have orders to begin their attack once that phalanx begins advancing. But once we engage, the whole unit must turn their attention to the man on the horse until they see him fall. Tell them to make sure they do not lose sight of him. He must be brought down."

"All of them, Sir? The whole unit is to aim for this one man?" questioned the young man who was still in his teens.

"All of them. When that man dies, it will turn the battle in our favor. Now go!"

The young man jumped out in front of the ranks and ran across in front of the men to deliver his message. Some of the men, not understanding the young man's mission, made jokes about the boy needing to relieve himself before the battle began.

Without taking his eyes off the Syrian phalanx, Judas said to Azarias, who was standing beside him, "Does everyone understand how we will take down this phalanx?"

"They understand," came the reply.

Just to reassure himself, Judas shouted across the ranks, "Now remember, men, we must do this as one man. No one get in front of everyone else."

Within a few minutes, the man on the horse had finished his speech before the troops. He trotted the horse down one side of the phalanx and took up a position just behind it. A drum began to beat somewhere, and the phalanx began to advance. Judas held his lines still. The sun rising in the east cast its blinding rays directly into the eyes of the Syrians advancing up the steady incline. Within a few seconds, several of the Syrian phalangites fell under the constant hail of arrows that had started coming from Jonathan and Eleazar's units. Amidst the cries of the men, Judas heard a sharp order barked out from behind the ranks. Immediately, the phalanx broke into a charge. The entire army advanced behind them.

More of the Syrians fell, but the phalanx continued its charge. Judas held his men back until they were but seconds away. Suddenly he turned to his own troops, raising his sword high into the air, and shouted, "No one quit fighting until the sun goes down. This day belongs to the army of God. Now charge!"

Judas started a slow descent toward the advancing phalanx, continuously picking up speed as he went. The line of men with drawn swords stayed right with him until they were running at full speed. Not only was the sun in the eyes of the Syrians who were fighting to protect themselves from the barrage of arrows from above, Judas had calculated that the terrain would allow his troops to advance at a greater speed than the Syrians would anticipate. Running downhill at full speed, the Jewish troops were moments away from the wall of deadly points of hundreds of *sarissae* held at chest level. Before the Syrians could react, the Jews dropped to the ground and slid under the extended sarissae into the feet of their enemies, slicing newly sharpened swords across their thighs above the *greaves*. Within moments, the front rank of the phalanx felt the upward thrust of the same Jewish swords, and their bodies were thrown back into their ranks behind them. The phalanx quickly fell apart.

Seeing their troops in man-to-man contact with the enemy, Jonathan followed Judas's orders and directed all his men to release their arrows upon the man on the horse that had been indicated to them. Seron was overwhelmed by the scores of arrows that came down upon him and his horse. Though he tried to protect himself with a shield he wrenched from the hands of a hypaspist standing below him, he caught two arrows in one leg and one in the upper arm on the side he had turned toward the front during the first barrage. His horse did not fare as well. Frantic with pain from multiple arrows sticking from his body, the horse leapt furiously and threw Seron to the ground. In the next hail of arrows that struck at the moment Seron hit the ground, the horse was overcome and dropped lifeless across its master, crushing the life from the ambitious young general.

Seeing their general die, the men closest to Seron turned to run but were hindered by their own ranks who were as yet unaware that Seron had fallen. Trying to push their way out of the field of battle, they began to fight their own comrades. Judas continued an unrelinquishing push from the front. Following his lead as well as the fierce slashing and stabbing of Azarias, who seemed to find pleasure with each slash, the Jewish warriors cut their way halfway through the phalanx before the men in the rear turned to escape their wrath. Looking into the dust-filled sunlight, to the remaining phalangites the army pouring down the hill appeared to be one of many thousands.

Within a few minutes, the entire Syrian army turned to flee down the Way of Beth-horon. This time, though, Judas did not halt the attack. They pursued the Syrian army for the entire day. Nethanel launched his small cavalry unit into the pursuit and cut down many more than would have been reached by the troops on foot. By the time the sun went down, over eight hundred Syrian bodies lay scattered along the Way of Beth-horon from Upper Beth-horon to Gimzo, a village only a short distance from Modin, the town where the resistance had been born.

That night, there was laughter and rejoicing in the camp at Mizpah. The men celebrated and danced until the sun came up the next morning. Very few of their own men had died in the fighting. A number had sustained wounds, but most of these were minor. This was seen by all as God's fighting their battles as he had fought for their forefathers. Now, surely, God would give them Jerusalem.

Chapter 38

Determined not to make the same mistake as before, the next morning Judas led the entire army out to renew the siege of Jerusalem. While the army was still some distance from the city, they saw a column of smoke billowing in the distance. When they came within sight of the city walls, Azarias was the first to realize the source of the smoke. The siege tower that had loomed for the past two months over the low trees that dotted the landscape on the western side of Jerusalem was no longer in sight.

Azarias, who was on foot near the front of the army, broke into a run. A few minutes later, he stood looking at the smoldering ruins of two months of work. Judas and Simon arrived a few moments later on horseback. Others on horseback had been sent to survey the countryside for immediate threats. The two men dismounted and approached the smoking pile of charred beams. Judas put his hand on Azarias's shoulder, but Azarias pulled away with a jerk and looked at Judas with tears of rage in his eyes.

"Is this the way it is, Judas? We come so close but never quite go the distance? We could have crossed the wall months ago, but you would not allow it. Now we are back where we started." Azarias fell into a lengthy tirade of criticism of the way Judas had managed the siege.

Judas allowed Azarias to continue his ranting until he had

run out of words with which to express his discontent. When the young man had finally calmed and just stood staring morosely at the smoldering rubble, Judas spoke in a quiet but firm voice.

"Azarias, you need to understand this. The battle for Jerusalem is not a battle we can afford to lose. We will gather every tool at our disposal, but we will not attack this city until I know we can make it incontestably ours."

"But we could have taken it!" retorted Azarias.

"No we couldn't!" rejoined Judas sharply. "We could have crossed the wall, but we could never have taken the city without enough troops to besiege the Acra at the same time. Azarias, you don't go into battle if you do not have the resources to win it."

The hotheaded young warrior offered no further argument but stared straight ahead. Judas put his hand on Azarias's shoulder again. This time Azarias did not pull away.

"Look, Azarias," said Judas in a more conciliatory tone. "I've never seen anyone who fights with the zeal you do. In the battle yesterday, I think half the reason the Syrians turned and ran was because they saw the bodies that you kept piling up in front of them. But not everyone fights like you. I have to weigh the possibilities of what an army can do, not one man. If all my men were like you, we could have taken Jerusalem by now. But most of these men are farmers and shepherds and the such. It's absolutely amazing what they have been able to accomplish. Twice, already, we have defeated well armed armies. But each time, we used the land itself as our ally. This time, the terrain is against us. It's a different battle."

Azarias still did not respond.

"Azarias," Judas continued after a short pause. "You and Joseph serve well together. You balance each other. Joseph has eyes that see, and you have a heart that feels. Together, you could command an army of your own. I see that happening in the future. The men look up to both of you. I've seen it. But never forget, we fight to win, not just kill. If I don't think we can reach our goal, we will not attack. If we lose the war, it doesn't matter how many Syrians we have killed in the process.

His anger subdued, Azarias reached up and clasped his hand over Judas's. "I will do anything you ask me to do, Judas, even at the cost of my own life. Always put me on the front. I was born for such a time as this. God made me to fight."

Azarias turned and walked away to rejoin the approaching troops. As they watched him walk away, Judas looked at Simon. "Do you think I told him right?"

Simon stared after the young man. "I fear that given too much responsibility, he may someday prove to be a liability. His emotion tends to overrule what little wisdom he has."

"That is why I want him working with Joseph," said Judas. "One can balance the other."

"Maybe you are right. I hope so. Otherwise, you may live to regret it. Wars are not won by people who just love to fight."

Judas looked again toward where Azarias was meeting up with his unit at the head of the army as he considered Simon's words. Simon counseled caution in dealing with this zealous young man. But then, thought Judas, Joseph and Azarias would relate to one another much as he and Simon related to each other. Judas knew that Simon balanced his own thoughts and actions. With Joseph at his side, the same could work for Azarias.

The army halted on the western side of Jerusalem and waited for the return of the riders who were scouting the perimeter. By early afternoon, most of the riders had returned and reported on what they had discovered.

Though they already knew that troops had come out from Jerusalem, the blackened remains of the siege tower lying scattered across the ground as evidence, the worst news came from Eleazar, who had explored the eastern side of the city. "I found the tracks of many horses as well as carts that seemed to come from the outside entrance of the Acra. I followed them first to Bahurim and then as far as Bethany. Both towns have been looted, stripped of all food supplies. Most of the people have left the towns, but I did find one man who told me that Syrian soldiers came along with some Jews who seemed to be working with the soldiers. They emptied the granaries onto carts and led these along with most of the livestock they could find back to Jerusalem. He also said some of the soldiers on horseback continued on toward Jericho."

Judas and the other men around him considered this news. "They are resupplied with food, at least for the people in the citadel. I doubt they care much about anyone else."

"What about these cavalry troops that went toward Jericho?" asked one of the men.

"They are going for help," said Judas. "They've gone north by way of the Jordan valley. We will have to cut off that access. An army could move down that valley before we would know it."

Though the Jerusalem garrison's activities had been a small success in comparison to the great victory the Jewish resistance had gained the day before, it proved a major setback for Judas's plans to move on the city. Still, Judas had to make sure that the garrison commander did not gain a sense of confidence from his accomplishments.

Toward late afternoon, Judas marched most of the army to the eastern side of the city and put them in formation along the base of the Mount of Olives. Only two hundred men remained behind. These remaining men he scattered around the city, placing them in smaller groups within sight of each city gate. Judas's main intent was to make a show of force within sight of the citadel.

With his army arrayed behind him, Judas slowly approached the eastern wall of the citadel on horseback with twenty other horsemen in two ranks behind him. The army moving into position had not gone unnoticed by Lysimachus, who watched from atop the wall as Judas approached.

"What do you want?" Lysimachus called to the approaching horsemen, his voice echoing back from the Mount of Olives.

"I want to speak with Lysimachus," shouted back Judas.

"I am Lysimachus. Who are you?"

"I am Judas ben Mattathias, leader of the armies of Israel."

"Are you the one they call the Maccabee?"

"I am the one. I am calling upon you to surrender Jerusalem. There is no need . . ." Judas stopped speaking momentarily as he watched an arrow curve across the sky and stick into the ground a few feet in front of him.

Lysimachus turned and shouted to the young archer who had shot the arrow. "Stop, you fool. I didn't give any order to shoot. Besides, he's too far out. You can't reach him from here."

At that instant, an arrow bounced off the stone parapet just inches away from where Lysimachus held his right hand. The ram's horn bow that Jonathan used proved itself far superior to the wooden ones used by the Syrians. Lysimachus looked back at Judas, a stunned expression on his face.

"An eye for an eye, Lysimachus," shouted Judas. "Jonathan could have killed you if he had wanted to. But there is no need for anyone to die today. Surrender the city, and your garrison and anyone else who wants to go with them can leave in peace."

"We have no need to surrender to you and your rebel army. We have men and weapons to resist anything you bring against us. And we are well supplied. It seems that going off to celebrate your holy day has proved quite costly to you. It allowed us to replenish our supply of food. We can last for months, a year if need be. By then, Antiochus will bring an army that will wipe you from the face of the earth."

Judas assumed a mocking tone. "Your king has tried that already. Twice."

"Twice?" The garrison commander looked at other men on the wall but only received shrugs and questioning looks in return.

"It seems you don't get much news," derided Judas. "Do you know a general named Seron?" Judas had learned the general's name as his troops had plundered his camp.

Lysimachus did not reply, but waited for Judas to continue.

"You will find his corpse, along with those of almost a thousand of his men, scattered along the Way of Beth-horon all the way to the sea."

When Judas said these words, a deafening cheer rose from the army arrayed behind him. The blood drained from the face of the garrison commander. After about a minute, Judas held up his hand to silence the roar behind him.

"Commander, I offer you again this chance to surrender. There is no need that you become like Seron." Judas paused before adding, "And Apollonius."

"I cannot surrender to you, Maccabee. Do what you must."

Lysimachus turned to descend the stairway from the rampart. As he did, Judas shouted after him. "One more thing, Lysimachus." The commander stopped and turned to hear what more this man he was beginning more and more to fear had to say.

"You have something of mine. If anything happens to her, if even a hair of her head is harmed, there is no wall and no army that can keep me from you." With these words, Judas pulled his horse around. The ranks behind him opened for him to pass through, then they too turned and followed. Judas motioned to the long line of troops arrayed across the base of the Mount of Olives. Slowly they faded back into the trees until not a single man remained in sight.

Lysimachus stood staring after the disappearing army that would hold him prisoner for months to come. Apollonius was dead. Now Seron was dead. If Antiochus did not send an army that could defeat this one they called the Maccabee, eventually he would have to find a way to deal with this man. Somehow, he needed to leave himself that possibility. His only hope was to care for the two women he was holding, but now one of those was sick. What would happen if she died?

Rebekah held her ear against the narrow opening. Faint as it was, she could make out the voices that were coming from outside the wall and echoing around the central courtyard of the citadel. She looked down and saw men in the courtyard looking up at the eastern rampart, listening intently to the exchange. Suddenly a roar resounded across the courtyard that sounded like thousands of voices. The stone walls of the fortress seemed to shake. Rebekah looked at her mother who lay motionless on the bed, her eyes turned toward Rebekah with a questioning look.

The roar died, and Rebekah held her ear against the opening again. A short while later, she stepped away from the window and knelt by Miriam's bed.

"Mother, it was him. It was Judas. I heard his voice." Excitement was in Rebekah's voice, but Miriam just lay on her bed and smiled a weak smile as Rebekah clasped her thin hand in her own.

"That roar. It was an army. Judas is here to take Jerusalem. Mother, it won't be long now."

Miriam still did not respond. Rebekah began to plead with her mother.

"Mother, you need to eat. If you don't, you will never get well."

Miriam tried to speak, but all she could do was part her lips to mouth her daughter's name. Rebekah looked quietly at her mother. One of Solomon's proverbs came to her mind. "A merry heart is a good medicine; but a broken spirit drieth the bones." Rebekah had watched her mother's health begin to decline the day she had pronounced Shimri dead. Now, within a few days, her own broken spirit would end her life.

Rebekah looked back at the narrow window from which she had heard Judas's voice. She had heard clearly his last challenge to Lysimachus. Hope was still alive.

Chapter 39

Antiochus had grown more sullen with each passing day. A week earlier he had returned from the eastern frontier, leaving his army under the command of Philip just west of the Euphrates. The king knew Philip to be a man of great political ambition and would hold the army intact during his absence. Antiochus had met stronger than expected resistance while trying to suppress the seditions in Persia. As a result, his army had grown discontent with the lack of plunder. If he was going to keep an army in the field, he would have to find means to reward them, so he had returned to Antioch to obtain whatever had been added to the royal coffers during the past months. However, he had found in the past week that the royal treasury would be of little use in this regard.

Now the king's surly disposition was festering to the point of open rage. Not only had the expected revenues from Judea not been forthcoming, the insurrection in that region had grown out of control. If a place as small and insignificant as Judea could rise up against Antiochus's rule, other corners of the empire could as well. This rebellion would not merely have to be crushed, it would have to be done in such a way as to strike terror in the hearts of anyone having similar aspirations.

Lysias watched the four officers leave the court. He stood in the open floor to the front and side of the king's throne. The remnants of Seron's army had begun arriving in Antioch the day before. Lysias had stood by the king as various groups of officers were brought in and interrogated. Besides the officers from Seron's defeated army, an envoy on the part of the garrison commander in Jerusalem had arrived in the company of a small cavalry unit. Lysias had talked to these alone.

"We have underestimated this Maccabee," said Lysias as the guard closed the tall doors to the hall, leaving them alone together.

"How can a fly from a hole like Judea cause so much trouble?" lamented Antiochus. "One swat should have taken care of him. But he has beaten back our armies and killed our generals. How can a mere peasant keep on doing these things?"

Lysias stared at the floor for a moment before commenting, "I wish he were on our side. He seems to be a very gifted man." Lysias's tone conveyed a sense of admiration for the Jewish leader.

Antiochus considered the governor's words for a moment. "Do you think he can be bought?"

Lysias's reply was quick and certain. "No. Not this one. He's not interested in money or land or anything like that. He just fights for this strange god of his. And the people love him for it."

"Surely he has a price. Every man has a price."

"We do have one thing." Lysias paused to consider how best to counsel the king with the information he was about to give.

"And what is that?" asked Antiochus, irritated at being kept waiting.

"We are holding the Maccabee's woman in the citadel in Jerusalem. The Maccabee has demanded her release and made threats of what he will do if anything happens to her."

Antiochus's mind quickly ran through various possibilities of how to use this woman to his advantage. "Can we bargain with her? Can we make a deal that we will release her if the resistance disbands?"

"No. This resistance is about more than the Maccabee's woman. The rebellion started well before we ever had her. I'm not sure how we can use her, but I know it won't be to make any deals."

Antiochus abandoned his idea of diplomacy, duplicitous as it was, and returned to his usual ruthlessness. "Then we must use her in such a way as to show this Maccabee that we are not afraid of him and that we will not give in to his threats. Strip this woman naked and hang her from citadel wall until the birds pluck her bones clean."

Reluctant to challenge the king too openly, yet knowing that wiser counsel was needed, Lysias commented slowly, "I would suggest a measure of caution. I fear that it is this kind of activity that has served to fuel the rebellion in the first place. If we do something of this nature, the people will be so enraged that our only choice will be their total destruction."

The king creased his brow deeply as he said in an icy tone, "Then we will destroy them. We must put an end to all this. Send in an army that is large enough to kill them all. I do not want a Jew left living in Judea. Make slaves of however many you want, but sell them outside of Judea. And destroy this precious city of theirs. Leave them nothing to return to. Let not a stone be left standing in Jerusalem. The only thing that should be left will be our own citadel."

"But, Sire, how can we finance an army that size? As you well know, the lack of tax revenue has left us with no reserves."

"Promise the men the land. If we wipe the Jews from Judea, we will need someone to occupy the land. Put the word out to the slavers. They are always ready to pay a tidy sum for a good slave. They can buy them from our own soldiers. Make great promises of the plunder, promise more than there is. You will have no problem raising an army on those terms."

Lysias knew that the king was right. The promise of plunder always worked to raise an army, especially among the mercenaries from the Greek states.

"I need to rejoin my army in the east," continued Antiochus. "When can you put an army in the field?"

Lysias would not make the mistakes that had been made

already. He knew the king would not favor a delay, but he would not be pushed into launching the campaign too soon. He searched for a way to make the delay seem reasonable. "Winter is upon us now. We will move into Judea in the spring. It will take that long to pull together the assets we will need to assure success. Nicanor and Gorgias have their armies here close to Antioch. Of course, we will need to hire many more mercenaries to augment their numbers. I will call Ptolemy from the north. He has a strong cavalry. By the time the full army is ready to march, and we have garnered the support of the slavers who will be the assurance of payment to the troops, winter will be over."

"How large an army will that make?"

Lysias stood for a moment as if seeing numbers in the air. "I estimate about forty thousand on foot and seven thousand cavalry."

"Good," said Antiochus, clearly impressed with the numbers. "Though most of my elephants are on the eastern frontier with Philip, some are still here in Antioch. Take them with you. They are always impressive in a fight."

"Thank you, Sire. I'm sure their very presence will make a statement to our own men as well as to our enemies."

"And one more thing," said Antiochus as he rose from the cushioned marble throne. "I'm leaving my son, young Antiochus, in your charge this time as I return to Persia. It is time that he learned how to wage war. I will not take him with me for if something were to happen to me and him at the same time, the Seleucid dynasty would be finished. I want him to remain here with you. Some day he will be king. Watching you deal with these Jews will show him the kinds of things he must do as king."

"But he's still a child, Sire," Lysias protested, seeking to avoid the encumbrance of managing the young man who had already developed a reputation of stubbornness.

"A child who will be king," retorted Antiochus. Without further word, Antiochus walked away into an adjoining wing of the palace.

Lysias stared after him as he went and whispered under his breath, "A king who can be killed by a friend as easily as by an enemy."

Rebekah sat on the floor quietly clutching her dead mother's hand for well over an hour before she rose and knocked on the door to inform the guard stationed by her chambers. When the door opened, Rebekah said to the guard in an emotionless voice, "My mother is dead." She then returned to her position beside Miriam's dead body.

The guard peered into the room for a few moments, his mouth hanging open. For eight months he had carried out his duty of guarding the door to the room that housed the two Jewish women. He did not know anything about them except that they were being held hostage because they were somehow important to the man they called the Maccabee. For eight months, from sunup to sundown each day he had stood in the dank, dark hall outside their chamber. At times, he had wondered who the real prisoners were, for he seldom saw the sun himself. He would only get a glimpse of the women when food and water were brought to them each day and the clay urn into which they relieved themselves was exchanged. Other than that, no one had visited them during the passing months. The guard found this curious, for he understood that the oldest woman's son, brother to the younger one, was living in the citadel and was an important man among the Jews who had adopted the king's laws of Hellenization.

The guard stared at Miriam's lifeless body a moment longer, looking for signs of life but seeing none. Rebekah did not look up from where she sat holding her mother's hand. A moment later she heard the door close behind her. The sound of the bolt turning in the lock rang somewhere on the edge of her consciousness. The room was still and empty.

A few minutes later she heard the bolt turn again. The guard pushed the door open wide and stood back out of the way for a Syrian officer to enter. The officer knelt by Miriam's bed across from Rebekah and placed his hand on Miriam's neck to feel for a pulse. Rebekah did not move except to roll her eyes up to look into the eyes of the Syrian. A few moments later, the Syrian took his hand from Miriam's neck and gave a shallow nod while pursing his lips to affirm what Rebekah already knew. As he was rising to his feet, he looked toward a sound in the doorway.

"Is she? Is she dead?"

Rebekah snapped her head around at the voice. It was Shimri. Shimri stood for a long while in the doorway looking down at his mother. As he began to walk slowly to the place where the Syrian officer had knelt, Rebekah's eyes followed him. The officer backed out of the way. Shimri squatted by the bed and reached out both arms as if to place them under Miriam's lifeless body to pick her up.

The stillness of the room was pierced as Rebekah suddenly threw herself across Miriam's body, elbows extended outward as to hold the body down. "Don't you touch her!" she screamed at Shimri in a voice rasping with venom.

Shimri jumped back, startled by his sister's actions. He started to reach out again toward the figure on the bed.

"Get away from her!" Rebekah screamed again. "You killed her. You killed Father. If you had the chance, you would kill Judas, too. Why do you hate everything that I love?" Tears of rage flowed down Rebekah's face.

"Rebekah. You don't understand," Shimri offered as a weak defense.

"I understand just fine. Everything that is good and right and decent, you're against. And you destroy anything that is not like you."

Shimri labored to bolster a firmer tone with his sister. "Rebekah. You do not know what you are talking about. Now move out of the way. We need to take mother and bury her."

Shimri reached toward his mother again. This time, Rebekah lunged at him screaming. "I said, 'Don't touch her!'"

The guard by the door jumped forward and grabbed Rebekah from behind to pull her off Shimri, trying all the while not to disturb the body over which all the fracas was occurring. He pulled her away from the bed, but not without some difficulty as she continued to struggle.

Shimri reached again for his mother's body when a voice boomed from the doorway. "Don't touch her!" Shimri looked up to see Lysimachus. Upon seeing the garrison commander, he stood up and faced him.

"Sir, it is my mother," Shimri began. "She needs to be taken . . ."

"She may have been a mother to you, but you have not been a son to her," blasted Lysimachus before Shimri could complete his sentence.

"But, Sir," protested Shimri, "you yourself have held her and my sister hostage. How can you say that . . ."

The commander cut Shimri off again. "I do what I do because we are at war. I must do what is expedient to our cause, which, by the way, also means that I tolerate the likes of you. But the devil himself would not betray his own mother."

Shimri searched for words with which to protest the commander's accusations, but seeing that the sentiments of the commander were clearly against him, he stormed out of the room past three other soldiers who had come with Lysimachus.

Lysimachus came and stood in front of Rebekah. "Release her," he commanded the guard who was still holding Rebekah by her arms from behind. The guard released his grip and stepped back. Rebekah stood without moving, her eyes cast down toward the floor.

Lysimachus examined the young woman in front of him. He had not seen her since the day she and her mother had been brought in eight months earlier, and that had only been from across the courtyard. Commanders of his stature seldom dealt directly with prisoners. This had been no different.

"Look at me," Lysimachus ordered Rebekah.

Rebekah slowly raised her eyes and looked defiantly at him without blinking. Lysimachus studied her face, now streaked with the paths of dried tears. He had a younger sister whom he had not seen for several years who would be about her same age. He wondered if his own sister had the kind of beauty that this woman did. Even in her present disheveled condition there was something in this woman that any man would desire. Rebekah's pale skin from not having seen the sun for eight months made her already intoxicating eyes all the darker. Her full lips were themselves an invitation for desire. Lysimachus understood why this woman was so important to Judas the Maccabee.

"May we take your mother to be buried now?" he said.

"Do I have a choice?" Rebekah replied bitterly.

Lysimachus did not respond. He allowed his eyes to drop from Rebekah's still defiant eyes to her thin figure.

"How do I know you won't just throw her in a pile to be burned somewhere?"

"You don't," Lysimachus said gently. "But you have my word. Your mother will be buried properly according to your own traditions. I am the commander here, and there is nothing that requires me to do this. But I do give you my word that it will be done."

Rebekah looked into the firm face of the man that had seen many battles and had himself pronounced the death sentences of others. She saw that even in a man like this, buried somewhere deep inside and struggling to get to the surface, was a sense of what was right and wrong. History, war, and politics had cast integrity into a seemingly insurmountable pit, but at rare times as this, a small glimmer of character rose to the surface of even the most hardened of men.

"I believe you," Rebekah finally said. "My father is buried in a cave on the western side of the city. I would like it if she could be buried there."

"It will be done," said Lysimachus. "The city is under siege, and my men can't leave without being attacked, but I will find someone of your own countrymen who will do it. They will not know who it is, but it will be done according to your desires."

"And do not allow my brother to attend the burial. He died to her long before she died to him. His presence would be a desecration, more so than any Gentile."

Lysimachus did not take offense at the implication in

Rebekah's reference to Gentiles. He simply said, "It will be done as you have said."

At the commander's orders, soldiers came in and bound Miriam's body in linen wrappings. Lysimachus followed them out of the room, leaving Rebekah alone once again. As the guard turned the key to lock the door, Lysimachus said to him, "I want you take this young woman out into the courtyard for an hour each day. Shackle her to yourself so that she cannot escape, but take her out where she can see the sun."

"Yes, Sir," the guard replied. As the commander disappeared into a side passage down the long gray hall, the guard added quietly, "Thank you, Sir," for now he, too, would see the sun again.

Chapter 40

It took only a few weeks for all of Judea to become aware of the army that would move against them out of Syria in the spring. Knowing it futile to attempt to hide the formation of an army of such size, Lysias sought ways to propagate the news of the coming campaign in hopes of destroying the previous resolve of the rebel fighters. Mercenaries poured into Antioch primarily from the Greek islands, but also from the towns of northern Judea where many of the Jewish citizens remained loyal to Antiochus. Lysias used some of these to spread the word to Sadducees and other known Syrian sympathizers who remained scattered throughout other towns in Judea.

When word of the campaign reached the ears of Judas, he pulled most of the army back to Mizpah, leaving a skeleton force under the command of Joseph and Azarias to continue the siege of Jerusalem. Judas knew they would accomplish little, but he hoped to isolate the city from outside communication. This effort, however, proved to be in vain.

Feeling himself out of favor with the garrison commander, Shimri escaped the city by the western gate one night on horseback. When stopped by some of Joseph's men, who did not know or recognize Shimri, the guileful young traitor addressed them in Aramaic and claimed to have an urgent message for Judas. The men allowed him to pass, but Shimri took a circuitous route for the next two days that eventually brought him to Samaria. It wasn't until he reached Samaria that he learned of the army being put together by Lysias. From Samaria he continued on to Antioch where he gained an audience with Lysias.

"You commanded a phalanx with Apollonius?" Lysias studied the young man who was making such great claims for himself. "Yes. It seems I do recall one of our cavalry officers mentioning a certain Antigonus being captain of a phalanx made entirely of Jews. What became of the men under your command?"

"Many died in the battle," responded Shimri, "but I managed to get most of them to safety in Jerusalem. They are there now, reinforcing the garrison there that is presently under siege by the rebels. The commander is very grateful for their presence."

"If the city is under siege, how did you make it out?" Lysias had learned not to trust the word of every man who courted his favor, especially the words of a man who, by his own admission, was a traitor to his own people.

"Lysimachus . . . the commander, Sir," said Shimri, showing familiarity with the garrison commander but feigning respect at the same time, "asked me if I would try to bring word to you of the present situation in Jerusalem. I pretended to be one of the rebels and managed to pass through their lines. The commander was unaware of the campaign you are presently planning. The siege has left the garrison completely cut off from news from Antioch."

Nothing the young man said contradicted what Lysias had learned from the messengers who had escaped Jerusalem when the rebels had withdrawn to confront Seron. Still, Lysias continued to raise questions in order to assure himself of the young man's authenticity.

"I have learned of a woman who is being held in the citadel. It is said that she is the wife of the rebel leader. Do you know anything about her?"

"She is my sister," came Shimri's quick response. Shimri

hoped this would somehow strengthen his position with the supreme governor.

"Your sister?" Lysias raised his eyebrows.

"Yes, Governor. But she is not Judas's wife. They were betrothed to be married, but it is a wedding that will never happen."

"How is it that your sister became our hostage?"

"I delivered her to the commander myself, along with my mother."

"Your mother? You delivered your own mother to us?"

"Yes, Sir. But she has since died. She was not in good health."

Lysias now understood what drove the young man standing before him, an unquenchable thirst for power. It was the same desire that drove Antiochus and many who served him to unmentionable cruelty. All sense of compassion was dead in such a man as this. No love remained for his family or his people, and Lysias was sure his people no longer held any love for him. Such marked enmity would serve Lysias's purposes well.

"How well do you know this Judas, the one they call the Maccabee?"

"We grew up together," said Shimri, now certain that he had won favor with the man second only to the king. "He was often in my home. I probably know him as well as anyone."

"Do you think you could lead us to him?"

"He has made his base at a town north of Jerusalem called Mizpah."

"But I don't just want to defeat his army. I want him. Not until we kill this hero of theirs with the mythological qualities the people have attributed to him can we crush the spirits of the people who follow him. I need to find this myth personally and humble him before the people in such a way that they will never have such false hopes again."

"How would you humble him, Sir?" Shimri tried to hide the sinister glee he felt boiling over in him, but it did not go unnoticed by Lysias.

"We will crucify him on the front wall of the temple in Jerusalem. The people will watch their hero slowly die and will realize that their god is too impotent to help him," said Lysias. Then he added, "Then we will destroy the temple."

Shimri paused, envisioning the scene Lysias had painted with his words. The man he had grown to hate more than any other, the man who had the kind of power that Shimri had always wanted, completely humbled. Breaking from his duplicitous reverie, Shimri said with an arrogant certainty to Lysias, "I will lead you to him, Sir. I managed to fool the rebels when I escaped Jerusalem, I can do it again. I will infiltrate their ranks and find him. But allow me one thing."

"What is that?" asked the governor, expecting a request for some sort of position, or possibly something of a material nature.

"Allow me to drive the nails."

Lysias stared at Shimri for a moment, wondering what caused this kind of hatred. After a moment, his lips widened to a smile. "Your request is granted." Shimri's smile widened to match that of the governor's.

Having found an unexpected ally, Lysias now grew more businesslike. "I will attach you to Gorgias, one of my generals. You will deal directly with him and with no one else. When our armies move into Judea, you will report to him and lead him to Judas. But first, I have a small task for you. If you can manage this, you will have already infiltrated the rebel ranks."

"What is it, Sir?" said Shimri, feeling suddenly bold enough to try anything.

"I must get a message to Lysimachus in Jerusalem. As in most siege situations, it is much easier to get out of the city than it is to get into it, so I don't expect you to enter the city. I am going to bind a sealed message around an arrow. At night, I need you to shoot the arrow over the citadel wall so that it falls into the courtyard. Someone will find it and take it to Lysimachus."

"That doesn't sound too difficult, Sir. I will become as one of the rebel archers who are presently besieging the city. At night I can easily slip out and shoot the arrow."

"Good," said Lysias. "It is important that the garrison know our plans so that they can support us from Jerusalem. Now, come with me. I will introduce you to Gorgias."

A little over a week later, just as the third watch of the night was beginning, a guard within the Acra heard a clatter on the stone pavement of the courtyard. Searching with a torch for the source of the sound, he found an unusual looking arrow. The head was blunted and the length of the shaft was wrapped in goat skin leather, tightly stitched from one end to the other. The guard could just make out writing on the leather by the light of the torch. It read, "For the eyes of Lysimachus, commander of the garrison of Jerusalem, only."

The guard wondered whether to hold the message until morning. The commander would not take well to being awakened in the middle of the night. However, if the message was of an urgent nature, the commander would hold responsible whoever delayed its communication to him. The guard ascended the stairs within the eastern wall of the citadel and awoke the commander's personal attendant. After hearing the guard explain the nature of his business, the attendant led the way to the commander's quarters. The attendant knocked loudly on the thick wooden door. He was about to knock a second time when the door flew open.

"What is it?" barked the commander, assuming they must be under attack.

The attendant showed no emotion, but simply said, "This guard has something for you, Sir." Once having done his service, the attendant backed away into the hallway.

Lysimachus glared at the guard, who was uncertain whether or not it was the proper time to speak. "Well?" snapped the commander crossly.

"This just fell in the courtyard, Sir," said the guard, still hoping his decision to awaken the commander was the right one. "It appears to be a message for you."

Lysimachus stared for a moment at the strange arrow the

guard was holding.

"I thought it might be urgent, Sir," said the guard, trying to explain his actions.

Lysimachus took the arrow from the guard and examined it closer. A moment later he looked at the guard and said simply, "Return to your duties," then closed the door.

Once alone in his chambers, Lysimachus took a sharp knife and split the stitching along the shaft of the arrow. Peeling away the goat skin, he found a sheet of thin parchment wound around the shaft. On unrolling the parchment, he saw immediately that it was a message from Lysias. He unrolled the parchment fully and spread it on a table, pulling an oil lamp closer so as to cast its light down upon the table. The message read:

> Lysias, Supreme Governor of the Provinces of Syria, Chief Minister of the Great King Antiochus Epiphanes.
> To Lysimachus, Commander of the King's Garrison over Judea.
>
> I salute you as a servant of our Great King Antiochus and commend you for your stand against the rebellion that has overtaken the region of Judea. I have recently received word of your valiant efforts through Antigonus, whom you sent to inform us of your present situation.

Lysimachus looked up from his reading with a frown. He had not seen the arrogant young Jew for several days, nor had he cared to. Still, he wondered how the young man had made it out of the city and all the way to Antioch. Returning to the parchment, he continued to read:

> I am sending you this missive to inform you of the king's directives. Due to the rebel activities that have led to the defeat of the armies led by the Syrian generals Apollonius and Seron during the past year, the king has ordered the destruction and enslavement of the entire

Jewish nation. An army is presently being prepared to invade Judea in the spring. This army will be almost fifty-thousand men and, unlike the previous efforts, will be capable of carrying out the king's orders.

You are called upon to serve the king in this campaign by working to destroy the morale of the people and to aid in the eventual destruction of Jerusalem. I have learned from Antigonus that you have in your custody the woman who is betrothed to the rebel leader. The king has ordered that when the invasion begins, you are to hang this woman from the wall of the Acra for all to see. There will be many other such displays made to dishearten and humiliate our enemies before this is over, but this one should strike at the heart of the rebel leader himself. With the help of the gods, this will serve to disrupt the ability he has already shown in warring against us.

Lysimachus first felt cold, not so much from the chill air of his chamber, but from how easily the governor was able to write about the destruction of a nation. He didn't think so much about battling armies. Men went into battle intending to kill and knowing they might be killed. He thought about the women and children who would die on a mercenary's sword just for the simple pleasure of watching them die, or of the ones who would be sold into slavery who would have been better off had they died.

When his mind turned toward the orders he had been given to kill the woman, however, his blood ran hot. The Jew, Antigonus, had informed the governor about his own sister. For the past several days, Lysimachus had watched out his window as the young Jewish beauty had strolled around the courtyard chained to a guard. He had found himself looking forward to her strolls each day, waiting secretly by his window to watch her every movement. Never before had he considered a Jew anything but a nuisance, but this woman had changed something in him. Something about the way she carried herself set her apart from other women, her strong will, and yet the gentleness she displayed, except when she had confronted her brother. She was an enigma to him. He knew he could never have her for his own. But could he kill her? If he did not obey orders, his own life would be forfeit.

The commander looked at the parchment in his hand. No one knew what was written there except himself and the man who wrote it. He held it toward the flame of the lamp but then pulled it back. Sinister though its message, this letter may one day prove to be his salvation.

Chapter 41

Judas was alerted as soon as the Syrian army began to move out from Antioch in the early spring. Not to be caught off guard again as he had with Seron, he had planted spies everywhere possible. Some had even joined the Syrian ranks, pretending to be Sadducees. These supposedly served as spies for Lysias, but when they made their covert incursions into Judea at his command, they came straight to Judas and reported everything they had learned.

By the time the massive army crossed the northern corner of the Great Plain of Meggido, Judas and his men watched its every move. As the army emerged onto the coastal plain, it seemed to stretch for miles. Thousands upon thousands of infantry and cavalry moved down the plain like a giant serpent. In the midst of the men and horses towered eight elephants. On top of each elephant was a rawhide-covered frame in which sat a pikeman and an archer. An Indian driver perched in front of the frame enclosing the two fighting men.

This army came with more than weapons of war, however. Sandwiched between the two main divisions were hundreds of wagons drawn by oxen. These wagons were separate from the usual baggage train that accompanied the divisions within the ranks. Some of the wagons were very elaborate, an indication of the wealth of their owners.

Judas and his men looked on curiously from the low-lying

hills where they hid. Jonathan, who was lying on the ridge beside Judas, was the first to inquire.

"What are those wagons? They don't look like anything we have seen with the other two armies. Do they have some new type weapon?"

Judas looked closer and spotted the rows of chains and iron shackles hanging on the outsides of some of the wagons. "Slave traders," he replied, suddenly realizing what he was seeing. "They're slave traders. One of our men in Antioch reported that slave traders would be coming. I didn't think there would be so many. Our spies were right. They intend to enslave the whole country." Judas continued to stare in amazement at the slow moving line of wagons that stretched farther than he could see.

Jonathan was still confused. "Will they haul the slaves away in those carts? Those seem rather well built for what I imagine would be used for slaves."

Judas laughed. "No, Brother. They're not going to let a Jew ride in a cart. Slaves have to walk, at the end of a whip. The idea is that the slaves would be chained together in a file behind each wagon. The wagon is for the owner." Judas pointed to one particular wagon. "There. Look at the man driving that wagon."

Jonathan squinted his eyes to better see across the distance. Perched at the front of the wagon was a rotund dark-haired man dressed in an embroidered silk robe. He was shouting angrily at a slave who was walking alongside the oxen in front.

"He looks a lot like Matthan who used to live in Modin," said Jonathan. "He looks like he would be rich."

"How much money do you think is in that wagon? He has come to do business with the soldiers who are here to capture our people as spoils of war." Judas turned to look at the other men who were with him. "Men. The Syrians have sent wagon loads of money into our land. The only problem is that there are fifty thousand soldiers guarding it. What do you think we should do?"

One of the other men watching the processional pass by

responded wryly, "I think we should take the money." Everyone burst out laughing, but Judas quickly stifled their fun for fear of their being heard.

Leaving some men to follow the progress of the enemy army, Judas returned to Mizpah. He sent Jonathan to Jerusalem to call in all the troops with Joseph and Azarias, leaving only a few whose sole task was to continue building campfires during the night to give the impression that troops still filled the countryside. Judas, meanwhile, sent riders to call troops from every corner of Judea. Several hundred came from the camp at Lebonah. Hundreds more poured in from other towns and villages.

The next day, Jonathan rode into Mizpah and leapt off his horse in front of where Judas was discussing tactics with Nethanel and Simon. "Judas," he said while trying to catch his breath. "You won't believe what I've seen."

Judas and the other two men waited while Jonathan took a deep breath. "I've seen Shimri, Rebekah's brother. He's with Joseph's men."

Judas frowned. "With Joseph's men? Did he see you?"

"He saw me, but I don't think he knows that I saw him. When I looked his way, he quickly turned away. Do you think he has changed sides?"

Judas pursed his lips after letting out an angry sigh. "Not Shimri. He was commanding the leading phalanx in Apollonius's army."

"I know," said Jonathan. "I remember you saying that you saw him. I just thought that maybe he . . ."

"No," said Judas brusquely. "If Shimri had had a change of heart, he would have come to me. Does Joseph or Azarias know about him?"

"I asked Joseph about him. Joseph didn't know much about him except that he joined them a few weeks back and seemed to fit in well with the men. He still goes by the name of Shimri, but that's a common name so I guess he didn't think it would give him away."

"If they lift up his tunic they'll find out how well he fits in," said Judas sarcastically.

Simon saw the confused look on Nethanel's face. "He had his circumcision reversed," explained Simon. Nethanel grimaced.

Judas looked at Jonathan. "Are Joseph and Azarias on their way here?"

"Yes. They broke camp as soon as I gave them the word."

"As soon as they arrive, I want you to tell both Joseph and Azarias to select two or three other men they know they can trust. Together with themselves, I want them to observe Shimri's every move and report to me. Shimri is here as a spy. If we watch him closely, we can use this to our advantage."

The Syrian army did not approach Jerusalem by the Way of Beth-horon as had Seron. Being superstitious, the generals considered it unwise to choose a route along which so many of their compatriots had met their violent end only a few months earlier. The same spirits that had blinded them in the face of the enemy's attack could still be around.

Eventually the Syrians turned inland and camped at Emmaus, south of the Way of Beth-horon. Word of where the Syrians had made their base quickly reached Judas and spread throughout the camp at Mizpah. The men who had seen the Syrian camp described the size of the enemy army to their friends. When they told of the elephants, fear fell upon many of the men.

Learning of the growing fear in his own camp, Judas climbed the tower as he had before the fight with Seron. After sounding the shofar, he waited until almost five thousand faces were looking up at him. He held up his hand, and a hush fell over the crowd.

"My fellow soldiers, you have all heard of the army that has entered our land. They have come, not merely to rule us, but to destroy and enslave us. If you have courage, if you have contempt for the danger that has come among us, we will defeat this enemy and we will regain our liberty. Many centuries ago, our forefather Gideon led out an army much larger than we have today against the Midianites. God told him to tell those who were afraid to go home. In the end, Gideon only had three hundred men, but with those three hundred he defeated an army that covered the land like locusts.

"I say to you today, if you are afraid to meet this enemy, go home. You will be an encumbrance to us. If you are newly married, or if you have recently acquired new homes or lands, return to your wives and lands that yet hold so firm a place in your hearts. If you have anything to live for other than the glory of Israel and her God, if you can accept another way of life other than the one God gave us, leave this camp and return to your homes. Anyone who fights this fight must choose to die rather than run.

"God did not set us apart from the other nations around us so we would be subject to them or enslaved by them. God set us apart that we may freely worship him. This fight is for that freedom. Should you die in this fight, you will have died fighting for the freedom to worship God. You will obtain everlasting glory. Set your mind on these things, for tomorrow, there must be no fear."

Judas descended from the tower without further word. Some murmuring rolled across the crowd, some questioning whether they should return to their homes and leave the fighting to others. A young soldier shouted out, "I have a new wife, but if I don't fight, she may become the slave of one of those Syrian bastards, or worse. I'll fight for her freedom, or I'll die trying."

Similar statements began to be heard from other corners of the camp. Within a couple of minutes, cries of war reverberated from one side of the camp to the other. Where fear had dominated a few moments earlier, a reckless courage now took hold. The army was not without its deserters, however. Over the next few hours, almost two hundred men quietly slipped away and returned to their homes. The only thing they had feared more than the Syrians was what would happen to them if they refused to fight. Once Judas had given them a way out, they took it, though they did not do it openly.

Among those who left the camp was Shimri. Azarias and

two other men followed him at a distance. It didn't take them long to realize that he was headed toward Emmaus. They took care to maintain enough distance from Shimri so that if the young traitor turned to look back, they could quickly drop to the ground and avoid being seen.

Just as night was falling, they came to the edge of the Syrian camp. Azarias and his two men came just close enough to see Shimri speak to a guard at the edge of the camp and then be escorted to what was obviously the tent of a general. Less than a half hour later, Shimri stepped from the tent at the side of a man they assumed to be the general. Shimri was now wearing the full gear of a Syrian cavalry officer. Horses were brought for each of them. The general shouted an order, and the air was suddenly pierced with the blast of a trumpet. In moments, the camp bustled with activity. Thousands of soldiers moved into marching formation followed by what appeared to be as many as a thousand cavalry.

"They are going to attack tonight!" exclaimed Azarias. "They think to surprise our camp in the middle of the night. We must tell Judas."

Already tired from having followed Shimri for half the day and not having eaten since morning, the three men ran for the next three hours until they reached the camp in Mizpah. Azarias burst into Judas's quarters where Judas had gathered his captains. "Judas, they're attacking tonight."

Judas motioned for someone to get water for Azarias. The other two men arrived a moment later, equally out of breath. They all drank and, between gulps, told what they had seen. Judas rolled out a tattered map drawn on goat skin. Together with the other men, he studied the way the enemy army would be advancing and the various ways to and from Emmaus. Looking up from the map, he said to the captains who were gathered around looking on, "Tell your men to add wood to their fires so that they will burn long and bright. Then prepare them for a fast march. The Syrians have done us a favor. They have split their army. We will attack the half that has remained at Emmaus before the sun comes up."

Immediately the captains left, and the entire camp sprang into action. Less than a half hour later, Mizpah was a ghost town surrounded by hundreds of brightly burning fires. It would not be accurate to say that Judas marched the army all night, for in actual fact, they ran most of the way. Taking a southerly course that brought them so close to Jerusalem that they could see the fires over the countryside that had been lit by the men left there by Joseph and Azarias, they turned west down a pass that would bring them to the enemy camp from a southeasterly direction. The army halted about two miles from Emmaus at the beginning of the fourth watch of the night. Only then were the men allowed to rest and take food and water.

By midnight, Gorgias had led his army within sight of the fires around Mizpah. He called the cavalry, a full thousand in number, to the front. Fifty were set apart to accompany Shimri to the known quarters of Judas. Orders were clear: Take the rebel leader alive. Shimri smiled as the general repeated the orders again. He relished the thought that it would be he who would stand before the people and deal the torturous blows that would destroy the myth they had created. He would be vindicated in the choices he had made.

Once in place, the Syrian army charged upon the camp. Sparks flew as a thousand horses trampled fires, knocked tents from their posts, and delivered masters with slicing swords that found no body on which to inflict a wound. Thousands of *pila*-carrying infantry charged in behind the cavalry. For several minutes, chaos reigned in the darkness throughout the camp. Some of the infantry were mistaken as the enemy by their own cavalry and at least a dozen met their deaths. When Gorgias realized the camp was empty, he had the trumpet sounded. After several minutes, the commotion stopped. Shimri found his way to the general's side.

"What has happened here?" demanded Gorgias. "Where is this rebel army that you said was here?"

"Somehow they were alerted to our coming," defended Shimri. "They have spies everywhere. They have fled to the hills. The hill country north of here, all the way to Lebonah where Apollonius met his end, has been the rebel stronghold from the very beginning. It is certain that they have fled."

Gorgias looked around at the scattered fires, some burning brightly, but many now dying coals after being trampled upon by men and horses. "Then they can't be far, their fires were burning too brightly." He called to the captains nearby. "Call your men into their ranks. We will continue our pursuit. Tell everyone to be alert for an ambush. If the gods be with us, they will not have time to organize any resistance before we are upon them."

Within minutes, the army was moving through the darkness at a rapid pace toward the Gophna Hills. It would not be apparent until the sun came up, which was yet hours away, that no army had traveled this road in the last day. A light rain had fallen two days earlier, and the signs of travel left in the ground since then were not the signs left by several thousand men.

Chapter 42

The sky had brightened just enough to make out the details of the sleeping army on the plain stretched out below the Jewish warriors hiding behind the stony ridge above Emmaus. Each captain had quietly moved his men into position and awaited the signal, a signal unlike any ever heard in battle. Jonathan and Eleazar gave each of their captains a specific target for their archers. Within seconds of the release of the archers' arrows, the signal would be heard from one end of the camp to the other.

Judas waited a few more minutes. He wanted to be sure the sky was light enough for his men to recognize the enemy. A few of the men in the camp below were beginning to stir. Perimeter guards, bleary-eyed from having been up most of the night, were giving way to their replacements. An occasional comment by one of the guards to his replacement resonated in the morning air, but for the most part, the camp remained quietly placid. The placidity, however, was quickly ended.

Judas waved to the watching eyes of Jonathan and Eleazar and their captains. Seconds later, as many as a thousand arrows arched across the dawn sky. A Syrian guard heard a whirring sound above his head and looked up, but the sky was yet too dim for him to see that the sound was the combined hum of hundreds of arrows streaking high above his head. His mind ran quickly through recesses of memory in search of a definition to a sound he had heard before. He suddenly realized what was happening and cried out to alert the camp, but his cry was not heard, for it was drowned out by a blast a hundred times more powerful.

The eight elephants that had been chained for the night in the middle of the camp suddenly trumpeted deafeningly as hundreds of arrows stuck into their thick hides. An elephant could rarely be brought down with arrows, but the pain exacted by the scores of pin-prick wounds drove them into a frantic rage. The chains that would normally hold a docile elephant in place were no match for the huge beasts now driven mad with the painful stings. The stampeding elephants crushed a number of Syrians who were unable to get out of their path. Smoldering coals left over from fires made the previous night were scattered into tents and baggage and ignited into flame. Many of the slave trader's wagons were overturned by the charging beasts as they searched desperately to escape the source of their agony.

The trumpet of the elephants signaled the rest of Judas's army into action. Five hundred men had been stationed in various positions around the outskirts of the camp to eliminate the threat of the cavalry. With the camp already in chaos, these men, armed not only with their swords, but with trumpets and shofars, cut the thousands of horses loose and caused them to stampede across the camp. Cavalrymen running from their tents were met by arrows that had now been turned upon them by the men under Jonathan and Eleazar's command.

Judas led the charge into the middle of the camp. Three thousand men poured over the ridge with loud cries and the blast of shofars. The elephants that were charging in their direction turned to escape the frightening noise and ran deeper into the Syrian camp. The Jewish fighters followed in their path and slaughtered the dazed Syrians.

Nicanor, the general in charge, ran from his tent to be confronted by bedlam on every side. In an instant he saw his camp being laid waste by charging elephants, stampeding horses, and what seemed to be an endless stream of screaming

Jews coming over the ridge. Immediately he assumed that the information given to him the night before had been wrong. If Gorgias had found the enemy camp, it had not been the only one. Where had these thousands now coming down upon him come from? And how many were there? He would not fight a battle with this degree of uncertainty. He called his trumpeters, and they sounded the retreat.

All morning long, the Jewish fighters pursued the Syrian army. They hounded their antagonists and left their corpses strewn along the ground all the way to the port at Jamnia. When they reached the coast, most of the Syrians turned north toward home, but others, thinking it a better means of escape, turned south toward Ashdod, but in so doing, cut the army in half yet again.

Judas would have pursued them further, but he remembered that Gorgias's army remained untouched. He sounded the call, and everyone returned to Emmaus where he knew Gorgias would return. Many of the men, aware of the wealth brought by the slave traders, wanted to begin to plunder the Syrian camp, but Judas reminded them that they had yet another army to confront. He promised them that once their victory was complete, the plunder would be theirs.

The men rounded up as many of the frightened horses as they could. Some of the elephants were still in the camp, but had worn themselves to exhaustion. Using the long *sarissae* left in the Syrian camp by the fleeing army, the men killed the pitiful beasts.

Toward late afternoon, word came to Judas that the other Syrian army was approaching from the northeast. Judas put his own army in array, spreading it out as much as possible so as to give a deceptive appearance of the numbers he had with him. Men who had never ridden a horse were given a horse to either sit upon or simply hold by the reins to give the appearance that they were cavalry. The foot soldiers on the front lines held *sarissae* gathered from the camp in vertical fashion. They had no intention of using them, but Judas had learned that the Syrians were often more impressed by show than substance.

When the fight began, the *sarissae* would be dropped and swords drawn. Riderless horses would be charged into the enemy ranks, and soldiers with swords slicing the legs from under their dazed enemy would follow in their train.

A sense of foreboding had grown in the mind of Gorgias from the first moment he had seen the smoke rising in the distance. He pulled back on the reins of his horse as they came to the top of the rise overlooking the plain. Officers on horseback came to either side, along with Shimri, who took up a position immediately beside the general. No one spoke for a long while. One officer said in amazement, "What kind of gods have done this?"

The bodies of hundreds of their comrades lay strewn in the debris across the smoke covered field. Here and there was the giant carcass of an elephant. Through the smoke, far across the plain, they saw what appeared to be thousands of soldiers with upraised *sarissae*. Behind the soldiers were hundreds, perhaps thousands, of horses.

"It's Judas," shouted Shimri. "We must prepare for battle."

"We can't beat them," said one of the officers quickly. "Our men are exhausted from marching all night and most of the day. And look what has already happened here."

"But we must," retorted Shimri.

Gorgias had fought to hold back the rage boiling within him up to this point. "Damn you, Jew. This is your fault. If you had not led us on this useless chase all night, this would never have happened."

"But now they are here. The enemy is in our sight," insisted Shimri.

"Don't you know what you are looking at?" screamed the general. "There were forty thousand men down there. What kind of army defeats an army this size? Everything you have told us has been wrong, where the enemy was, how many of the enemy, everything. They've even managed to slaughter the elephants. Do you know what it takes to kill an elephant in battle?"

"But if we just . . ."

Gorgias drew his sword and put the tip of it to Shimri's throat. "I should kill you now. For all we know, you are one of them."

Shimri bristled. "If you kill me, you will answer to Lysias. Need I remind you that it is he who put me in your service?"

Gorgias held his sword at Shimri's throat a moment longer, staring into the eyes of the young Jew he suddenly hated. "If I pay for this, you will pay more." He withdrew his sword and shoved it back into its scabbard.

Gorgias gave orders to turn the army back toward Mizpah and then through Lebonah to Samaria. Gorgias would have made camp for the night in Mizpah, but many of his men feared the gods of Judea, having seen what had been done to their comrades at Emmaus, so they marched until they had passed Lebonah, well into the night.

When it was dark enough to escape undetected, Shimri slipped away into the night and headed east across the Jordan into Perea. He knew Lysias would listen to Gorgias and probably have him put to death as a spy. Suddenly, Shimri was a man without a country. He dared not return to Jerusalem, for Lysimachus had already made plain his feelings about Shimri. As he pushed the horse through the night, distancing himself from the Syrian army, Shimri repeatedly told himself that the course of events had not been his fault. He had been loyal in every way. He had even turned his own family over to them. Now he had no family, and he had no country. All had been lost, at least for now.

Once his scouts had assured him that the enemy army was well in retreat, Judas allowed the men to plunder the Syrian camp. The amount of gold and silver found in the wagons of the slave traders far exceeded their expectations. At Simon's advice, Judas called upon the men to bring a tenth of it to be kept for the work that needed to be done on the temple. Once the army rested, they would march on Jerusalem.

Lysimachus stood upon the northwestern tower of the

citadel staring beyond the city that lay below, out toward the countryside in the direction of Emmaus. He formed a picture in his mind of the description the officers who had come to him from Gorgias had given of the battlefield. For a few hours, the rebels had left the city unguarded and the officers had managed to bring a report. The rebel army had attacked and defeated a well-equipped army of forty thousand men. If ever they had the capability of entering Jerusalem, now was that time. By tomorrow morning he would see the dust raised by thousands of feet marching on Jerusalem.

"You're not thinking about surrendering to this rebel, are you?" said Menelaus from a few feet away.

The garrison commander did not answer immediately. That the traitorous high priest should be choked by his own fear for a few moments brought him some degree of pleasure. Menelaus had far more to be afraid of than did Lysimachus. It was one thing to be an officer following orders. It was quite another to voluntarily sell out one's own people for the sake of personal profit.

"What are you thinking, Lysimachus?" Menelaus grew more worried when no answer was immediately forthcoming.

Lysimachus continued to stare across the countryside, but finally answered matter-of-factly, "No, I will not surrender. At least, not yet." Menelaus breathed a sigh of relief, something that did not go unnoticed by the commander. Lysimachus did not care at all how Menelaus felt. In fact, for a fleeting moment, he envisioned himself throwing Menelaus from the tower to the pavement below.

Shutting out his own sentiments with the discipline of a military officer, he explained to the high priest the reason for his present position, though he felt no real need to explain himself to the man for whom he felt such disdain. "I know Lysias. He will not let this stand. He will move quickly to come against the rebels again, only this time, he will lead the army himself. Gorgias's army is still intact. They didn't even enter the fight. We don't know what remains of Nicanor's force, but there must be many left.

Thousands may have died, but thousands also lived, enough to attack again. Lysias has direct orders from the king to destroy Judea. He will come. And he will come with a vengeance."

Chapter 43

The next day, Judas marched the entire army to the walls of Jerusalem. Jubilant shouts echoed through the ranks when they came within sight of the city. The comparatively few casualties they had suffered the previous day were quickly forgotten. Those numbered among the Hasidim were especially joyful as Passover was just days away. The thought of observing Passover at the temple held them in a state of euphoria.

Their elation quickly died, however, at the sting of Syrian arrows, many launched from the bows of other Jews. Lysimachus called every able-bodied man into service. The Sadducees and other Syrian loyalists who had taken refuge in the Acra were given weapons and put under the command of a Syrian captain. They lined the city walls day and night and shot down upon anyone who came near.

Azarias, assured by Judas that this time the army would take the city, set about again building a siege tower. However, threats from other regions of the country called much of the army away.

Lysias sent small units into Judea from various directions to keep the Jews divided until he was able to form the army that would finish the job of destroying the country. This time, he determined that he would take no slaves. The race would be exterminated: men, women and children. Small units of Syrian troops coming out of Samaria began raiding the Jewish towns and villages in the north. Other raids came from troops garrisoned in the coastal cities. The bands of marauders were not able to inflict very much damage as a whole, but their attacks could not go unanswered, for whenever they raided even the smallest village, Jews died, often being made sport of in the killing process.

Judas sent troops wherever there was a threat. Within a few months, most of the towns felt secure again. The cost, however, was that the army was left scattered over much of the country.

Jerusalem remained an unattainable goal. More than a full year passed. Then one day, the word came. An army had moved out of Antioch, this one larger than the last, perhaps as many as sixty thousand. At its head was Lysias himself.

Judas knew that he could not protect the country and confront this army at the same time, so he called for the evacuation of the towns that were closest to the Syrian controlled areas. For several days, a constant stream of men, women, children, livestock, and carts piled with household goods lined the roads leading into the highland towns from Mizpah to Bethlehem. This not only took the people out of harm's way, but also brought together the largest army Judas had assembled, almost ten thousand men.

Lysias moved his massive army slowly down the coastal plain. He moved the army only a few miles each day, hoping that Judas would come out against him on the plain. Lysias had in his company the king's son, the young Antiochus Eupator, only nine years old. By the king's orders, Lysias was to acquaint the young man with battle. It was Lysias's intent to show Antiochus the Greek style of making war in its most sophisticated form.

Judas refused to accommodate Lysias, however, knowing that the flatlands of the plain were the perfect element for the Syrian phalanx. Infuriated by the refusal of the Jews to meet him in open battle, Lysias tried to provoke a response by razing every town he came close to along the way. Since the towns had been vacated, all the Syrian army could do was destroy property, which Judas assured the people could be rebuilt.

Lysias sent sizeable cavalry units across the hills from the plains in repeated attempts to reach Jerusalem with word of the Syrian army that was now in the land, but each attempt was thwarted as the air suddenly filled with hundreds of arrows. Lysias was unable to make a move of which Judas was unaware.

Having taken a month to move down the coastal plain, Lysias found himself pressed by the approach of winter. He knew his army of mercenaries, most of who were accustomed to the temperate climate of the Greek isles, would rebel and begin to desert if the weather grew too cold. Pushing the army considerably farther south than Emmaus, where Gorgias and Nicanor had turned inland, Lysias made an eastern loop toward Beth-zur so as to approach Jerusalem from the south. This brought the response from Judas that Lysias had hoped to have on the plains.

During the night, two thousand Jewish archers took up positions on the hills north of Beth-zur on either side of the ravine through which the Syrian army would have to pass to get to Jerusalem. Judas stood in the middle of the ravine, backed by three thousand men armed with swords and *pila*. Nethanel held five hundred men on horseback just over a ridge behind the archers who would make way for a charge from the wing. The rest of the army awaited in the hills on either side to fight the flanking attempts that Judas expected from the Syrians.

The Syrian army had just begun to break camp when shouts rang through the ravine that the Jews were assembled for battle. Lysias immediately had the trumpet sounded and assembled the army to go out to meet them. Once the army was assembled, Lysias, in the company of a standard bearer and trumpeter, took Antiochus and found a position on a hill looking up the ravine. The young boy was excited much in the same way as if he had been attending a sporting event.

A tightly gathered phalanx led the Syrian army as they slowly advanced up the confines of the ravine. Behind them, in a formation Judas had come to expect, was a unit of *hypaspists*, followed by archers and cavalry. As the phalanx picked up speed, Judas signaled to the men on the hills. Arrows began to rain down from above upon the phalanx as the archers started their assault. As soon as Judas saw the phalangites raise their shields to protect themselves from the missiles falling from the sky, he shouted a charge and he and the men around him broke into a run toward the phalanx. They launched *pila* one after another. Some of the men had as many as four *pila* that they launched into the enemy before drawing their swords and throwing themselves into the midst of the phalanx. Many of the phalangites having already fallen under the arrows and *pila*, the uneven ground broke their ranks further.

A trumpet sounded and the Syrian archers began to release arrows over the heads of the phalanx into the men that had not yet made it to the front. Before they could release their second barrage, Nethanel led his horsemen over the hill into the left wing of the archers.

Later, when Judas would look back at the memory of this battle, he knew it must have been the hand of God that moved his eyes to see through the ranks of fighting men to what he saw in the next instant. While it pierced him to the core of his being, it may very well have affected the outcome of the day more than any other single moment of the battle. With uplifted arm, Nethanel was ready to swing his sword into the neck of the first archer he reached when a *pilum* flew from somewhere in the ranks of the Syrian hypaspists squarely into Nethanel's chest, piercing him through. Nethanel's eyes suddenly bulged and his entire body went tense. A moment later, a second *pilum* took him from his horse. In that moment, all the air went out of Judas. Nethanel had been a source of strength for Judas from the moment he had met him that first day in Mizpah. Nethanel had loved Mattathias as a son would love his father. Nethanel was what Israel was all about, standing strong for God.

Azarias saw Judas standing frozen in the midst of the chaos all around, pain written all over his face. "What is it Judas?" he shouted. "What's wrong?"

Judas quickly retrieved his senses. "Nethanel!" he shouted amidst the shouts and cries all around them as he pointed where Nethanel had been. "Nethanel's down. They killed him!"

"What?" shouted Azarias.

"They killed Nethanel! I just saw him go down!"

Azarias looked in the direction where the Jewish horsemen were battling in the midst of the archers, others of them continuing to fall to spears and arrows. Azarias shouted to the men around him. "They killed Nethanel!" In that moment, a contagious rage overtook the Jewish fighters that spread across the field of battle with word of Nethanel's death. Every man there holding a sword for Israel loved Nethanel. To many, he was as much their hero as was Judas.

Judas suddenly lunged between the ranks of the phalangites with his sword in one hand and a dagger in the other. Azarias plowed through the ranks with him. Their men followed in their train.

From on the hill, Lysias looked on in amazement. The boy Antiochus looked on the pandemonium in the valley below gleefully. Lysias scolded him. "There is nothing to be happy about here. We are losing this battle." The demeanor of the child immediately changed. Lysias continued to stare at the Jewish men cutting through his phalanx with a speed he had never seen before. Something had happened after the battle had started that had suddenly given the enemy an almost superhuman power, but he did not know what it was. "I have never seen men fight with such spirit. They don't seem to care whether they live or die. It's as though the gods have put them under some kind of spell so that they fight without the least amount of fear. Who can fight such men as these?"

Lysias was not ready to give up the fight, however. He sent word to his cavalry to skirt the battlefield to attack the enemy flank. The cavalry never made it to the flank, but were met by the swords and spears of the troops Judas had placed in anticipation of just such a move. The battle raged until the middle of the afternoon. Finally, estimating that as many as five thousand of his men had fallen before the rebels, Lysias sounded the retreat.

The arrogant young Antiochus looked at his mentor, "Why do you quit? My father would not quit."

Lysias fought to keep from striking the next king from his horse. "It will take a larger army than this to defeat the gods of this land. We will gather such an army." Lysias paused for a moment before adding, "Then you can lead it."

The face of the nine-year-old broke out into a broad grin at the thought of commanding an army of his own. Lysias took one last look at the battlefield that was crimson with the blood of his men. Good men die in fields of blood, he said to himself, and foolish children rule empires. He pulled his horse around to join the retreating army, and the boy followed.

At the sound of the trumpet, the embattled front of the Syrian ranks turned to flee, but their way was blocked by their own troops who were leaving the field at a slower pace. More of them died. Archers continued to hound them from the hillsides for the next hour, but eventually the field cleared.

The sounds of distant skirmishes still making their way to his ears, Judas stood in the midst of the field looking around at the blood-soaked men who struggled to hold themselves erect. They stood surrounded by thousands of corpses of both friends and enemies. Everyone was gasping for air. Some dropped to the ground, unable to stand any longer. Judas saw one man who had had his clothes torn completely from him in the heat of battle. He stood completely naked, painted in blood, staring around the field with a dazed expression on his face, his hand still holding tightly to his sword. Even surrounded by so much death, a man managed to gasp out a joke to him. "Joab, you look like a Greek, standing around naked like that." Joab didn't care, at least not for the moment.

Judas tried to understand the battlefield. It was no longer easy to tell what had happened where. He walked along, stepping over bodies, turning up dead faces, until he came to what he was looking for. He rolled over Nethanel's body onto his back and sat down on the ground beside him. In a few minutes, Simon came and stood over Judas, placing his hand on his shoulder. "Do you remember when we first met him?" said Simon quietly.

Judas shook his head affirmatively. "It's what started all this. When Apelles killed that young couple and their baby. That's the day Father made the decision to fight the Syrians. That's the day we met Nethanel."

No one spoke for a long while. Other men began to gather around. Simon finally said, "He was the one that named you the Maccabee."

When Simon said that, Judas broke into sobs and shook as he wept. Many other tears were shed by the men around him. One of the heroes of Israel had fallen. Tonight, they would mourn him. Tomorrow, they would avenge him.

Judas looked up from his weeping to see Azarias's bloodstained figure standing in the last rays of the afternoon sun. While tears still ran down his face, he spoke as the general once again, "Azarias, tomorrow we will take Jerusalem. There will be no further delay."

"But how will we enter the city?" said Azarias, not having the strength to hope. "I'm sure the garrison from the city has destroyed our siege engines like they did before. How will we get in?"

Judas wiped the tears from his cheeks and stood up. "Get as many men as you need. Round up every horse you can find and every Syrian cavalry uniform you can put your hands on. Strip them from the bodies in this field if you need to. Tomorrow we will enter Jerusalem through the western gate. They will open the gates and welcome us as we enter."

Azarias immediately understood the plan. A reserve of energy that he did not know he possessed suddenly coursed through his veins. "Yes, Sir," he said with a broad smile. He turned and walked quickly away. Two other men who had been standing in the group quickly followed him. Together they began calling others together for the task ahead of them. Tomorrow, they would enter Jerusalem.

Peering from the crevice of a huge boulder on a hill just

east of the battlefield, yet far removed from the danger, Shimri looked down upon the valley carpeted with bodies. In the distance to the south, he could see the retreating army. He recognized the standard as that born by Lysias.

For several months, Shimri had gone from town to town in Perea. He never dared remain in a town overnight, for he always feared for his life. If he claimed to be a Jew, the people hated him out of a history of enmity that went back centuries. If he expressed Syrian loyalties, they liked him even less, for they were weary of the power that continuously drained them of everything but a subsistence level of life.

Finally, Shimri had returned to Judea, living, as he saw it, like an animal in the wilderness. Not really knowing how to live off the land, he survived mainly from stealing. He would slip into villages during the night and take whatever he could. For a time, he took up with a marauding group of highway bandits who would lay in wait for unprotected travelers. This did not satisfy him though.

Shimri had an unquenchable thirst for the life he had tasted during the days before the insurrection had begun. How he relished those days when he had wrestled in the gymnasium, sometimes before cheering crowds. Afterwards, he would stand naked over the man he had vanquished, his well-sculpted, oiled body shining gloriously for all to see. He had been welcomed many times into the homes of men of great wealth. He had eaten their meat and drunk their wine. And the women. He had tasted of the love of more than one. The temple prostitutes that Antiochus had brought to Jerusalem all knew him by name. It was not the life his father had taught him, but it was the life he wanted. It was the life he had set out to make his own.

But everything had changed on that fateful day almost three years earlier. That old priest, Mattathias, his own father's friend, had launched a rebellion in a little insignificant place like Modin. He had dared hope that the rebellion was short-lived when word had come of Mattathias's death, but Judas had taken up the cause and the whole country had followed after him. How he hated Judas! He hated everything he stood for, and he hated anyone who loved him, even if it was his own flesh and blood.

Shimri climbed from among the rocks where he was hiding and mounted the horse that was tied behind the ridge. He turned the horse in the direction of Jerusalem and kicked his heels into its sides. It had been a year and a half since he had seen Lysimachus. Perhaps Lysimachus was not even commander of the garrison any more. If so, so much the better. But if Lysimachus was still in charge, Shimri would lie his way into the commander's favor. He refused to live like an animal any longer.

Chapter 44

By midmorning the next day, almost seven hundred men on horseback were assembled at the northern end of the camp. Each was dressed in the body armor of a Syrian cavalryman. Many wore cuirasses still stained with the blood of their enemies. Those in the front of the formation wore greaves upon their legs so as to appear in everyway as authentic cavalrymen.

Judas, Simon, Joseph, and Azarias led the procession toward Jerusalem. Behind Judas, a strong young horseman held a standard high on a pole. It was identical to the one carried by Lysias's standard bearer, or at least as close to the original as could be fabricated in a few hours time.

Obed, the smith from Modin, had worked through the night to create the standard that would identify them as Lysias's cavalry. When he brought the finished product to Judas in the morning, some of the men complained that it was an idol and that it would be blasphemy to march behind it. Indeed, at the top of the standard, was a bronze statue of Zeus. Judas looked at the statue for a moment then asked Obed if he could hammer a hole through the chest of the statue and pierce it through with an arrow. In a few minutes, Obed presented them with a Zeus that had been shot through with an arrow. The arrow would be difficult to see from a distance, but it was clearly visible from up close.

Judas held the standard up and called out to those around him, "Men, don't you remember what Torah says Moses did in the wilderness? When the people had sinned, and God sent serpents into their midst that bit them, and some of the people died? God told Moses to put a serpent of bronze on a long pole, that if the people would look upon the serpent, they would not die. The serpent is all that is evil. The bronze, just like the bronze used in the altar where sacrifices are made in the temple, shows God's judgment upon it. The people had to agree with God that their evil deserved judgment.

"It is no different today. Serpents have invaded our land. They have brought idols into our land and have seduced our people into every kind of evil. Today, by the hands he has chosen as instruments of his vengeance, our own hands, God is bringing judgment upon this evil.

"Look upon this idol, this evil, pierced through with the arrow of judgment. There is an idol just like this one, only much larger, in the holy place of the temple in Jerusalem. I have seen it with my own eyes. Today we ride through the gates of Jerusalem that this evil might be judged and the holy place cleansed. Before the new moon, we will worship there once again."

Shouts rang from every side as men attached new meaning to the standard under which they rode. This was not the standard of Lysias. It was the standard showing Lysias and his evil king brought to their knees in defeat.

Judas mounted his horse and led the way. Within moments, the earth thundered behind him. Behind the thunder of seven hundred horses marched thousands of bruised and battered men who had reason to fight one more battle.

"You just disappeared a year and half ago. How do I know where you have been? How do I know that you come from Lysias now?" said Lysimachus heatedly. The commander's disdain for the young traitor had grown every time he had watched Rebekah enjoying the morning sun in the citadel courtyard. He had hoped after such a long time that perhaps he was dead. Lysimachus still remembered vividly the message from Lysias that had mentioned Antigonus's presence with him, the same message that had ordered that Rebekah be put to death with the launching of the invasion in the previous year. But Lysimachus could see no way this hateful young Jew would be aware of his having this information, so he feigned ignorance.

Shimri's mind worked quickly to put together responses to the questions the commander was posing. He had worked every angle as he had lain awake the night before in an effort to anticipate whatever question Lysimachus might ask. In some measure, he was glad the commander had refused to see him until this morning, for it had given him additional time to plan his strategy, a strategy he now employed. "Over a year ago, an arrow with a message from Lysias was brought to you."

Lysimachus blanched. "How do you know about that?"

Menelaus, who had been sitting quietly to one side up to this point, raised his head and looked at Lysimachus through narrowed eyes. This was the first he had heard of any such communication from Lysias.

"It came from my bow," said Shimri insolently, seeing by the look on the commander's face that he had chosen the right approach to manipulate the situation.

Lysimachus was aware of Menelaus's questioning looks but refused to look his way. Instead, he studied Shimri's face for a long moment. How much did Shimri know of what Lysias had written? If Lysimachus said the wrong thing at this point, he could hang himself with his own words, that is, if Lysias chose a method as civil as hanging. The supreme governor had been known to make cruel examples of the few who had dared disobey his orders in the past.

"Then you know what was in that message," said Lysimachus, probing to see what Shimri knew.

Shimri was coy in his response. "I know what was in the governor's mind when he wrote it."

Lysimachus hated the game Shimri was playing, but he knew that if he asked too much, he would arouse suspicion.

The commander rose from his seat and walked over to the window. Looking out onto the courtyard, he saw that Rebekah's guard had just led her outside. Shimri had said nothing of Rebekah. Did he think her dead, or did he just not care?

Lysimachus was mentally groping for a way to make Shimri reveal further what he knew when the door suddenly burst open. Lysimachus turned quickly from the window and was about to reprimand whoever it was that had entered in such a brusque fashion.

"Commander," announced a burly officer, "Syrian cavalry are arriving at the western gate. The standard is that of Lysias. They should be at the inner gate of the Acra within moments."

"They are already in the city?" questioned Lysimachus. His heart sank. Shimri suddenly became the least of his worries. If Lysias was here and gained direct knowledge of his failure to comply with orders, he was already dead.

"Yes, Sir," responded the officer. "The guards opened the gate as soon as they recognized the governor's standard. He has hundreds of cavalry with him."

"But it can't be," exclaimed Shimri. "I saw Lysias retreat toward the south from Beth-zur yesterday. There are thousands of rebels between him and Jerusalem filling the only pass by which he could get here so soon."

"You *saw* him. I thought you were *with* him." Lysimachus looked accusingly at Shimri, whose mind raced for an explanation.

"I . . . I was already on my way here," Shimri stammered. "I mean . . . he sent me just as he gave the order to retreat. I looked back from a hilltop later in the afternoon and saw the army clearly heading south."

Lysimachus was about to accuse the young traitor again when a panting guard burst past the officer that was standing in the doorway. He looked nervously from Lysimachus to the officer who had previously entered, not sure whom he should address. In another instant, he snapped to attention and blurted out a barrage of words that left everyone momentarily stunned.

"Sir, it's a trick. It's not Lysias. It's the Maccabee. Our guards at the western gate did not realize it until it was too late. They tried to close the gate, but some got in before they could. Now the rebels are pouring into the city."

Menelaus was now on his feet, his eyes wide with fear. "They must be stopped," he shouted out frantically.

Shimri, momentarily vindicated in having been correct in saying that it could not be Lysias, felt a sudden boldness swell within him. He would have been more fearful had it been Lysias, for his duplicity would be brought into the open, and he would surely die for it. Against the rebels, however, he might yet find a way to work matters to his advantage. "Commander," he said as if he himself were in command, "you must stop the accesses to the temple. The mount is a veritable fortress. If they make it there, it will be almost impossible to overpower them."

Lysimachus's face grew red. He looked at the young guard who had brought the calamitous message. The commander pointed first at him and then beyond him to another guard standing outside the door. "You and you," he said. "Take this man and put him in irons." Lysimachus pointed at Shimri. "He is either a deserter or a spy. I don't know which. We will find out in due time."

Shimri backed away as the two guards approached him. "You can't be doing this!" he protested vehemently. "Lysias will hear of this!"

Lysimachus said not another word to Shimri. He simply said to the two guards who had now taken hold of Shimri on each side, "Take him away."

The two guards struggled with Shimri as they dragged him from the room. As Shimri's continued shouts of protest faded from their hearing, Lysimachus spoke to the officer who had initially entered the room. Two other officers had since arrived, and the words were meant for them as well. "Send two hundred troops to the western access of the temple mount. Block the other accesses with fifty men each. Send what little cavalry we have left to the western gate of the city. We must close that gate."

The officers stood for a moment, possibly thinking the commander would say more. Lysimachus barked irritably, "Now go! Do it now or we are all dead!" The officers immediately ran to call together their troops.

Menelaus watched silently as Lysimachus began putting on his armor with the aid of an attendant. The commander in no way acknowledged that the high priest was even still in the room. Once Lysimachus had strapped on his sword and was about to leave, Menelaus asked, "Will you be able to stop them?"

Lysimachus stopped and stared at Menelaus as if looking through him. "I have just sent several hundred men to their death. They will not be able to stop this army, but they may buy enough time for our people who are scattered over the city to make it to the citadel. Antigonus was right. The rebels will try to take the temple first. Perhaps it will give us enough time. But then, who knows what will happen? An army that can defeat Lysias can also break through these walls."

Lysimachus turned to leave, but Menelaus stopped him with another question. "Commander, that message that the young man spoke of, the one from Lysias a year ago, what was it?"

Lysimachus turned back to Menelaus with a piercing look. "It was a military matter. It didn't concern you."

"But I have a right to know," objected the high priest. "I am responsible for the king's revenues which the military has been unable to protect. I demand that you tell me."

Lysimachus stared at Menelaus. His first impulse was to shout profanities at the insolent high priest, but he chose a deeper insult instead. He simply left the room without responding.

When the sudden commotion had started in the courtyard, Rebekah's guard had rushed her back inside. "What is it?" she demanded as he pushed her gently along. "What's going on?"

"I'm not sure. I heard someone say the rebels have entered the city," replied the guard. Over the months he had developed a quiet respect for the attractive Jewish woman who remained steadily in his charge. When around the other soldiers who knew of his assignment, he would joke about her with all manner of vulgarities, but when alone, he treated her with respect.

"Is Judas with them?" she questioned as they moved along the hall to her chamber.

"I don't know, but someone did say something about the Maccabee leading them." The guard knew well that the one Rebekah so fondly called by the name of Judas was the one others spoke of with fear and respect as the Maccabee. "Now I must close you in your room. All the guards have been called to assemble in the courtyard."

As she heard the bolt turn in the door, Rebekah ran to the window and looked down into the courtyard. Within what seemed only moments, she saw ranks of soldiers armed with spears and shields spread across the pavement. Orders were shouted out by officers and the ranks tightened up and broke into a march that was more of a trot. They exited the citadel through the broad gateway that led into the city.

A few minutes later, she saw yet more armed soldiers assemble into ranks. Even with his helmet, Rebekah recognized her own guard amongst them. Lysimachus took a position on a stand in front of the soldiers. Rebekah had seen him often peering at her from his window ever since the day her mother had died. She knew he was Judas's sworn enemy, yet somehow she pitied the man. It was as though he was in a place that he did not choose to be. Yet here he was, barking out orders to fight against, and if possible, to kill the Maccabee.

Rebekah stared out the window for more than an hour. She could hear chaotic noises wafting over the wall and echoing around the inner court. There was fighting in the streets not far from the citadel, perhaps on the temple mount itself. The last assembly of troops she had seen in the courtyard seemed to have remained within the citadel to defend it. From what she could see from her vantage point, there were probably two to three hundred troops. All the others had been sent outside the walls, all sent to fight against the man she loved, the man she had not seen for almost three years. Memories of the past and hopes for their future together had kept her spirits alive. Now she was watching men go out who wanted to wipe the memory of him from the earth.

Though there were already hundreds of the traitorous Jews who had taken permanent refuge in the citadel, hundreds more began to fill the courtyard. Many of these were not actually Jews, but rather Syrian merchants who had taken up residence in the city. It was difficult to tell them apart, for they all wore the Greek style of dress. There was much animated conversation among the new arrivals, but the sounds were so chaotic as they reached her ears that Rebekah was able to discern little of what was said. What she could tell, however, was that the people were both angry and afraid. And she heard many times the word *Maccabee*.

Finally pulling herself away from the window, she lay on her bed and stared at the ceiling. The constant din of the crowd below continued to pour through the window, but Rebekah no longer heard it. The image in her mind spoke far louder than the voices of traitors. Judas was only streets away. He would come for her. He had conquered armies. The walls of the Acra would not stop him from getting to her.

Chapter 45

Judas kicked his heels hard into his horse as he saw the massive gates that had opened before them only moments earlier begin to close. The men behind him followed his lead. About forty men managed to get into the city before the heavy gates met in the middle and anxious Syrian soldiers fought to brace them against the onslaught coming from without. Judas spun his horse around and charged at the men laboring to secure the gates. "We must keep the gates open!" he shouted to the others. "Otherwise we are trapped."

Arrows had already begun to rain down upon them from atop the wall on either side. Under the arch of the gateway the men were protected from the arrows, but some who were out in the open fell under the hail of the deadly missiles. Unable to endure exposure to the arrows, the men leapt from their horses and ran for the narrow stairways giving access to the top of the wall. Within moments, their swords were slashing through the line of archers, most of whom were Jews who had been living in the Acra but placed there by the garrison commander during the siege. Most of the archers had no weapons beyond the bows and arrows they carried, and those that did have swords had little experience with them.

Judas and several others charged their horses into the soldiers working to secure the gates, slicing their swords into any they could reach. Those that fell were trampled under the feet of the horses. Within moments, the gates were opening again. Men on horseback poured into the city. Above the clatter of hundreds of hoofs could be heard the shouts of jubilant men, thrilled to again be entering the city that held deep meaning in the heart of every Jew.

Judas had begun leading the column of horsemen deeper into the city toward the temple mount when about sixty Syrian cavalry poured from a side street behind him, attacking the column from the side. Their orders had been to close the gate, but they would never make it that far. Judas turned his men around and encircled the Syrians. Shouts and cries from man and beast alike echoed through the narrow streets. Blood splattered against the walls of dwellings on either side of the fight as men and horses thrust themselves upon one another with deadly force. Within minutes, what had been left of the Syrian cavalry garrisoned at Jerusalem was no more.

Now wary of what other threats might lie elsewhere in the city, Judas proceeded with caution. He knew from the confrontation with the cavalry that Lysimachus had already received word of their presence in Jerusalem. Judas slowed his advance toward the mount until the rest of the army made its way into the city. He sent units of a hundred each to take possession of the city gates on the southern end and the northwest corner. Though he had left two thousand men at Beth-zur to assure that Lysias did not turn back, thousands were still going to walk through those gates for the first time in three years within the hour.

As they proceeded slowly through the streets, Judas noticed changes in the city. The streets, now empty because people had either abandoned their homes months earlier or were now sitting silent and afraid behind closed doors, were dirty from the litter that had amassed during the years of siege. Some dwellings had their doors broken in, a sign of the iron hand with which the Syrian garrison had ruled the city. Amidst the physical decay of the city, though, appeared signs of a decay that reached right into the heart of the nation. In almost every wide opening where streets came together stood a pagan shrine.

The shrines were clean and well maintained. Some had figures of Zeus much like the one on the now discarded standard Obed had made, but others had idols that Judas did not recognize. The men with Judas were quick to throw the idols into the street and trample them under the feet of their horses.

Within an hour, the rest of the army began entering the city. The units Judas had sent to open the other gates had found little difficulty in overcoming the resistance. Joyful shouts resounded throughout the western quarters as troops swarmed through the streets. Only when they finally came within sight of the western access to the temple mount did the joyous clamor subside.

Judas halted the procession toward the temple mount and studied the new situation. At the top of the long avenue that led steadily upward to the wide arch that opened onto the broad pavement running down the south side of the temple courts was a contingent of Syrian infantry. Though the tight confines of the avenue that was walled on both sides did not allow them to be in their typical formation, Judas recognized by the wall of *sarissae* in front of them that these men were trained for fighting as a phalanx. This was probably the same phalanx that had carried out the massacre in the temple court three years earlier since the city had been under siege much of the time since then.

A hush fell over the crowd of men on horseback behind Judas. The occasional snort or clatter of hooves of a restless steed interrupted the silence. For what seemed to be several minutes both sides eyed one another. There seemed to be no hurry by either side to engage in battle. The Syrians knew they were grossly outnumbered. The Jews were simply tired of fighting.

"What do you think the other entrances would be like?" asked Simon, hoping for an easier way though already knowing the answer to his question.

"They will be just like this," Judas said. "The Syrians know that once we take the mount, we cannot be moved." Judas turned to the others and said, "Wait here," then he prodded his horse closer to the phalanx.

"Who is in charge here?" Judas shouted.

A stout captain with a gravelly voice stepped from the corner of the front rank and shouted back, "I am."

"We have several thousand men who have it in their hearts to walk in the temple court today. You're in our way."

"I have orders to hold this position," came back the gravelly voice.

"There is no need for you and your men to die today," said Judas.

There was a long silence. The captain, along with his men, looked nervously up the street where they could not see the end of the column of horsemen. He turned his attention back to Judas. "Are you the Maccabee?"

"I'm the one," said Judas.

The already fearful phalangites now moved to near panic. Some were on the verge of running. Detecting this, the captain shouted out at them, "Stay your positions!" He looked again at Judas and let out the sigh of a man resigned to defeat. "Well, Maccabee, I have my orders."

Judas looked at the captain for a long while. No matter who it came from, courage was to be admired. Or perhaps this was not courage, but rather fear of a greater evil. Judas had heard how the Syrians dealt with cowards. He too let out a deep sigh and pulled his horse around and came back to the others.

Judas dismounted as he spoke. "Today, we will be the ones carrying out the massacre. They leave us no choice." He looked up at Joseph and Azarias. "Joseph and Azarias, you take every man on horse and block both entrances to the Acra, both the one in the city and the one that opens toward the Mount of Olives. Allow no one to leave."

Judas then looked up at Simon. "Call up four hundred men with spears and at least three hundred archers."

The clatter of hundreds of horses' hoofs shook the ground over the next few minutes, but then the sound gradually receded. For several minutes longer, Judas stood with only a few men at his side watching the Syrian troops. The Syrians looked from one to the other, wondering what was happening. They could easily have attacked and defeated the small group of Jews remaining in front of them, but they heard the echoes through the streets of thousands of advancing troops. The sounds seemed to come from every side.

A few minutes later, Jonathan arrived beside Judas accompanied by several hundred archers. Judas gave Jonathan instructions on how he wanted to attack. Once the spear throwers were standing in reserve on either side, Jonathan began the attack just as Judas had said. He separated his archers into groups of seventy. Some would shoot their arrows up so that they fell straight down upon the Syrian troops. Others would shoot straight into the troops in a horizontal fashion.

For a quarter hour, without cease, arrows fell like rain upon the doomed phalangites. The Syrian troops attempted to hold their shields in a turtle formation so as to protect themselves from all sides, but trying to hold the heavy and cumbersome *sarissae* at the same time caused gaps in their protection. The sheer volume of missiles launched meant that occasionally one of them would attain its target. Once a man fell, even if it was from a simple leg wound, a greater hole was opened up through which other arrows immediately flew. Other soldiers fell, precipitating an even greater opening. The phalangites struggled to maintain their protective cover, but one by one they fell before the hail of deadly missiles. By the time the archers ran out of arrows, a fourth of the Syrians were dead and most of the rest were wounded and barely able to fight. Judas then sent in the spear throwers. Within a few minutes, the phalanx had been destroyed.

Judas led the charge through the archway onto the mount. Immediately to the right they saw a much smaller unit of Syrians in the first archway that gave access to the mount from the south, an access near where the Acra bordered the temple mount. The Syrians tried desperately to turn to face the enemy now pouring in behind them. The scene repeated itself in another access farther in. Within minutes, the hundreds of

Jewish men pouring in from the west had eliminated this new threat.

When the last sign of resistance was gone, amidst shouts of victory, the men ran toward the entrance of the outer court of the temple, the court in which the massacre had taken place three years earlier. When they gained their first sight of the temple, the shouts of joy quickly died. A few moments later, several hundred men, with hundreds more arriving by the minute, stood silently staring at a sight that brought grief to every heart.

The place where all had memories of joy and celebration in the worship of God was now deserted. Weeds grew between the stones in the pavement. The doors to the temple hung open, one torn partially from its hinges, still bearing the marks of having been cut through by Syrian spears three years earlier. The altar was broken down on one side, most of its spilled contents having long been washed away by the rains and snows.

Judas led the way closer to the temple and peered in. The great statue of Zeus still loomed in the middle of the great inner court, though just as with everything else, it too was in a state of deterioration. Rather than turning this into a temple in which they would worship their god, the Syrians had chosen to turn it into a symbol of the impotence of the god of the people they dominated. So they had desecrated the temple and left it desolate. Weeds even grew inside the temple itself. The great veil that had hung before the most holy place was now gone.

Many of the Hasidim began to wail. Some tore their clothes as they often did when lamenting a great loss. Others scraped ashes from inside the broken down altar and sprinkled them on their heads.

From atop the steps leading to the temple, Judas looked out across the sea of men who now stood in the temple court, some standing in quiet astonishment, others lamenting loudly. "Men of Israel," he called out. "Today God has brought us back to this place. No one has been able to withstand us. But our work is not finished. This place will not be a temple again until it becomes the place that we can worship God in the way he has told us to. With God's help, let us make it such again. God will help us, just as he did our fathers when they returned from the time of their exile in Babylon. Let us begin today. Let all the men who are gifted and experienced with work in wood, stone, fabrics, and bronze and gold come to me now so that the work may begin this very hour. Let men from the tribe of Levi come that we may again purify this place. Before the new moon, we will dedicate this temple anew to the worship of our God."

The laments and complaints began to change to voices of victory once again. One by one, men started coming forward volunteering for the work of refurbishing the temple. Simon agreed to take charge of preparing for the rededication. He assigned men their various tasks. Some who had no special skill volunteered to remove the articles that had been defiled by the Gentiles. That very afternoon, before the sun went down, men had destroyed the statue of Zeus and had completely torn apart the already broken down and defiled altar upon which the pig had been offered in sacrifice. It would be replaced with an altar of uncut stones according to the word God had given Moses.

Leaving the responsibility of the temple in the hands of Simon, Judas left to join Joseph and Azarias, for from the temple mount he had seen archers lining the ramparts of the Acra, shooting arrows down upon the troops outside its walls. No doubt, they would have shot those coming into the temple court had those entering not kept their distance from where the Acra bordered the temple mount. Before leaving the mount, Judas stationed archers on the paved expanse on the south side of the temple to release arrows upon anyone on the Acra wall who might make such an attempt. He sent some men to collect the hundreds of arrows that lay on the ground around the Syrian phalanx they had destroyed upon entering the temple area. With these arrows, his archers were able to maintain a steady barrage of missiles upon the men on the walls until the sun went down.

Judas's real concern, however, was not with what stood upon the citadel walls. They were only a threat to whoever came close enough and within their line of sight, something easily avoided. What held his heart was the one who sat within those walls. He had no way of really knowing whether or not Rebekah was still alive, but he felt sure that if she had died, his enemies would have found some way to inform him of it.

Menelaus made his way silently through the dark, dank hall underneath the northern wall of the Acra, holding a torch out before him. He came to an opening where a guard sat warming himself by a low-burning brazier.

"What are you doing here?" demanded the guard as he rose from his seat and reached for a spear that had been leaning against the wall.

"I'm here to see the prisoner," replied Menelaus in an authoritative tone.

"What about?"

"Open the door. I don't have to tell you what about," ordered Menelaus haughtily.

"I have orders to allow no one to see him without word from the commander." The guard clutched the spear in both hands but did not point it at Menelaus.

"Do you know who I am?"

"Yes," the guard answered without hesitation. "You are the high priest of these Jews."

"That's correct. I am also the king's tax collector. I have the power to do whatever I please to bring revenue into the king's coffers. This man has information I need to carry out that duty. If you prevent me from doing my duty, you will not answer to the commander, you will answer to the king."

The guard hesitated for a moment then reluctantly turned and unlocked the heavy door behind him with a key he had at the end of a leather thong tied to his belt. When he stepped aside, Menelaus stepped through the doorway into the dark cell. He looked around the stone walls, getting a feel for the austere conditions prisoners endured. High on one wall, next to the ceiling, was a small grated opening. This hole through the thick stone opened just above the pavement in the courtyard and allowed a diffused light to filter into the cell during daylight hours. However, the sun had long since gone down, and now the cell was bathed in blackness except for the flickering light of Menelaus's torch.

Shimri rose from the dirt floor on which he had been sitting, squinting at the light from the torch. He tried to look around the light to see who held it. When Menelaus saw this, he held it to one side to illuminate his own face.

"High Priest," said Shimri, calling Menelaus by title. "What are you doing here?"

Menelaus came close to Shimri. Suddenly realizing that the guard was standing in the doorway, he turned and said harshly, "Leave us. Close the door until I call for you." The guard shrugged and backed out of the doorway. A moment later, Menelaus and Shimri heard the bolt turn in the lock.

The high priest turned back to Shimri and spoke in a low voice, looking back at the door as he spoke to communicate to Shimri that the guard was probably listening from the other side. He spoke in Aramaic just to be safe. "I am here because I think we can help each other."

Shimri leaned forward and spoke quickly, using Aramaic as well. "First, tell me what is happening outside."

Menelaus sighed impatiently. "The rebels have taken the temple. They are in control of the city. The only thing they don't have is the Acra."

Shimri dropped his head in fear and disgust. Looking up again, he said, "How can I help?"

"Lysimachus is weak. He is on the verge of surrendering the Acra. But if the Acra is ever given into the hands of the rebels, they will forever possess this city. Our day will be over, and we will be without a homeland. Somehow, he must be convinced to hold on against the rebels until Lysias sends another force against these brigands."

"But what can I do?" asked Shimri, looking into the dark eyes of the high priest that only reflected the flickering flame of the torch.

"What was in that message that Lysias sent a year ago?"

Shimri stared at Menelaus, puzzled by the question.

Menelaus continued. "When you spoke of it to Lysimachus, it disturbed him."

"You saw it too," said Shimri quickly, suddenly reliving the moments earlier in the day. "His face went white as a corpse when I mentioned it."

"Exactly. And I could tell by what he said right after that that he was trying to find out what you knew without giving himself away. Later I asked him what was in it, and he refused to tell me."

Menelaus waited for Shimri to respond. Shimri looked from side to side as if to find the answer in the darkness around them. Finally he shook his head. "I don't know. I don't know what was in it. Lysias gave it to me sewn in leather around an arrow that I was to shoot over the citadel wall. I did exactly that. The best I know, and it's nothing specific, it contained orders of how he would coordinate the activities here with the campaign made by Gorgias and Nicanor last year."

Menelaus raised his head, staring into the darkness as he pondered what Shimri had just said. "I don't know of anything Lysimachus did during that time, nothing out of the ordinary." He dropped his eyes to the floor and stood silent for a long while. Gradually, a realization seemed to take hold of the high priest. "That's it," he said slowly as he put his thoughts together. "The commander disobeyed orders. There was something he was supposed to do, but he didn't do it. He has as much to fear from Lysias as he does from the rebels, that is, if Lysias ever knew. Whatever it is that the commander was supposed to do, no one knows about it except him and Lysias. The thought that someone else may know who could inform Lysias that he did not comply makes him afraid."

"Lysimachus? Afraid?" Shimri had difficulty believing the commander feared anything.

"Have you seen the way the Syrians deal with their soldiers who disobey orders, even officers?"

Shimri shook his head.

"It's not a quick death. It's meant as an example to others."

Menelaus spoke with great satisfaction. He had found the leverage he had been seeking to manipulate the situation they now found themselves in.

Before turning to leave, Menelaus took Shimri's hand and said, "You have given me what I need. I will have you out of here soon. Hold to your dream of wealth and power. One day it will be yours, young Antigonus . . . or should I say Shimri."

"You know my Hebrew name?" Shimri was surprised.

"I have always known who you are. I knew your father." Menelaus looked at the ambitious young man for a moment then added, "You made the right choice. This is a new age. The old ways must be done away with. Stay strong. Your day will come."

The high priest shouted at the door for the guard. A moment later, Shimri stood alone in the darkness, his ambitions still very much alive.

Chapter 46

During the next three days, what was left of the garrison tested the resolve of the men holding them prisoner within their own fortress at least once a day, sometimes as many as three times in a day. Their efforts were easily anticipated. Hundreds of archers would suddenly appear on the walls and towers as the giant gates would be pushed open. A small phalanx would exit the gates in a rapid march into whatever resistance they met.

Joseph commanded the troops that watched the citadel gate which opened into the city, while Azarias watched the gate opening toward the Mount of Olives. At first, their troops suffered some casualties. They would charge into the phalanx under the hail of arrows from above only to find it necessary to turn and flee when they met the wall of *sarissae*. They quickly learned, however, that once the phalanx got beyond the range of the archers who worked to hinder those who came against it, the phalanx was much easier to deal with.

By the second day, every time the alert was given that archers were again lining the walls, the men quickly distanced themselves from the wall. The archers launched their missiles uselessly while those on the ground outside waited patiently until whoever came through the gates was outside their range. Then the unit that came out was met with a force that overwhelmed them, usually with hundreds of *pila* that pierced both shield and soldier. By the fourth day, the garrison made no more attempts to leave the citadel. Arrows did continue to fly from its ramparts, however. Had it not been for the constant volley of arrows from outside, those on the inside would probably have found their supply depleted. The constant exchange continued even though there was little success for either side.

On the fifth day, the people standing atop the eastern wall of the Acra watched in horror as a giant battering ram was rolled from the cover of the trees on the Mount of Olives. Azarias had discovered that the siege tower he had built months earlier, while it had not been destroyed as before when they had lifted the siege to do battle against Lysias, was useless for attacking the Acra due to the higher walls. The massive wheels, however, did prove to be of use. He had these brought from the western side of the city where the tower had been built and set on stout beams for axles. Then he set as many tree trunks as could be bound together upon the axles. The huge wooden wheels lifted the front of the ram just high enough off the ground to clear the steps that led up to the outer gates of the citadel.

Lysimachus came out onto the rampart to see the new threat being pushed from the trees. When Judas recognized the commander, he came from the trees on horseback, followed by over a hundred archers on foot.

"Lysimachus," called Judas. "These archers are only for my protection. If you will not use yours against me, I will not use mine against you. I just want to talk. Do we have an understanding?"

The garrison commander shouted back, "We do." He turned and shouted to those who lined the wall with him, "Whoever releases the first arrow will die by my sword."

Judas walked his horse forward, alert to every movement on the wall. He recognized the face of Menelaus peering over the parapet of the tower on the northeast corner. When he felt he was as close as he needed to be, he called out to the commander again. "Lysimachus, I am in possession of the city and the country. We have defeated the armies of Apollonius, Seron, Nicanor, and Lysias. Whatever your king has sent against us, we have defeated. The walls of the Acra will not protect you."

Lysimachus ignored everything that Judas had said for he had anticipated it already. He went straight to the only leverage he knew he had. "Maccabee, your woman is safe and well. I have seen to it."

Judas's heart leapt in such a way that it took his breath. For a moment he could not speak. He looked at the archers on either side as he blinked back tears that tried to force their way into his eyes. He had not seen Rebekah for three years. He tried to form an image of her in his mind but had difficulty doing so.

Lysimachus was still speaking, and Judas almost missed what he said due to the emotions that were overwhelming him. "I regret her mother's passing. It was not my doing."

Judas came quickly to his senses. "What happened to Miriam?" he demanded.

"She wasted away and finally died. It was not by anything we did. Rebekah will tell you that. We buried her in the way Rebekah asked us to."

Judas was now confused by this commander he had built up such a hatred for who now seemed to speak tenderly of Rebekah's mother, even giving her a proper burial at her death. This was not the heart of the man he had fashioned in his thoughts, the man he despised with every fiber of his being. He now called Rebekah by name. How often did a Gentile even care to know the name of a Jew?

"Lysimachus," said Judas, embraced by a hope beyond anything he could have imagined only moments earlier, "I offer you and all the people in the citadel safe passage out of Judea if you will surrender."

Lysimachus looked down at Judas for a long while before speaking again. Surrender was never easy for a commander. "What guarantee can you give me that we will leave Judea safely?"

"You have my word."

Lysimachus looked from side to side, examining the expressions of the people lining the wall with him. "That may be good enough for me, but I think my people may want something more. Come back tomorrow at this time and we will discuss the details. We will meet in the middle of the field on which you stand. Bring with you twenty armed men. I will do the same. Let none of your troops other than the twenty come closer than the Mount of Olives. I will allow none of my troops to leave the citadel, excepting the twenty. We will set terms for the surrender then. Until tomorrow. Shalom!"

Judas was taken aback by the Syrian's use of the Hebrew word, but he repeated back to him, "Until tomorrow. Shalom!" Judas turned his horse and galloped across the field into the trees on the Mount of Olives. The archers trotted behind, looking over their shoulders lest a sudden hail of arrows come from the citadel wall.

Lysimachus left the rampart and was immediately joined by Menelaus, who followed him to his chambers. "You cannot surrender the Acra!" Menelaus said vehemently

"I can, and I must," rejoined the commander. "If I don't, we are all dead. You saw the ram they just rolled out. You've also seen how many men are out there for almost a week now. How long do you think we can stand up to them?"

"Lysias will come soon. He will not allow the Acra to be taken."

"The army that surrounds us now defeated Lysias only a week ago," shouted Lysimachus as they entered into his chambers. "Are you so foolish as to think he will appear in Jerusalem in the next few days?"

Menelaus had waited until this moment to say what he had been holding in his mental arsenal for the past five days. "If you had followed Lysias's orders, perhaps we wouldn't be in this situation now."

Lysimachus froze. "What are you talking about?"

"I spoke with the young Jew you are presently holding in your dungeon, the young Antigonus. Now I know why you put him there. He knows something." Menelaus paused, watching the commander's expression, then added, "And now *I* know."

"You know nothing," retorted Lysimachus. "Whatever he told you, it's all lies. What were you doing down there anyway? The guard was given orders that no one was to see him. I will have him flogged."

"Lies?" said Menelaus, reveling in the moment. "We will find out when we finally do see Lysias, whether it's here or in Antioch."

"Yes, we will," barked Lysimachus. "Now leave me. I do not want to see your face again today. You and everyone like you disgust me. Now get out."

Menelaus said no more. He was sure he had gotten his point across. When he left the room, Lysimachus walked over to close the door behind him. An attendant was about to enter, but the commander told him to wait outside. "I want to be alone for a while," he said and closed the door in the attendant's face. He walked to a small wooden writing table from which he picked up a dagger. Removing it from its sheath, he ran his fingers down the blade as he stared blankly into space, unable to still the images that flashed through his mind, mental pictures of the faces of Judas, Rebekah, Menelaus, Shimri, and finally Lysias. In a sudden burst of frustration he rammed the blade of the knife into the table top. He felt like a cornered animal. There was simply no way out.

Late in the night, Rebekah felt a hand on her shoulder. Startled, she sat quickly up on her bed and drew back. In the dim light of an oil lamp, she recognized that it was the garrison commander leaning over her. She was afraid for a moment. She knew well of the abuses that went on between soldiers and their prisoners, especially female prisoners. Her fears were quickly laid to rest.

"Don't be afraid," Lysimachus said quietly. "I'm not here to hurt you. I need to talk to you."

Rebekah just looked at him, not knowing what to say. Finally, she just gave a short nod of her head.

Lysimachus set the lamp on a table and pulled a stool by

the bed where he seated himself facing Rebekah. Rebekah sat on the bed with her arms wrapped around herself to ward off the chill Kislev air that found its way into the room. "Rebekah, have I ever treated you badly? Have I ever harmed you in any way?"

Rebekah looked at the commander through eyes that would melt any man, confused with what the late night interrogation was about. Finally she shook her head from side to side.

Lysimachus paused as if he wanted to say something else but then held up his hand. "Rebekah, do you read Greek?"

Only now did Rebekah notice that Lysimachus had been holding a rolled up parchment. "Yes," she responded timidly. "Strangely enough, my brother taught me to read Greek when I was young. My father taught me Hebrew, but Shimri convinced me that it would be good to know Greek."

Lysimachus held a puzzled look on his face for a moment. "Shimri? You have another brother?"

"Oh, no," explained Rebekah. "I only have the one, or at least I did. Now I suppose I really have no brother. The one you call Antigonus, that's Shimri."

Lysimachus showed understanding for what Rebekah had said with a gentle shake of the head and a pursing of the lips as he dropped his eyes to the parchment in his hand. He realized more and more the pain that had been brought into this young woman's life by no choice of her own. Lysimachus held out the parchment to Rebekah. "I received this over a year ago. As you will see, I never followed through with it. But I want you to read it for yourself. You will understand why in a few moments. Now read."

Rebekah took the parchment from the commander and held it so that it caught the light of the lamp. She moved her lips silently as she read, rereading certain sentences to make sure she had understood correctly. At one point she put her hand to her mouth in disbelief. After several minutes she looked up at the commander.

"You were supposed to kill me, but you didn't." Rebekah's face was filled with questions.

Lysimachus put his hand to his chin pensively. "There was a time when I could have. To me you were nothing more than a game piece or another spin of the dreidel in this game kings and generals play. But by the time I received this, it had all changed, ever since that day your mother died. It was like I saw your heart that day. I saw that you could love, and I saw that you could hate. For the first time, you became a person to me. And I found that there was nothing in you that I could despise. Neither could I simply ignore you."

Lysimachus wanted to reach out and touch Rebekah but kept himself from it. Instead, he just looked at her sadly. "I've watched you each day as you have walked in the courtyard. I know you've seen me at my window." He paused for a long while then added. "In another life, in another world, I could love you, but not in this one. The gods, it seems, will not allow it."

Rebekah stared at Lysimachus with wide, unblinking eyes. She could not believe what she was hearing as this Gentile commander, known for sending men to their death, opened the secrets of his heart, secrets that involved tender feelings about her. For an instant, she wanted to reach out and touch him as well, not as a gesture of intimacy, but rather to show sympathy and provide comfort, but she dared not.

Lysimachus could no longer bear looking into Rebekah's eyes. He looked away to one side and then allowed his eyes to survey the room about them. "Tomorrow, this will all be over for you," he said, "and you will see me no more. Neither will I see you. I will miss seeing you, but that doesn't really matter where I am going."

Rebekah leaned her head forward, "Where are you going?"

"That doesn't matter. What really matters is that you will be free. Now listen closely to me because there may still be someone who would try to kill you. I'm fearful that others may know of this message, and they would think by killing you they would gain favor with Lysias. They would see it as a strike against Judas. That is how Lysias saw it when he wrote this. Therefore, your life is still in jeopardy."

Lysimachus paused to make sure Rebekah was receiving everything he was saying. "What would you have me do?" asked Rebekah, hanging on every word.

"In the morning, your guard will come to take you for your daily walk in the courtyard a little later than usual. You will be shackled to him like you always are. But when you get to the courtyard, he will bring you to a unit of armed soldiers. Do not be afraid. They will not harm you. They will take you to freedom."

Rebekah's emotions became a confusion of overwhelming joy and intense fear. A picture formed in her mind. During the past three years, more than once she had seen units of soldiers march out of the citadel with a shackled man in their midst. The man had been marching to his own execution. "Will you be there?" she asked.

Lysimachus nodded his head. "I will be there. I will protect you."

Rebekah's fears melted. This man could have killed her a year earlier and would have been commended for it. He would not harm her now.

The commander suddenly remembered the parchment that Rebekah was still holding. "One other thing," he said. "Keep this letter with you. It is very important that you have it with you tomorrow."

Rebekah looked down again at the paper that carried such a cruel message. "I will. I will have it with me. I think I understand why."

Lysimachus stood up and walked slowly to the door as Rebekah followed him with her eyes. As he opened the door, he looked back at Rebekah still sitting on the narrow bed. He stood for a moment staring at her. His sad eyes combed over her thin but still shapely form before settling on her dark eyes. "Another life, another world," he said somberly. Then he stepped out into the dark hall and closed the door.

Rebekah listened to the bolt turn in the lock. It mattered little that the night had only entered the third watch, all sleep had been chased from her eyes. Tomorrow, she would be free.

Chapter 47

The sun had almost reached its zenith the next morning when Lysimachus assembled the small company that would escort him onto the field. He had deliberately remained in his personal quarters up to this moment to avoid having to deal with Menelaus. The high priest had made more than one attempt to see him, but the guard standing by the commander's chamber door had refused him access.

As soon as Lysimachus walked out upon the courtyard, the irate Menelaus confronted him. "You have no right to surrender the Acra. If you do, it will be treason against the king."

Lysimachus spoke in a very flat tone. "I not only have the right, I have the responsibility to save the lives of the people here."

"Perhaps some of the people don't want you saving them," ranted Menelaus. "If they lose the Acra, they lose Jerusalem, they lose their country. I say to you again, you have no right just to give it away. You must hold on until Lysias comes."

Lysimachus gave no further response, which infuriated Menelaus even more. To be refused was maddening, but to be ignored was the ultimate insult, especially for a man of Menelaus's temperament.

Within moments of Lysimachus's arrival before his troops, Rebekah arrived, chained to her guard. The unit was in four ranks of five men each. The commander ordered a gap between the third and fourth rank. He placed Rebekah in the middle of this gap, still chained to the guard.

Menelaus watched indignantly. "You are going to give her to them, aren't you? You fool! She is the only leverage we have left."

"She is still in chains," said Lysimachus in a matter-of-fact tone, hoping against hope that he could deceive the high priest into silence. "When the Maccabee sees her for the first time in three years, I will have something to bargain with."

"Then why not stand her on the wall with a knife at her throat? Why march her right out in front of him when you know there are hundreds of troops just in the trees on the other side of the field? You *are* going to give her over. I *know* you are. Then what hope do you think there will be for any of us?" Menelaus's anger had become a seething rage.

Still without raising his voice, Lysimachus addressed the high priest as one would address a subordinate. "My dear Menelaus, have you not ever wondered what it is that has driven this man, the Maccabee, all these years?"

"He's driven by his god, or so he thinks," Menelaus replied curtly. "Look at the first place he went when his army entered the city, the temple. That should tell you."

"But even the gods will use a woman to accomplish their own ends. Have you forgotten what history says happened at Troy?"

"Nothing but fanciful stories." Menelaus spit on the ground. "Besides, if thinking about this woman has sustained him all this time, why not just kill her and leave him with nothing."

"Killing her would make it worse. Then we would die for sure," chided Lysimachus, weary of the discussion.

Menelaus stared at Lysimachus, a wild expression growing across his face. He began to speak slowly and deliberately. "I think I'm beginning to understand. You have grown soft for this woman. This is what Lysias ordered, isn't it? You were already supposed to have done it." Suddenly, Menelaus whipped a small dagger from his waistband as he shouted, "I will kill the bitch myself." He lunged into the opening between the ranks toward Rebekah.

Rebekah's eyes widened in terror. Before Menelaus had taken a second step, however, the guard to whom Rebekah was chained had drawn his sword and had the point digging into the skin at the base of the high priest's neck. An instant later, the points of several *pila* were poised around him as well.

Lysimachus called out to an officer that was standing nearby. "Captain, place this man in irons. Put him with the other prisoner until I return. He is to have no interaction with anyone. There must be no distraction from what we have to do today."

The officer, who did not like the pompous Jew at all, was glad to oblige. He took Menelaus by the arm and effortlessly wrested the dagger from his hand. Menelaus would have resisted, but the weapons aimed precariously at his body prevented any movement. A few moments later, he was descending into the bowels of the Acra with a spear at his back, shouting curses as he went.

A shout from the northeastern tower rang through the courtyard. "Commander, the rebel unit just came out of the trees."

Lysimachus order the gates opened. With his second in command at his side, a Macedonian named Delonius, Lysimachus led the march away from the citadel into the open field. Rebekah walked hidden in the ranks of large, fully armed men. Their shields prevented anyone from seeing her through the ranks.

As Judas approached the Syrian unit, he led a group that looked much like the unit that was coming to meet him. They, too, wore body armor and carried shields and spears that had been taken from the bodies of some of the many Syrians they had killed in past battles.

Judas stopped his men at a point he estimated to be an equal distance between the citadel and the Mount of Olives. As he watched the Syrian unit approach, he looked from side to side for possible dangers. Toward his right was the city wall, behind which lay the outer courts of the temple. His eyes traced the base of the wall, trying to pick out the place where he, along with Simon, his father and many others, had come out of the tunnel under the mount three years earlier. Despite all that had transpired in the interim, the events of that day remained vivid in his mind. It was the first time he had ever killed a man. He had no idea how many he had killed since then. How ironic, he thought, that three years of fighting should begin and end at the same approximate place.

Lysimachus called his unit to a halt about fifty paces from where Judas waited. For a long while, both men and the units of soldiers behind them just stood and stared at each other. Seeing Delonius standing by Lysimachus and surveying the troops behind them as best he could, Judas called out, "I think you have more than twenty men."

A wry smile appeared on the commander's lips. "Forgive me. I wanted my second in command to witness what is said here today. Besides, I think with the number of men you have behind those trees, it makes little difference."

Judas nodded and returned the smile. Sensing the rebel leader's accepting posture, Lysimachus slowly drew out his sword and handed it to a man in the rank behind him and ordered Delonius to do the same. Unarmed, they walked to the center of the open ground between the opposing units. When Judas saw this, he drew out his own sword and thrust it into the ground before going forward to meet them.

The three men stared into each other's eyes for a long while before speaking. A cold winter breeze blew across the open field, but it was hardly felt due to the present tension. Judas had never been in the position of negotiation and was unsure how to proceed. He wished Simon were there. Simon always knew what to say in situations such as this. But Simon was involved in activities more important to the heart of the nation.

"How do we begin this?" Judas finally said.

Lysimachus went straight to the point. "You have offered us safe passage out of Judea. You have given your word that our people will be safe, but some of our people are not so trusting. We have about three hundred men of the garrison left in the citadel, but there are well over a thousand Jews with Syrian loyalties. These are the ones that are the most untrusting."

A shadow crossed Judas's demeanor at the mention of the thousand traitors. To Judas, as Mattathias had taught him, these were the people who had brought about the ruin of the nation. Still, he had given his word. Yet he did not know exactly how to give the assurances that were being requested. "What do you suggest?" he finally asked.

Lysimachus had already formed a plan in his mind. "Allow the people to leave and proceed by the Jericho road fully armed."

"Fully armed?" Judas frowned. "How do we know you won't attack us?"

"We would be foolish to attack you, you so outnumber us. Most of these people have no experience in battle, and there are some women and children."

Judas studied his opponent's face but could read nothing. "Our allowing this would be a gesture of trust on our part. What gesture do you give us in return?"

Lysimachus turned and motioned to his troops. Judas tensed momentarily as he saw the troops parting in the middle, thinking there might be archers with drawn bows behind the ranks or some other more sinister threat. Suddenly his heart raced. His breathing became irregular, more so than when facing battle.

Rebekah's guard removed her shackles. Though they had hardly spoken during the three years, Rebekah put her hand on the guard's arm and said to him, "Thank you for watching over me these three years." The burly guard's lip quivered as he fought back tears, shaken by the unexpected words of kindness.

Rebekah walked between the soldiers to the middle of field. Judas felt his whole body tremble. It was all he could do to refrain from running and grabbing Rebekah up in his arms. He told himself there would be plenty of time for that later.

Nevertheless, he fought back tears. Rebekah's tears flowed freely down each cheek as she came and stood in front of him. For a long while, they just looked at each other as if no one else were around.

Lysimachus interrupted the reunion. "Rebekah, show him the letter."

Not taking her eyes off Judas, Rebekah pulled the parchment from the folds of her cloak, the same letter that Lysimachus had brought to her during the night. She handed it to Judas and the two of them began to speak in Aramaic as she explained its meaning. When Judas had finished reading, having fully understood, he looked at Lysimachus, then at Delonius. He was not sure what he should say in front of Delonius. He knew that what Lysimachus had done was an offense punishable by death. His throat became tight as he whispered the simple words, "Thank you." The commander nodded slightly, a sad yet settled expression on his face.

Judas composed himself. "I will pull my army back. Your people may leave by the outer gates of the Acra and take the road to Jericho. They may be fully armed as you have requested. They have three days. If they have not left Judea in that time, they will be considered a threat and will be dealt with appropriately."

"That is all we ask," returned Lysimachus. The commander then addressed his second in command, "Do you understand these terms, Delonius?"

Delonius was confused as to why the commander had posed this question to him, but he responded affirmatively. Lysimachus exchanged final glances with both Judas and Rebekah. Their eyes communicated a message that did not need to be spoken. Then he turned, followed by Delonius, and rejoined his troops.

As Lysimachus led the unit back to the gates of the Acra, he heard a mirthful whoop suddenly arise from the field behind him. His lips turned up slightly as he pictured in his mind the joy that was being experienced by those he had considered his enemies, but the sadness never left his eyes.

Lysimachus dismissed the troops as soon as they had attained the citadel courtyard. At his request, Delonius accompanied him to his quarters.

"Delonius," said Lysimachus, "I've seen that you have the respect of the men. Most of them are Macedonian as yourself, and that seems to your advantage. Do you think that with these three hundred troops you can march this crowd all the way to Antioch, or at least to some other city in Syria?"

"Yes, Sir," answered Delonius, confused by the way Lysimachus had worded his question. "But the men have the highest esteem for you, Commander. You will be there."

"I won't be coming with you," said Lysimachus as they continued down the passageway leading to his quarters.

Delonius stopped in his tracks as the commander continued to walk. "Not coming? What will you do? You are not joining the rebels, are you?"

Lysimachus turned to see the surprised look on his subordinate's face. "No. I would never be a traitor. I've seen too many traitors in the last few years, and I despise them all." They began to walk again as Lysimachus continued. "I can't tell you at the moment, but you will understand soon what it is that I must do."

They arrived at the commander's chambers where an attendant opened the door and stood to one side. Lysimachus looked at Delonius, whose mind was racing through all the possibilities of what his commander might be speaking of. "Right now," said Lysimachus, "I want you to go release the two men we have in the dungeon. I do not like or trust either of them, but they are looked upon as leaders by the Jews who are here in the Acra. What actually happens in these next couple of days will be up to the three of you. Now go, and bring them here."

Delonius left, still in a state of confusion. As Lysimachus entered his quarters he asked the attendant to wait outside. "I just need some time alone," he said. "When the captain returns with the two prisoners, you may allow them in." The attendant departed, closing the door as he left.

Lysimachus stood alone in the room. After a few seconds,

he loosened his breastplate and dropped it to the floor. He walked slowly to the window and looked out onto the courtyard. In his mind, he pictured Rebekah in the morning sunlight where he would see her each day. In a strange sort of way, for him, those were good memories. He heard a captain from below calling orders to some of his troops and was brought suddenly to his senses. There would be little time before Delonius would return with Menelaus and . . . what was the other Jew's real name . . . Shimri. That's what Rebekah had called him. How could a man betray his own sister? Lysimachus thought of his own sister, a sister he would never see again. He prayed that the gods would forgive him. He prayed also to Rebekah's god. Her god seemed to be different from the god of the other Jews he knew. Her god had a strength the other's seemed to know nothing about. He could tell it by Rebekah's gentle nature. She trusted her god.

The commander seated himself at the table where he had sat many times writing out correspondence in his duties as the garrison commander. He pulled the dagger from where it had remained stuck in the tabletop from the day before. Gripping it tightly with his left hand and placing the palm of his right hand under the ball of the handle with the knife facing upward, he pointed the sharp tip of the blade into the soft flesh just under his sternum. Perspiring heavily, Lysimachus paused for only a moment as he drew in a deep breath. Then, with a sudden and intense push with both hands, he rammed the dagger into his heart.

A few moments later, the attendant opened the door to usher in Delonius and the two men who had just been released from the dungeon. The attendant froze momentarily then ran to where the commander lay in a contorted position on the floor, the chair having fallen over from the weight his dead body had exerted on its arm. The other three men slowly entered the room. No one needed to tell them that Lysimachus was dead. Delonius, instantly and involuntarily promoted to garrison commander, noticed the demeanor of the two Jews. He did not like what he saw. He realized immediately, that his life had suddenly grown more difficult.

Chapter 48

The sounds of jubilation as Judas entered the cover of the trees on the Mount of Olives with Rebekah at his side surpassed the shouts of victory after any of the battles that had been won. Men crowded around, pressing against one another to get a look. Some women who had joined the camp to cook for the men maintaining the siege pressed between the men to get a look at Rebekah. For three years, they had sent prayers up to God for their two sisters held captive in the citadel. The day before, the word of Miriam's death had brought a quiet depression over the camp. But today, the same camp was ecstatic.

Rebekah, who was not accustomed to such attention as was Judas, hung her head shyly. Judas, however, kept raising his fist in a sign of victory as he pulled Rebekah close to his side with his other hand. Shouts did not cease to ring out over the hillside.

Hardly had the shouts begun to die when Eleazar worked his way through the crowd on horseback. He smiled from ear to ear at the sight of Rebekah. He just sat there looking at her for a while, hardly able to believe it. Judas knew he had not pushed through the crowd on horseback just for a look at Rebekah, though. He called out above the din that still filled their ears from every side. "Eleazar, what is it?"

Eleazar suddenly remembered why he had come. "Judas,

Simon says for you to come. He says everything is ready for the dedication of the temple." As soon as the words had gotten out of Eleazar's mouth, a great cheer erupted from the crowd. After years of darkness, experiencing the betrayal of their countrymen, living in fear, fleeing cruelty that seemed to know no bounds, and seeing continuous bloodshed, losing friends and brothers even when victorious, today everything was good. No one had died, their sister whom some had once thought dead had been returned to them, and the temple through which they touched the very throne of God would now be restored to its former glory.

After the crowd had quieted enough for him to be heard, Judas shouted to Eleazar, "Eleazar, send riders all over Judea. Tell the people to come. In two days, we will declare a Sabbath and dedicate the temple in solemn assembly. Then, just as we have celebrated the feast of tabernacles in past generations, we will celebrate a new feast before the Lord for a solid week, for God has given us a great victory."

The crowd exploded with sound again as it parted so Eleazar could be on his way to spread the word. Within the hour, men on horseback were seen racing down every road and path in Judea. By nightfall, people were already pouring into the city – men, women, and children. Many were leading sheep or goats to be offered upon the new altar. Not since the return of Israel from Babylon when Ezra and Nehemiah had presided over the dedication of the rebuilt temple had Jerusalem seen such an influx of joyful people into its walls.

Two days later, Judas stood with Simon in the temple surveying the work that had been carried out with such joy and diligence over the past six days. They both wore the consecrated clothes of priests. Other Levites of the priestly lines stood to one side, consecrated with holy oil and ready to serve the people in their renewed worship of God.

To the left upon entering the temple stood the solid gold lampstand that stood as tall as a man. Obed, the smith from Modin, had worked day and night, hammering and fashioning it from a solid piece of gold. The original lampstand, as with all the other furniture of the temple, had been taken away by Antiochus when he had stripped the temple on his return from Egypt years earlier. A cruse of the special oil for the lampstand had been found in the rubble of the vandalized priest's quarters with its seal still unbroken. That oil now made the seven lamps on the stand glow brightly.

To the right was the newly built table for the showbread. Craftsmen had fashioned it from acacia wood and overlaid it with gold according to the specifications given in the Torah. Bread had been placed on the table at the same time that the lamps had been lit that morning, bread that represented the presence of God.

In front of the great veil that hung once again in front of the most holy place was the gold-overlaid altar of incense. The fragrance of the holy incense filled the air, a fragrance unlike any other, for the incense was a blend of spices that was permitted only for worship in the temple, to show the absolute uniqueness of God. Anyone else found making incense by the same formula would be cut from the people of Israel.

Motioning to the others to follow, Judas pushed open the massive doors that had been repaired. As the men filed out, their white priestly robes glowing in the morning sun, cries of joy broke out among the throng that filled the court. Judas looked across the court to the special place where the women stood during times as this. Though there were hundreds of other women in the crowd, Rebekah was the only one Judas really saw. The other women honored her by giving her a place in front.

The court was filled shoulder-to-shoulder with men, most of them Hasidim, though there were many others. Seemingly spontaneously, the crowd broke out into one of the songs of the *Hallel*. How different it was from the day, exactly three years earlier to the day, when the court had been filled with the murdered bodies of their brothers.

Judas looked down at the bottom of the steps leading up to the temple. There, standing at the front of the crowd was Lucas, the old man who had been a slave his whole life. Tears were streaming from Lucas's eyes. He tried to sing with the others, but emotion would not allow him. Never having lived free, he now stood in the front rank of free men before the very house of God.

Judas looked across the crowd trying to pick out other faces he knew from among the thousands. Many faces were familiar, others just part of the joyful crowd. He could not see Jonathan or Eleazar, but he did spot John standing with Leah close to where the women stood. He knew that Oren and Jadon were somewhere in the throng, but he could not pick them out. To one side, he saw three of the four slaves who had once carried Apelles's litter. One of the slaves had died in the battle against Nicanor, but the others had accounted for themselves well as adopted sons of Israel. Today, they would begin to experience in a much deeper way what it meant to be a Jew.

Neither Joseph nor Azarias were there, for they had volunteered to keep watch with their troops over the gates of Acra, which till this moment had remained closed. The people inside had just one day left to safely leave Judea.

Judas thought of others as he listened to the joyful words of the *Hallel*, others who were not there. Judas felt the absence of Nethanel, the Hasidim warrior who had been closer than a brother. Nethanel had poured out his life in battle just for a day such as this. Most of all, Judas missed Mattathias, the father who had taught him to love God and to never compromise with the enemies of God, though it cost his very life. How he wished he were here now, leading this great multitude gathered before the place that God himself had designated as the place to which his people would turn to seek his face.

Judas raised up his hands to quiet the crowd. It took several minutes for the noise to finally die enough for him to be heard. When he finally did begin to speak, every person remained perfectly still so as to hear every word.

"Sons and daughters of Israel," Judas's strong voice rang out across the court, "long ago, even before we were born, a great darkness entered our land. That darkness grew until many of our people abandoned the God of our fathers and adulterated themselves with the worship of the gods of the nations that surround us. Finally, the light of our nation went out as this place was stripped and made desolate by the abominations that were committed here.

"But three years ago, my father, Mattathias ben Hasmoneus, stood up to the powers of this darkness and informed them that there is still a God in Israel. Today, after three years of having seen God fight our battles, I tell you that inside the walls of this temple, the lamp burns once again."

A cheer erupted with these words and Judas waited until it died away to continue.

"We must never again exchange the light for the darkness. Today, we are here to rededicate this temple to the worship of the one true God. Let us never again depart from him. Let us never again compromise his laws. Let us repent of those past deeds that nearly destroyed us, and let us always walk in the light of God's righteous law.

"That we may always remember this, today I proclaim a new celebration. On this day, the twenty-fifth day of Kislev, for generations to come, we will come to this place and celebrate before the Lord. We will celebrate with feasting and with hymns and psalms for eight days, so that we may never forget. We will celebrate with lights, so that we may remember that once, there was a darkness that almost destroyed us."

When Judas had finished, Simon unrolled the scroll of the Torah and read from the Law of Moses for almost three hours just as Ezra had as is recorded in the book of Nehemiah. The people remained quiet and attentive. When he finished, he led the people in a prayer of confession, repentance, and dedication. Many wept as he spoke of the sin that had almost led to their destruction. All voiced agreement as he prayed words of dedication.

Just after noon, the other priests came forward and began offering sacrifices on the newly erected altar. As in the days when Solomon dedicated the original temple, they found that the sacrifices were too many for the one altar, so they set apart another section of the courtyard for additional sacrifices. By evening, the people had begun to feast before the Lord.

Taking to heart Judas's words that this would be a celebration of light, many of the men put candles on the ends of their spears and stood them in cracks between the stones. As night came on, the temple courts as well as streets all over Jerusalem were ablaze with light. The joy was unlike anything anyone could remember in their lifetime.

At the edge of the joy and light that covered the city, however, there stood a small colony of darkness. From the gloomy shadow of the northwestern tower of the Acra, three men stared morosely at the blazing lights covering the temple mount. It seemed to them that the celebration would go on all night. They did not know at the time that there would be many similar nights to follow.

The Macedonian grumbled to the two Jews, "If we do not leave tomorrow, there will be no time left. I was there when the Maccabee said we had only three days."

"We must not surrender the Acra," insisted Menelaus. "This is the king's stronghold in Judea. If this is lost, Judea is lost."

"But if we all die, it's lost anyway," rejoined Delonius, mentally cursing the dead Lysimachus for having put him in this position. "That huge battering ram is still out there, and I have no doubt they will use it."

Shimri spoke up at this point. "Then we must destroy the ram."

Delonius hated Shimri more than he did the high priest, for it had been Shimri with his many stories of battle, most of which were lies, who had managed to persuade the people to resist Delonius's attempts to abandon the Acra. "How do you propose that we do that?"

"Burn it," said Shimri. "Some men can slip out there tonight and pour enough oil on it so that, once they set fire to it, no one can stop it."

"They will only build another one," rejoined the Macedonian.

"By then, we will have help from Antioch," insisted Menelaus, as he had many times already.

Delonius saw that he was in a contest he could not win. If he tried to lead the garrison out of the citadel, the very people he had protected these months would resist him to the point of bloodshed. If he did nothing, the men presently celebrating in the lights of the temple court would break into the citadel within days. After long deliberation, he agreed to do as the two Jews asked.

Toward the end of the third watch of the night, after the city had grown quiet, several men slipped out of the Acra under a moonless sky. One carried a jar in which a low flame burned on an oil soaked wick. The others carried jars of oil. Several minutes later, the great wooden battering ram that had remained in the field between the Acra and Mount of Olives burst into flames from end to end.

Chaotic shouts broke through the still night as scores of men ran from the trees on the Mount of Olives. There was little they could do however. The ground was too hard to throw dirt upon the burning ram, and there was no water close by. Most of the perpetrators of the arson managed to make their way safely back through the citadel gates. Some, however, left the scene by way of the road to Jericho. Within days, they would appear in the court of Lysias.

Seven days later, on the eighth day of the celebration, Judas stood once again before the people. He again reminded them of how throughout their history God had fought for Israel so long as Israel had remained dedicated to his laws. Judas exhorted the people to remain faithful so that they might never again have to endure the cruelties that had been thrust upon them during their time of apostasy.

When Judas left the temple steps, he made his way through the crowd to where Rebekah was waiting. He had hardly let her out of his sight during the past week. In a few days, they would be married. A dream he had held in his heart from childhood would come true.

But something he had never dreamed of now weighed heavily upon him, the weight of a nation so prone to go astray. He would turn the leading of the nation over to Simon, as Mattathias had said upon his deathbed, but he knew there were battles that yet had to be fought. Until the entire land was pure, the people would see him as their leader.

As Judas took hold of the hand of the woman he loved, he looked past her to the towers of the Acra. The Acra stood like a cancer in the midst of a city that had suddenly come to life again. Seeing that the people inside would not leave, Judas had created a buffer zone around it. All communication with those inside was declared unlawful. He knew that allies of those within would someday come. It was always that way, wars from within and wars from without. The two worked together.

Judas thought upon the many times his father had told him of the real danger to Israel. It was what took root in the hearts of the people. The evil in a man's heart would always find an ally in the world around him. A week earlier, Judas had led the people as they joyously rededicated the temple to God. But a rededicated temple was meaningless without the personal dedication of every man and woman who worshiped there. Only when it happened in each individual heart would there be a true *Hanukkah** in Israel.

* Hanukkah means *dedication*.

Author's Historical Notes

A work of historical fiction is just that, history and fiction. It is important, however, that the reader not be misled into thinking that some of the fictional elements of the story were actual events or persons. Therefore, I have added these brief notes to clarify anything that might be wrongly interpreted.

The primary historical sources of the story you have just read are the two apocryphal books *1 Maccabees* and *2 Maccabees* and the book *The Antiquities of the Jews* by the ancient Jewish historian Flavius Josephus. Any scripture quotes in this book are authentic and are from the 1917 English translation of the *Tanakh (Old Testament)*.

The account given in the *Prologue* of Alexander the Great is a narrative retelling of what Josephus penned almost two millennia ago. Many have considered this "deal" Alexander made with the Jews upon seeing what he had previously experienced in a dream to be more legend than history. However, I have simply taken Josephus at his word and have made no judgment as to the accuracy of the history as he recorded it.

It seems in order here to give a brief overview of what

happened between Alexander and the time of Mattathias ben Hasmoneus and his sons. Alexander's death in 323 BCE sparked a frenzy of ambition and greed among the powerful men who had served with him. By the time the dust had settled fifty years later, three major successors held power: Antigonas in Macedonia, Seleucus and his heirs in Syria, and Ptolemy in Egypt. Judea fell under the rule of Ptolemy. The Ptolemies, while encouraging the Hellenization that had been Alexander's dream, generally allowed the Jews to retain their religious practices.

In 198 BCE, Judea passed under the control of the Seleucids of Syria, the king at that time being Antiochus III. It was Antiochus IV, called Epiphanes, who grew impatient with the Hellenization process in Judea. He believed a complete Hellenization would unify his kingdom, that chances of rebellion would be reduced if the people were all of one culture. His effort at forced Hellenization proved to be one of the grave miscalculations of history.

The story of Mattathias ben Hasmoneus, according to the sources cited above, begins with his attack upon Apelles, the Syrian officer sent to Modin to enforce the sacrifice on the pagan altar. The historical sources record Mattathias's killing of the man who came forward to offer the sacrifice when Mattathias refused Apelles's orders. Mattathias then killed Apelles. (The name Matthan is my creation since he is unnamed in the histories. Apelles is the actual name of the Syrian officer according to Josephus.) Josephus also records Mattathias and his sons killing a number of the soldiers who were with Apelles before fleeing to the Gophna Hills.

The general story up to the attack in Modin is my own creation, though elements within it have historical importance. The recording of the attack in Modin in the histories gives no indication of whether it was planned or spontaneous. The success of the attack has led me to believe it was planned well in advance, therefore I have written into the story the possible events that would have led up to this attack.

It is recorded history that Antiochus had a pig sacrificed on the altar at the temple in Jerusalem three years to the day before Judas rededicated the temple, this latter being the event now celebrated as Hanukkah. Whether or not Mattathias actually witnessed this event is unknown. The bloodshed on that particular day is my addition to the story, though such things were not uncommon in the reign of terror that Antiochus carried out upon the whole country.

It became unlawful to practice Judaism in any of its forms. Anyone found in possession of scrolls of the scriptures was put to death. The sources record that parents who had their children circumcised were put to death and the babes hung around their necks. The stories told by Joseph and Nethanel in *Chapter 13* of the old man Eleazar who was beaten to death by the Syrians for not eating the meat sacrificed to the idol and of the woman whose seven sons were tortured to death are taken directly from *2 Maccabees*.

The nude exercising in the gymnasium that was particularly offensive to the Jewish mind is recorded by Josephus. The most notable aspect of it was that it caused the young Jewish men to find ways to reverse their circumcisions so that they did not appear Jewish.

The particular events I have related in order to portray the political, cultural, and religious climate as given above are, as I have stated before, fiction. The climate it describes – nudity in the gymnasium, prohibition of Jewish practices, enforced worship of other gods, and murderous cruelty and bloodshed – is as it really was.

Perhaps I became the most fanciful in the telling of the escape through the tunnel under the temple. However, even here there may be a small glimmer of truth. The tractate *Shekalim* of the *Mishna* records: "Once a priest was engaged there, and he noticed that one of the paving-stones on one place appeared different from the others. He went out to tell others of it; but he had not yet finished speaking when he gave up the ghost, thereby it was known to a certainty that the ark of the covenant was hidden there." The tunnels under the temple mount have caused no small degree of tension in the present

Palestinian-Israeli conflict. There is a tunnel actually called the Hasmonean Tunnel, but it seems to have been an aqueduct that was carved just outside the temple mount by the Hasmonean kings who were descendants of Simon, figures who will be introduced in future volumes of the ongoing story of the Hasmonean family.

Mattathias and his sons fought many skirmishes after setting up their base in the Gophna Hills, though they are only spoken of in general terms in the histories. Mattathias preached in the towns and villages, and there was a purifying process that went on. Pagan altars were overthrown, and many who refused to repent and return to the ways of their fathers were put to death, both overtly and covertly.

The Syrian forces continued to fight against them. The account in *Chapter 24* of the people being suffocated in the caves, refusing to fight on the Sabbath is told by both Josephus and in *1 Maccabees*. At this point Mattathias persuaded the people that they were permitted to defend themselves on the Sabbath.

Just before Mattathias's death, he gave the authority to Judas to lead the army and to Simon to rule the nation. Judas becomes the dominate figure in the histories. The four major battles against Apollonius, Seron, Nicanor, and Lysias are straight out of the histories. The location of each battle is also accurate. The account of Gorgias's attempt to attack Judas's army at Mizpah during the night is also from the sources, with Judas leaving the camp and attacking Nicanor the next morning.

The Acra, the citadel in Jerusalem, is important to the story as it was the Syrian stronghold. The garrison there was composed primarily of Macedonian mercenaries. The citadel itself became the refuge for as many as two thousand of the Hellenistic Jews.

Finally, it is important to note who were actual historical characters, and who were products of my imagination. All the Syrian rulers, generals, and officers are authentic and did basically what they are said to have done with the exception of

Lysimachus, the garrison commander, and Delonius, who was only introduced near the end of the book. There was, of course, a commander of the garrison, but his name is unknown to us.

Menelaus was the high priest. In the next volume, it will be seen that even the Syrians recognized him to be some of the problem in their attempt to rule Judea, all which is recorded by Josephus.

Mattathias and his five sons really did exist and were all active in the war, and there is more to be told about them in the next volume. Judas is called Judas Maccabeus in *1 Maccabees*, the oldest history, which employs the Greek form of the name. Jews usually refer to him in the Hebrew form Judah Maccabee because of the negative connotation often attached to the name Judas due to Judas Iscariot who betrayed Jesus Christ (even though the Greek form Judas was a very common name in that day). I have gone with the name Judas the Maccabee – Judas, because it is the form used in the oldest histories; and Maccabee, because it is a description rather than a name and emphasizes the most probable meaning of that name, the hammer.

Nethanel, Oren, Jadon, and the citizens of Modin who joined in the fight are all fictitious. Joseph and Azarias are recorded in the histories as having become generals in command of the army guarding Jerusalem, as will be seen in the next volume. The Hasidim were a real group as described in the text.

Lucas is an imaginary figure, but his place in the story serves to give further historical context. The Romans were rising in power, having defeated Hannibal and were making their strength known against the Greek states. The battle of Pydna, fought in 168 BCE, was a major battle in which the Roman legions proved their superiority to the Macedonian phalanx.

Hananiah's family – Miriam, Rebekah, and Shimri – are all products of fiction. Shimri is representative of the many that sold their loyalties to the Syrians. I have used the character of Rebekah to make Judas a little more human. A legendary status is often attributed to heroic figures such as Judas. I wanted everyone to see that these were real people with real emotions, real loves and genuine hates. Nothing is recorded concerning the wives of any of Mattathias's sons, though we do know that at least some of the brothers had wives and children. The descendants of Simon eventually rule the nation as will be described in future volumes.

Glossary

dreidel: a four-sided top with a Hebrew letter on each side employed as a playful gambling device. In the present day, children often play with the dreidel at Hanukkah due to the tradition of its use during the times of the Maccabees as described in this book. The present dreidel contains the four Hebrew letters for the phrase *Nes Gadol Hayah Sham*, "A great miracle happened there."

greave: metal armor that was worn over the lower leg.

Hasidim: a Jewish party that arose sometime during the second or third century BCE. The word means the *pious ones*. The Hasidim remained faithful to Torah and the Jewish traditions.

Hellenization: The effort initiated by Alexander the Great and continued by his successors to spread the Greek culture and language throughout the world.

hypaspist: an infantryman within the Greek fighting system who, while appearing much like a *phalangite*, carried a shorter spear intended for thrusting and did not fight in the phalanx formation.

hoplite: the basic infantry unit in the Greek fighting system. The word hoplite is often used interchangeably with *phalangite*, a member of a phalanx.

Kislev: the third month of the Hebrew calendar which falls in late autumn or early winter. During the years 167-164 BCE, the time covered in this book, Kislev basically corresponded to the month of November in the Gregorian calendar that most of the world presently uses.

Maccabee: The name originally applied to Judas, the middle son of Mattathias ben Hasmoneus, who became the head of the freedom movement at Mattathias's death. The key figures in the movement that continued after Judas's death continued to be called the *Maccabees*. Most scholars hold that the word itself comes from the Hebrew word meaning *hammer*.

Mishna: a collection of Jewish traditions which was completed about 200 CE.

phalangite: a member of a phalanx.

phalanx: a formation of armed infantry that was employed in ancient Greek warfare. The phalanx formed a notable part of Alexander the Great's battlefield strategy. The basic unit during the time of Alexander consisted of 256 men in sixteen files, sixteen men deep. Each man carried a long pike called a *sarissa* which was about fifteen feet long. When in tight array, the points of the *sarissae* of the first five files would extend well beyond the first file of *phalangites*.

pilum (pl. pila): a thrusting spear that consisted of a heavy wooden shaft into which was mounted an iron rod, the end of the rod being shaped and sharpened to form the head of the spear.

Sadducee: a member of the Jewish party that arose during the third century BCE. The Sadducees rejected many of the traditional Jewish doctrines and favored *Hellenization*.

sarissa (pl. sarrisae): a long pike (about fifteen feet) that was carried by the members of a *phalanx*.

watch (of the night): one of four equal divisions of the night.

CPSIA information can be obtained at www.ICGtesting.com
Printed in the USA
BVOW08s2303170715

408916BV00001B/55/P